100 People to Meet Before You Die

Travel to Exotic Cultures

100 People to Meet Before You Die

Travel to Exotic Cultures

Jackie Chase

AdventureTravelPress.com

"100 People to Meet Before You Die" Travel to Exotic Cultures
Jackie Chase

AdventureTravelPress.com. FL, USA

Ordering Information:
Quantity sales. Special discounts are available on quantity purchases by corporations, associations, and others. For details, contact the "Special Sales Department" at the E-mail address above.

"100 People to Meet Before You Die" Travel to Exotic Cultures by Jackie Chase
Color Print: ISBN- 978-1-937630-94-2
E-book: ISBN- 978-1-937630-97-3
*****Grayscale Print: ISBN 978-1-937630-95-9**

www.WorldTravelDiva.com and www.CulturesOfTheWorld.com

Publisher's Cataloging-In-Publication Data
(Prepared by The Donohue Group, Inc.)

Names: Chase, Jackie, author, photographer.
Title: 100 people to meet before you die : travel to exotic cultures / Jackie Chase.
Other Titles: One hundred people to meet before you die
Description: FL, USA : AdventureTravelPress.com, [2016]
Identifiers: LCCN 2014935901 | ISBN 978-1-937630-94-2 (color print) | ISBN 978-1-937630-95-9 (grayscale print) | ISBN 978-1-937630-97-3 (ebook)
Subjects: LCSH: Chase, Jackie--Travel. | Indigenous peoples--Asia--Social life and customs--Anecdotes. | Indigenous peoples--Africa--Social life and customs--Anecdotes. | Indigenous peoples--Ecuador--Social life and customs--Anecdotes. | Indigenous peoples--Panama--Social life and customs--Anecdotes. | Travel--Asia--Anecdotes. | Travel--Africa--Anecdotes. | Travel--Ecuador--Anecdotes. | Travel--Panama--Anecdotes.
Classification: LCC G156.5.H47 C43 2016 (print) | LCC G156.5.H47 (ebook) | DDC 909.04--dc23

"100 People to Meet before You Die" Contents

by Jackie Chase

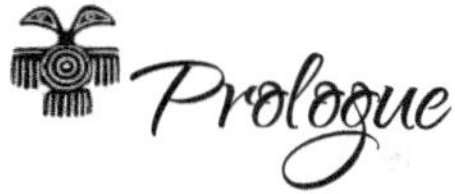

Prologue

"Only those who risk going too far can possibly find out how far they can go."
T.S. Eliot.

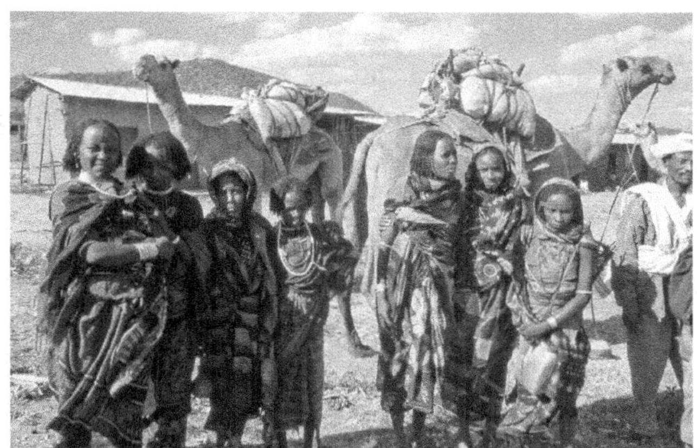

Berber transporting salt from Somalia to Ethiopia

Have you ever thought about becoming the hero of your own life story? On the horizon, there exists an invisible line between reality and our dreams. Have you had a yearning to ride by camel, experiencing saddle sores and searing heat, in order to know first-hand the life lived by nomadic desert tribes in Mali? Would you relish crawling through snakes disguised as vines in the steamy jungles of New Guinea to share huts with former headhunting warriors, while preparing your mind for sights that include dances you will never see on Broadway? Perhaps your love of water tempts you to consider the tranquility of remote rivers, accessible by a lone canoe, where tree sloths sleep for days. Or does your kind of adventure include visiting a regime where your attempted email gets intercepted by the government and never reaches home to say you survived okay, but you know you'll see village life that few foreigners can witness?

Does the China you crave require renting a bicycle because the transportation to remote villages by other means does not exist? Do you prefer to move from place to place by elephant, allowing for participation in the local scene? What if your fearless SUV driver maneuvered your vehicle into the virgin jungles of Ethiopia in order for you to stare down the AK-47s guarding the privacy of native tribes who seldom see a white-skinned woman, sacrificing the entire exterior of the vehicle to gunfire in the process?

Or do your milder moments cause you to dream of Bali, the perfect island, where the religion has evolved over many centuries, and the princedoms which exist today allow you to stay for less than $100 per night in the palace compound with the prince, a man descended from a continuous line of ancestors over 800 years?

If any of these experiences pique your adventurous spirit, then perhaps the following chapters could guide your planning for your next vacation.

On the other hand, you might like to experience the same thrills through the eye of the author's camera and her penciled journal notes while relaxing in the most comfy chair of your cozy home. You may wish to have a personal encounter with more than a hundred new friends that you never thought you could meet. These stories suggest both the primitive and the comfortable path to knowing and understanding cultures whose fascinating traditions may soon succumb to the tsunami of modern influences. Whether curled up in a hammock on an Amazon riverboat, or in the safety of your favorite armchair, accept the infection of the travel bug with enthusiasm and understanding. Reading this book can fill your opened mind with the enticing riches of our world and make the case for immersion in cultures that will do away with preconceptions and prejudice. Each of you, at little expense, can vicariously travel to exotic cultures as you live inside these pages. [Please remember, this is not an anthropology text or a complete guide to travel in each of these areas. It is the author's experience shared with you as a reporter of her journeys.]

CHAPTER ONE

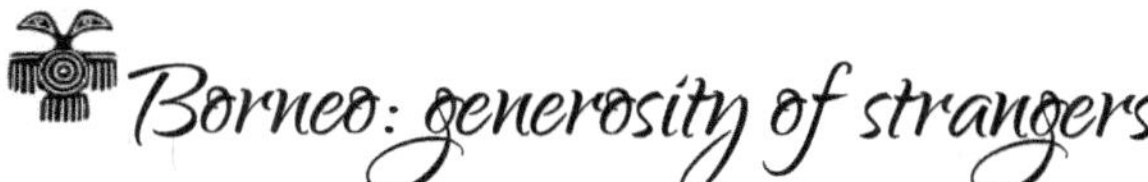

Borneo: generosity of strangers

"The most beautiful thing we can experience is the mysterious."
Albert Einstein.

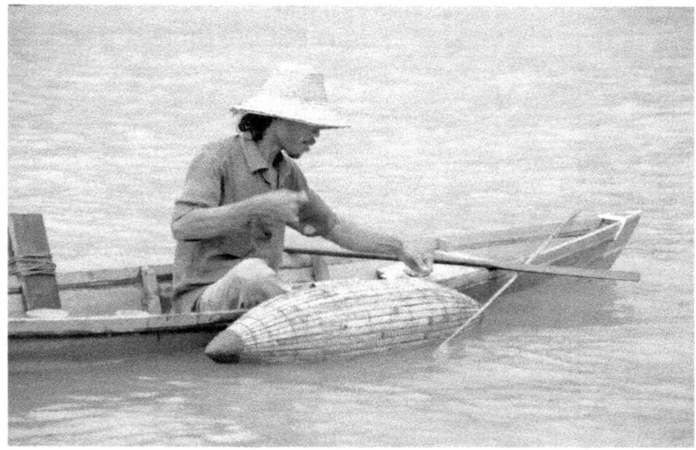

Fish traps

Sitting cross-legged on the floor of the canoe, my elbows scraping the raw splintery sides, I felt the intensity of Borneo on my skin. Small and sweaty, my guide strained his muscular arms to paddle hard, propelling the canoe around a river bend, well-traveled and cut deep in the mud. As the expanse of the brown lake water widened, an occasional view of water buffalo or a pair of freshwater dolphins offered diversion during the four hours I sat scrunched in the narrows of the leaky canoe. My legs felt like Jell-O. The smell of leaking fuel burned my nostrils. Water paths two feet wide cut through the tall coconut grass. Easily shaken loose by movement in the water, the shallow grass roots gave the engine reason to call for help. The silent boat driver maneuvered the wobbly canoe with skill as razor sharp slivers of coconut grass crisscrossed my arms in red. Standing took precise balance. The probability of windblown hair and the fresh scent of grass tempted me to risk the balancing act. The driver watched me struggling to stand in the bobbing canoe, and his smiles of encouragement removed my apprehension.

He shifted directions and, faster than a heartbeat, a family appeared on a wooden porch blocking our path! Individual homes also came into view, floating on the water as I watched, spellbound, feeling the up and down movement of our boat. A floating village full of life had mysteriously materialized in the middle of miles and miles of swampy grassland. We heard laughter and noticed a young man getting his haircut. As we paddled close to a porch to tie up, the laughter of the natives changed to curious but welcoming stares.

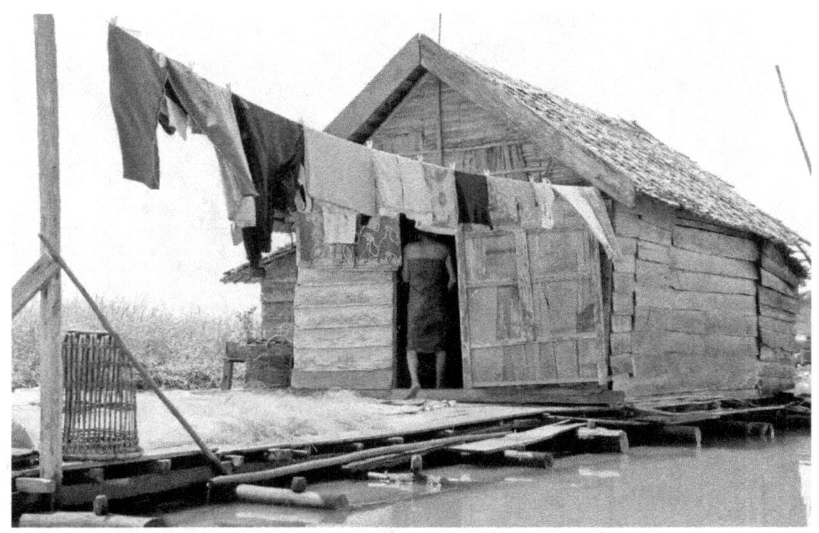

Nearby water grass helps stabilize floating homes

The portable villages consisted of bamboo huts built on floating, wooden-log platforms anchored by three or four unstable bamboo poles set upright in the shallow, swampy water. Patches of coconut grass surrounded the floating houses, but even a gentle breeze caused a change in their direction. Homes have open doors and windows to allow air to circulate to keep them cool. The water provides a natural boundary of protection against any unwanted animal intrusion. Narrow river paths offer communication arteries with neighboring villages. After a few hours of visiting different homes, my boatman motioned me back to the canoe. Children hid their faces from me with their hands, peeking between their fingers, giggling.

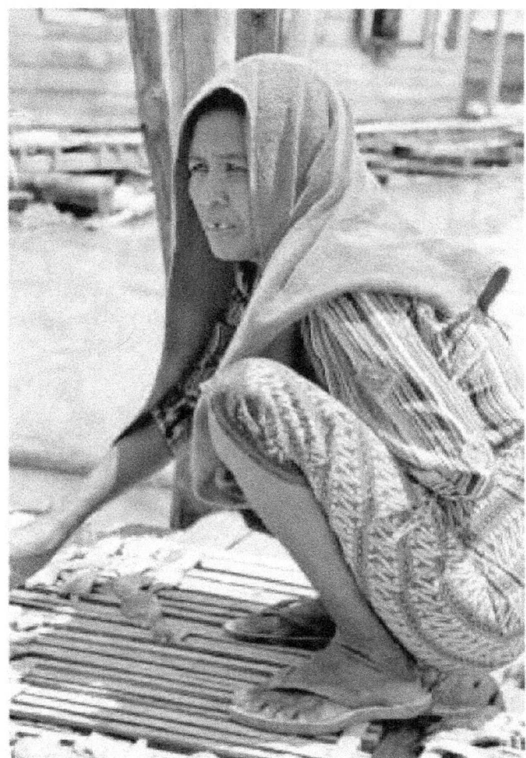

Checking fish drying in the sun

A man already seated in the boat extended a hard and calloused hand to help brace my juggling act of camera bag, sandals, and unsteady feet as I searched for the best place to sit in the canoe. Lives adrift on this shallow lake continue to follow patterns taught from generation to generation. As we set off, the floating village disappeared in the blink of an eye, leaving me with a sense of appreciation of the continuity of life.

Guardians of the earth, known as indigenous or native people, understand nature and its resources. Generation to generation, parents instill knowledge and guidance to their children and grandchildren in the ways of living. Lifestyles and dialects abound in Borneo, the world's third largest island. The majority of inhabitants live along the riverbanks of the jungles and coastal towns. The name, Dayak, means inland, or interior, and describes 450 ethnic groups. In decades past, the tattoo-covered Dayaks lived as savage headhunters, carrying poisonous blowpipes in forbidden, isolated jungles with slippery, wet vines, teeming with creatures baring ferocious black teeth.

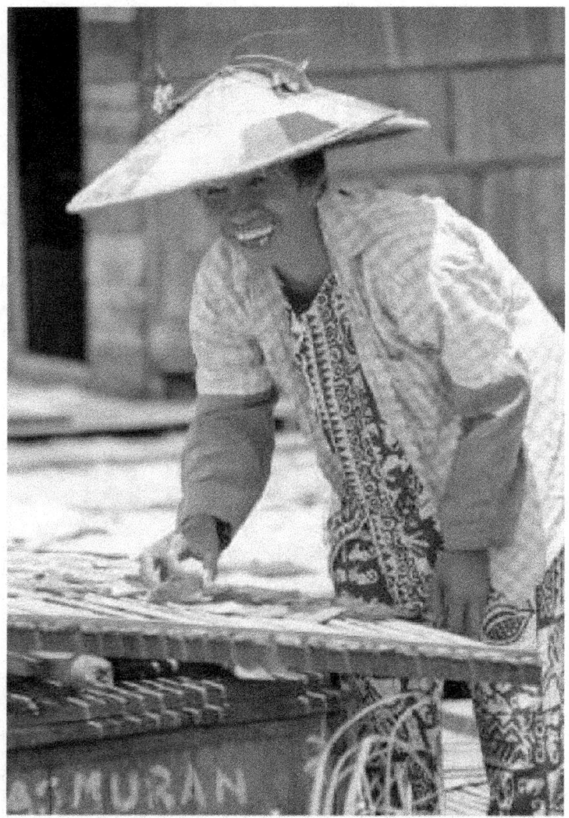

Turning over the day's catch drying in the sun

The "River of Diamonds," the translation of the Malaysian word "Kalimantan," lies on the Indonesian half of the island of Borneo, supporting four million people. Borneo invites exploration of large areas of tropical rainforest through the island's highways of powerful rivers. Locals use the rivers for trade and communication, while tourists arrive in Balikpapan to make river arrangements to see the Dayak peoples. The fast-growing mangroves cause the island to increase in size each year in the shallow Makassar Straits.

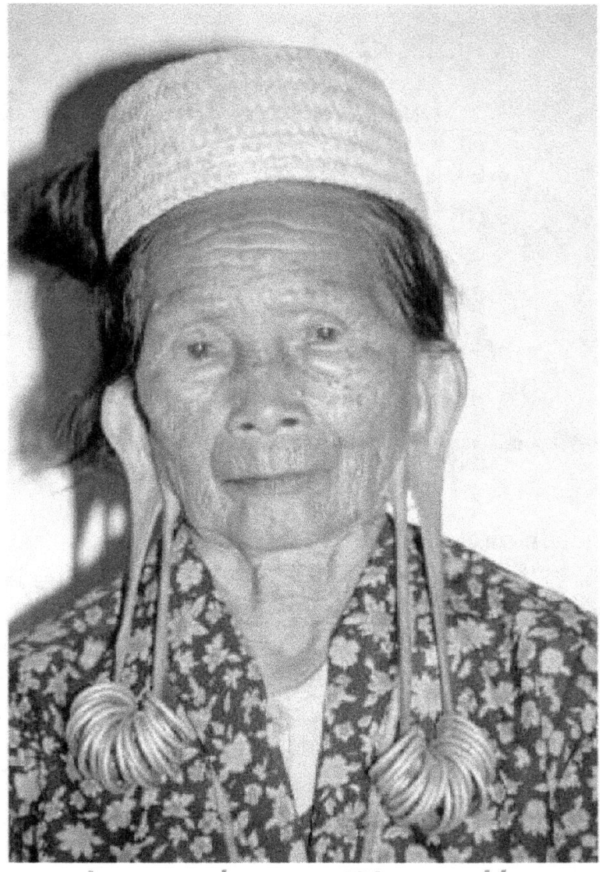

Long-eared woman, 100 years old

Long-eared women, along with orangutans, hide in jungles abundant with shouting hornbills atop black orchids. Traditional longhouses nestle against globally unique ecoregions.

World Wildlife Federation defines an ecoregion as a "large unit of land or water containing a geographically distinct assemblage of species, natural communities, and environmental conditions."

Locals go about their traditional lives, unaware of the modern world, as it converts native vegetation to agricultural lands, oil palm plantations, and commercial logging grounds.

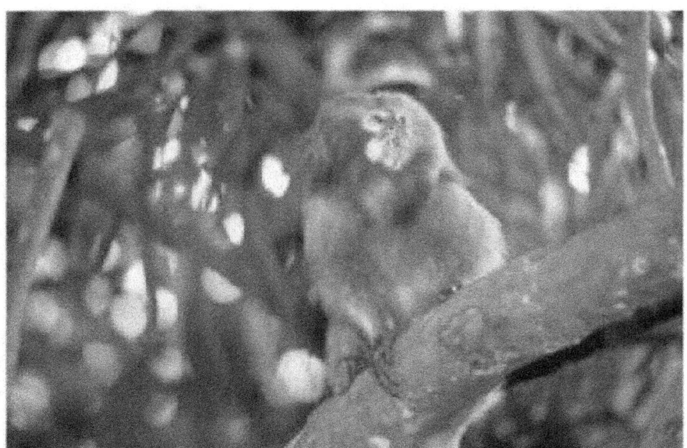

Proboscis monkey

The Dayak headhunters today live in peace, growing rice, using slash and burn techniques, gathering rattan for weaving, and working for timber companies. They hunt with dogs for wild pigs and with blowpipes for small game. Minimal cash flows between these people.

Spirits saturate the Dayak's mythological way of living. Managing these spirits, whether harmful or beneficial, requires knowledge learned from ancestors based on customs, animal sacrifice, and the use of complex, artistic presentations.

Hypnotizing eyes and mouths full of sharp teeth decorate coffins, masks, and shields to frighten human enemies and harmful spirits.

In times past, heads from headhunting guaranteed the tribes successful farming and wealth and brought good health that helped in manipulating the spirits in daily life.

Although headhunting stopped after World War II, men today still feel undressed if they do not carry a blowpipe and *mandua,* or knife, attached to their belt.

Spirits guide the villagers in making everyday decisions. Villagers blacken their teeth with the application of the dry distilled oil of coconut shells. Black teeth make the mouth appear empty. Seeing an empty mouth, the spirits will believe the "toothless" people pulled out their teeth as a gift to the spirits.

Tattoos memorialize images of dreams, spirits, and traditional lifestyles. Often a couple will tattoo each other, with the husband drawing the characters and the wife using a mallet and carbonized wood dyes to color the tattoos. Tattoos integrate life and life after death.

After death, Dayaks believe the individual's soul searches through the black afterlife for ancestors in heaven. The obstacles along the way, including the River of Death, bring the soul frustration. Tattoos from a previous life allow a spirit traveler to use the bridge across the obscure waters of darkness.

Successful headhunters wore hand tattoos, and those women considered good mothers and wives endured multiple tattoos on wrists, feet, and ankles.

Proper tattoos protect souls from Maligang, the guardian of the bridge, who lures some into the mouth of Patan, the giant fish living under the muddy log bridge. After death, tattoos start shining, illuminating the path on the other side toward a final resting place.

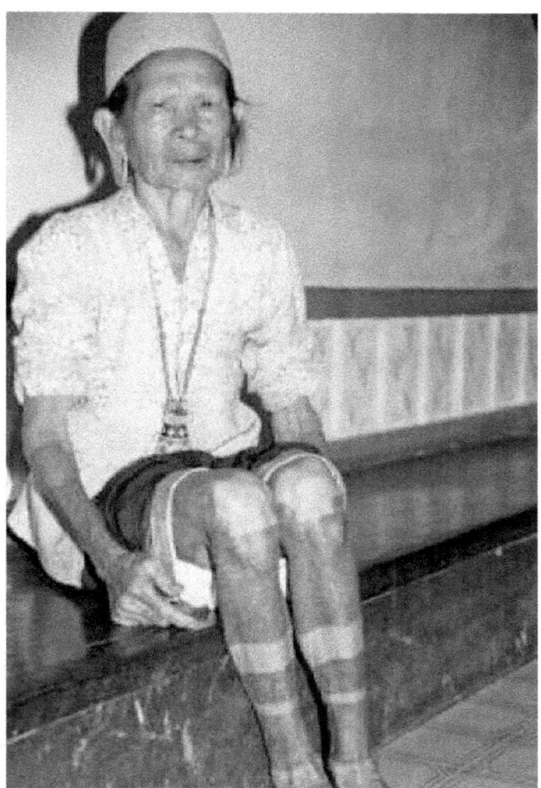

Extensive tattooed legs and arms

An old legend told of a mother and father crocodile unable to have children. The father crocodile captured a Murut tribal woman and carried her to the bottom of the river. Using the advice given by the tribal woman, the crocodile mother laid eggs, and the father returned the Murut woman to the village. To prevent future crocodile attacks, the crocodile father recommended tattoos of crocodiles.

The fragile Benuaq Dayak, wrinkled and sagging with stories, shivered, tugged at her sarong, and retied it. The guide listened as I studied the intricate tattooed designs on her legs. With a voice warm with memories, the little woman shared her culture with me, and my guide translated. I looked at the guide and remarked, "Why so many tattoos?" He turned to the woman and asked her. She told us that they began during her teenage years. Elders of the village used a heavy tree branch and pounded a three-pronged stick over ashes covering the design. Wealthier families used designs with more details. Villagers believed the more tattoos a woman displayed, the more courage she had.

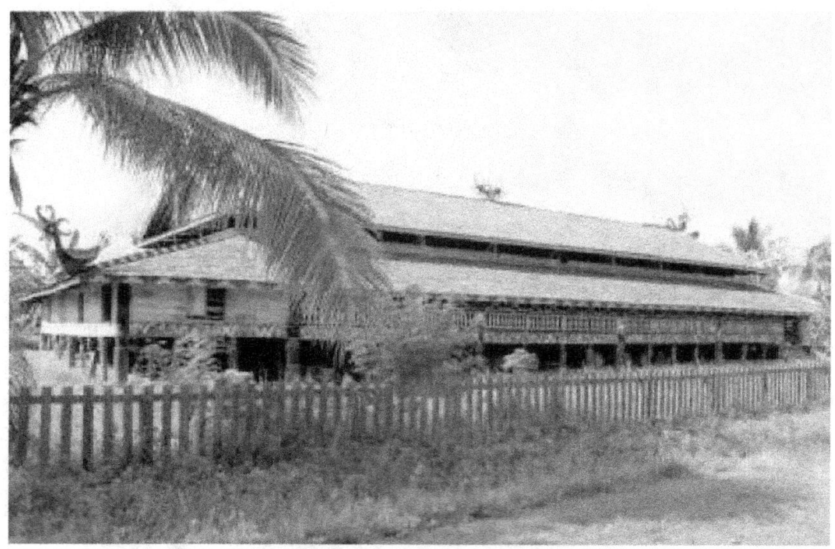

The longhouse, a jungle hotel

Stilted traditional homes, called longhouses, sometimes stretching sixty feet, safeguard villagers from flooding rivers and attacking enemies. The four-foot-high space underneath provides a sanctuary from the sun for children making mud pies, women resting in hammocks, and shelter for live animals. The *amin,* or household, of many families live in one of these communal wood structures with separate living space for each family. A hallway the entire length of the structure allows space for weaving, for cooking, for an area for children to play, and for meeting to plan the day, functioning as a village street. The longhouse beats like the heart of the community. Each village protects its longhouse with totem poles carved with images of birds, animals, and savages to scare away evil spirits and enemies.

Today's tourists can board a double-decker wood houseboat or river-bus on the Mahakam River for a peaceful float through towering jungle growth, through gorges, and for visits to the Dayaks. The unspoiled residents continue to preserve their native way of life, and stops at coastal villages abound with opportunities for tourists to fill their journals. Local men load and unload freight, with the boat sounding a loud, familiar horn, urging action to those running late, yet wanting to board.

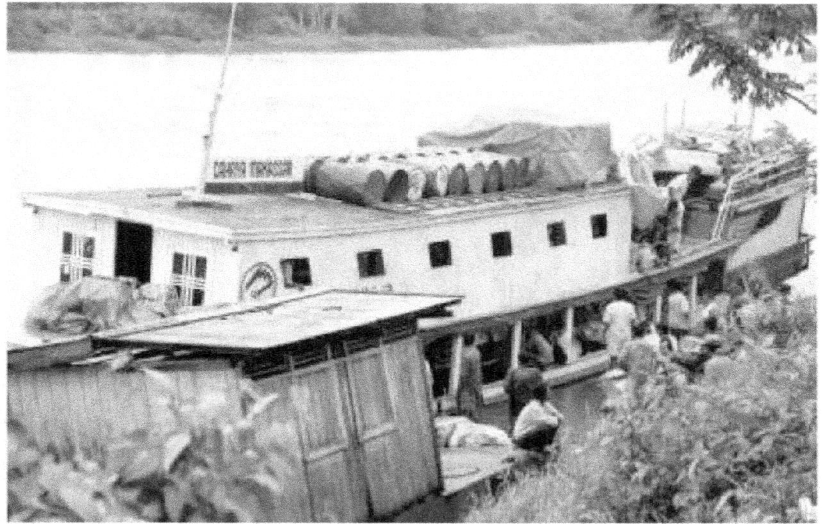

Two-deck riverboat

Visions of adventure filled my head as I watched the boat bobbing with activity. A tangible sense of trepidation marked the beginning of the river voyage. On board, the ticket taker pointed to piles of two-foot-wide, woven-grass mats. The boatman motioned me to one of the mats, and there I sat, crouched under a window, waiting for the trip to begin.

Boat engines roared with their first gulps of fuel and river water. People began boarding with children and cloth-wrapped bundles of food, much like Huckleberry Finn must have carried, crowding my own carved-out niche. Apprehension enveloped me, as expectations of the next twenty-four hours materialized before my eyes. My ticket said first class. I realized what first class meant after seeing the second-class deck below. The surrounding chaos and confusion hid cracks and chipped paint on the decks and walls.

Parents teetered, holding babies on one knee, the other half of their laps balancing baskets of tobacco leaves, vegetables, and well-worn, yellow, lard buckets rinsed clean for storage of sticky rice.

Chickens, their legs tied with filthy strings, wriggled atop baby pigs squealing for momma and protesting the jabbing bare feet, knees, and elbows encircling them. Snooping around the boat after it began its long journey, I began to realize my adventure rested here, not at the next stop.

Without means to communicate, I wondered how to interact with people each day as the sun came up out of the river.

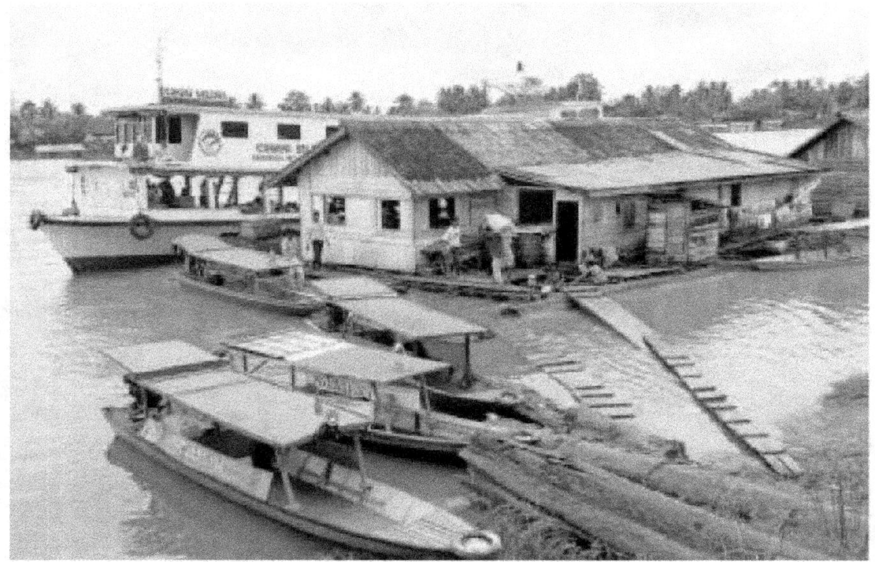

Slippery walkway to riverboat

The feeling of claustrophobia consumed me. A good book and my journal might keep me company on the top deck. They offered my best escape from "no English spoken," the lack of safe food to eat, and little diversion.

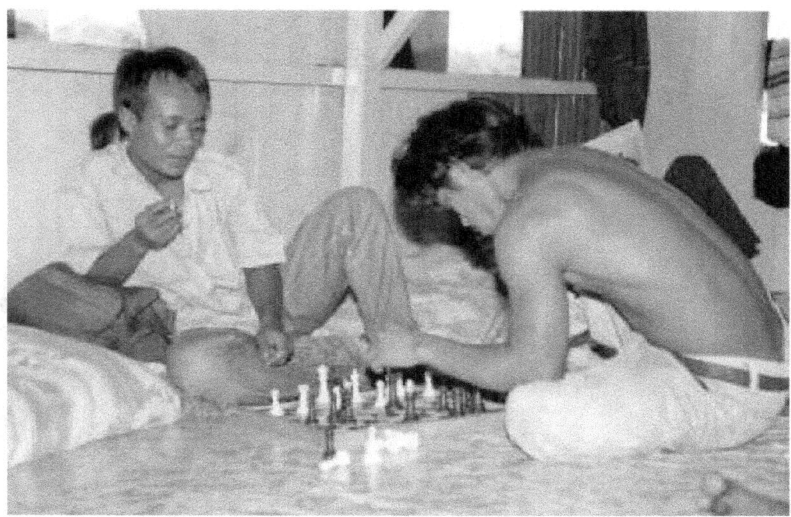

Making new friends during river travel

Within hours of leaving the main docks of Loajanan on the Mahakam, the strangeness of the situation changed. People began sharing stories, food, and card games.

A group of men motioned for me to join in their game of cards. Sharing crackers with the mother and baby next to my quarter-inch thick mattress opened the door for such welcoming acts from my fellow travelers.

From that point on, the more than one-hundred people on the boat accepted me not as a stranger but a silent friend. I joined in games, played checkers with bottle lids on imaginary boards on the floor, laughed as children drew animals using my markers, and spent hours on the tiny front deck alone, writing, reading, and reflecting.

The roof of the boat remained available for storage of motorcycles, mattresses, packed rice sacks, and chickens, waiting their turn for the boiling pots in the warung, or makeshift kitchen.

Teapots, baskets of rock-hard breads and watered down condiments danced on the kitchen's table, located above the engine room.

I relaxed on the rooftop, using sacks of rice for a chair, listening to a symphony of handmade instruments being played below me, and echoing against the riverbanks.

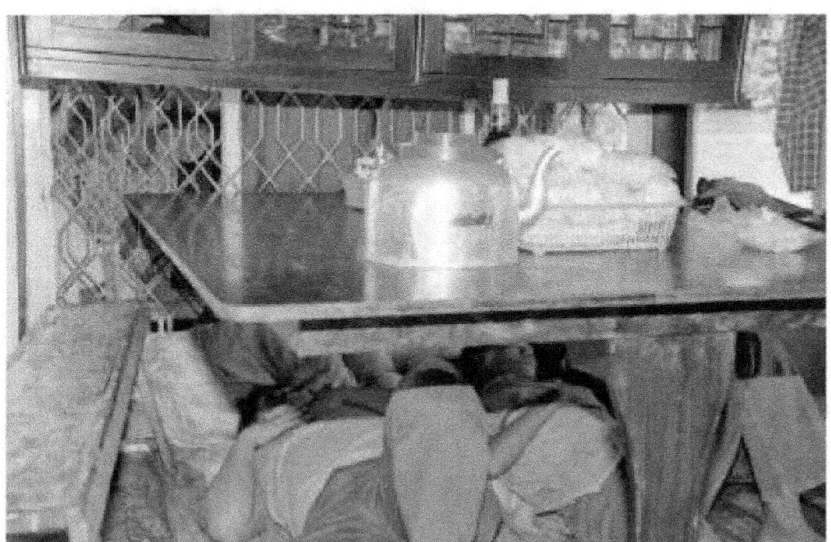

Naptime for kitchen help on the riverboat

The busiest area of the boat consisted of four walls around a hole in the deck utilized as the toilet, shower, or laundry area. After a half day of intense heat, even the warm-water shower felt refreshing to me. The shower consisted of a long hose filled with river water used to cool the engine.

Stepping around the hole in the floor called for caution. I lathered my entire body, looking forward to the warm rinse. Seconds later my shoulders banged the wood wall and a loud siren announced the arrival of the boat at a new dock as it shifted its speed. Oh no!

The engine stopping meant no rinse water for my white-with-lather hair and body. Holes in the walls allowed me to watch the loading of satellite dishes, wire crates of chickens, bushels of tobacco leaves and even two mattresses carried to the top deck.

As I stood there naked and covered with drying soap, noise from the engine startled me from my trance. I watched as the wavering planks to the boat slid back to land. Suddenly, hot water shot out of the hose with such force that the end of the hose fell down the hole into the river.

I scrambled down on my hands and knees, snatched the hose back, and then quickly rinsed myself free of soap. I washed all my clothing after rinsing my hair. Earlier in the day, a few other members of the boat ride had hung clothing on a makeshift clothesline on the top deck. These harsh conditions brought people together laughing, sharing, and caring. The impact of this boat adventure opened my thinking about strangers in a faraway place.

People's lives are commonly linked with food, clothing, shelter, love, religion, sharing, and smiling. However, it was the interaction with the local people that opened communication. Culture conditions us in particular patterns of communication, and I feared that the people on the boat would not take the time to open their hearts to someone so unfamiliar.

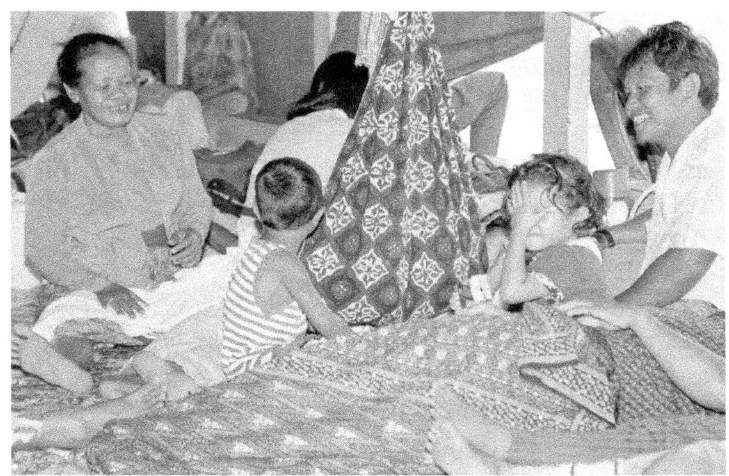

Crowded boat: second class for locals

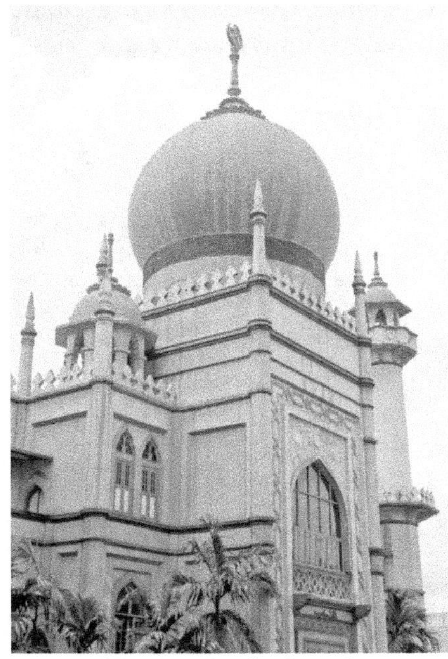

Mosque in the jungle

A tiny bench located outside a window just big enough to crawl through offered a perfect place for journal writing on the bow of the boat. Locals thought the area off limits as they never interrupted this little private space. While writing one morning, I squinted at a huge ball of fire in the distance. The sun brought the top of the mosque to life with blinding light.

Calls to prayer from the mosques of the Muslim river people offer a strange interruption from the constant hum of engines. Second-growth jungle choked the sophisticated structures with their gold spires, shocking those floating lazily past on the river. About two-thirds of the population of Borneo remain Muslim, living in coastal areas relying on river trading and fishing. The Dutch encouraged missionaries to convert the inland Dayaks to Christianity. Animosity remains today between the coastal Muslims and the missionary-converted Christians of the interior. Inland Dayaks speak a number of tribal languages, in contrast to the coastal Muslims who speak regional dialects of Malay. Muslims use military and political systems to control the interior tribes.

Indigenous peoples have known for centuries how to use jungle plants for healing. For example, bark from the cinchona tree contains quinine to treat malaria. *Tubo curanine*, a chemical from the bark and stem of local vines, provides uses in many western societies as a muscle relaxant, to treat tetanus and multiple sclerosis, and for eye surgery.

Contact from the outside world brings a variety of new diseases, once unknown to indigenous peoples. Governments set up periodic clinics with doctors giving polio, smallpox, mumps, and measles vaccines.

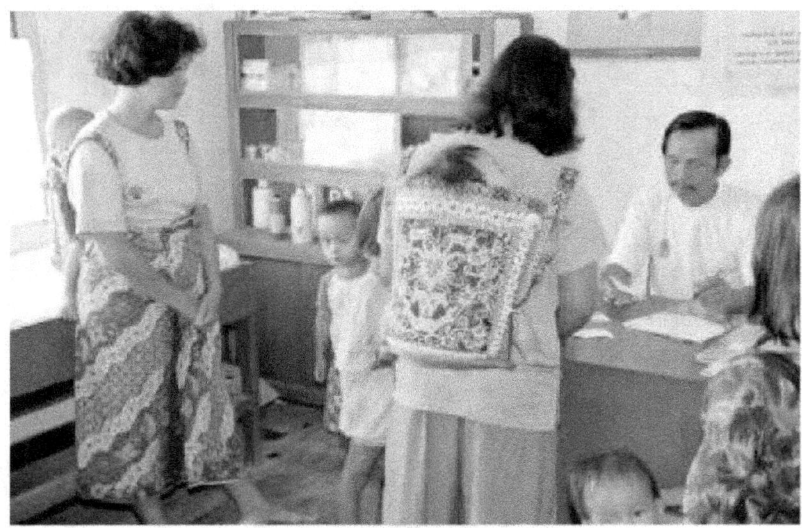

Jungle health clinic

Unique to central Borneo, the *ba,* or traditional baby carrier, worn on the mother's back, carries a child up to three-years old. Beaded carriers illustrate designs of spirit faces under lines of shells, teeth charms, and tiny tiger bells from centuries past. Hand-woven, plaited rattan forms the basis for glass-beaded panels. A half circle of wood forms a seat for support of the child, using wood braces of carved figures. Motifs on the carriers reflect social status. The nobility adorn baby carriers with motifs of human and spirit faces. Common tribes use geometric designs.

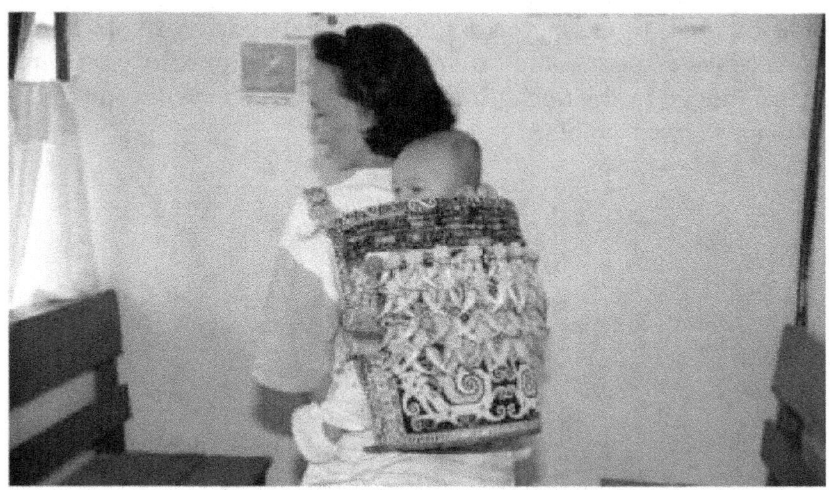

Baby carrier with magic amulets

Kenyahs believe the ba protects the child's soul, still innocent and free to meander. The child may die if the soul decides to wander, giving in to the temptation of spirits. Beaded designs satisfy the soul and keep it close to home. To ward off physical dangers facing children, women weave magical shields of teeth, claws, and beads into the carrier. Mystical carvings on blackened wood might depict a crocodile over a man's body, with monkeys sitting on the croc's tail. The combination of amulets makes a clinking or clicking sound, warning the mother of threatening situations and annoying mischievous spirits.

Morning village life stirred with activity. Women stood in single file outside a new wood structure, the once-a-month clinic. A man wearing a white coat immunized a rash-covered baby. I tried to ask the women questions, but they just shook their heads and smiled, unable to understand me. I picked up a baby carrier lying on its side and asked about the shells. My fingers counted out my age before I pointed to the amulets on the top row of the carrier, hoping someone would understand that I wanted to know the age of the baby carrier. A young mother grabbed my pencil and wrote in perfect letters the words “orang keturunan.” After returning home, I translated the words into "a person from descent of the ancestors who lived in the jungles." The baby carriers wrapped the children in such a loving embrace from parents, ancestors, and beautiful traditions.

I crossed Jempang Lake in a canoe to reach the Mancong Village along the Ohong River to visit the Benuaq indigenous communities. The floating villages hid in tall coconut grass and required the help of a boat driver to visit. A welcome dance in the rebuilt longhouse in Mancong included the chief and his people. Medicine men, or witch doctors, wore riotous patterned skirts, necklaces, and headdresses of beads and streamers from nature, as a *gamelan,* or local instrument, played in the background. Bamboo flutes, drums, and gongs completed the musical ensemble.

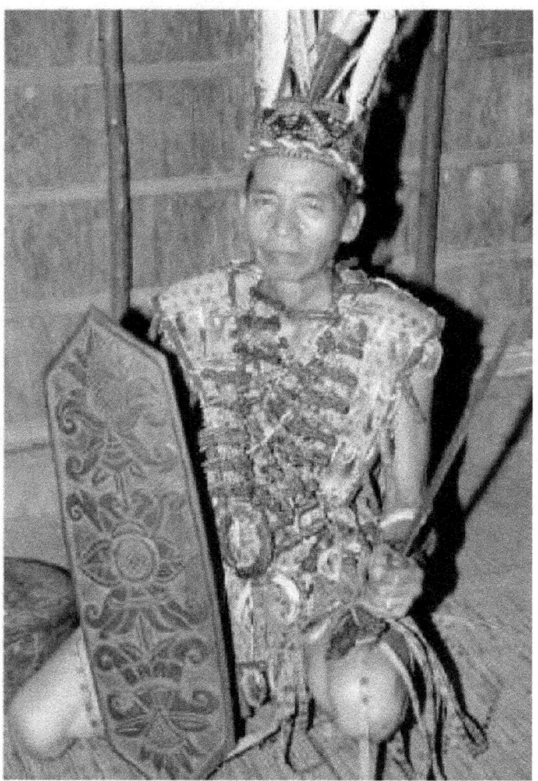

Tribal Chief prepared for warfare

Treks to smaller villages offer the possibility of watching a *belian,* or witch doctor, dressed in leaves, dancing in a circle of flames, asking the spirits for a cure for a patient. The Benuaq Dayaks prefer the cures of ancestors to the medications of more modern government clinics. Often young boys perform the traditional *behempas,* or fighting technique, using shields of wicker and sticks made from rattan. The chief may offer his visitors the opportunity to try a blowpipe.

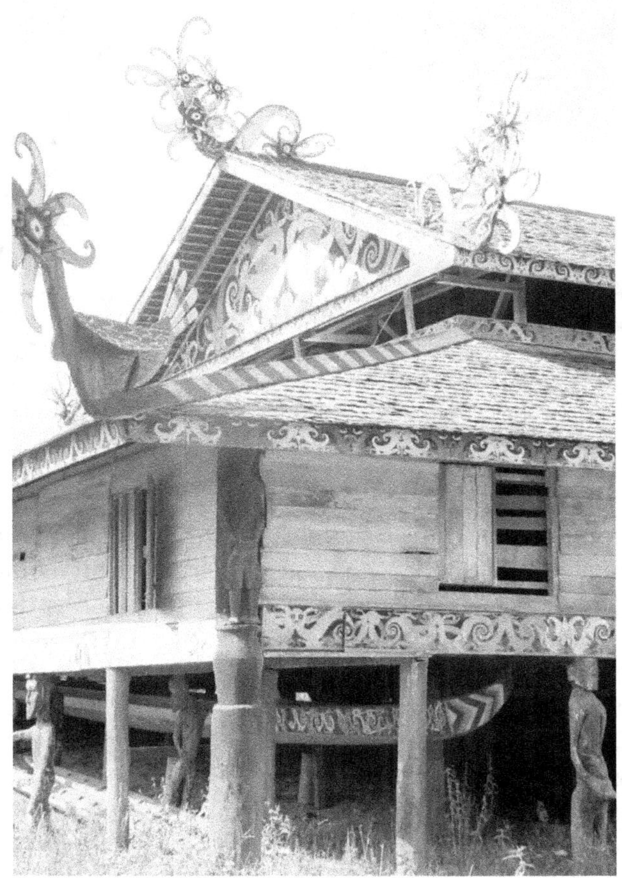

Ornate carvings decorate longhouse

After relaxing in your traditional longhouse guest room, you can peruse the selections of hand-carvings, beads, *itak* hand-woven cloth, baskets, drums made with deer hide, *mandau,* or knives, blowpipes, and traditional baby carriers, all for sale. As you move on to Tanjung Isuy, macaques, kingfishers, proboscis monkeys and monitor lizards appear.

A week on the Mahakam River will open your eyes to the real Borneo. Twice a day, families head to the river for bathing and washing clothes. Most men and women wear a sarong to bathe. After washing, and with years of practice, they slip the wet sarong off while almost simultaneously wrapping a clean, dry sarong over themselves.

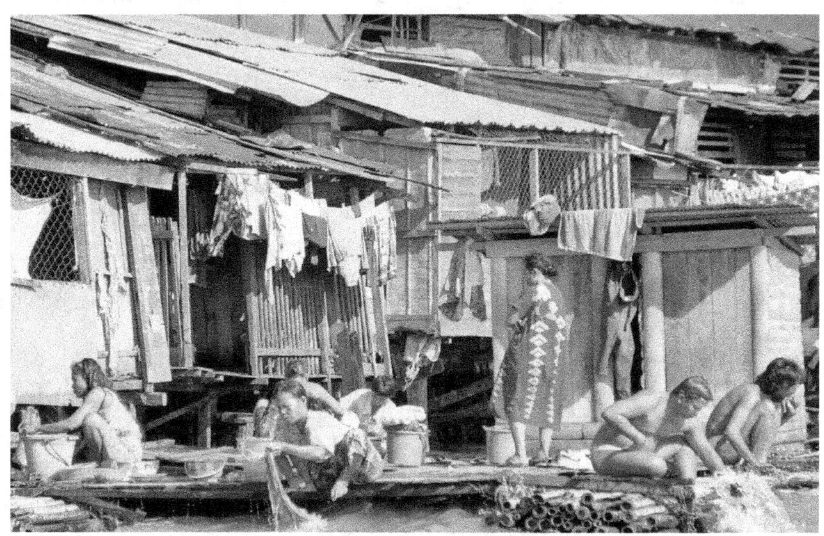

Bath time at sunset

Traveling inland gives you the opportunity to meet the long-eared women. Though this custom is no longer in practice, there are still women living deep in the interior of the jungles, in places which take time and patience to find, who practiced this custom as young girls.

The women inserted thin pieces of tree branches into holes made in the bottom of the earlobes of young girls. As time passed, thicker and thicker pieces of branches kept the holes open, and they attached brass weights to the branches in order to stretch the skin down. They inserted brass earrings of increasing circumference until, decades later, the bottom of the ear lobe hung inches below a woman's shoulders.

Kenyah Dayak women maintain the rice crop, which sustains village life. Spirits determine the crop's success or failure. The impressionable soul of the rice needs special attention.

Men of the village carve unique handles on blades with images of beastly figures, and they give these special knives to women during the courting period. Women use the elaborate knives to harvest the rice.

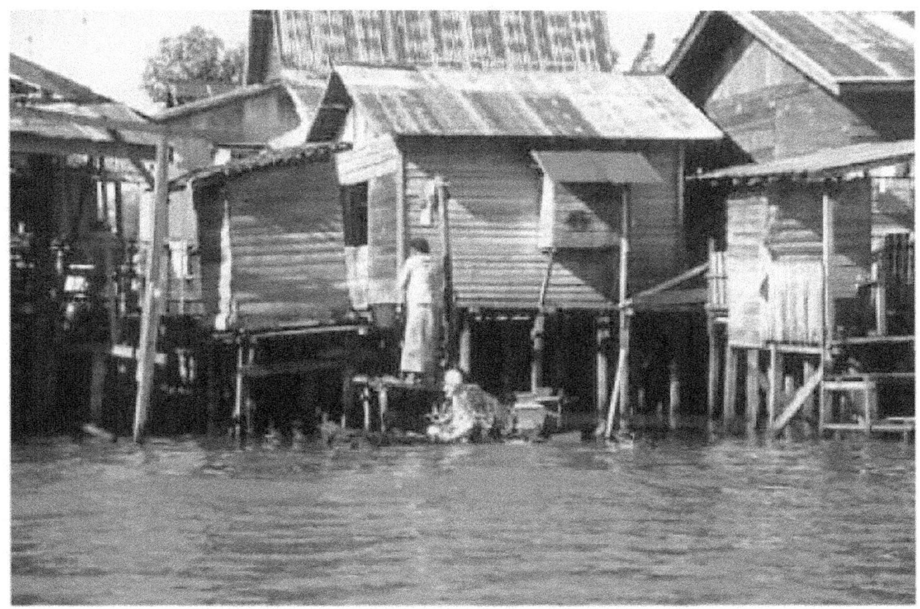

Bath time outside a river home

Borneo beadwork symbolizes a complex mixture of art, ritual, and everyday routines. Beads possess magical qualities and serve as amulets for protection.

The jungle highway, the muddy Mahakam, provides an opportunity for traders looking to obtain imported beads for basketwork and baby carriers.

Kayan and Kenyah Dayaks carry the name of bead traders of the forests.

A teenage Kayan can go to work for a lumber or oil company for a few years and bring back collected beads and enough money to live on forever.

Until the twentieth century, the most sought-after bead, referred to as the *lukut sekala,* offered opportunities in trading a bead for a human slave.

Lukut described a special class of bead used as an engagement or marriage gift and in other social transactions.

The lukut sekalas originated in the historic Islamic or Viking cultures.

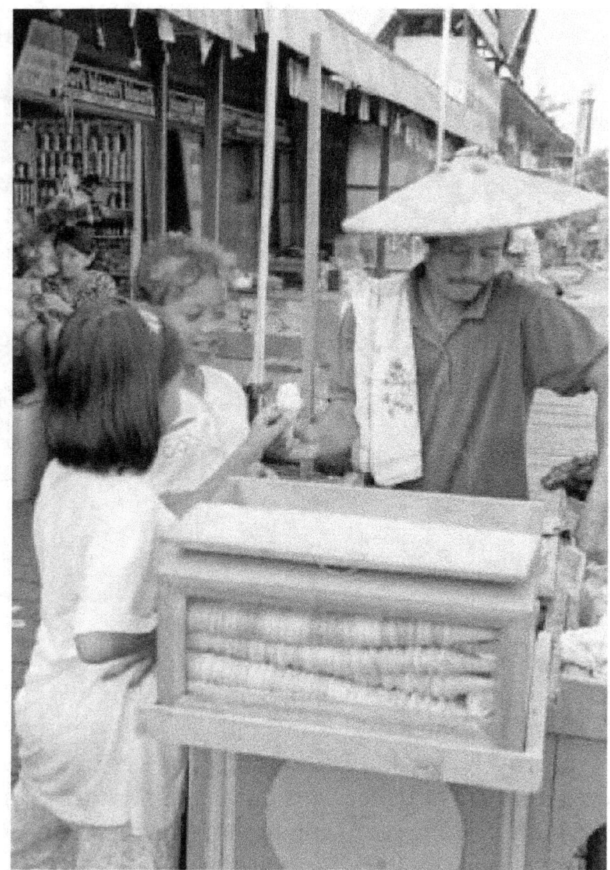

Ice cream cart

The Kayan tribe has a unique wedding procession. Both the bride and groom begin the ceremony in their own longhouse, each having several small groups of friends to represent them.

A man leading the bride's group in procession beats a *mebang*, or brass gong, which shields the bride from any evil noises. The women sing songs, called *nena,* of history, fantasy, fortune, ambition, and approval as they walk to the groom's amin.

The women honor the groom and each of his friends with a *jako,* or cigarette. The groom's family gives each woman a sarong to place over her shoulder as she returns to the bride's amin.

Two more groups from the bride's party follow the same steps, this time delivering *selap,* or betel nuts, and *bura,* or rice wine. The women wear the sarongs as a symbol of friendship with the groom's family.

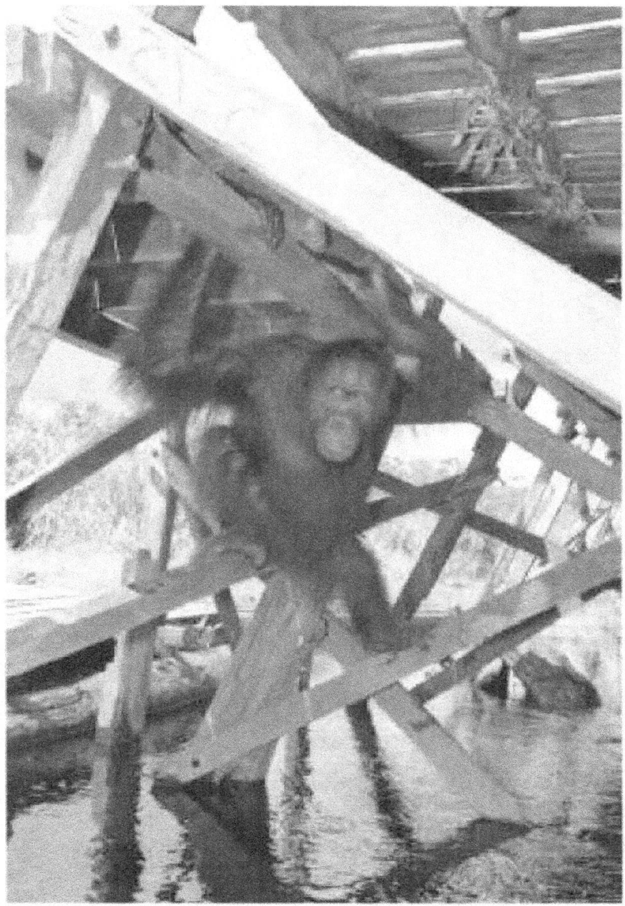

Brown eyes greeting author's arrival

As if a jolt of lightning struck the ground before me, his wild eyes caught mine. My heart, on double-time, pounded.

Rubber tire boat buoys bumped the wood-rafted dock. The breeze lost its fight with the stillness trapped in this jungle opening. Clambering between the rafters of the dock, the biggest orangutan I had ever encountered moved towards me. Did he want me, or my bowl of rice?

"Oh captain, my captain!" I called out, signaling to the river-man the urgency of the situation.

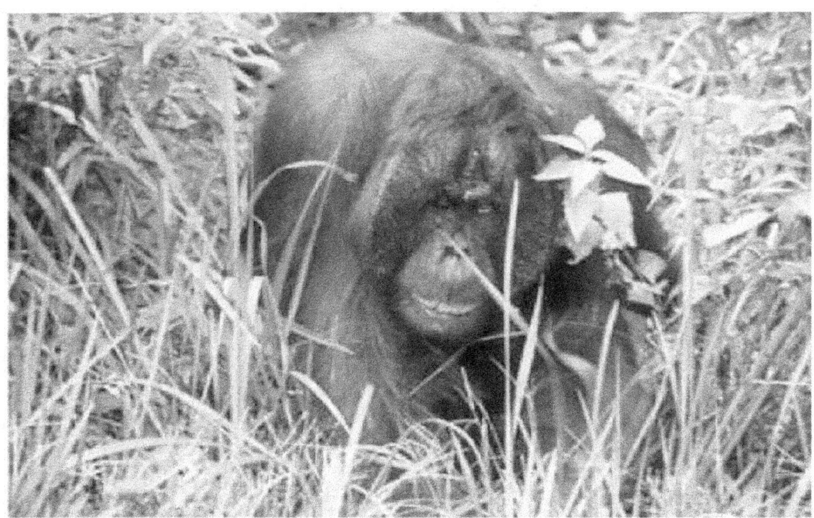

Orang meeting author head on

I had given the captain of my ***kloteck***, or tiny boat, this nickname earlier, knowing he had never heard of the famous poem of the same title by Walt Whitman. Pulling himself up through the kitchen hatch, he reached below for a thermos of hot coffee to splash in those wild eyes if it became necessary. Orangs do not like fire or even hot water.

Barefoot and with adrenaline flowing, I grabbed my camera and climbed out onto the dock. The corner of my eye saw the thermos steaming behind me. Taking baby steps forward, I trained my camera on the orang and shot a roll of film while he sat, motionless, watching me.

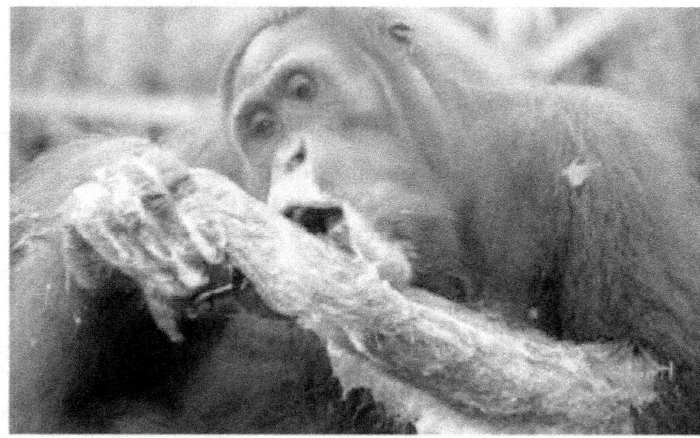

Orang lathering himself with shampoo

The last day of my adventure with the orangs found me bathing in the orange-tinted river. My reaction to the smell from the sulfur-rich soil disappeared within hours of arrival, but my bath-time lathering with orange bubbles highlighted the trip.

The same orangutan, which had greeted me the first day, watched intently as I bathed.

With deliberate steps, his lumbering two-hundred-pound body moved closer and closer. With long, furry arms, he reached for the shampoo bottle and proceeded to pour shampoo over himself. His long fingers rubbed the soap until thick lather formed. Copying every movement I made, the beast shampooed, and then he added a little trick of his own. He licked his arms clean!

The Tanjung Puting National Park in the south of Borneo offers protection for orangutans by the government. Many people try to raise cute baby orangs and find them difficult to care for as they mature. Poachers try to snatch the babies for zoos.

The government returns the poached orangs, half-grown or sick, to the park under the care of watchful scientists. The park provides powdered milk and bananas while introducing them back into the jungle.

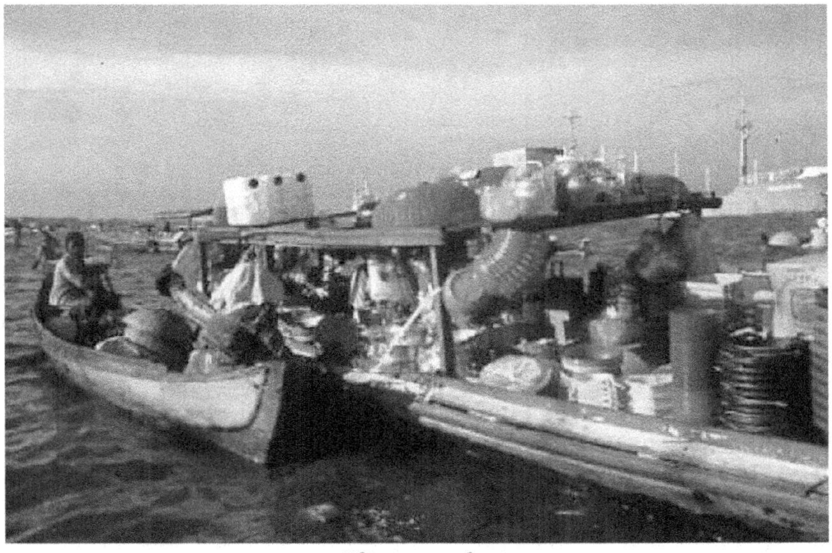

River market

Leaving with several hours of river travel ahead gave me quiet time to absorb the impact of this unusual park. Trying to write in my journal turned into a chore as darkness fell inches at a time on the boat. Suddenly, as if someone turned on a switch, millions of *konang-konang,* or fireflies, lit the narrow river path.

Happy for our departure, the jungle wanted to provide light for our safe journey through tangles of vines unseen in the darkness. The experiences reflected in the eyes of the people I met in Borneo included those passed on from people who lived hundreds of years before them and were as much a part of their lives as the color of their skin and the smiles on their faces. The challenges of this voyage continue to manufacture memories for me, while the chance for building bridges to create even more enriching opportunities stirs my sensibilities.

CHAPTER TWO

Kenya: Unable to Hear the Tolling of Time's Bell

"There are years that ask questions and years that answer." Zora Hurston.

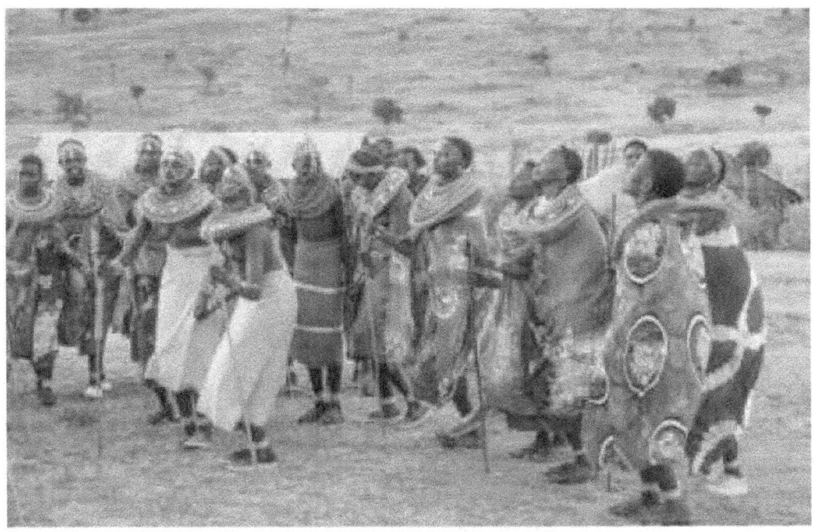

Samburu wedding festival in desert

The agency charged extra for an armed driver for the trip north from Nairobi toward Ethiopia and Somalia. Newspaper headlines reading, "Americans Robbed Again," warned of the lack of security along the dusty northern roads. One rumor passed along from hotel to hotel hinted that robbers killed a white woman for her money and passport.

Although I paid for an armed guard, the driver said he had no guns. The driver assured me of a safe trip and lacked any concern for robbers or hijackers. The grungy left-over-from-some-war vehicle had lost its doors and seat covers, so comfort and cleanliness were not on my travel menu.

Miles and miles of hard-packed sand filled the horizon without a sign of a village or even tire tracks.

Shapes of camels followed by strange-looking donkeys caught my eye between my squinting and blinking through the fierce energy of the sun.

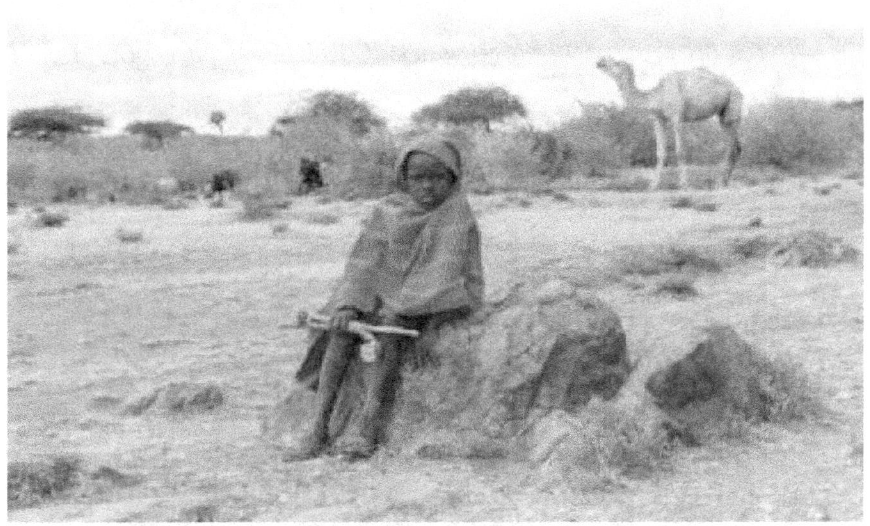

Child alone in desert tending his herd of goats

"People walk for many days to find water. Would you like to see a watering hole?" the driver turned to ask, ignoring his driving tasks, easily managed by a blind man.

Hours of dust covered my clothing and skin, and the idea of stopping to see something other than sand sounded great.

Camels belched and groaned in the distance as we approached several Turkana women filling goatskin water pouches.

In Ethiopia, the Tuareq families I stayed with for a few days in the desert showed me how they take the skin of a goat, turn it inside out, and stitch up the leg areas. They bind the neck opening with a thin piece of skin used for the drawstring closing.

The Tuareqs used the waterproof bags for carrying water for days in the desert.

Donkeys stood motionless while women arranged weird-looking woven carriers that hung on each side of the donkeys' backs, like huge envelopes.

The filled skins propped on top of each other occupied the carriers, leaving no room for riders.

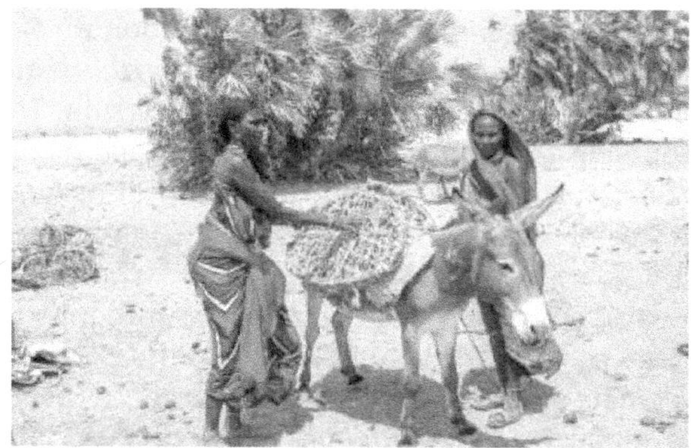

Filling water containers for three-day journey home

Loud, red-patterned fabrics wrapped around women's heads and shoulders warned the sun to back off.

How did the women walk in their tight-fitting sarongs of clashing oranges and pinks?

They draped fabric across their faces, leaving only their eyes exposed to us as our beat-up vehicle approached.

Uncomfortable with my stares, or perhaps because their donkeys had all the weight they could carry, the women began their barefoot journey home.

A diet of cattle milk and blood gives sustenance for the Turkana who think nothing of walking twenty miles in one day.

Millet and gourds supplement the diet during the rare, rainy seasons.

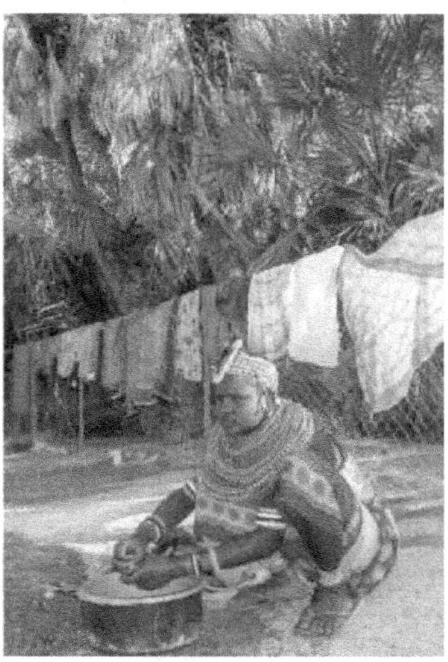

Turkana doing laundry in hot spring

Unlike the ever-changing shapes of the northern Sahara Desert, the heart of the Chalbi Desert lay undisturbed. An occasional gazelle, giraffe, scrub bush barren of leaves, or human dotted the vast, sand horizon. The Kurungu Camp looked deserted outside the town of South Horr, so we moved on. The Forest Camp, the last alternative for overnight protection, sat as quiet and isolated as the previous site. The night's agenda called for setting up tents and a cooking fire.

My calendar dictated that we move farther north the next morning. Indigenous peoples, artists at battling sustenance from the parched landscape, stay with their water camels on the life-giving Lake Turkana, the largest desert lake in the world. Also known as the Jade Sea, the lake appears like a rare, brilliant, green stone.

The crusty, brown earth of the Chalbi Desert wins the battle for space with drought on its side. Each year the lake dwindles in size. Practicing nomadic tribes materialize like a mirage, oblivious to the approaching ways of Western society in the beat-up vehicle creating a dust cloud in the distance.

The sandy terrain cluttered with stones changed to black lava rocks. I quickly noticed my bottom was no longer bouncing on the hard springs buried in the seat. Such a nice change to ride smoothly and without the dust of the desert stinging my face. The volcanic wasteland donated little more than scrub vegetation for the El Molo's huts, similar to igloos.

Unlike most tribes of Kenya who depend on cattle or camels for their livelihood, the El Molo eat fish, with a crocodile or hippo, if lucky. Fresh, grilled fish sounded perfect for dinner. Eating the donated fish that might have sat in the sun for two days gave me a sick feeling.

Acacia roots provide material for harpoons. Shade on the lake side of huts provided an afternoon resting spot for mending Doum palm fiber nets. Shaved heads were prevalent as ringlets of beads wrapped the foreheads of faces, pretty enough to model for any magazine. Women with outstretched legs, hidden by mounds of fishing net, leaned against their huts in the shade.

Children pretended to sail the high seas, pulling sticks through the black, lava-stone beach while balancing on rafts of Doum Palm branches tied with fiber ropes. The El Molo people live on the shores of Lake Turkana in small clusters.

El Molos once faced extinction, but due to their increased contact with western society, modern medicines, and intermarriage with neighboring Samburu and Turkana tribes, the tribe's population continues to increase.

They do not depend on livestock for their survival. Men and women wear numerous metal elbow and wrist bracelets in addition to collecting colorful beads.

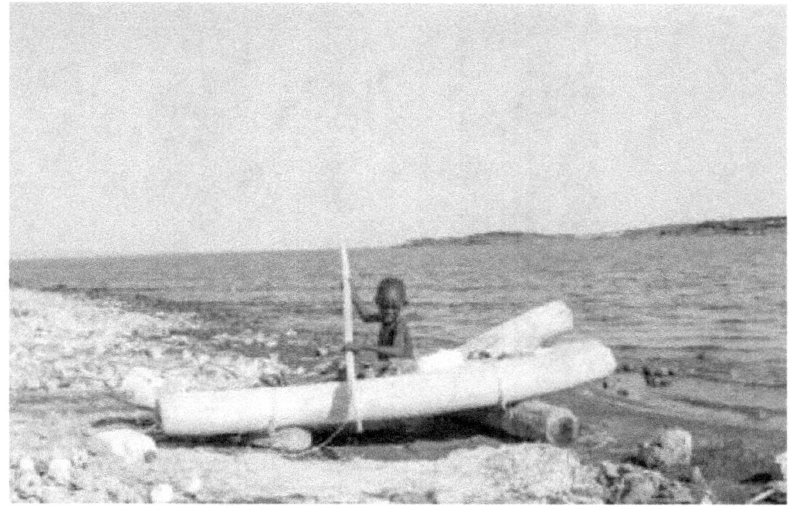

El Molo child playing in a boat on Lake Turkana

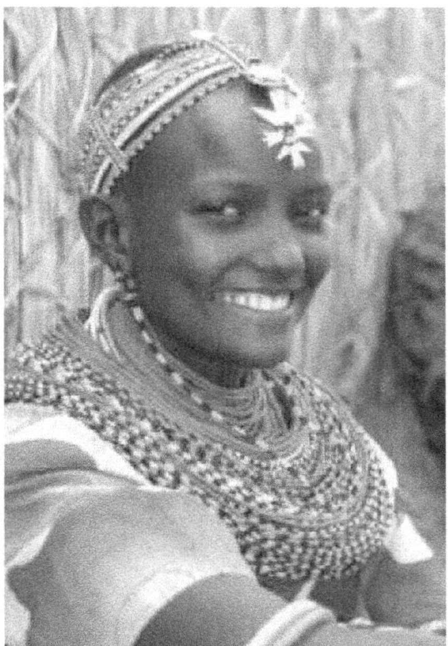

El Molo living on Lake Turkana

Paul, the driver, said, "The El Molo name came from a Maasai word meaning those who make a living from sources other than cattle. They trade fish with the camel herders to survive."

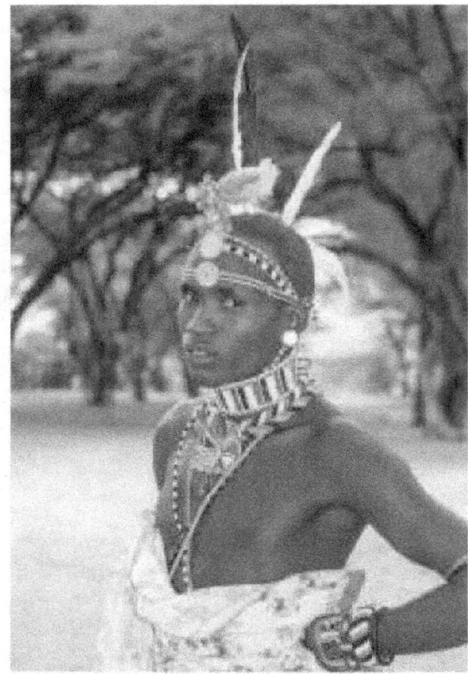

Rendille tribal man

"The sun is sinking fast," I hinted to Paul in case we needed to move on to another village for the night.

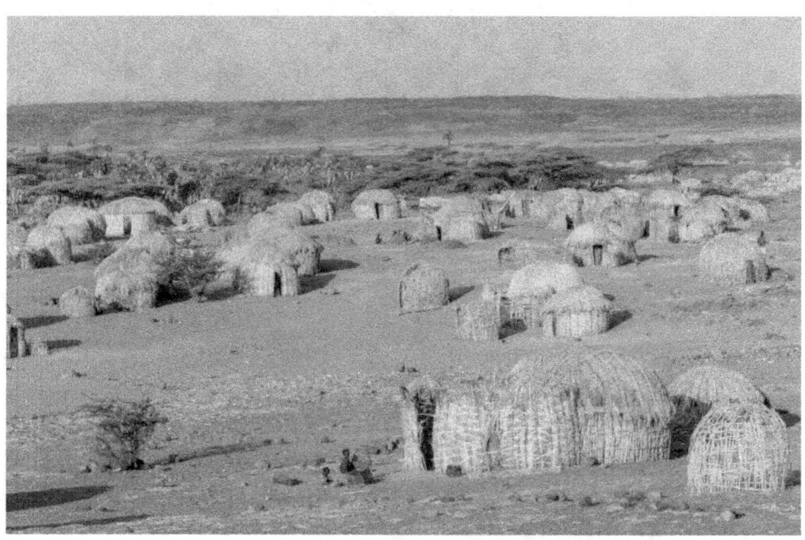

Rendille village

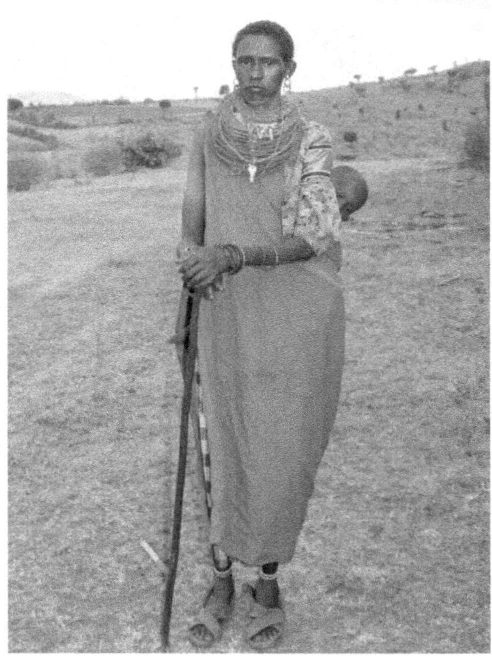

Samburu mother and child

Paul motioned for me to climb aboard followed by, "The Turkana tribe live in a large, welcoming village, very near, with a hot spring for bathing."

Rain falls an average of once in five years, which made me question leaving the one permanent source of water in the area.

Paul changed directions from north to east, heading toward Marsabit, and somehow, without even a tree for a landmark, Paul found this remarkable group of huts almost hidden by dead scrub bushes spilling over their roofs.

A few Turkana tribesmen welcomed the rare sight of a bare-legged white-skinned woman, wearing heavy purple-and-turquoise hiking boots. A young boy offered private hut, complete with a log bed and a thin single layer of fabric for a mattress.

Along with the darkness, a cool chill settled all around.

Paul served me a reddish-brown soup with white floating things on the surface and presented me with a handful of candles.

Heavy-duty protein bars, averaging 30 grams of protein each, made a super second choice for dinner.

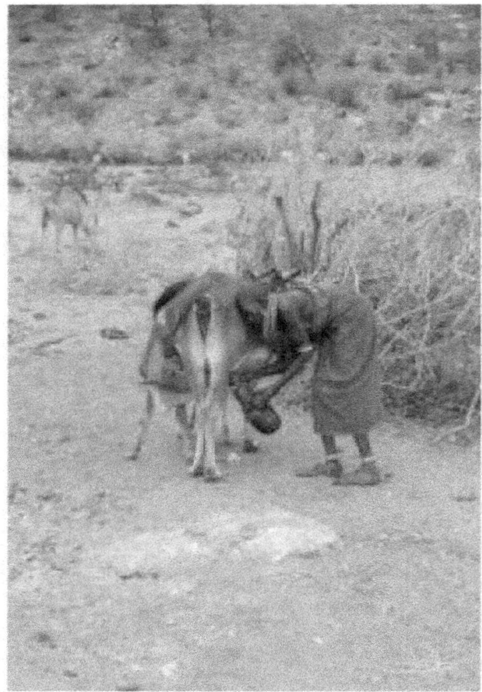

Milking a cow

The flashlight I carried extended my reading time until a young man knocked on the outside of the hut. He spoke little English.

I understood him to say I could watch some local dancing. I followed him for about fifteen minutes, tripping on stones and berating myself for leaving my flashlight behind.

My clothing calmed my shivers while I wondered how much farther. The young man pointed to a horizontal log and walked away leaving me alone, scared, and wanting the security of my little candlelit hut. I sat down and chanting started.

A blast of wind crossed my face. Several men jumped up and down inches from my feet.

They jumped higher and higher, causing the sand to loosen and spit at my legs. Why no women? And dancing at midnight?

A boy squatted near the log, making motions for me to scoot over. He explained in broken English the meaning of the songs. The men sang about their fathers protecting livestock and families. A half-hour later, the boy stood, reaching for my hand while turning away from the dancers. I was not sure he was the same boy who led me to this place.

No light from the moon or flashlight meant following his lead. His tight grip kept me balanced as rocks and ruts caught me off guard.

His jerking motions forced me over dry cracks in the desert landscape. The door handle of my hut, a rag tacked into place with a sliver of wood, eventually took the place of the boy's hand.

The wobbly tree-branch bed never looked more comforting.

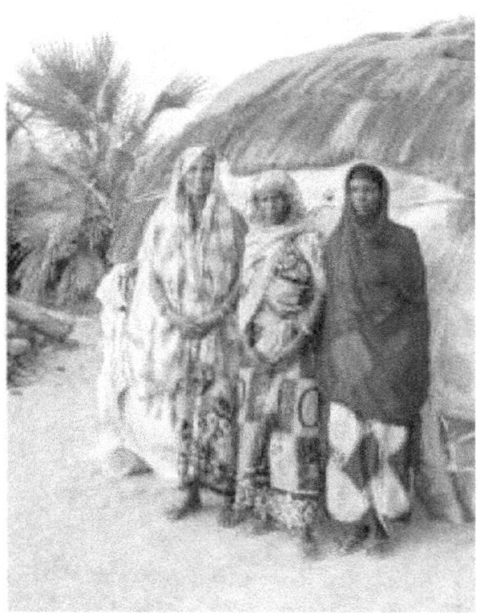

Ready to prepare dinner

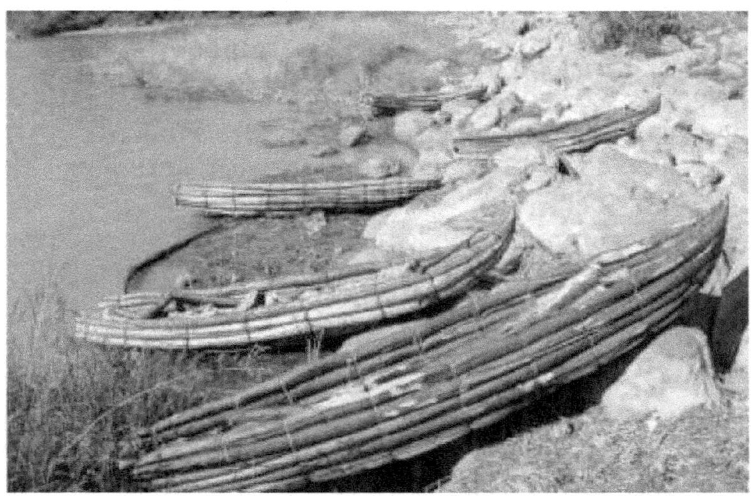

Njemp boats

Isolation has protected the El Molo, Borana, Rendille, Gabbra, Pokot, Samburu, and Turkana tribes from the effects of the twenty-first century in the past.

New technologies like GPS and cell towers now make their way into the lives of the last true nomadic tribes.

The Turkana we left behind waved, wearing nothing more than ostrich-plumed headdresses, yet, incongruously, they held cell phones in their hands.

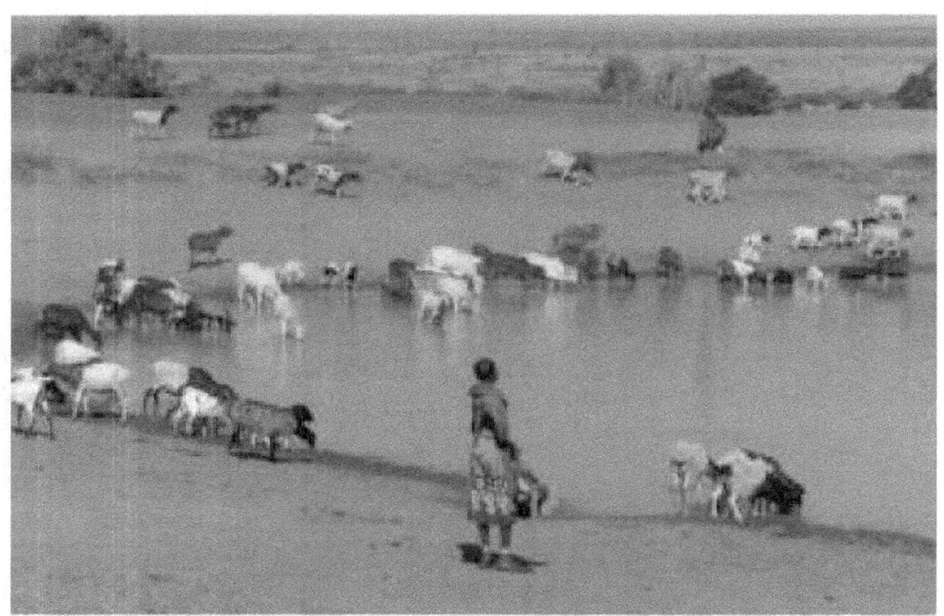

Child watering her herd of goats

The Chalbi Desert lies motionless with its hard-packed, bleak and barren crust, unlike the dusty flowing dunes of the northern Sahara.

The Gabbra and the Rendille, unlike the neighboring Turkana, act as guardians of their traditional existence.

As if quarantined from the modern world, their ancient lives continue with folklore and practices like the singing wells.

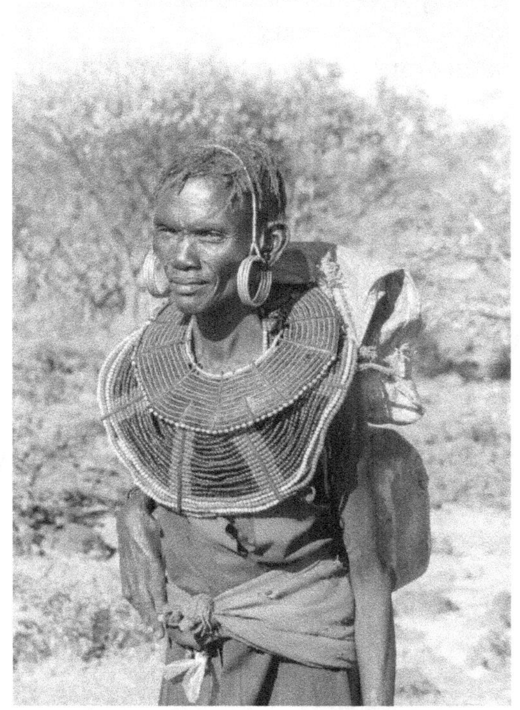

Pokot walking home from market

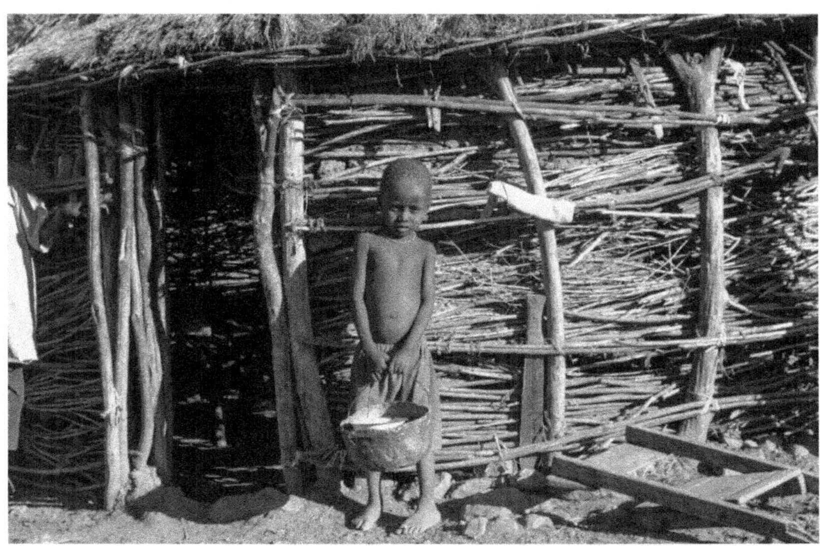

Helping with dinner

The cool of the morning offers the best viewing time for the primitive custom of obtaining water from fifty-foot wells dug in the hard-packed earth. The steps down into the well wind around and around to the bottom, and women line up every other step as they lift the water in wood buckets hand over hand. Soft chanting echoes to the background clacking of the wooden bells, adorning the necks of camels waiting patiently above.

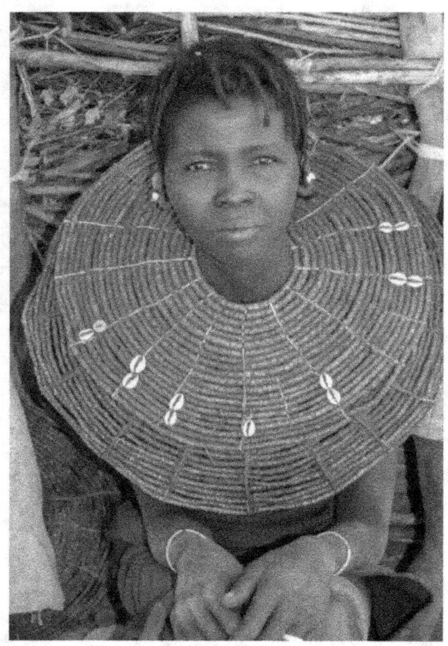

Unmarried Pokot

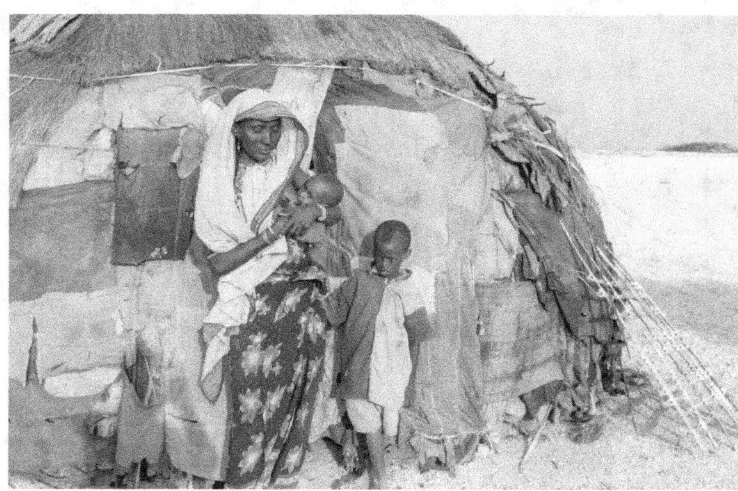

Proud mother

The vast sea of pebbles stretched in every direction to where the sky meets the earth.

The afternoon heat had begun its wearing down process that pulled us toward a hotel for the night, offering two huts with beds of tree branch legs and coverless mattresses.

Two women wrapped in yards of colorful fabrics smiled while plopping chickens down in the sand and pointing to the huts.

They spoke a language unfamiliar to either my guide or me, but they acknowledged through their smiles and their pointing towards the huts that we needed a place to sleep and food to eat.

Whether Rendille or Gabbra, their beauty stood in sharp contrast to the earth-tone colors of the day.

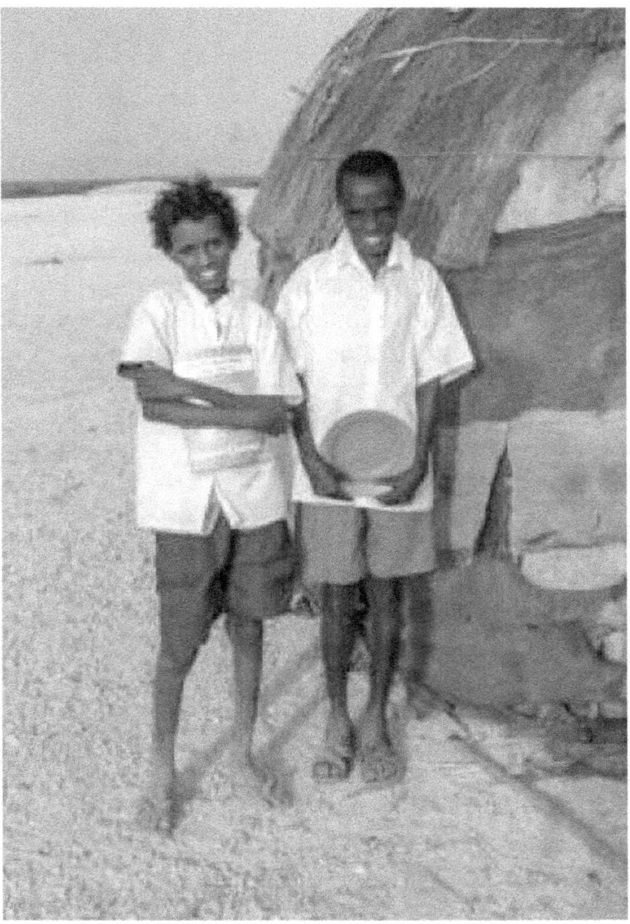

Returning from desert school

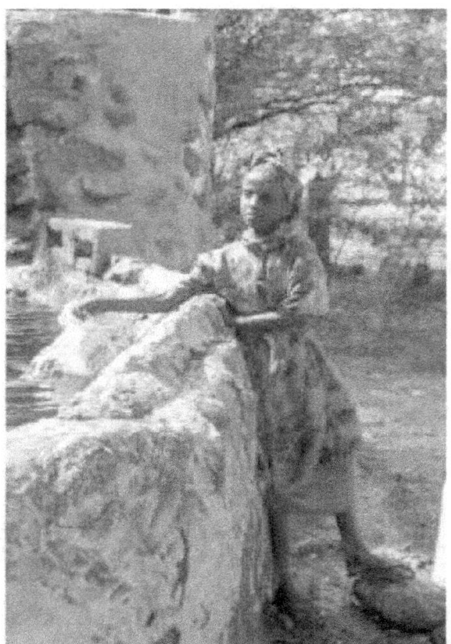

Deaf girl filling jugs at local well

I knew of the desert long before this sojourn began, including the scary little sand flies carrying a killer disease called Kalazaaris, and the eyeless Siafu ants with their impressive jaws. Also called Safari ants, they swarm in large armies feasting on everything in their path.

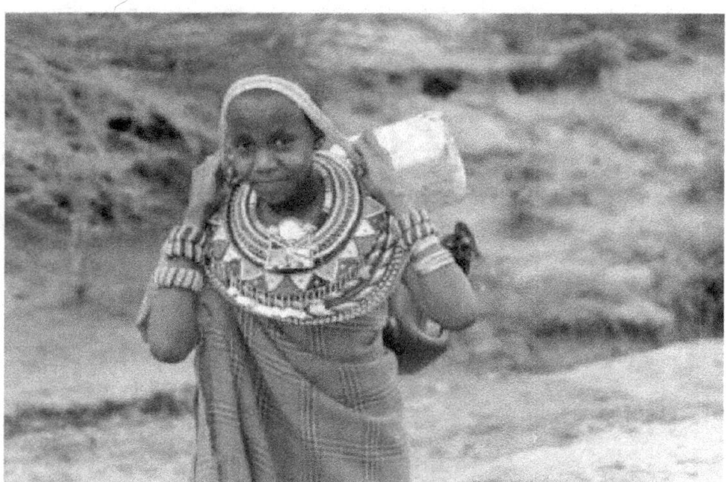

Tried to teach her to blow bubbles with gum

The acacia tree, known as the Whistling Thorn, surrounded the backs of the huts, creating a wall of thorns. Thorns, hollow and three-inches long protruded from bright purple bulbs. The dark hollows offered a safe home for stinging ants. The wind dries the thorns, creating tiny whistling flutes, more than enough reason to want to sleep off the ground tucked safe inside the false security of my mosquito net. The tree-branch roof of my hut offered a perfect place to attach the strings of the net.

My flashlight and toothbrush, the focal points of the room, were ready for darkness to fall.

A walk before bed took me to a resting stop for camels. About a hundred or more, groaning for shade and water, filled an opening in the circle of invasive Prosopis bushes. The spiny thick bushes, taller than the camels, made a perfect jail for their night's rest.

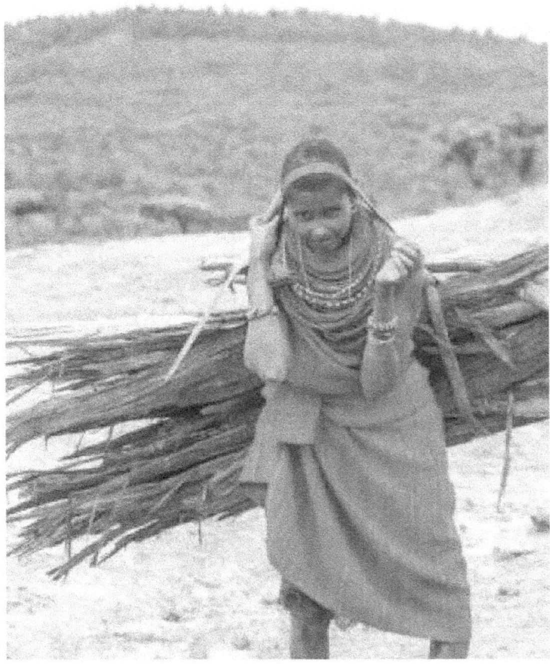

Carrying firewood back to Pokot village

I walked into the third hut designed for cooking and sleeping, and I was caught off guard. The women, still draped in their beautiful fabrics, knelt on the dirt floor scraping and cleaning a bloody mess of a chicken (I guessed).

Little foil pouches of tuna have saved my life all over the world. I never knew how depressing those packets would appear after eating one a day for over a month as I did in China. With a stomach growling for a fresh salad or even a grilled chicken breast from the Colonel, I left the hut to find my journal for some note-taking before dark. By noon the next day, I wished I didn't have a stomach.

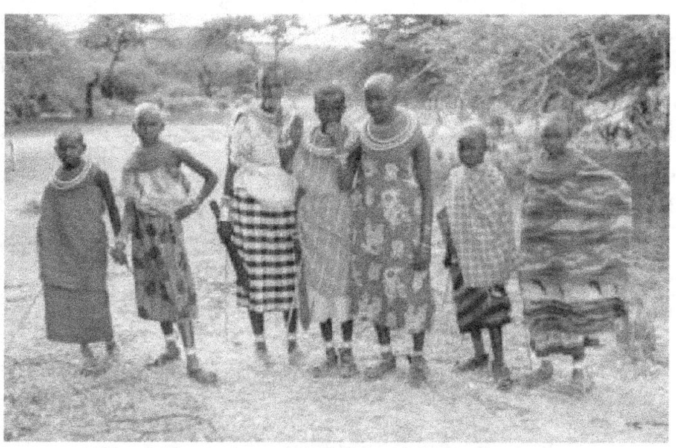

First time to see white-skinned woman

Paul tried to soothe me with, "Maybe we can make Marsabit, the next real town, before sunset."

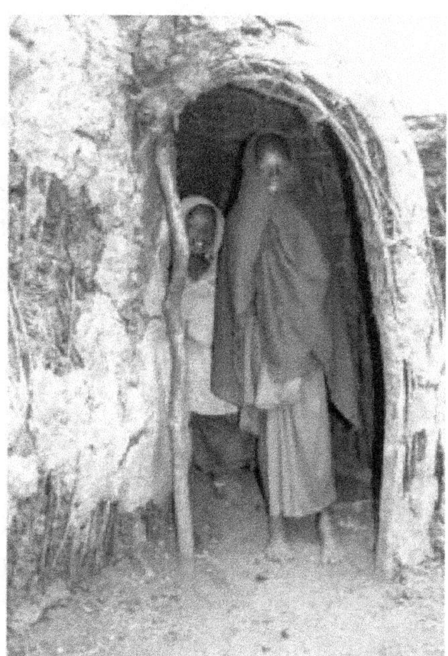

Peeking out from a Maasai hut

Clean sheets, a real squat toilet with a door, and bubbling soda in a glass bottle kept me alive for two days while I tried to recover from a bacterium those chicken ladies passed on to me, although I never touched their chicken!

The third day I learned my lesson well after visiting the local hospital. If I ever, ever get sick again, I will find the nearest hospital immediately.

For the price of a soda back home, the local doctors will treat you with medicine known only to them. Familiar with this problem, they have figured out what to do for immediate help.

A camel safari stirred my level of excitement, which meant my illness had met its match, and the thrill of the next adventure could take its place.

Rumors of camels slobbering and biting warned me to keep my boots on. Allowing three men and five camels to guide me into the wild, arid lands of Africa came easy for me. The traditional desert vehicle offered a peaceful inroad into the raw terrain of northern Kenya.

Each day, the panorama around me appeared as if painted like a mural on my sunglasses. Often, a giraffe or herd of zebras pranced across the path. At night, the men established a campsite. I did what I could to find spare bits of wood for a fire or set up the tents.

The camel's movement up, and back down hard, gives your whole body a workout, but in particular, the behind, with a few added blisters.

A clerk in a travel goods store showed me his best-selling item, a blue flannel pillowcase folded into a tiny little pouch. Amazing, the things we take for granted, like pillows!

Budget hotels and camel saddles sometimes need an extra pillow stuffed with your favorite tee shirt. This pillowcase held all my loose clothing together for padding, and after hours of my sitting on the clothing, it lost its fluff and ended up flat like the saddle.

Nighttime offered me much-needed relief from the day of bobbing up and down like a boat.

Sunrise meant instant coffee. Water came from the shallow stream where the camels traipsed, drank for what seemed like hours, and proceeded to pee.

Boiling water for half an hour kills anything, they say! Before the temperature reached its peak, the group had started the desert day.

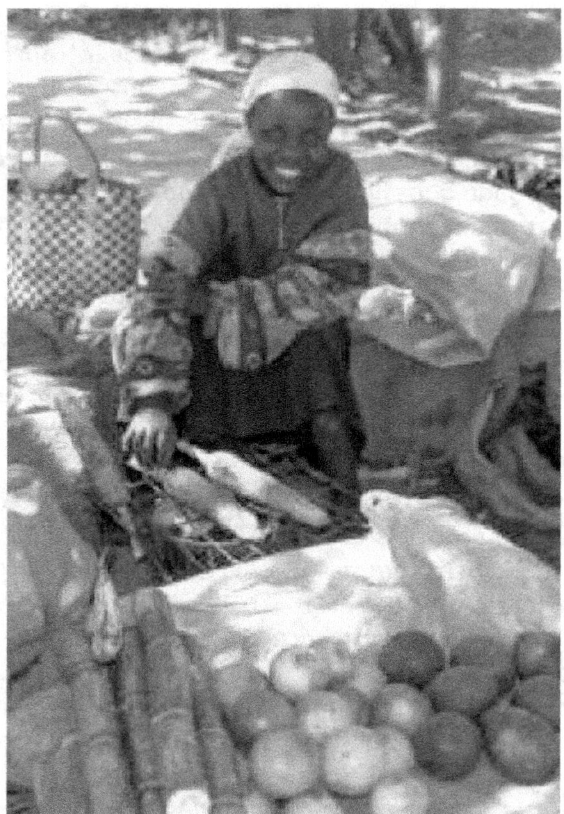

Selling corn on the roadside

In the distance, bright colors melted into the horizon like a mirage. A group of children scattered like jackrabbits on a prairie at the sight of our five camels, one carrying a white-skinned rider. One of the dark-skinned guides yelled in the Samburu language for the young teenagers to come back and meet a new friend. People with shaved heads, and sunshine-colored fabrics wound around their tiny bodies, peeked out at me from behind scrub bushes.

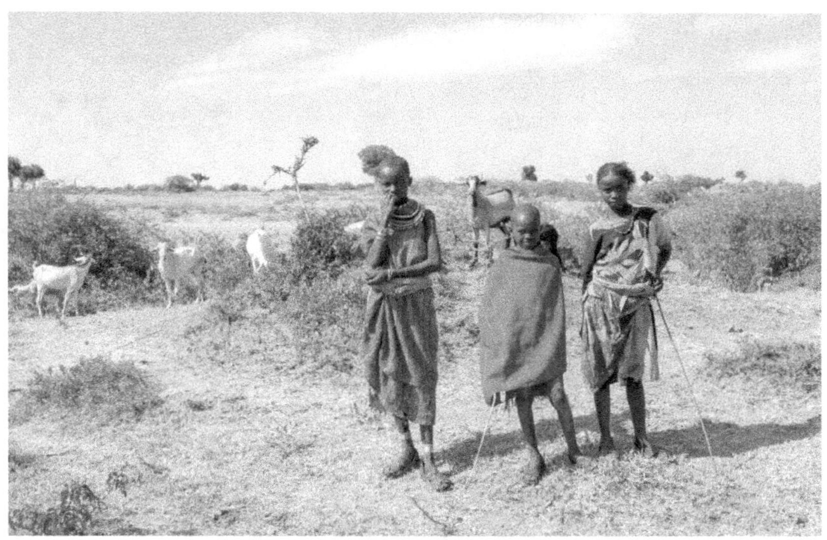

Samburu children watching their herd of goats

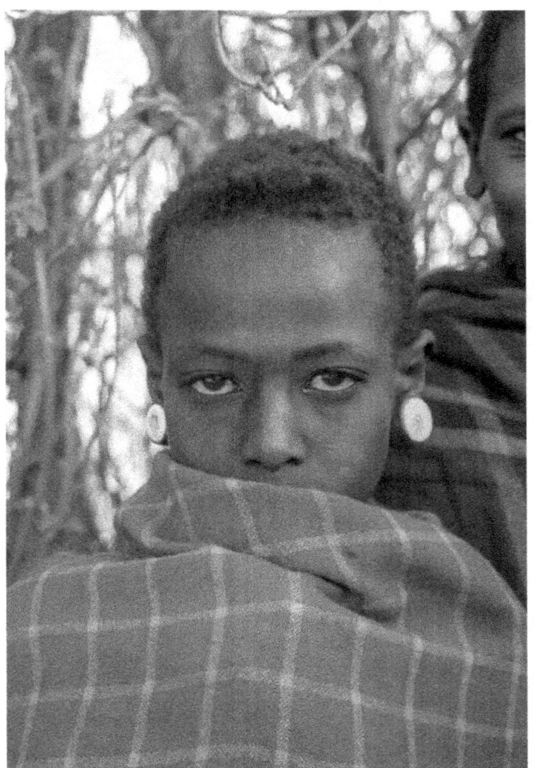

Samburu watching wedding festival

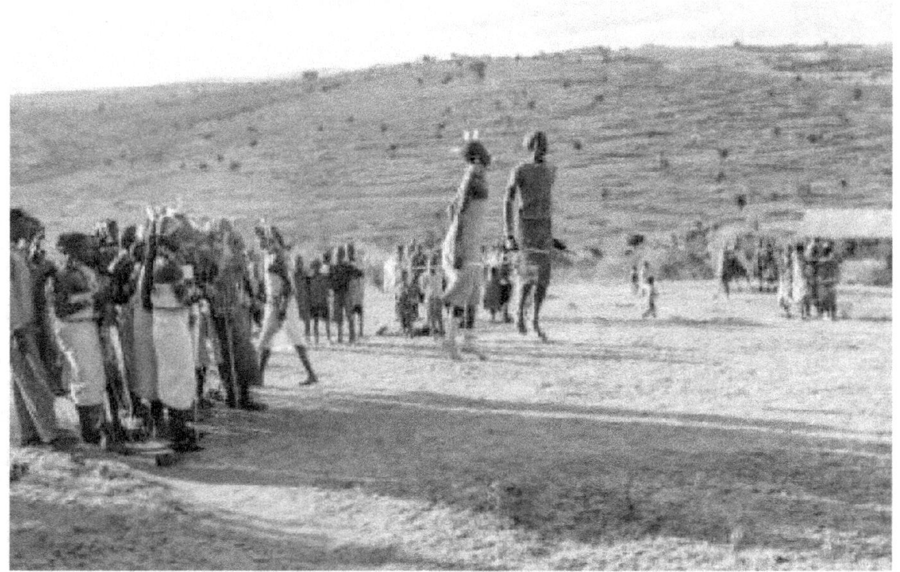

Samburu men jumping high

Choices fill our everyday lives. Money spent for three weeks of travel can bring the desert mirages to life. That same money could be spent on remodeling the bathroom.

CHAPTER THREE

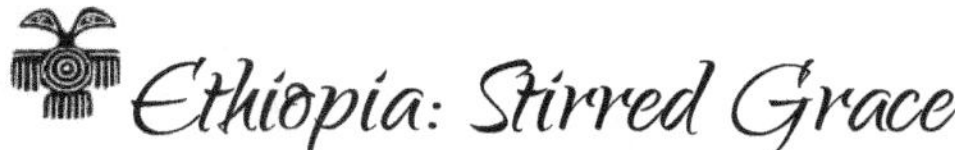

Ethiopia: Stirred Grace

"Not I nor anyone else can travel that road for you. You must travel it for yourself." Walt Whitman

Paint a picture of a dry desert with starving people, and Ethiopia comes to mind. Ethiopia, one of the most compelling countries in Africa, opens pathways that allow us to step back in time.

The word "history" found its initial breath millions of years ago with the first human remains unearthed near the capital, Addis Abba.

Away from the scramble of city life, ripples of vivid lime to dark pine feed the eye.

Tourists interested in the Christian monuments and rock-hewn churches of the north wander the ancient alleyways lost in the fifteenth century.

Halfway around the world, Ethiopia's geography and culture feel eons away from the wheat fields of Kansas.

Twice the size of Texas, Ethiopia offers geographical variety, with altitudes ranging from below sea level to heights of 4620m/15,000ft, creating one of the hottest places on earth, giving Ethiopia the nickname of "Roof of Africa."

Looking for an anthropological expedition? Make contact with primitive tribes in the southwest, the richest concentration of aboriginal tribes in the entirety of Africa.

These primitive tribes share ethics, values, and goals of non-materialistic traditions.

Compensated with the symbolic and ornamental wealth on their embellished bodies, people live satisfied and balanced lives.

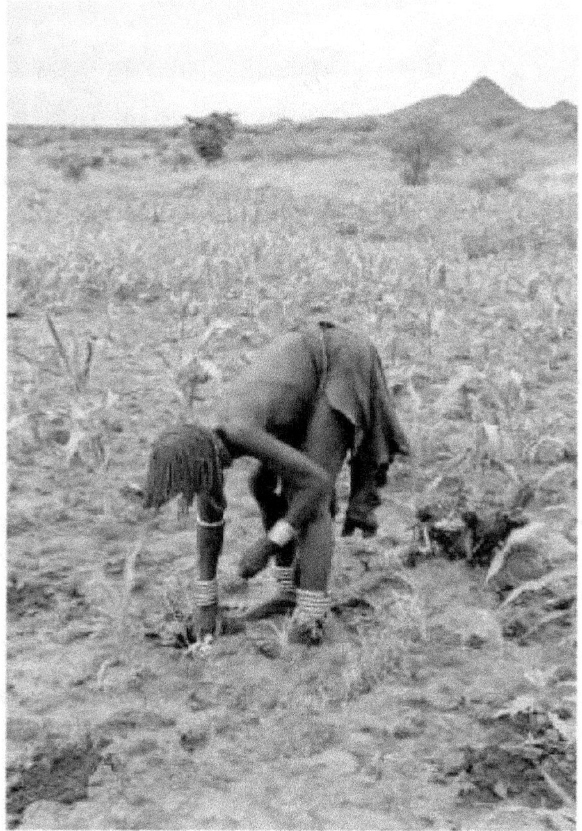
Hammer tribal planting corn

Variations of traditions range from the practical to the exotic in the population of rural villages.

The environment dictates simplicity and practicality in living quarters, like small mud huts with grass tops for the nomadic or semi-nomadic tribes.

Animal skins embellished with shells and bottle caps cover bodies coated in red paint for decoration, with hairstyles I'll leave to the imagination.

A natural affinity for beauty gives the Ethiopians a reason for breathtaking clothing, hairstyles, and, most of all, jewelry.

The Ethiopians pursue a heritage that remains vital to their cultural ethics and religious rituals, often reflected in their garments and style.

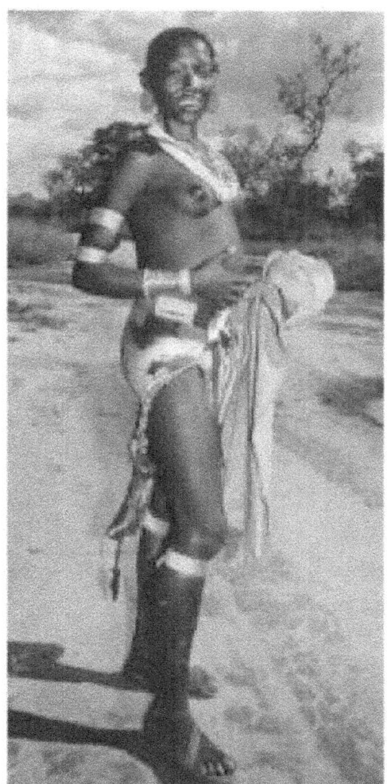

Tsamy walking from Konso wearing animal skins

The Mursi, Hammer, Karo, Konso, Galeb, and Borana tribes all coexist in a cracked and craggy environment, forgotten by the rest of the world. Here, the visitor can see the Africa of yesterday. In their hidden cloisters, these tribesmen's symbolic customs flourish through body adornment. The power of nature dominates while strong ties link them to the Omo River as their main life source.

***

Green patches of maize, cotton, and sorghum, and villages, like little brown buttons separated by the stitching of fence borders, completed the seen-from-the-sky quilt. In the center of each village, a yellow circle contained the second-hand of a clock ticking. While the plane sank from the sky, I could see cattle tied side-by-side, their bellies rubbing and their heads down, walking in a circle, grinding maze. Baboon families scattered around the grass runway, a welcome end to the ten-passenger flight from Addis to Arba Minch, the beginning of my sojourn to villages not found on common maps.

* * *

Girma, my guide, driver, cook, friend, and interpreter, greeted me with a smiled sigh of relief after waiting two days for my flight, delayed for reasons that changed faster than the ripples on water.

My bag of tricks included the following: water purifier, enough cans of tuna to cause an overweight charge, a new tent tricking me into believing the waterproof tag, enough batteries to open a store, (though this did not help the new flashlight with the broken bulb), and lots of hope.

I arrived, ready to camp in the raw Africa that greeted me.

Girma promised a hotel of some sort if possible. For eight birr ($1), the first night's hotel consisted of an empty room with no screens.

Malarial mosquitoes buzzed my neck, which meant setting up the tent inside the room.

Shutters and doors had broken locks or none at all. How could I squeeze all my gear, boots, and body into a one-man tent?

For further protection from the gang of mosquitoes waiting for a bare-skin feast, I left my long sleeves, pants, and socks on, and woke up drenched in sticky, wet perspiration from the intense heat of the closed-in space.

A bush in the jungle offered more privacy than the wood platform with a hole in the middle for a toilet.

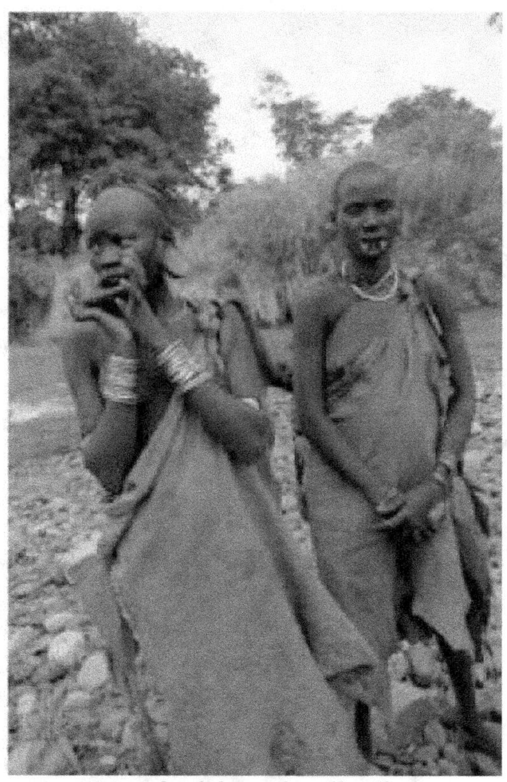

Mursi without her lip disc

The Mursi, one of the most peculiar native peoples of Ethiopia, live as herdsmen and warriors. Myths, symbols, and superstitions influence the Mursi's way of conveying their significance.

Girls start their ritual mutilations around age ten to begin the process to achieve womanhood. Without drugs or modern tools, the Mursi extract the two, lower-incisor teeth to make room for the lip plates, a common tradition for the Mursi women.

Skilled women pierce the ears of teenagers for insertion of clay and wood disks.

After the teen becomes fifteen, one of the women of her family makes an incision in her lower lip to allow for stretching of the opening until it is large enough for insertion of a small lip plate.

About six months before marriage, stretching continues with larger plates inserted into the pierced lip. The elasticity of the lip increases in time, allowing easy removal of the plates.

Women must wear discs when men are present, but take them out when sleeping or eating alone.

The Mursi suggest three reasons for the adoption of the unnatural custom. Men believed the strange behavior would discourage slave traders from taking their women, the same reason the Palaung women wear brass rings around their necks in Thailand.

The superstitious believed the ugly discs kept evil spirits from entering the body. The size of the disc designates the bride price or number of cattle acceptable for the future wife's hand in marriage.

The woman, wearing many arm bracelets and large lip discs, demands maybe fifty cattle for her parents. Other traditions include scarification of the body and face along with wild-as-one's-imagination body paintings. These acts may attract the opposite sex.

Men compete for recognition of masculinity and strength. The young men love a sport called *donga,* or stick fighting. Winners earn status among their peers.

Some have the opportunity to win a girl's hand in marriage. Villages come together, and winning fighters challenge each other.

The aggressive reputation of the Mursi plagues outsiders, most often the Bana tribes, over disputes of trespassing, stolen cattle, or revenge for evil spells supposedly cast over their herds.

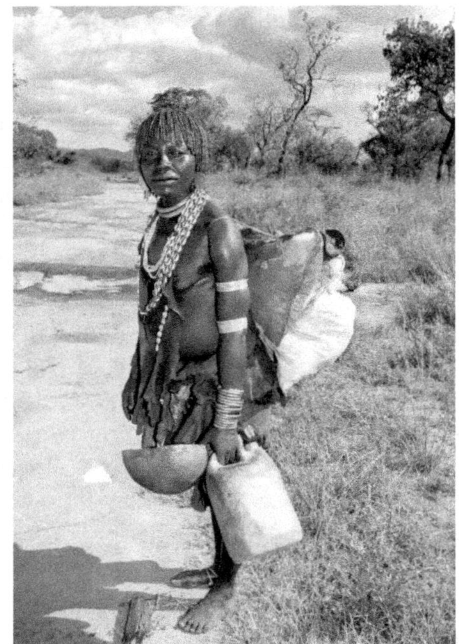

Carrying market purchase

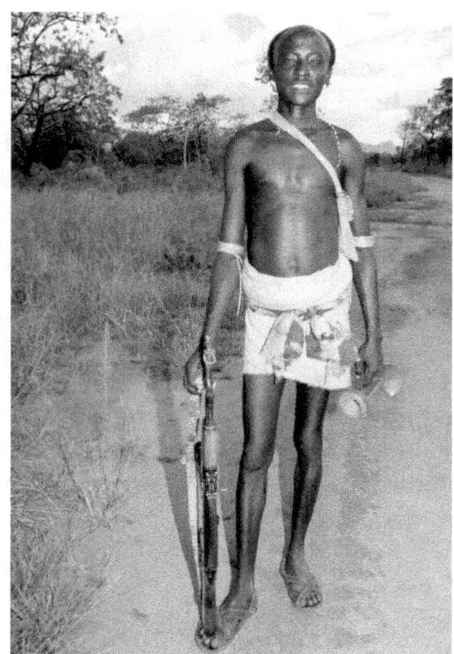

Tribal man carrying his rifle

South of the Mursi village, on the edge of the Mago National Park, lies the Village of Duss, home of the Karo people. An endangered people with less than a thousand surviving, the Karo do creative body paintings using available white chalk, pulverized iron ore, black charcoal, and yellow mineral rock. Women scarify their chests, as they believe the skin holds sensual appeal for men. They decorate animal skin coverings with cowrie shells, beads, soda bottle lids, and even the metal pop-top lids from soda cans. Villagers cut hair in a bowl shape and cover it in red clay. Both men and women pierce the lower lip to insert objects like small sticks or nails.

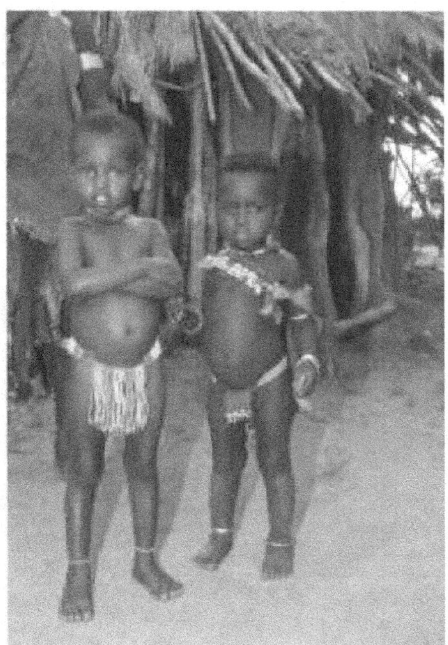

Children playing in the market area

Men spend much more time on their hairstyles. After a part to divide the hair in half, a man weaves the front section into braids to hang down over the forehead. He gathers the back section into a ball and covers it with a cap of mud. Holes punched in softened bark make spaces for ostrich feathers.

Men wash their bodies in ashes mixed with fat, which helps fight mosquitoes and the tsetse fly, and the ashes demonstrate virility in festivals and combats with neighboring clans.

Scarification on a man's chest shows he has killed a dangerous animal or enemy. Using knives, razors, or sharp branches, they cut the flesh and later rub ash into the wounds to cause the scars to swell.

Former nomads, the Karo, differ from all other groups around the Omo River as they have settled in one village. A Karo man may take as many wives as he can afford, but often settles for two or three.

Mangled pieces of the bridge lie visible on the river bottom. A construction worker yelled something in foreign words, which my driver translated, "You can cross the River Omo in your four-wheel to reach the Mursi Village."

Halfway across the swift current the Amharic word for "help" echoed through the jungle. I wondered if I should have believed the email from the agency hiring my driver, telling me to abort the Mursi trip. Due to El Nino's harsh side effects, previous clients had to leave the area by helicopter, and I feared now that I might follow them out of this country in the same way.

The worker transferred the chain from a metal bridge railing to our Land Cruiser and hopped into a nearby tractor, shouting at it as he coaxed it forward, pulling our vehicle behind it.

My driver, Girma, explained, "We will try an opening in the jungle down the road leading to the village where the Mursi women with their five-inch clay-lip-disks live."

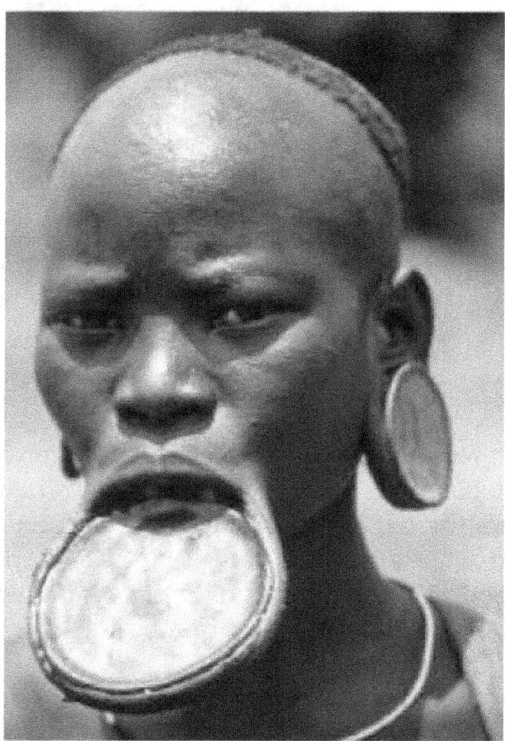

Lip disc on Mursi woman

Within minutes, the jungle branches, vines, and insects stuck to the car like honey. I had to give up trying to wipe away the constant salty trickles of sweat, blurring my vision. I was using up my toilet paper for the job, and toilet paper is a much-needed necessity for other purposes. Intense humidity and high temperatures shut down both the air conditioner and our hopes of reaching the mysterious Mursi people. With the windows closed for protection from the clawing vines and hordes of black biting flies, we gave our attention to the dry, riverbed crevices we had to maneuver.

A familiar smell distracted me from my watch for problems ahead. My concerns changed course after seeing the back and side windows covered in something oily and wet. Girma ignored my questions about the smell while slowing for two men wearing skimpy loincloths and shouldering AK47s. Girma tried to rationalize his reason for allowing the men to ride with us by saying, "The men will help build temporary, tree-branch bridges for the tires where the jungle has given way to the flooding waters."

The doors held tight by the wild and free jungle meant the men had to climb in through the driver's-side window. Both men climbed over the front seat awkwardly, with private parts flopping about. Their hands clenched the headrests so hard their skin turned white, and I could almost hear one man's jaw drop down to his belly with anxiety at seeing his surroundings. In and out of the window, the two men and Girma climbed in order to cut tree branches to connect the wide openings.

Minutes later, three naked men with Kalashnikovs, also called Russian AK-47 semi-automatic rifles, stood with perfect posture behind a fallen tree, stationed there to protest our passing. Adventure travel put to the test! Spirited, naked men waving rifles? Girma wrinkled his eyebrows as if to question my concern. Truckloads of these rifles cross the border from Sudan and Somalia. Locals increase their status when they carry a gun rather than a spear. My driver offered them a few coins, and they disappeared before a river stopped the vehicle once again. The Mursi people have a reputation for demanding money and food.

"When we reach the river close to their village," Girma said, "we will wait for them to visit us. Their curiosity levels match ours; plus, they hope to receive some money for showing off their lip plates and painted naked bodies." Girma spoke as if he had memorized the words before the trip.

Most of the villagers materialized like whispering aliens, and the women pulled their loose lip-skin out and around clay disks. Shiny ebony bodies appeared from behind trees, crossing the shallow river toward us. I knew they could hear my heart beating fast and could sense my fear. My dream of crossing the boundaries of the civilized stood before me, embodied in these people, tugging at my hair, shirt pockets, and camera strap. Rough pieces of tree bark had rubbed their bodies clean of hair. Intricate white designs hid the nakedness of those bodies.

The sun played with the metal decorating the animal-skin loincloths on the women.

A woman came close and stood still as if to offer herself for a photo. I snapped a few pictures. She took the lip plate out of her lip, offered it to me and held up her fingers. Girma said she wanted a ten-birr note ($.80). I knew I had to pay for every photograph when they increased the number of fingers held up with each click.

The tribes understood the reason for my presence. If I could reward these people for giving me their time while continuing their traditional ways, perhaps in some small way I could contribute to the preservation of their culture.

But sometimes the tribes took advantage of strangers due to some tourists tossing hundred-birr notes ($8) at them for a couple of photos.

Tribals soon learn the value of money and expect the next visitor to pay the same. When the tourists say no, dangerous situations occur. And that's what happened to me and Girma that day.

An argument started between two women and a man. Apparently, the man thought he might miss some payment since I took a photo of the woman who was not his wife. After a half hour of trying to communicate with my driver and watching my photography antics, the Mursi chief asked Girma for the equivalent of twenty dollars.

A group of men circled the car waving spears and rifles. Girma reached for two boxes of crackers to pass out and, with caution, opened the car door. I followed his actions.

A live encounter with the Mursi tribe could provide a frightening experience not worth the effort of getting there. Leaving under this kind of stress caused a sensation of needles pricking my arms and face. Burning, salty sweat kept me from seeing the real aggression in the Mursis' eyes.

The driver ignored the crowd around the vehicle while creeping forward. Dead ahead, the three naked men, now wearing loincloths, pointed the guns in our direction while standing again behind another dead tree.

They caught the *birr,* or Ethiopian currency, in midair as Girma tossed it toward them and proceeded around the dead tree.

The driver explained that last week they had killed a park scout! We searched for the dip in the tree canopy, evidence of the previous tree felling.

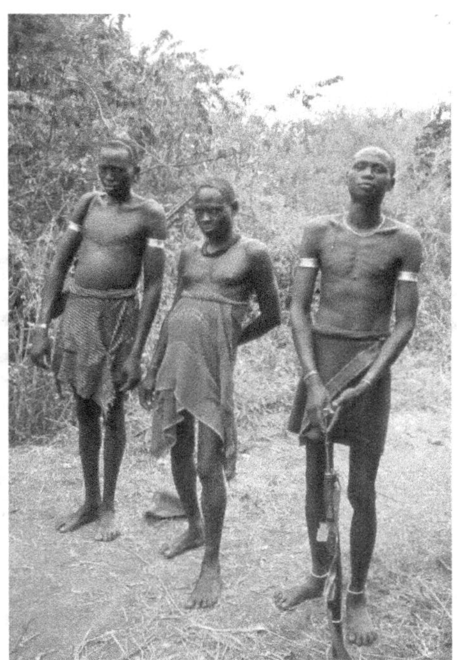

Mursi men in loincloths blocking the path with AK47s

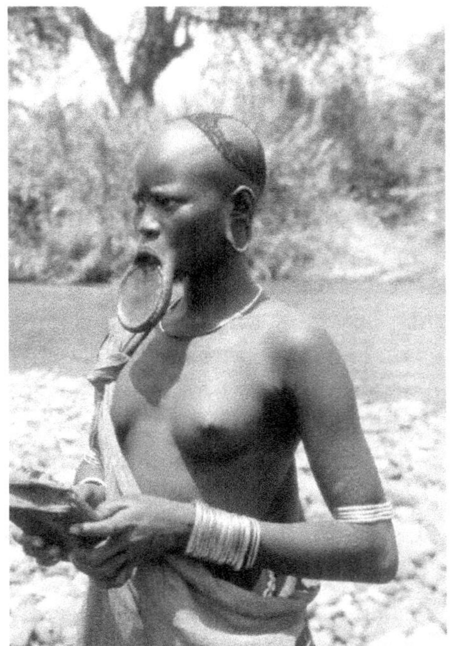

Mursi playing handmade musical instrument

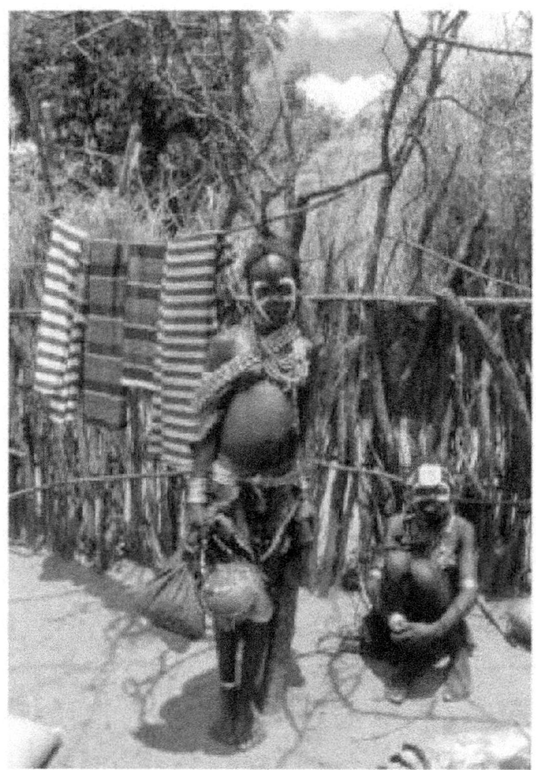

Young girls selling gourds

A rough, dirt road never looked so good until we left the car for some fresh air.

With tears in his eyes, my young driver circled the clawed, dented, and diesel-fuel-covered car. The jungle growth had worked hard to try to keep the vehicle from entering its playground.

Headlights, taillights, bumpers, and trim pieces looked like an angry weightlifter had slammed his heaviest weights at the vehicle.

Thorn bushes fought with broken branches, competing for the challenge of leaving their imprint of black, horizontal stripes across every door.

All of the five-gallon, diesel-fuel containers remained tied to the misshapen luggage rack, crushed to a fourth of their original size.

Three weeks of fuel washed the car while we dealt with men with guns.

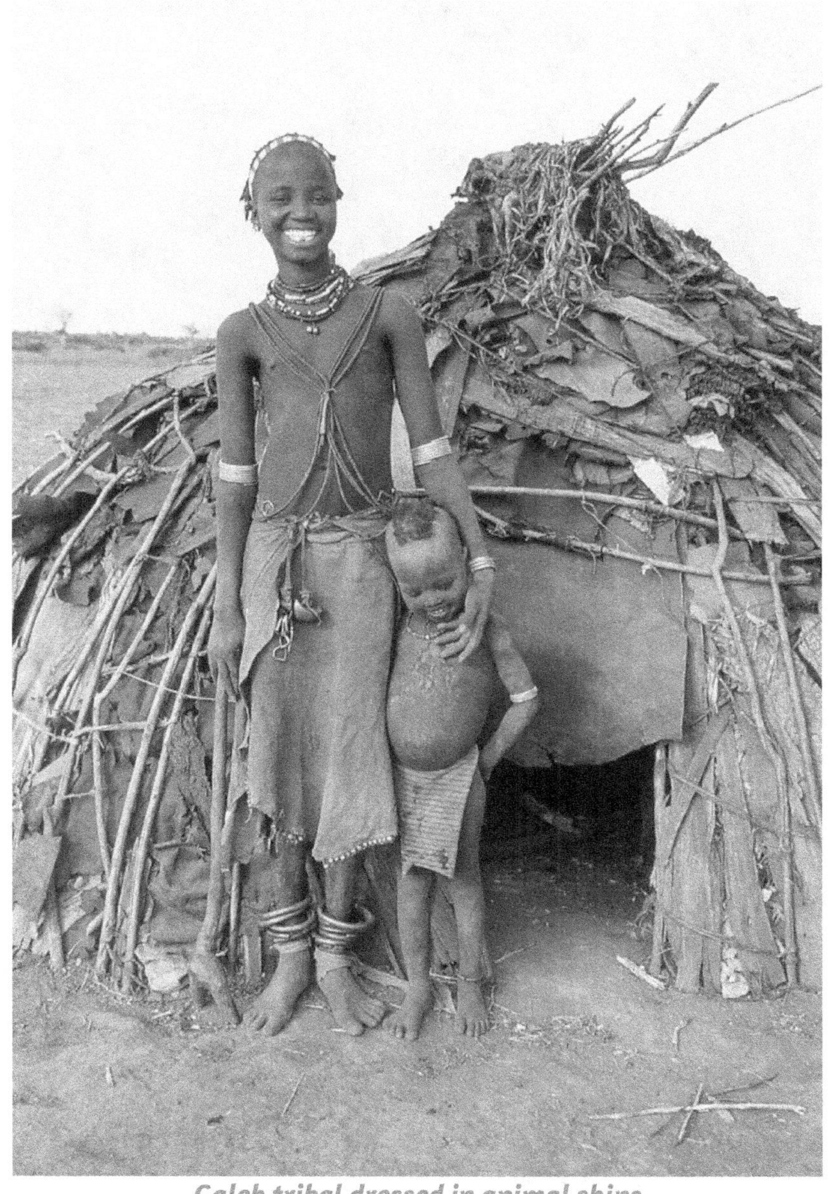

Galeb tribal dressed in animal skins

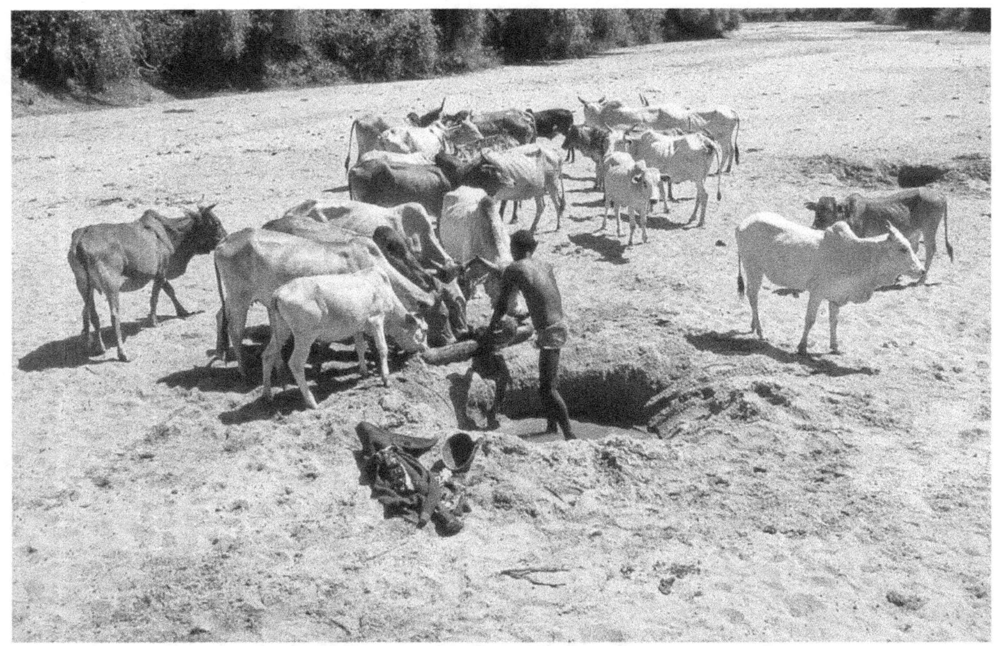

Digging for water in a dry riverbed

I never thought much about what might have happened to us, nor at the time did I worry when I saw the almost ferocious look on the men's faces, as they gathered around the 4X4, chanting for money. Traveling to meet indigenous societies requires a vast amount of trust and patience for one's driver and all of humankind. If some gypsy could have predicted that situation beforehand, perhaps I would have thought twice about trying to find the Mursi.

***

Drinking very hot bottled water while eating peanut butter on rolls, both Girma and I reflected on the events with the Mursi, the battered vehicle, and our own exhaustion. Girma laughed, saying the small river had dried up, and his earlier promises to me of a cool river to dip in would have to wait. Covered in sweat, leaves, dead bugs and dust, I pinched him as we stopped on the banks of a muddy stream. Cooling off, although not cleaning off, triggered my joyful splash into the water, heard for miles around.

Not an hour into the flat scrub bush jungle, I saw smoke. Girma called it the "Devils Wind" and kept driving toward it. If it's like a tornado, why drive into it? Topping a hill, our vehicle faced hordes of animals racing fast enough to beat the red-hot flames, grumbling and hissing. Dead savannah grass, the underbrush of the thickets, and thorny Acacia trees, fed the fire as fast as it could consume them. The sandy clearing offered little help for turning around until Girma shifted into four-wheel drive. Their "interstate system" consists of dry riverbeds and sometimes a cattle trail.

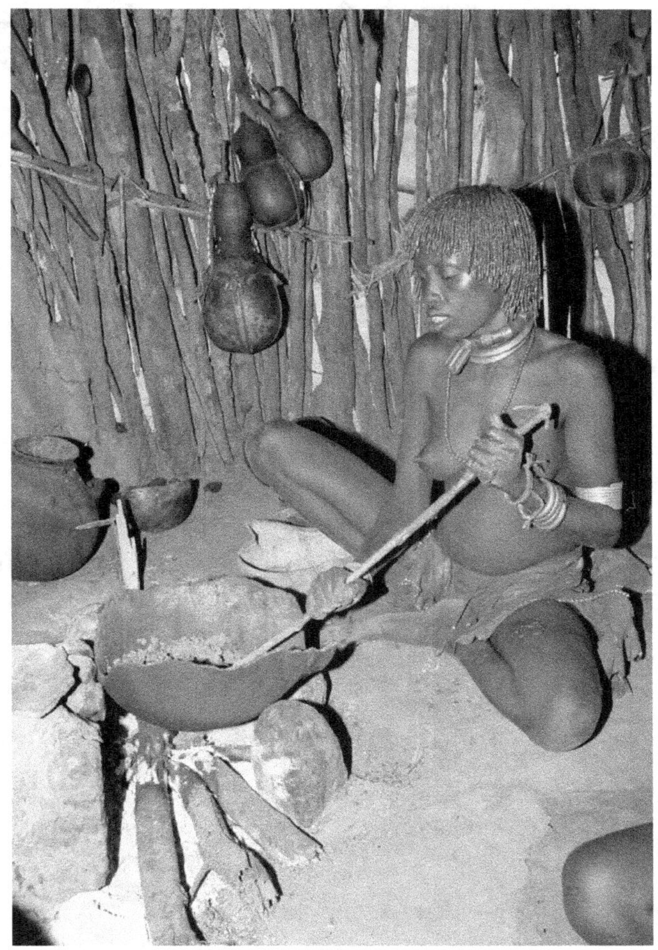

Cooking inside hut

Girma said, "No need to warn the park rangers. They can do nothing to stop the fire, so we will turn around and go back to Jinka for more fuel and then travel down to the villages of Demeka and Turmi to meet the Bana and Hammar peoples."

Looking back, I noticed the two red spots of flames blended into one long line of red.

Fifteen minutes later sprinkles cleared our car of the dusty day, while giving the fire what it deserved!

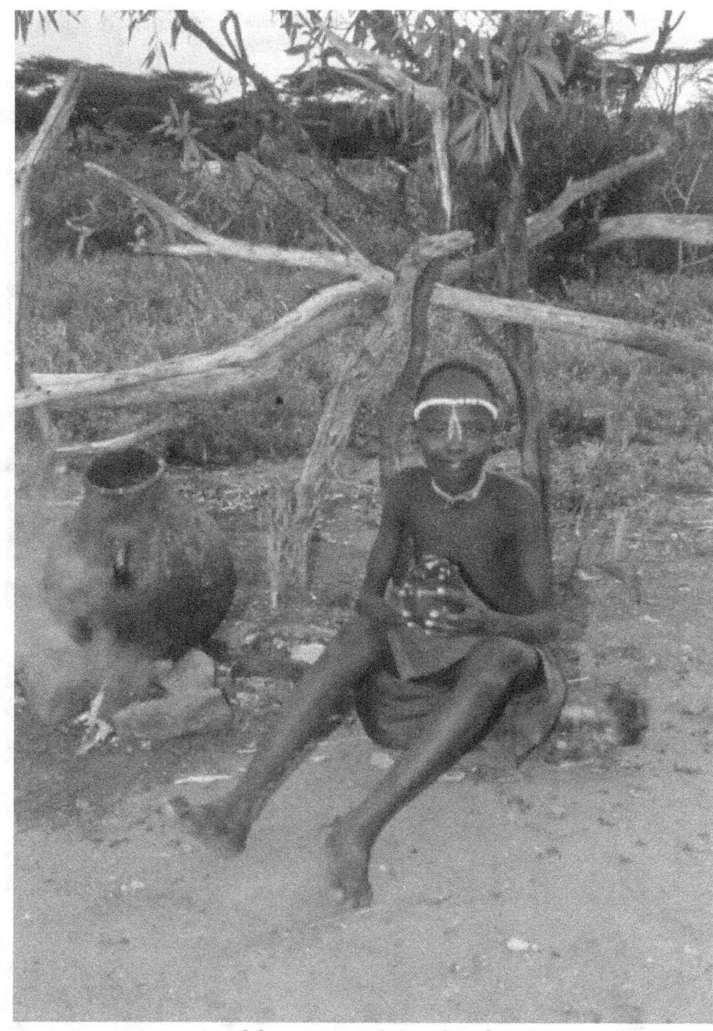

Cooking oxen dung for food

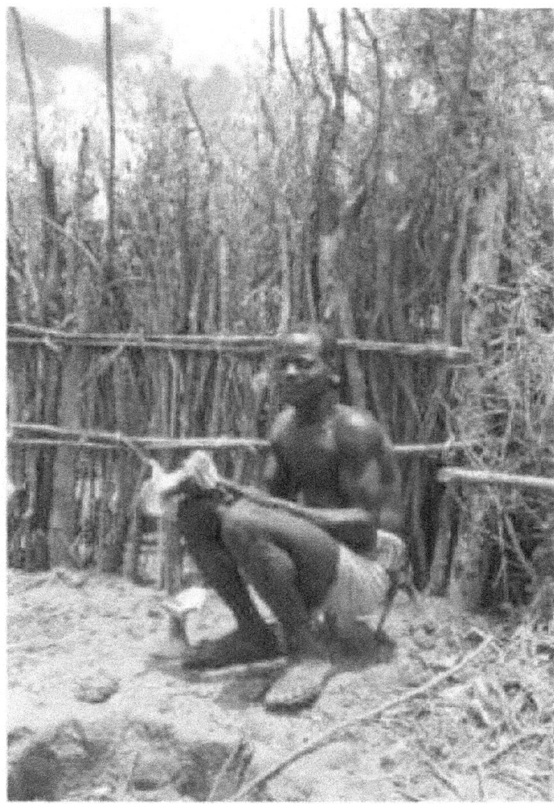

Boy carving neck stools

Descending into the Great Rift Valley toward Kenya and Sudan meant leaving the shadowy treescapes and fertile cotton fields to head into the classical sandy earth and mud-colored brush.

The remote location of Southern Ethiopia creates difficulties when the traveler attempts to find villages, as roads turn into dry, rocky riverbeds with no village in sight.

Ethiopians use the flour from *teff,* or staple grain, to bake *injera,* or large pancake-like breads, served on the table. Meats consist of muscle and gristle.

The injera holds the food, and, using his or her fingers, diners tear off portions of *injera* and roll up food pieces. Did Girma miss eating his customary staple of *injera*?

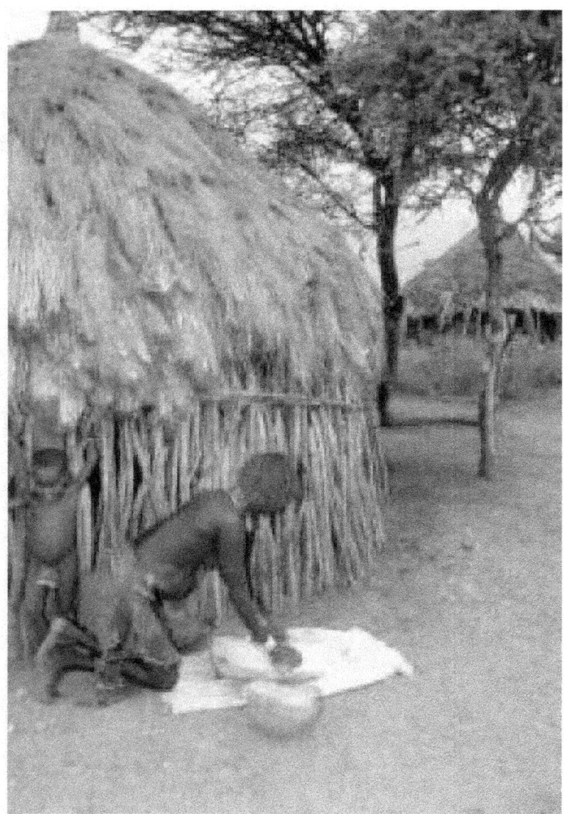

Grinding maze on a stone

Camping in Ethiopia requires skills beyond those of the standard canoe trips of my college days in the Midwest. Thieves and baboons rank highest of the camper's concerns. Girma traced the edge of the windshield while explaining the best way for thieves to get into the vehicle without leaving notice. Later, when you miss your camera, documents, and hiking boots, you see evidence of the careful removal of the windshield glass. So even inside the car, you tie the equipment together with extra caution for hiding valuables.

Baboons look cute when six weeks old. I know. I babysat one owned by a pet shop owner. They live in large families and love to carry loose items away in the middle of their day (your night.) Nighttime trips to the jungle toilet will challenge your confidence even when attempted with an armed guard.

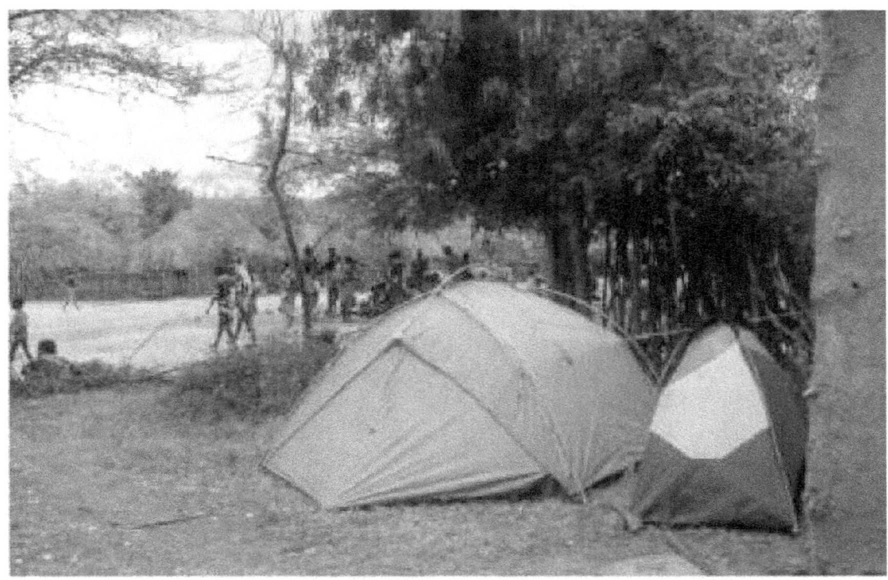

The leaky purple tent

A group of trees and bushes almost in a circle caught our attention as we searched for a suitable campsite.

The oncoming dusk urged us to set up camp quickly, and I liked the enclosure, surrounded by this tree fence, and a football field's distance to the local government-placed well for bathing and cooking water.

Tents in place, gear stored and locked tight, we took a quick walk through the nearby village before another boring spaghetti dinner.

I introduced myself to the chief as he casually emptied his honey trap. Smoke, along with a smell so intrusive I had to pinch my nose, came from a black gourd balanced on a bed of black and red embers.

The chief's son boiled oxen dung in a calabash, or oversized gourd, and added honey as the final ingredient before this spiritual liquid could bring good luck at dinner!

In his hands, the young boy held a black ball. I never did ask or figure out its use or composition.

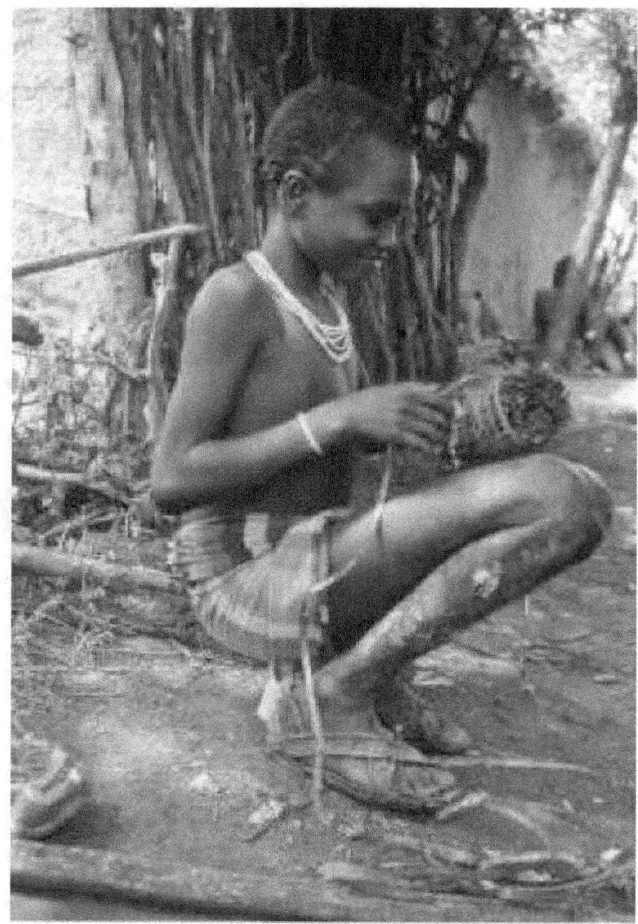

Wrapping bundles of firewood

When it comes to protecting my health on a fourth-world trip like this, my paranoia develops. Extensive research provided me with tips on boiling water for at least thirty minutes before use for cooking or drinking.

The previous year my teenage daughter, Katherine, and I spent a month living with the Stone Age peoples of New Guinea and used this method of purifying water for all our tea made from muddy, brown, river water.

We avoided any problems with sickness. I taught Girma that the thirty minutes starts after the bubbles appear. We played a timing game each day. After boiling the spaghetti and sprinkling it with instant tomatoes, he poured water direct from the well over the pasta!

So much for a spaghetti dinner for me! Another empty can of tuna to bury with the rest of the garbage in the morning.

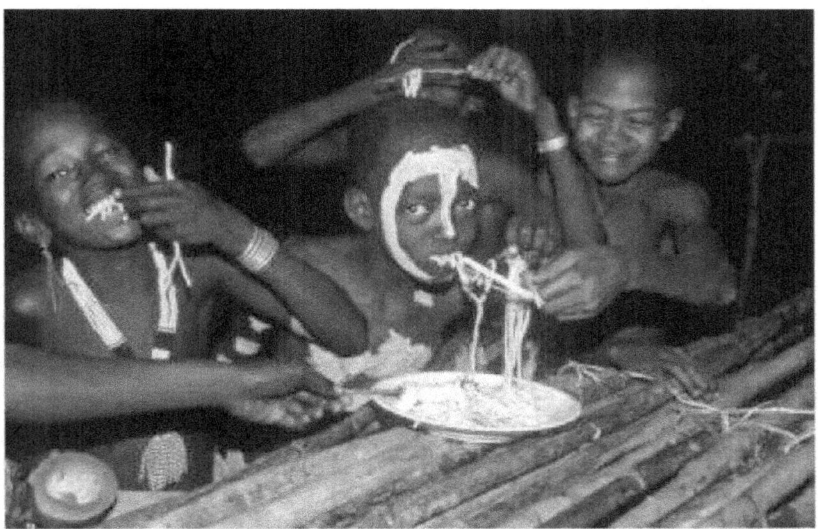

Tribal boys tasting author's leftover spaghetti for the first time

Girma insisted that tribal onlookers keep their distance and use the small opening into our camping circle as the stay-back line. To avoid wasting our excess spaghetti (the dry pasta expands with the moisture in the air), Girma invited some children who were peering into our camp to join him for dinner. Villagers, hoping for a glimpse into another world, hid behind bushes or gathered in groups to point at my weird clothing, boots, or wild, purple-and-pink tent. Girma showed the boys how to take a stick and wind the pasta around it, but they found it easier to shove it into their mouths with their fingers. What fun watching pasta hanging from their mouths. Sharing western foods, I experience guilt, as I would prefer not to tempt these young minds with new ideas in the ways of living. This comedy caused us all to laugh with each bite taken!

Do not believe those ads that guarantee a sound and restful night sleeping on self-inflating, half-inch-thick, sleeping pads. Sticks and stones reminded me all night of my age and my growing dislike of camping while I lay on my too-thin pad. Memories still return, as I recall the hours spent listening to those lions and colabus monkeys, who jumped trees faster than you could blink your eye.

The first time I tried to bathe created a scene, as I did not understand the traditions for using the well. This cement well, government-placed, had an open-ended trough so water rolled off the end. With my shirt stretched out on the ground, I thought a sponge- bath sounded appealing, a chance to cool my body. Off came my shirt while I fidgeted with the pump. Two young men appeared like ghosts and tried to take my place pumping the handle.

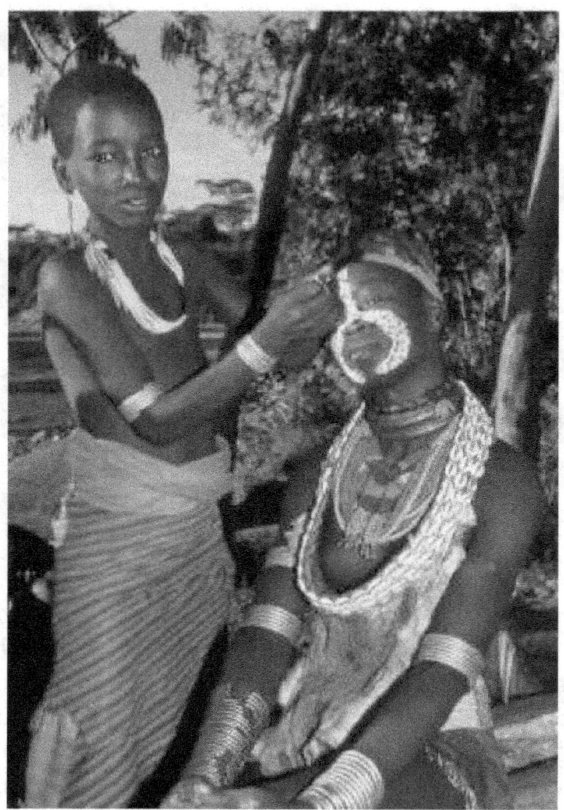

Painting faces at the well

"Go away, go away," I demanded, but their looks of bewilderment gave me reason to grab my shirt and run back to camp.

"Their custom becomes their duty. Men have the responsibility of pumping the handle and women gather the water. Those boys tried to help you," my guide told me.

I walked back to the well and found about eight kids chatting and giggling. My appearance changed the noise level to zero as they stared at this white-skinned woman in long pants and strange-looking boots. Besides, I was carrying a polyester camping towel and odd containers filled with white liquid.

My smiles gave them permission to get back to their face and body painting, using small twigs as brushes dipped in white chalk and red ochre powder. I soon faded to invisible, sitting on a clump of dead vines as I caught their fun on film.

Coffee plantations in the remote, high plateaus and my location, recorded by tiny landmarks on the GPS, turned into memories as the 4X4 sank its tires into knee-deep ruts. The last of the river water, abandoned by the crocodiles, made many canoes homeless. Nevertheless, the landscape grew thick with people, somehow surviving.

Termite nests, towering thirty feet above, provided shade for the Hamar people and offered a way to escape the sizzle of the desert heat. The unrelenting surroundings contribute to maintaining the ancient customs of exotic people like the Hamar in the area of Turmi.

Broad savannahs spotted with thorn bushes and cacti provide a harsh environment for the support of the Hamar's cattle.

Beekeeping and pottery keep hands busy, singing to soothe their cattle and. building fires at night to warm them. The Hamar live for their cattle. Young men move their cattle to grazing areas around the crocodile-infested waters of the Omo River.

When their roots and grains run out, they depend on cattle’s milk and blood from the neck for survival. Packs of wild jackals or hyena, and cattle raiding threaten the lives of both the cattle and their young guardians.

Villagers measure a family's wealth by the number of cattle owned. Famine, drought, needing a few more cattle for a wedding dowry, or taking weapons of the men killed calls for cattle raiding.

Cattle serve as the Hamar's living bank account, and without cattle, a young man cannot get married, as a bride price can cost as much as fifty cattle.

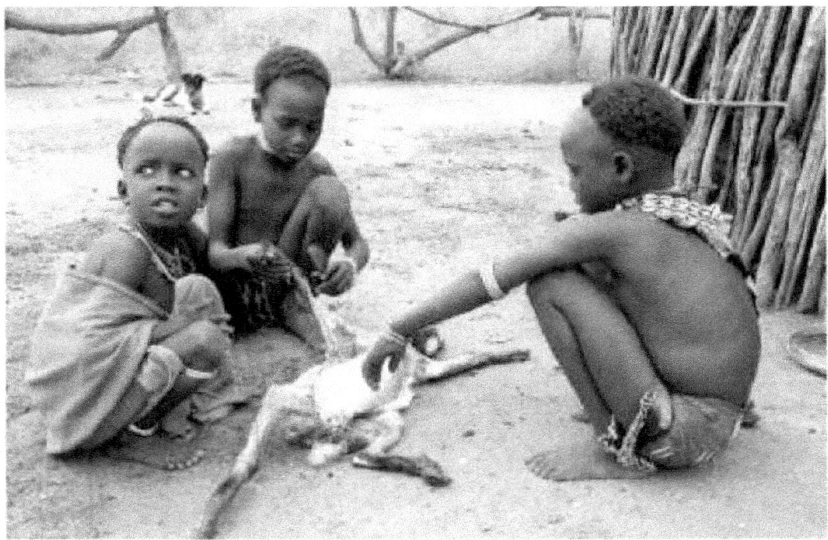

Turmi children skinning a goat for food

Part of the culture for these people includes raids to kill a man from another tribe. Killing, for ownership of water rights, for access to a prized lion, or to avenge the theft of cattle would cause the Mursi/Bana, the Karo/Bume or the Hammer/Galeb tribes to fight back and forth.

Men gain high status within communities for killing a man or large animal such as a buffalo, elephant, or lion. To kill a man takes less effort. Many warriors turn their backs on the traditional weapon, the spear.

The celebration for killing an enemy starts with the sacrifice of a goat for blood to wash away the man's guilt for having killed another man. A man cannot marry until he has killed an enemy or large game animal.

A significant part of the killing ritual involves scarification. The elders hire a scarrist when they can afford to hire one, and she cuts crude designs on the killer's upper body and uses the *garanti* plant, or dead spirits food, to heal the wound.

To reach manhood, the young boy has to pass the *bullah,* or bull-jumping ceremony. A dozen or more cattle are lined up, side by side, and covered in dung. Success in jumping up and running across all the cattle backs ensures the boy a new wife and tribal acceptance.

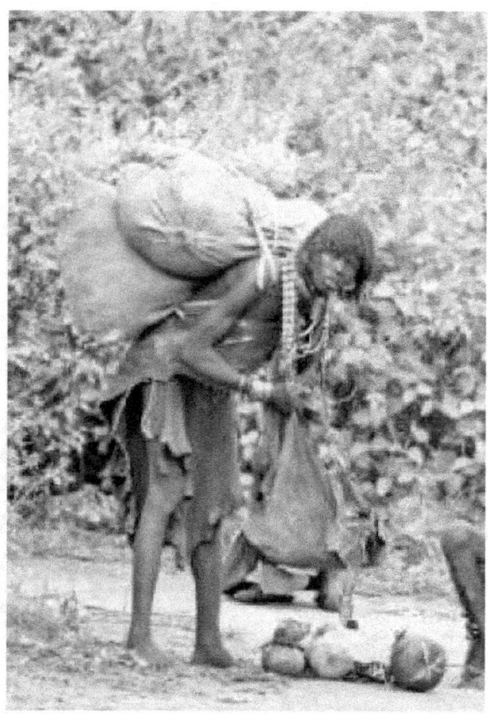

Hammar woman carrying a heavy load

Both male and female tribe members show their love for physical beauty through hair grooming. Women rub fat and red ochre paint into their hair and wear it in *goscha,* or short ringlets. Men who have killed a dangerous animal or enemy wear a cap made of mud. Softened bark with holes or tiny goat bones holds ostrich feathers. Most men carry a *borkoto,* or carved stool, to protect their hairstyles. Carving their own borkotos, boys as young as eight sit in the markets.

Engaged or married women wear *essente,* or iron necklaces, which stay on their necks for a lifetime. A first wife carries a *binyere,* or phallic protrusion attached to the front of the necklace. The village *garsho,* or blacksmith, closes the neck circles with a hammer and closes the arm and leg rings on the women. Years ago, twenty-five rings cost one cow. If a woman dies before her husband, he removes the rings from her severed body parts so he can give them to his new wife.

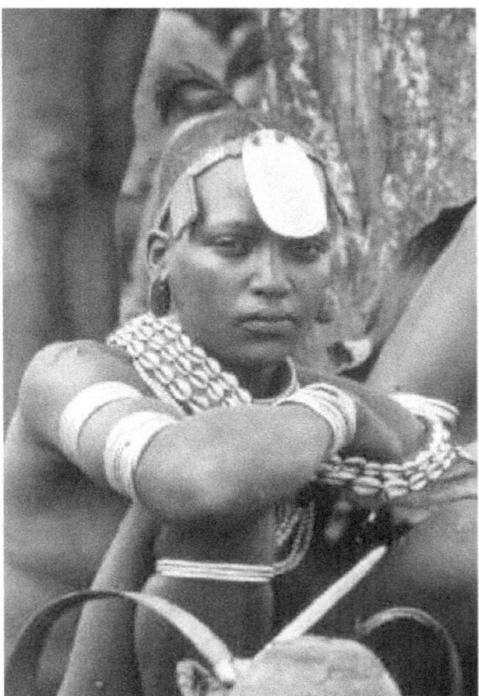

Proud and beautiful tribal woman

A group of villagers hung around our campsite day and night, trying to sell me ancient artifacts belonging to deceased tribal members, or maybe hoping for a few birr notes for a photograph. A woman, bent in half from the heavy load on her back, stood watching, while Girma packed the 4X4, and I collapsed the tents. Two young boys, with smiles, inviting me to join them, helped the heavy-laden woman move her burdensome bags to the ground.

One pointed to her heavy brass bracelets that circled from her wrists to her elbows and pointed to my arm with questioning looks. Although I didn't say yes, he proceeded to pry open her bracelets one by one with a rock as each had a quarter-inch opening. After pounding and prying with the rock, he took his shoe made from a rubber tire and shoved it into the opening.

He tugged so hard trying to separate the brass opening enough for her wrist to slip out that he broke his shoe in half. He squeezed her wrist out and mine in. The bracelets cling tight on the skin and don't move around, so he pushed them to my elbow and pounded them closed. By the time the opening for the ninth bracelet closed, the inside of my wrist had bled and some of the skin on my arm hung in bloody ribbons.

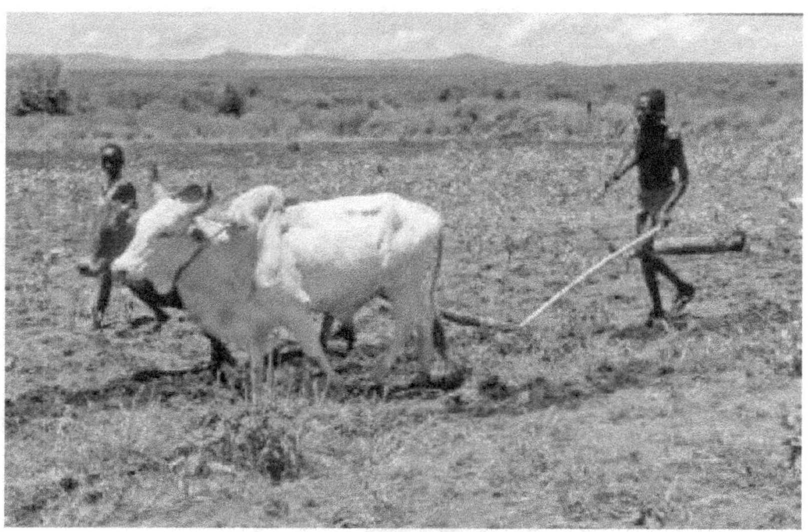

Oxen plowing

People die from infections in a tropical environment. I do not get paranoid with worry; otherwise, I guess I would not have traveled to this wild, remote place, but the extra care these boys had taken with me caused me concern. The jewelry exhibits status and wealth. Rings worn, from the wrist to the shoulders and on the legs, could mean a high status in a village. The group exhibited pride as they stepped back to see my reaction. I did not understand why they shared this tradition with me, an outsider. I offered the woman some birr, and she shook her head. In a country of beggars, drought, and severe hardship, I wanted her somehow to know my appreciation for her friendship.

"Girma, do we have food we won't eat on this trip?" Two boxes of cornflakes took up space in the food box along with a large box of powdered milk. Hot milk with cornflakes sounded disgusting, so I asked him if I could give that to the woman in trade for the lifetime memories she gave me.

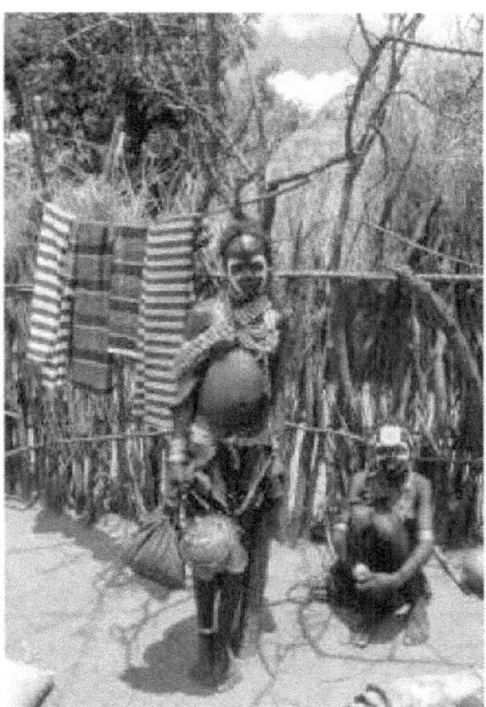

Selling gourds in tribal market

The Ethiopian government attempts to control tribal life. Federal officials work their influence to win the support of village chiefs in the hopes of abolishing all harmful traditional practices.

Government organizations prohibit certain practices like *Minga,* a belief that certain things bring bad luck.

A child, born out of wedlock, deformed, or who had its front teeth grow in before its bottom teeth, will die of exposure after his mother abandons him in the forest, desert, or river.

Other regulations outlaw female circumcision, scarifications, piercings for lip plates, stick fighting, cattle jumping, and the whipping of women in ceremonies.

To witness these traditions, tourists spend their money to cross vast and uncomfortable distances.

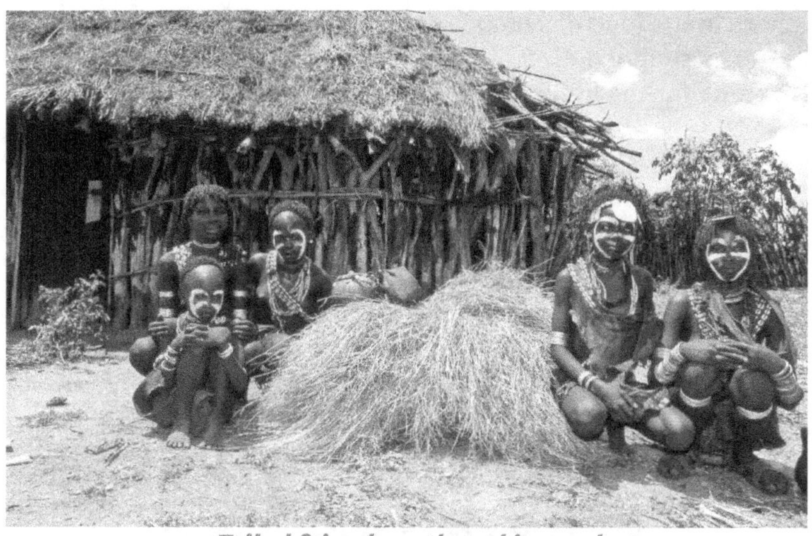

Tribal friends gathered in market

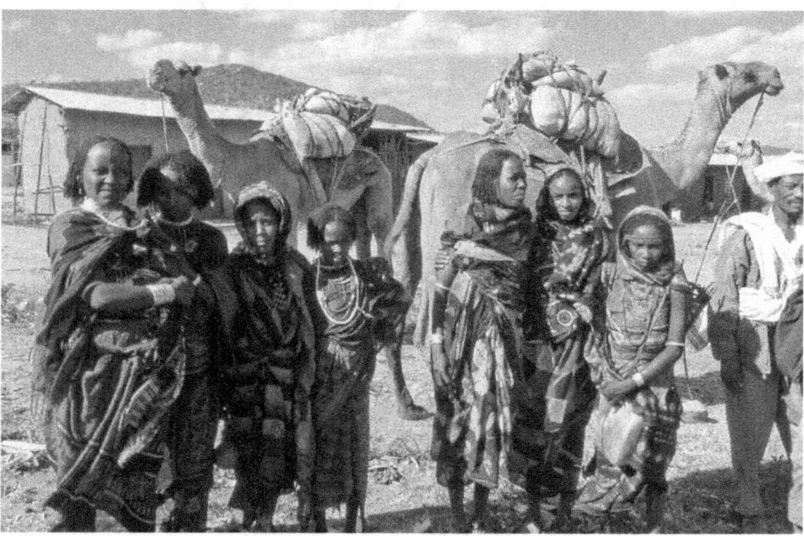

Berber women bringing salt to market from Somalia

A few times on this trip, I have seen 4X4s with white-skinned people inside. Initially, I wondered where they camped, for some kind of reality check or means of pinching me to prove that I lived this dream. Pausing, I asked myself if I felt lonesome or needed their company.

Did I want to hear about events in the world spoken in English? I live on my computer back home like young people today live on their phones but the thought of checking email or wondering about world events didn't enter my mind here in this primitive place.

Meeting with unusual challenges, setting up campsites, visiting with the locals, and finding places to wash my clothing and body consumed my time and energy.

Whether curious or begging, the tribal people and their constant attention drained me. Solo travel demands a great deal of patience.

Girma never seemed to leave me alone unless I made a point to tell him that I needed privacy in the bush. I don't think I ever felt loneliness in spite of this trip's exhausting physical and emotional demands.

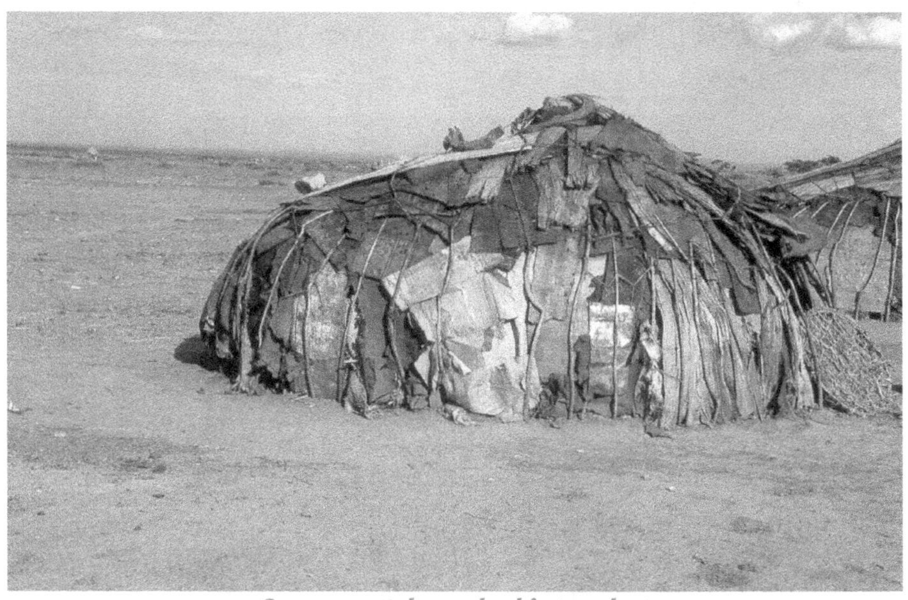

Scraps patch worked into a hut

A timeless culture, colliding with modern day sensibilities, offered me a glimpse back in time through the living tribes I met in village after village.

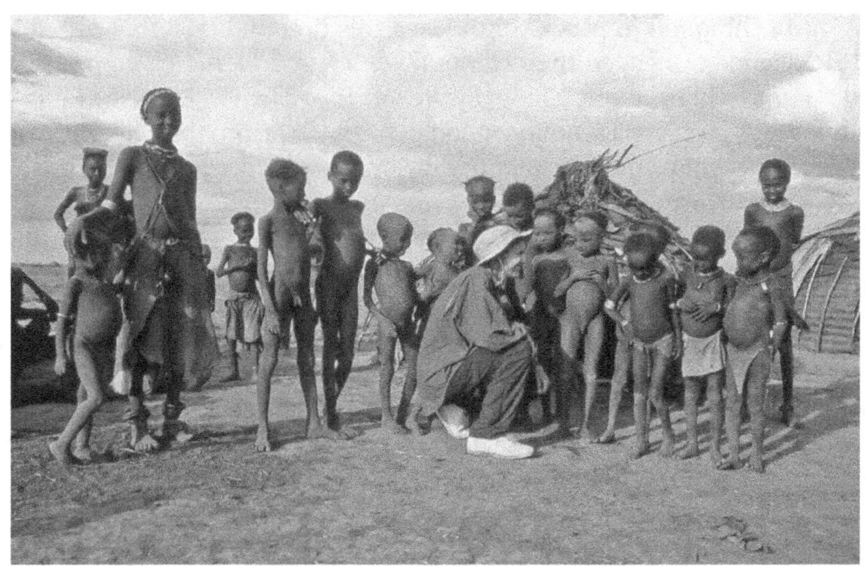

Author talking with Galeb children

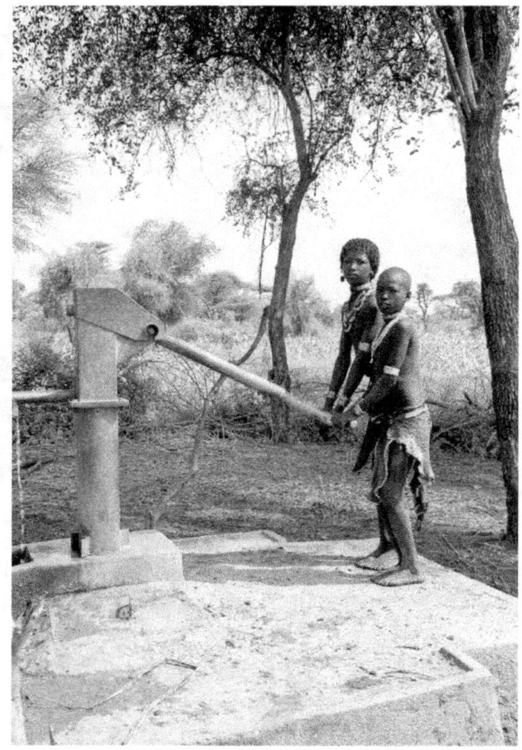

Karo sisters pumping water from a local Konso well

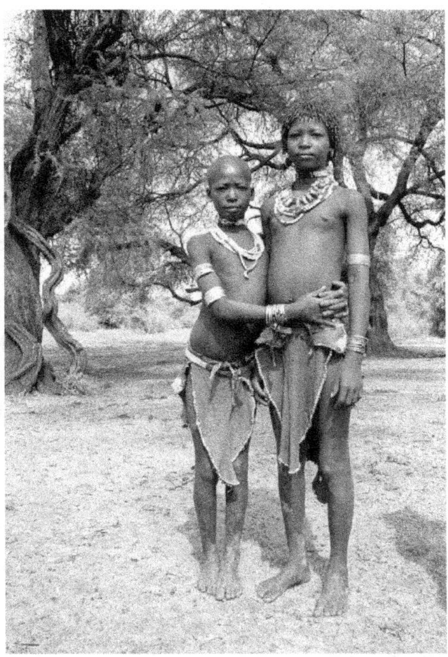

Karo girls shave their heads until they pass through puberty

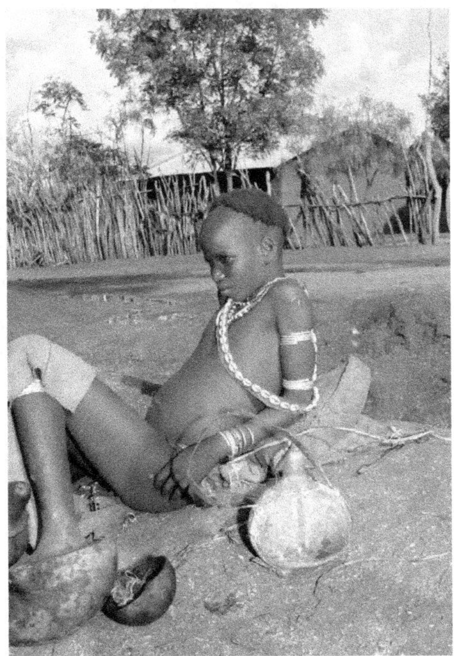

Hammar teenager, with shaved head, resting in Demeka market

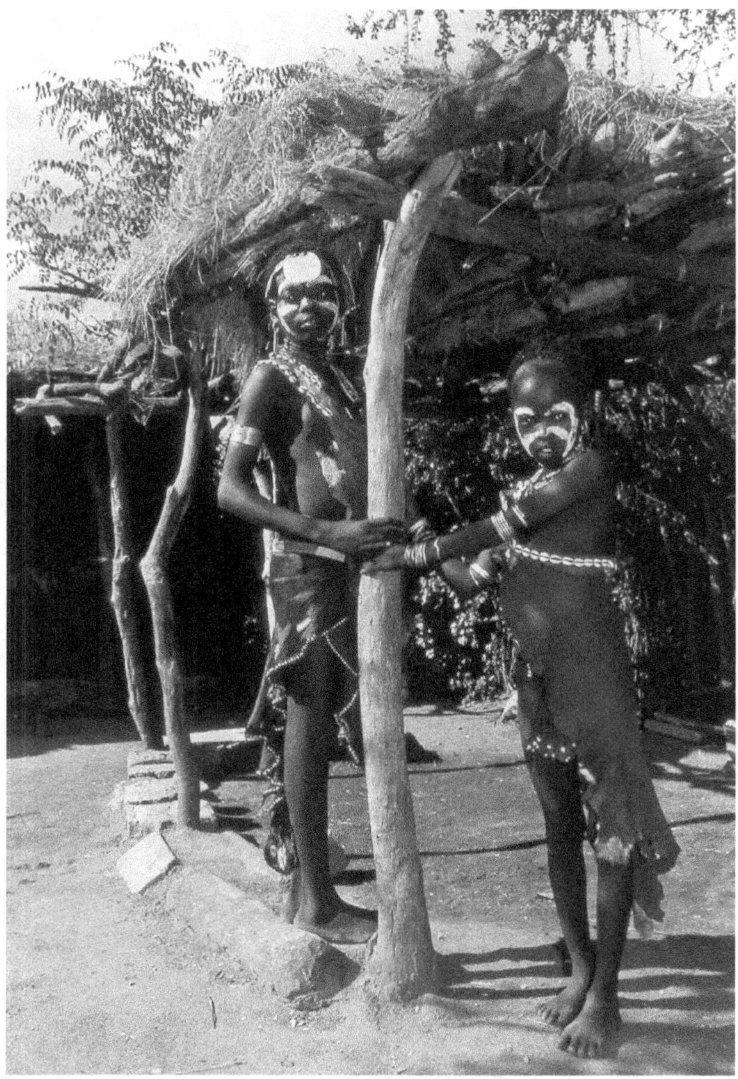

Painted faces

CHAPTER FOUR

Bali: Threads of Religion

"We all should know that diversity makes for a rich tapestry, and we must understand that all the threads of the tapestry are equal in value no matter what their color." Maya Angelou

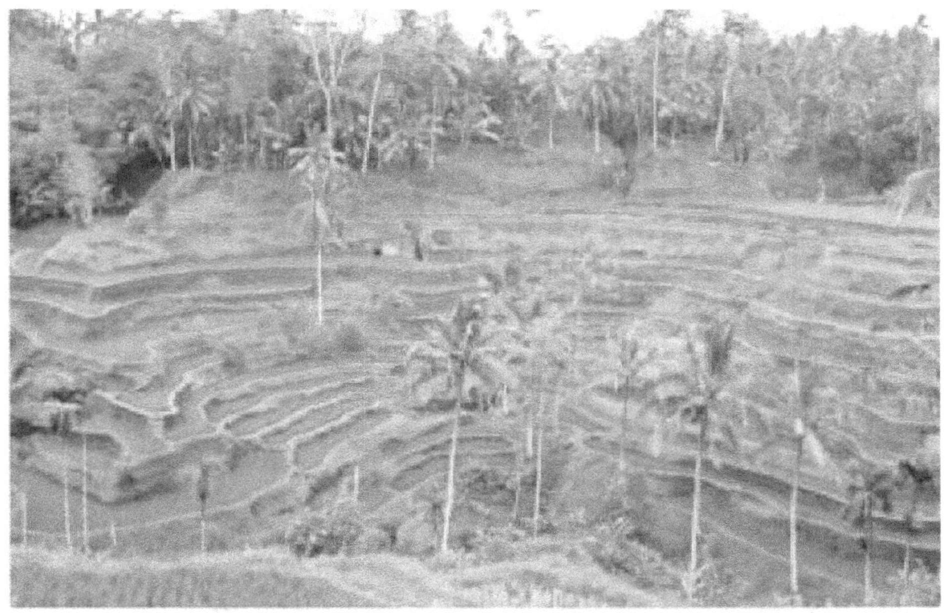

Otherworldly landscapes dot the countryside

The heart's definition of Bali creates visions of tranquility nourished by rituals, whispered conversation inside temples, and people wrapped in graceful sarongs. Bali's animated charm captures your attention minutes after arrival.

A more significant task involves integrating into the deeper, spiritual energy of the people.

Planes land minutes from the social swirl of Kuta, a chaotic blend of leisure options. Budget ten-dollar-a-night hotels adjoin sidewalk restaurants displaying chalkboard menus of the freshest local dishes, exploding with flavors from nearby markets.

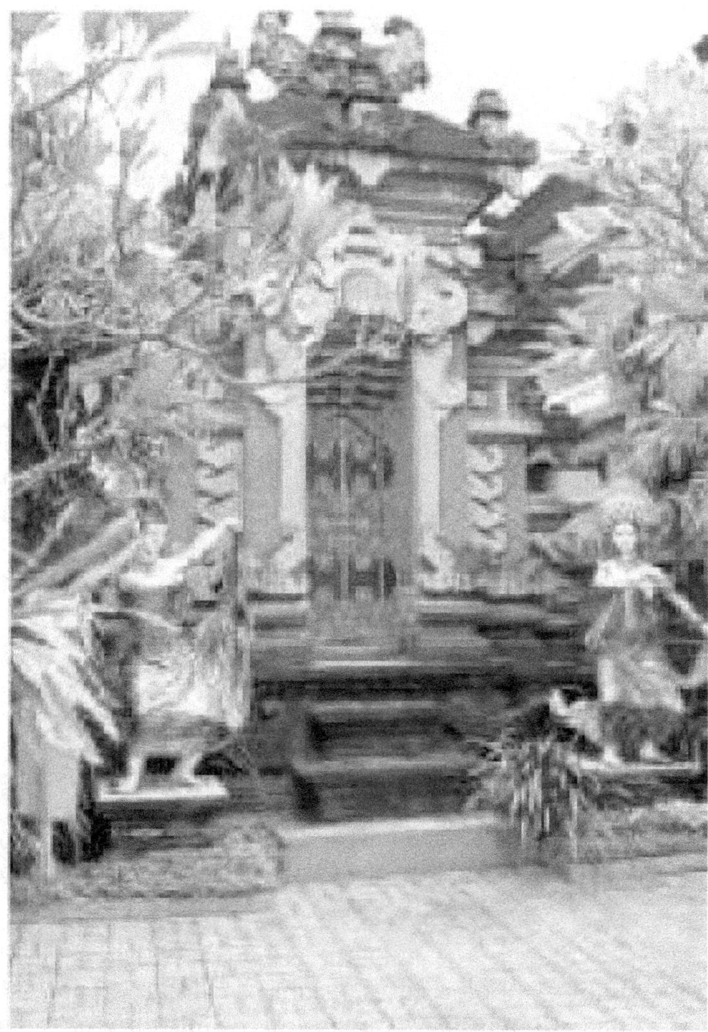

Typical entrance to hotel or home

Luxurious beach resorts offer their secret spa and massage pleasures for the body, along with famous chefs preparing pleasing dishes from around the world. The visitor's thoughts turn right side up again when no longer intoxicated by the armies of shopkeepers begging for business. Feet need a rest after those asphalt-shopping meccas of boutiques and galleries have worn soles and attitudes to a frazzle. The enthusiasm returns as images of iridescent rice fields, bewitching dance performances, and black sand beaches shake away the unbalanced frenzy of Kuta.

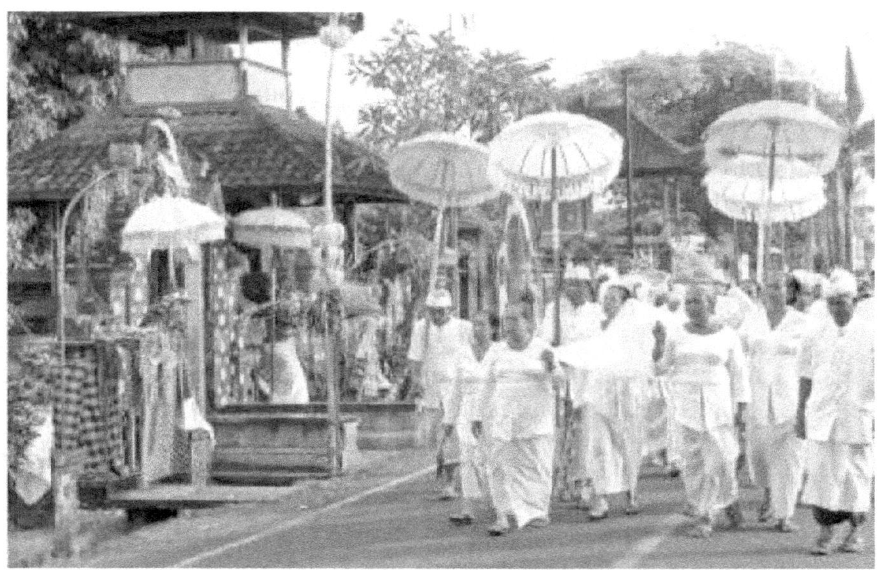

Walking to temple

***

"Yes, please?" asked a boy, wearing white, balancing a silver tray with fruit, cups, and a teapot.

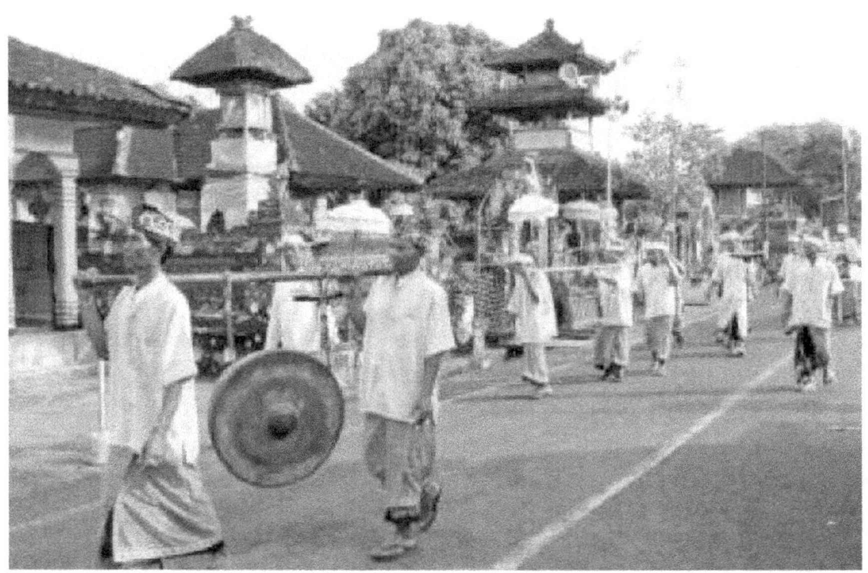

Temple procession with instruments

"Do you have a room?" I responded while eyeing the courtyard of the palace compound. I could not imagine why the prince would allow foreign visitors to stay in his palace. The research I had done suggested stopping in the town of Tabanan, finding the palace, and asking for a room. The young boy first showed me a room filled with antiques, paintings, and sculptures from diverse sources. The musty smell caused the boy to lead me to a second room, lost behind a green wall of vines, alive with lizards startled at the intrusion.

Magical in every way was the second room that spoke to me in a hundred different languages. The bed, so high it needed steps, came from the pages of "The Princess and the Pea." Centuries-old linen curtains draped from the top rails of the canopy frame. Fragrant, pink flower petals dotted the bed cover. Wild and careless paintings crowded the walls.

Pillows and shawls, painted with wild colors outlined in gold, tumbled from ornately carved benches. Invitations to relax seeped from padded, velvet windowsills.

Sculpted pieces crowded every inch of space, leaving little room to walk to the garden-like bathroom with the sky for a mural. Using the toilet made me feel like I'd climbed behind a waterfall as thick vines hung from the roof. The sunken tub boasted brass fixtures, and walking on the pebbled floor while barefoot completed my sensuous experience.

A woman came to the room with a silver bowl of fruit next to a serving of hot tea. I pointed to the other buildings with a motion of walking, and she nodded.

I felt comfortable that she gave me permission to wander the palace grounds. The large, walled compound contained many smaller, walled-in living areas, each separated by wood walls with stairs leading up to doors opening into the next area. Exposed living areas with gold *lamé* chests and velvet-covered, carved furniture lined the stone paths.

Surprised and embarrassed, I wandered into a studio full of paintings, tables, brushes, palettes, and oils, where I chanced on a man who introduced himself as the prince!

He spoke English well and invited me to join him for tea. My curiosity burned like fire although I felt chills from the excitement breaking out on my arms. A long, batiked piece of fabric, called a *kamben,* wrapped the lower half of his otherwise naked body. Grey hair in a long braid touched his waistline.

Our conversation went on into the evening, covering subjects from our mothers to local presidents. He wanted to learn more about the world, as well as develop better English skills. His invitation to join him for dinner gave me a feeling of acceptance.

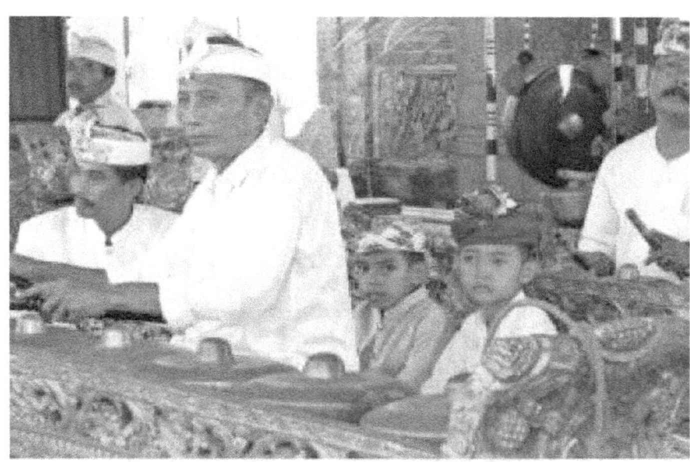

Watching father play his instrument

Throughout dinner, I noticed the left hand remained motionless except for locating pictures in a photo album, which led me to ask, "Are you right-handed?"

The prince almost whispered as if embarrassed for my lack of knowledge of his culture, "Our left hand is impure. We use our right hand for shaking hands, passing, receiving, and eating."

For dessert, he shared photos of his family, a delicacy better than any home-made apple pie. My next invitation, to join the prince and his wife for worship at the local temple the following morning, kept me awake all night.

"You must wear our clothing," explained the prince after breakfast. "On holidays, we pray and give offerings with hundreds of local people."

I agreed, and the prince left me alone with his wife, who looked at my khaki, nylon, travel pants, with weird zippers above the knees to convert to shorts, and forced a smile. Another woman appeared with a long piece of fabric and proceeded to wrap it around my waist. The wife unbuttoned my nylon travel shirt after wrapping the sarong over the nylon pants. A lacey white blouse, a yellow sash for the waist, and a narrow piece of fabric to secure my hair completed the outfit. No suggestions for shoes. Their small feet equaled the size of my hands, so I decided to unpack my Western-sized flip-flops. The prince came out and told me to walk to the temple for some wonderful photographs of the women carrying three-foot-tall baskets of food on their heads. Dressed like the locals, I could join a traditional parade into the temple. Later, after an incredible experience, I connected with the prince and his wife in their car. The prince told me to follow his lead as we sat in front of the temple, our hands filled with rose petals and sticks of lit incense.

My Indian style of sitting on the ground embarrassed me as the prince pointed to his calves, which he had positioned perfectly under his thighs. He began making circles with his hands, followed by tossing a rose petal toward the shrine before us. I followed his movements until he bent his forehead to the ground for prayer, which my back refused to mimic.

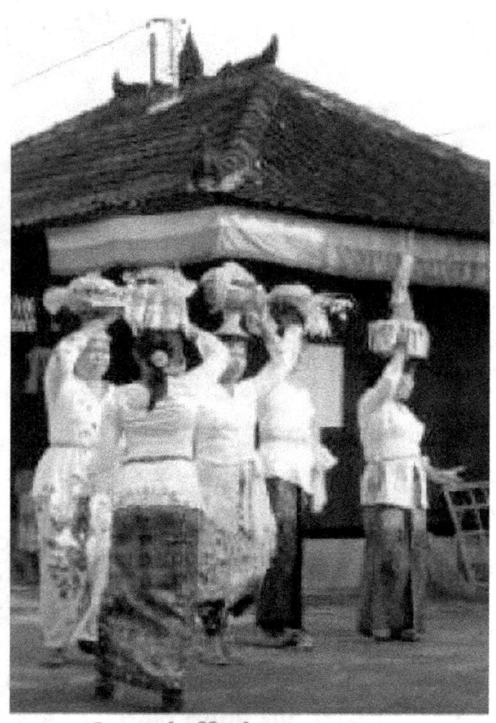

Sacred offerings

Trying to stand gracefully did not work either, as I fell to the side, dropping the incense. I recovered, found my way behind the prince's wife, and shook hands with those offering theirs to mine.

That evening for dinner, the prince's father had a plate delivered beside mine. Dressed in a bright yellow *kamben* around his waist and an official jacket, bearing medals and ribbons of honor, he sat across from me, laying some maps and books on the table. He wanted to talk about my country's government, and I tried to explain that I did not keep up with politics but would love to know more about his country. He pulled his kamben up and refolded it tight around his waist. His natural smile told me that he accepted my invitation for him to share. After about an hour of talk, I asked, "Tell me about the huge kites on the walls of some of the compounds."

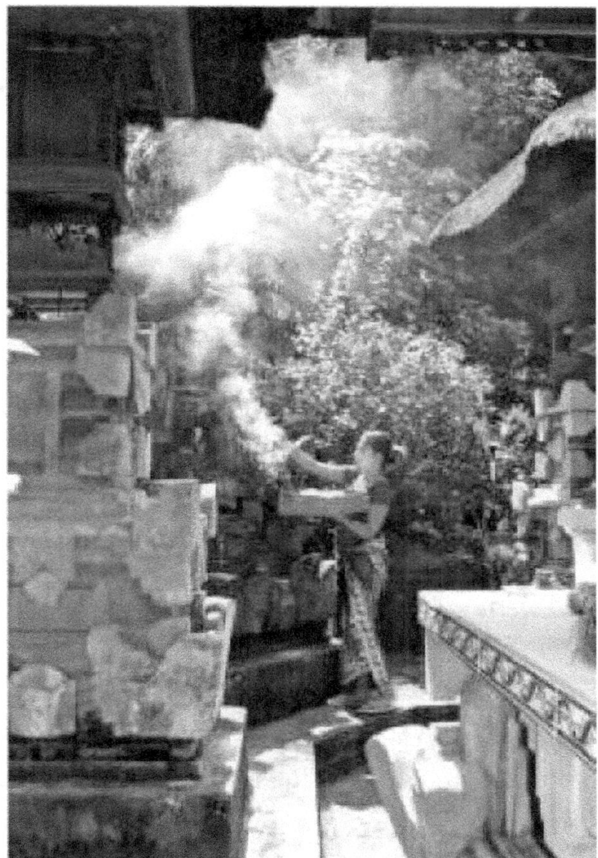

Lighting incense as an offering to spirits

"I helped organize the national kite festival many years ago, when we built kites wide enough to stretch across the dirt roadways. When cars became more abundant, the drivers did not like having to wait while a handful of men manipulated the kites toward the beach. In time the kites became smaller and smaller. I could teach you how to build a kite and take you to the beach to fly it during the next kite festival in July."

"Yes, what an honor. I will write and let you know if I can make that date."

I do not like regrets, and I hope that the next time such an extraordinary opportunity opens its doors, I will rush there with wings on my feet!

In one of the books the prince's father carried to my table, I found a wonderful folktale symbolizing the humility of the Balinese.

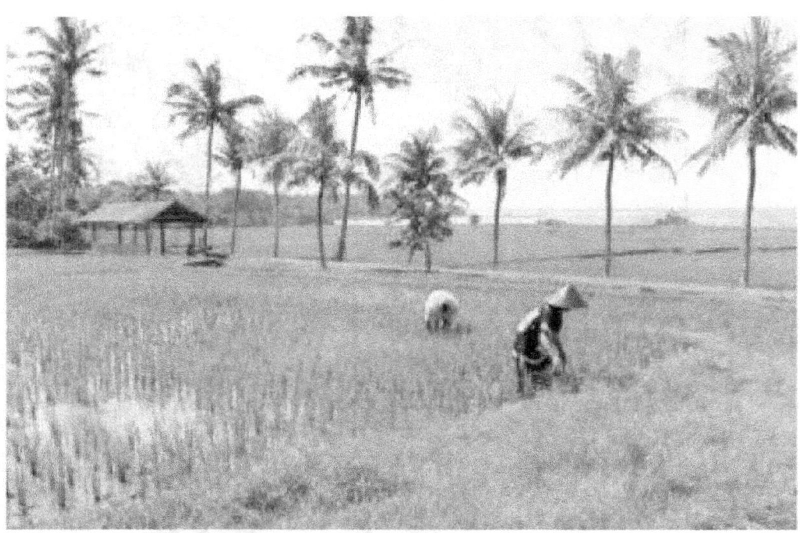

The start of a peaceful workday

One day a Gecko went to the Village Chief and complained: "Oh, sir, can you help me? Will you speak to the Firefly? He keeps me awake all night, flashing his light in my eyes."

Now, the Village Chief, who liked to sound important, said, "I will look into this matter. Come back one week from today for my answer. "The Village Chief called the Firefly and asked quite kindly, "Tell me, why do you have to worry people by flashing your light?"

And the Firefly, a very humble little fellow, put out his torch, folded his wings, and said, "Oh mighty sir, I pass on the message. I hear the Woodpecker going tong-tong-tong on the tree trunk—and I think it sounds like a *kul-kul,* warning the village to awaken."

The Village Chief, anxious to get to the bottom of all this, called the Woodpecker: "What do you mean, causing all this trouble?"

But the Woodpecker fluffed up his feathers and answered: "Your worship, I heard the frog in the rice field going kwak kwak. .k. .wa. .k, and I said to myself, 'the signal for an earthquake,' so I pass the warning." The Village Chief, now becoming fed up, called the Frog. The Frog hopped up to the Village Chief, made a bow, and said, "I know why you sent for me, but so help me, I wanted to stop Big Black Beetle from carrying loads of filth down the street. Most unhygienic, I must say."

"Oh," said the Village Chief, popping a wad of betel nut in his mouth, "wait till I have a word with Big Black Beetle."

Now when the Beetle crawled into Village Chief's office, he showed signs of anger. "My Village Chief," he said, wiping his feelers humbly on the carpet, "obviously, I can't please everyone. Do you think carrying filth down the road gives me pleasure? Far from it. But someone has to clean up after the Water Buffalo has dropped a pat in the middle of the road."

"That's it!" roared the Village Chief, who feared the cockfight in the next village would start before he arrived. "Bring in the Water Buffalo!"

The Water Buffalo, frustrated and anxious, came to the Village Chief. "So, that's all the thanks I get for filling up that hole in the road?" he snorted. "Do it yourself next time the Rain washes one of the stones away."

Of course, the Village Chief had to speak to the Rain. The Rain, embarrassed by the Chief's lecture, spat hailstones at the Village Chief.

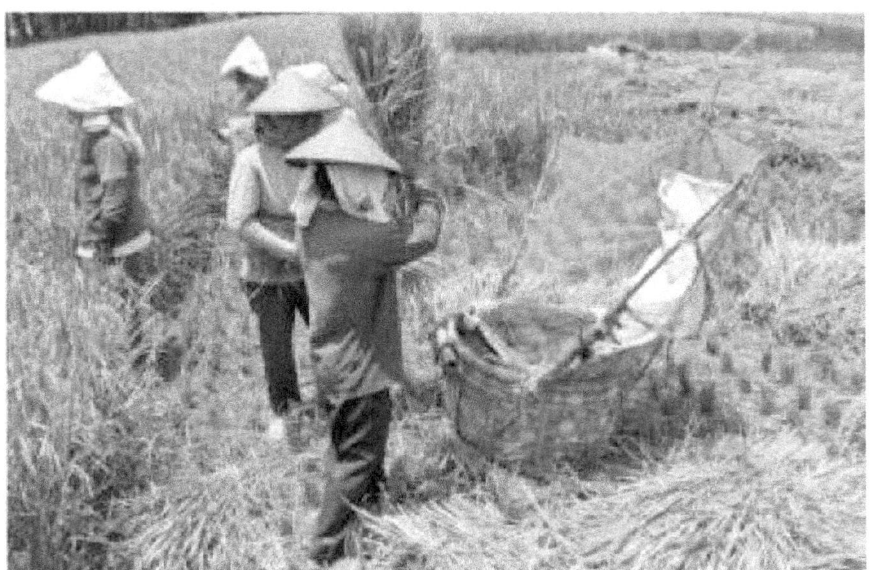

Pounding rice to release kernels

"I like that!" thundered the Rain. "For weeks, the Gecko sent offerings to the gods to send Rain because without Rain the mosquitoes go away and without mosquitoes the Gecko goes hungry. Speak to the Gecko and leave me alone," and the Rain departed in a flash of lightning.

When the Gecko returned, the Village Chief gave him a stern look and said, "Go and live at peace with your neighbors. For all of us have our problems."

A series of ceremonies and rituals add to the dignity of Balinese life, which fortifies the variety and richness of the culture. The observable demonstrations of perfected atonement, temple worship, tooth-filing rituals, and intricate cremations go together to seduce and magnetize the visitor. The interrelationship between Bali's unique religious traditions and its passion to connect this to everyday life thrives in its people.

Ask a Balinese his idea of heaven and he will reply, "Bali." Reflections come back to me of that first day, standing outside my charming hotel room when a man's finger touched his lips, signaling silence, and said, "Please respect our worship area."

Mansukh Patel states, "If you can cultivate a state of silence, the most challenging problems in your life will suddenly become manageable."

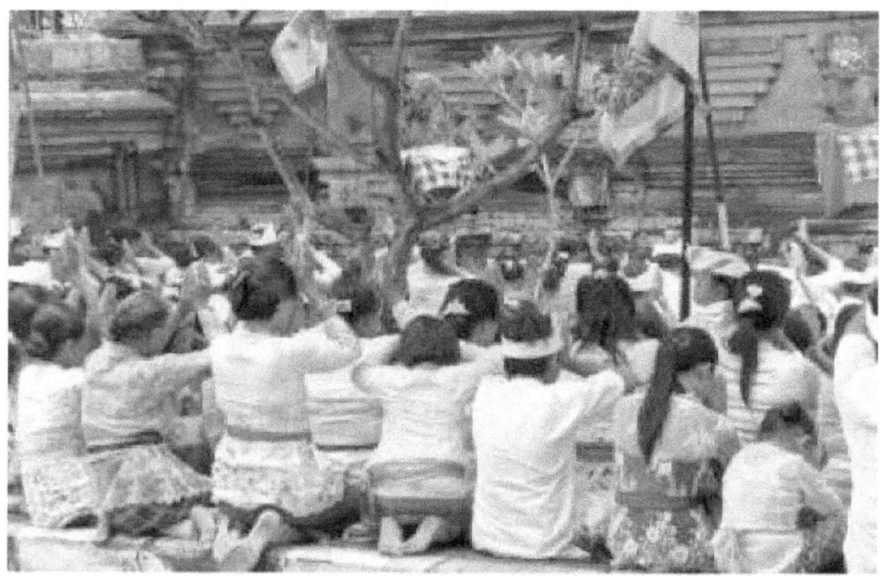

Praying the day before Nyepi begins

Mahatma Gandhi observed a Day of Silence every Monday, saying, "In the attitude of silence, the soul finds the path in a clearer light."

The absorption of these new ideas rewards the traveler here. When you arrive in Bali, you may or may not meet a prince, but options abound throughout the island.

Hotels, balancing on volcano craters, offer views of sandy ribbons on both sides of the island when your endurance for nightclubbing and expensive distractions seems exhausted.

Little island hideaways wait patiently for the sound of the ferryboat arriving with a passenger or two.

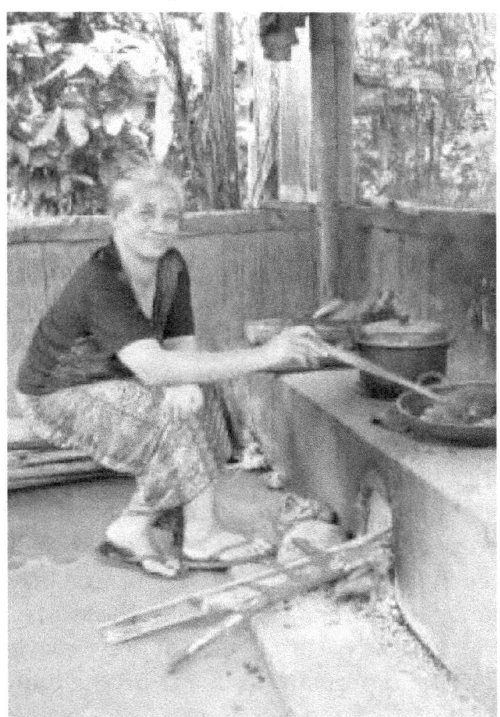

Roasting coffee beans

The tapping sound of the carver's mallet signals a wood carver's workshop, offering a class. Workshops to please any interest abound in Bali from creating delectable food entrees, batik dyeing, weaving on traditional looms, and even coconut tree climbing. In the past, these artistic abilities slanted toward the gods and spiritual worship.

To appease the tourist market, artists have moved into all levels of creativity. Artists work together, not concerned so much about personal recognition when carving the stone statues and gates. They delight in going beyond the traditional with whimsical mythological creatures.

Locals create the necessities of clothing, food, and other offerings with all levels of art forms. Typically, men have had the obligation to continue sophisticated art forms, including music. Women funneled their creativeness into the traditional rituals of making offerings several times a day. Designing these gifts to higher beings and affirming an appreciation for good fortune (while soothing ill-behaved, or vicious, devilish spirits, playing with the rhythms of life) takes fifty percent of a woman's day. Cakes, fruits, and flowers make pyramids on women's heads as they walk to temples before festivals. Once presented to the gods and their essence consumed, the perishable objects again remain balanced on heads for the long journey home and the evening meal. The production of offerings each day defines the commitment the Balinese make to their exotic tradition.

Walking the streets of Ubud, the cultural capital of Bali, my feet tiptoed with caution among the hundreds of homemade coconut leaf baskets, lining the sidewalks in front of businesses and homes. The strong, recognizable odor of burning incense, and the sweet flowery smells from offerings exposed some of the invisible layers of life, so faithfully ingrained in the dynamic culture of Bali. Cracks in the stone-walled compounds offered me a sneak preview of women lighting their incense while with devoted compassion, sprinkling droplets of water over the shrines. Their hands moved in ritualistic motions, passed down by ancestors, interrupting spirals of smoke. The vibrant culture still lives and breathes in stones and trees.

Offerings, stacked high at corner intersections to decrease the number of accidents, often spilled over into the streets. Motorcycles lined the curbs, like a game of dominoes, each blessed with offerings placed on the seat. Every morning and evening, homes and businesses make these offerings to local spirits. Blessings for different objects occur on special days of the week. Metal objects like cars receive offerings to prevent accidents on the day designated for metal objects.

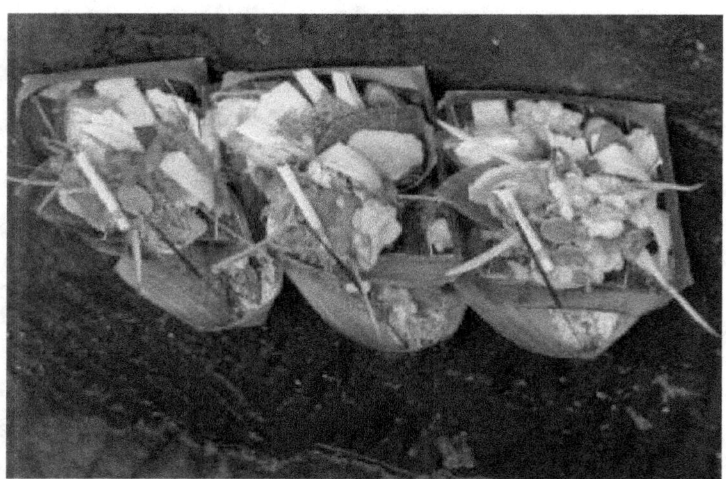

Spiritual offerings

Jagged sidewalks reminded me of jungle walking, tripping over roots, and avoiding the occasional snake or colony of ants which can eat a horse in two hours. Metal grates with holes covered the sewer system, running under the sidewalks. The local custom calls for leaving shoes outside before entering a shop or home. Baskets of offerings and endless numbers of shoes outside a busy restaurant could cause visitors or customers a visit to the hospital!

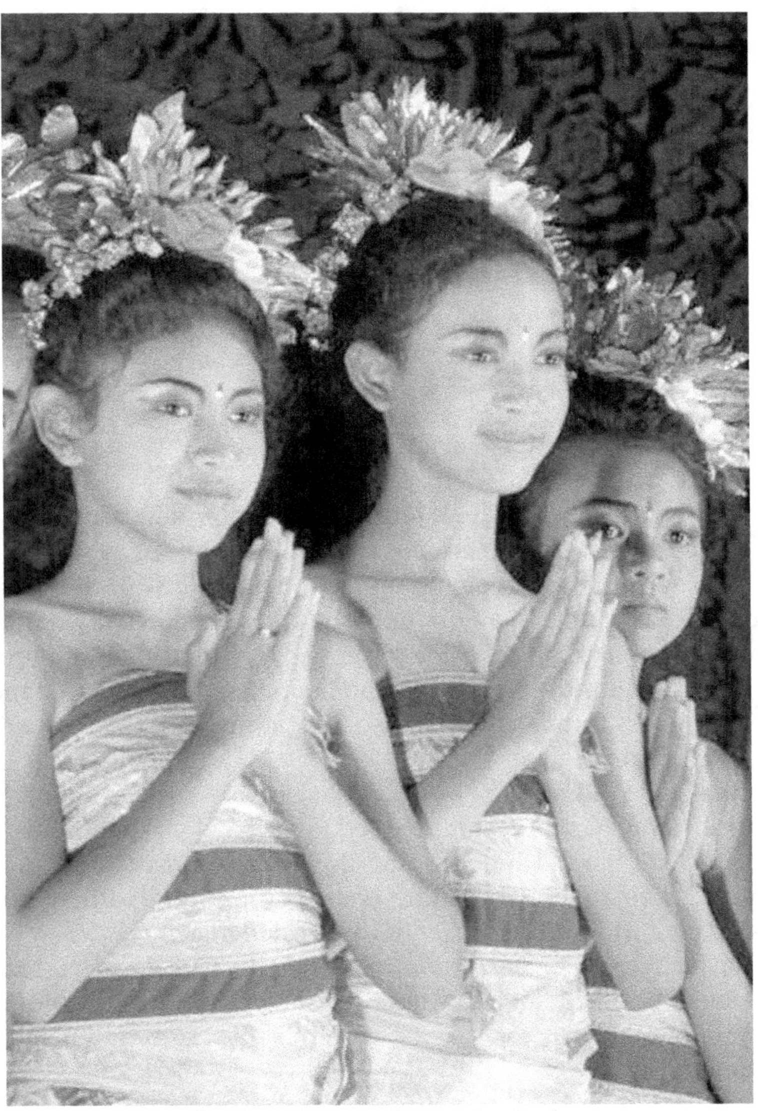

Performing to please the Gods

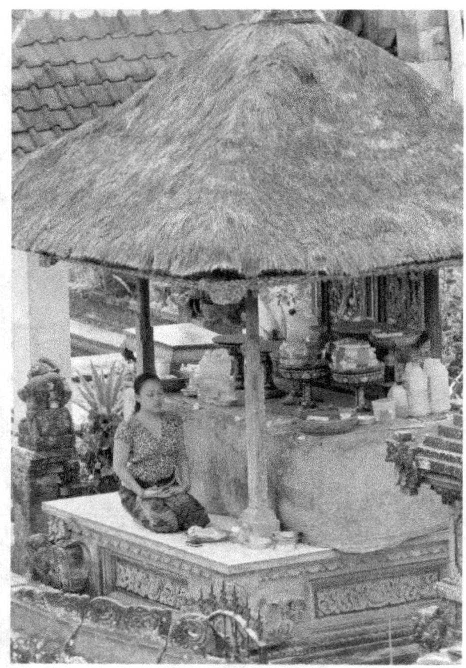

Small family temple

My camera, like my soul, wanted constant attention. Dangling from my shoulder, the strap put the camera out of mind but not out of sight.

"No," an older man said, coming up from behind me as I stepped over the short rail, teetering under the gate opposite my new hotel room. Each family compound has a small area set aside for prayer. I had no idea that area was off limits to strangers. Inside the walled compound, small, carved-stone shrines, hungry for prayers, rituals, and those ubiquitous offerings stood proudly against the elements of time.

I remembered an old saying, "When words become unclear, I shall focus with photographs. When images become inadequate, I shall be content with silence."

Balinese beliefs blend Hinduism and Buddhism, and the people believe in reincarnation. Their souls, reborn into another life after death, allow half the spirit to stay on earth and the other half to reside in heaven.

Yearning for *moksa,* or perfection, the soul passes into successive reincarnations through physical bodies or temporary caretakers. After death the soul, in its newfound freedom, prepares for its imminent return as a newborn member of a family.

The karma accumulated during life results from the consequences of obedience to demanding rituals.

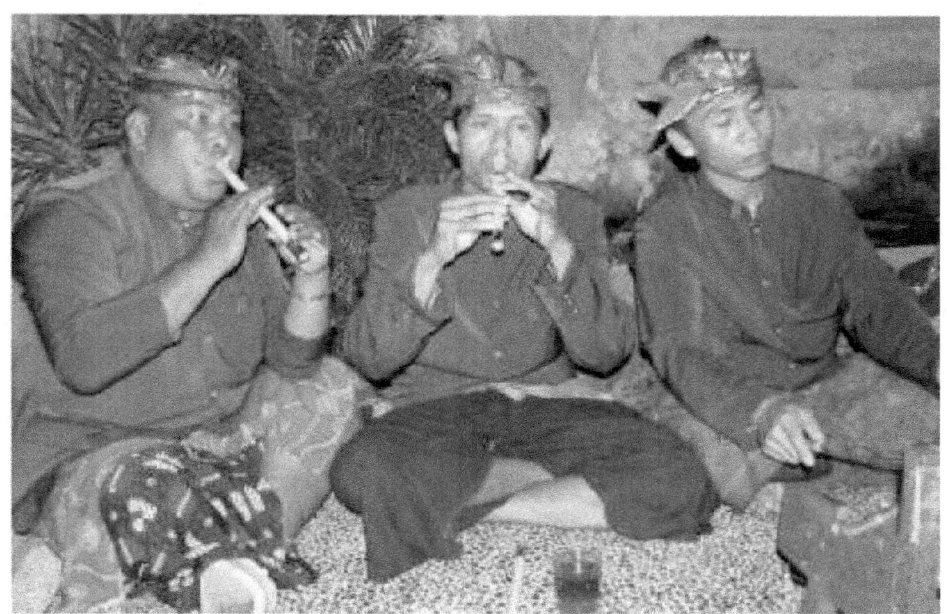

Sidewalk musicians

Balinese homes have walled-in areas, containing many small spirit houses and shrines, called *sanggah*, the Hindu word for temple.

Shrines consist of ornate carvings of stone or wood with coconut-thatched roofs.*Bebali,* or sacred fabrics, purify sacred places and offer protection from bad spirits and illness.

Spirits of dead family members live in shrines. The people appease specific gods with offerings of elaborate plates of food, prayers to invite the deceased spirit into the shrine, and *bebali* fabric wrapped around the bottom half of the shrine.

Convenient to my hotel compound, sat the Tutmak. It is a culture-watching open-air restaurant, famous for its flair, and its international food. Any table in the place offers views of the busy street with locals carrying baskets on their heads, children walking home from school, or shopkeepers giving offerings to the shrines wrapped in *pelong* cloth, or black-and-white checkered design.

Across the street, two shrines wrapped in the pelong appeared alive and breathing, with their main bodies clutching baskets of rice and tiny cups of tea. Incense offerings tumbled upwards, greeted by diversions of umbrellas, wavering over the top of the shrine.

All over the city, you will observe black-and-white cloth draped around trees, stones, statues, and pavilions or anywhere a spirit might dwell.

The host with big brown eyes, serving my breakfast of scrambled eggs and tomatoes, toast, tea, and banana pancakes, knew a few words in English.

I have tasted banana pancakes, a Third World wonder, in rural China, Laos, Burma, and now here in Bali.

The Bali version tastes like traditional crepes made with thin, sweet batter, filled with chunks of bananas.

Brown eyes wondered why I wanted both the eggs and pancakes, as I would have to pay more since the room rate included just one free dish.

"Mau makan kue dadar minta," I blurted, as I refreshed my memory of this phrase from my notebook. "I would like to eat banana pancakes, please," a great translation, always good to have with you!

Laughing, I shared with my host, "I eat a lot for breakfast, and your pancakes taste better than mine back home!" He may not have understood my words, but he laughed, in any case.

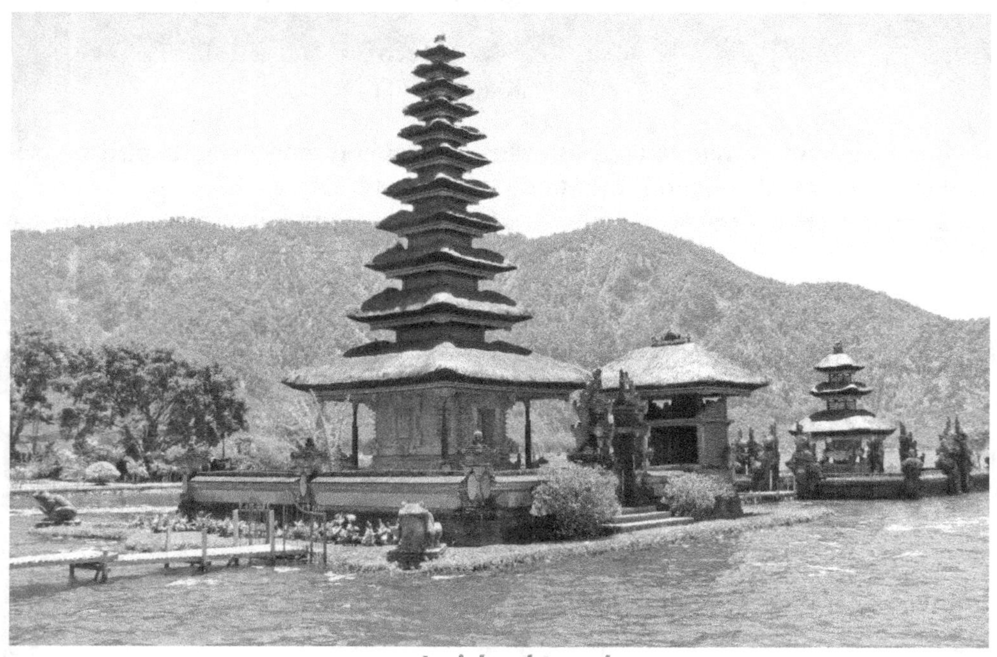

An island temple

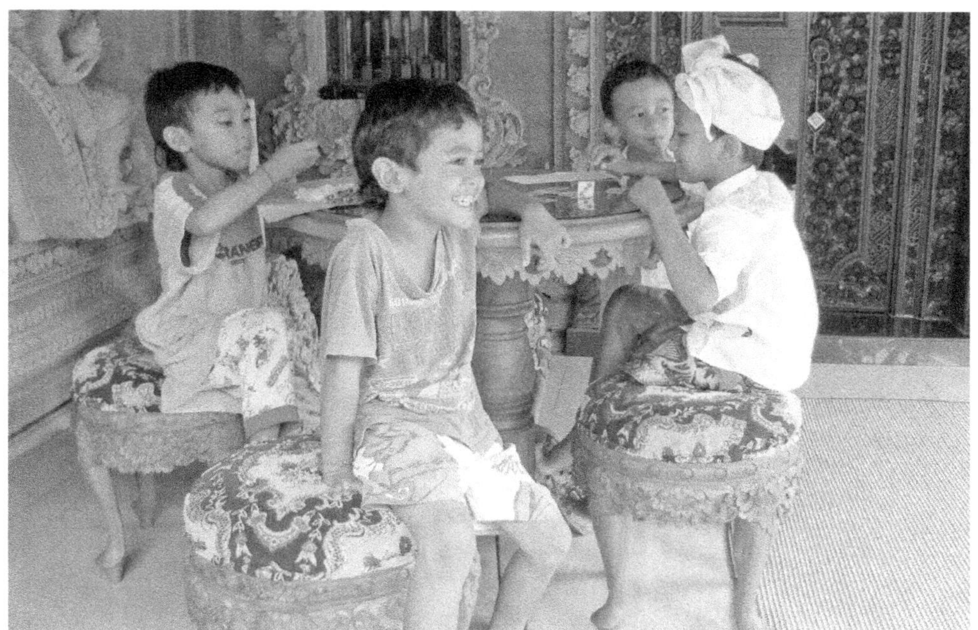

Fun after school

I pointed to the walled compound where I saw a young girl going through a set of rituals with her hands and arms after lighting incense and setting a basket of tiny offerings on top of the tallest shrine.

"Only family," his words matched feelings of the older gentleman earlier that morning when I tried to step over the railing into the private compound. Laundry day meant finding some sunshine for my sink-washed clothes.

The same girl I had seen sacrificing walked past me, balancing a basket on her head full of offerings.

She placed a small, leaf-woven basket, filled with rice and flower petals at the entrance of doors and gates.

She lit incense, sprinkled holy water, and murmured a few words in Balinese while she made circling movements with her hands around the incense.

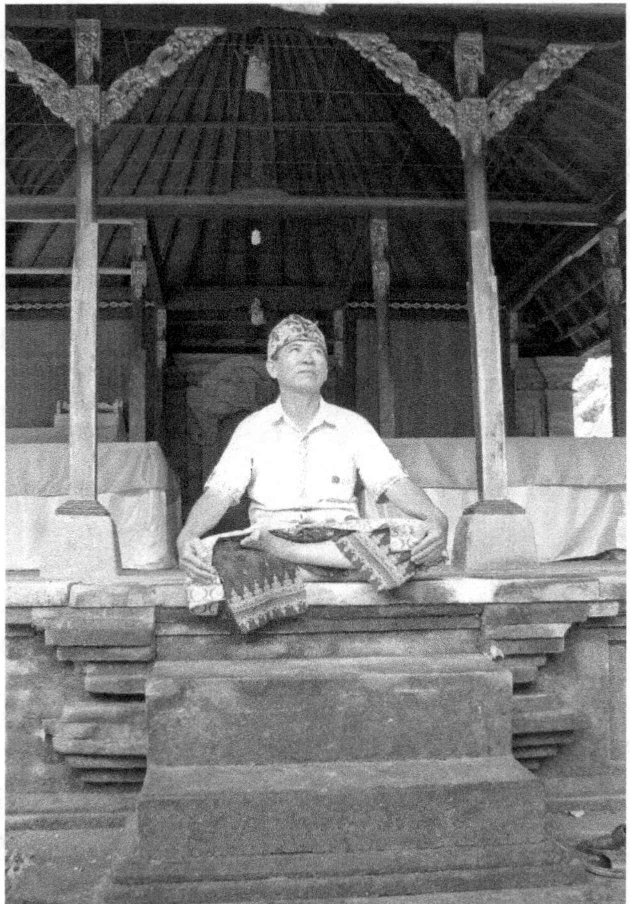

Meditating at Elephant Cave

Crossing the street, I sometimes met motorcycles coming out of nowhere. No traffic lights or stop signs gave traffic the right of way, meaning that I had to look both ways and run!

Bali offers cheap and easy travel except for one thundering issue: traffic uses the left side of the road. You can enjoy carefree driving until the corner opens to a two-lane street, and you want to turn right from your left-hand lane.

Another foreigner had the same problem: coming towards me from the right lane, he had misjudged and directed his motorbike straight at mine. We crashed, and both of us hit the asphalt on our sides. Policemen arrived.

Dealings with foreigners promote huge audiences, and people rushed to the road to watch the show. Local government guards its reputation, and, therefore, someone would have to pay for this situation.

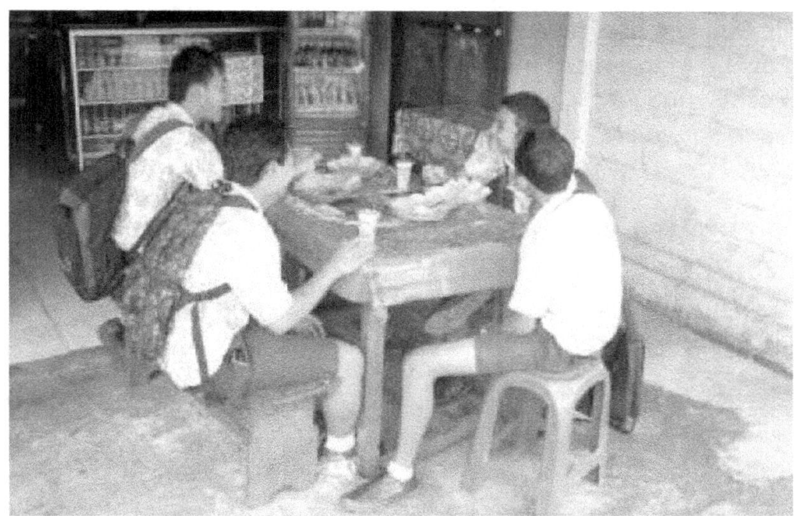

Schoolboys taking lunch break

The girlfriend of the young boy came up on her motorbike from behind us and told the police, "No broken bones and no dents on the bikes, so please let us all go home."

Trickles of blood ran down the boy's bare legs, covered with loose skin hanging over pieces of sandy pebbles. My wrist started throbbing and already the swelling was causing me concern. After the police had questioned each of us in private, they declared our freedom. Walking the bike back to the hotel, I wondered why I made the decision to rent a motorbike for three dollars for the day when a car and driver cost ten!

The outside layers of a culture catch sightseers off-guard, often hiding the true essence of a people. Travelers need an emotional tolerance for feathering in the old traditions with the new. It's best to focus on the real jewel for journeying so far from home: the people.

The nucleus of traditions and spiritual energy appeared as a scene, unfolding right across the street! Hunched over and limping, a middle-aged man dragged a cart to the corner, balancing it on two upright tree branches.

"*Lima, Lima Eskirim*." His words bounced off the sidewalk, catching children from all directions.

His ritual celebrated the ending of the school day. Uniformed children, accompanied by elders, envied the older kids' freedom to stop for ice cream, run and skip through mud puddles, or kick a ball back and forth, confusing traffic. I'd jotted the numbers one through ten on the first page of my catch-all notebook, and these notes often came in handy.

I knew Balinese shortened the extra digits when talking or writing numbers. Looking at the man's makeshift cardboard sign, I assumed the ice cream might cost five cents, and I watched as the children swallowed up my view of the man. The children squealed with laughter as they reached out their hands, begging for a cone.

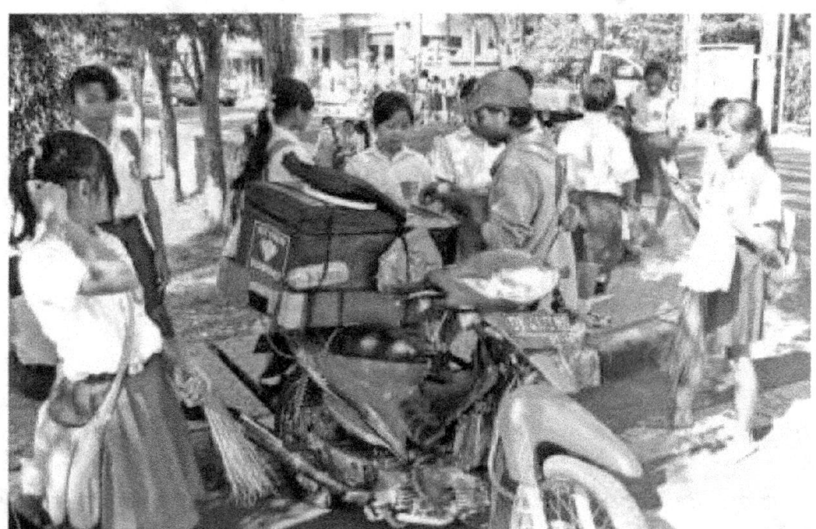

Ice cream seller across the street from school

Sunset awakens street vendors, anxious for tourists to buy tickets to local Balinese dances after gaining their attention with coupons from restaurants. Groups of young girls attract attention along sidewalks with brochures offering body massages, facials, and milk baths.

The massage in Bali resembles a new art form. A shower, open to the sky, begins the experience. The hostess sprinkles rose petals on ice-cold stone floors, and lights candles to warm the emotions, as clients anticipate the promised relaxation process.

Apprehensive of the sexual exploitation sometimes ascribed to the massage parlor reputation, I replaced my clothing with a tiny twelve-inch-long piece of fabric, attached by Velcro around my waist, and I found the darkened room. Monks dressed in saffron robes, leaning against stone temple walls came to mind as Balinese music and fragrant incense played with my imagination and senses. For four dollars, the professional one-hour massage topped any winning lottery ticket I could imagine. The next few days I tried the facial, plus a soak in an aromatherapy bathtub filled with warm water, herbs, and milk topped with rose petals and sunshine.

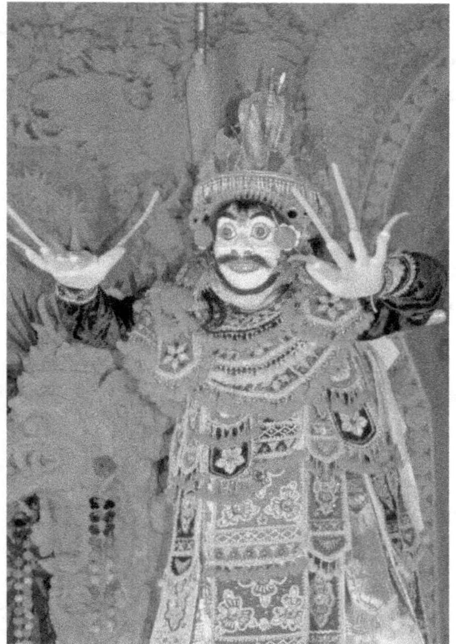

Rangda, everyone's nightmare

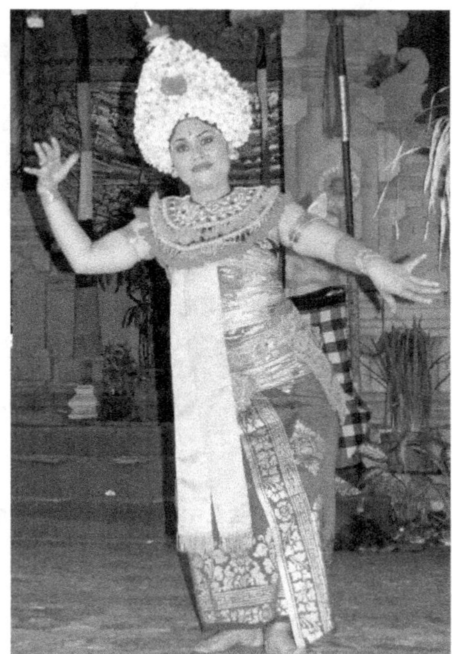

Hands emphasize graceful complexity

Ubud, known as the arts center of the island, provides the perfect location for local dances like the famous Barong dance. Ask any Balinese the name of the character in their worst nightmare and the witchlike character named Rangda brings wrinkled eyebrows.

Masks, carvings, and batik wall hangings depict Rangda, representing evil. Long sharp fingernails reach from the stage as Rangda appears in the Barong dance. Crazy hair, fangs as long as fingers, and an even longer tongue cast a shadow over the freaky bulging eyes. Her loud cackles carry supernatural powers, and the locals believe sacred prayers protect them from her.

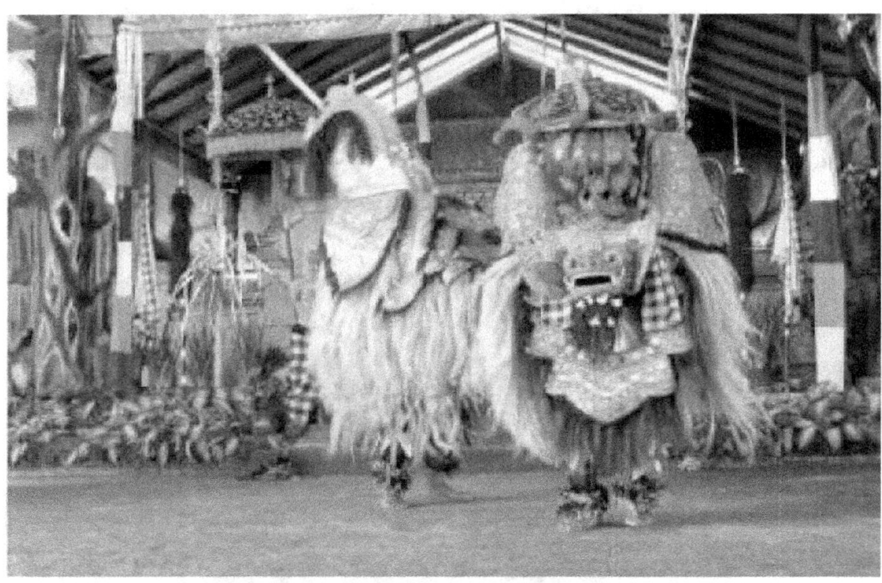

Barong, half dog and half lion, propelled by two men inside

Legong dancers begin their career when about four years old. Chosen for their supple physiques and beauty, they work hard until retiring in their mid-teens.

Brilliant yellow and green fabric strips form a snug wrap around their chests and upper bodies.

Heavy makeup accents eyes and lips.

Gilded layers of leaves create crowns for their heads with frangipani blossoms attached to the hair they have wound in tight buns at the back of their heads.

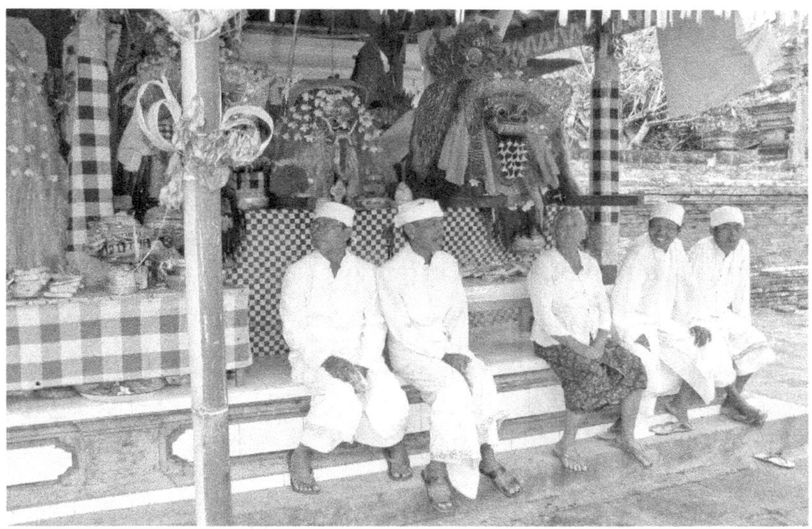

Relaxing after a ceremony

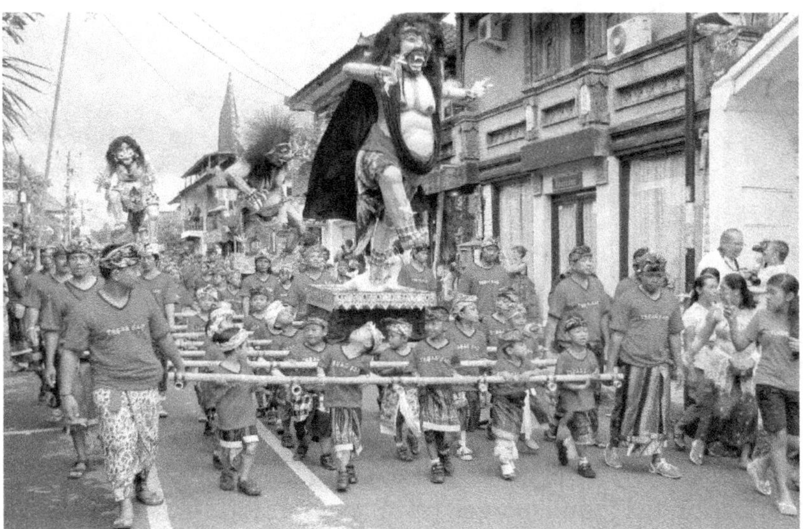

Scaring the bad spirits away with Ogoh Ogoh effigies

Festival time offers an opportunity to feed the soul. Ancestral traditions come alive as human puppets prance and mimic dragon movements.

My visit to Bali fell between two special Balinese holy days called Galungan and Kuningan.

Phases of the moon and 210 days comprise the Balinese calendar, which dictates when the holidays occur every six to seven months.

Ancestor spirits arrive from heaven on the Galungan holiday to visit with their family. Families make decorations for weeks in preparation.

Visions of carved fruits, iced cakes, and platters, embellished with garnishes of grace and love, build their anticipation.

Music from day-long entertainment softens the air. Noises from carts with wobbly, wood wheels, clattering over cobblestone streets disappear.

Ten days later, Kuningan, the day that marks the end of Galungan, offers more celebrations with prayers and offerings, signaling the spirits returning to heaven.

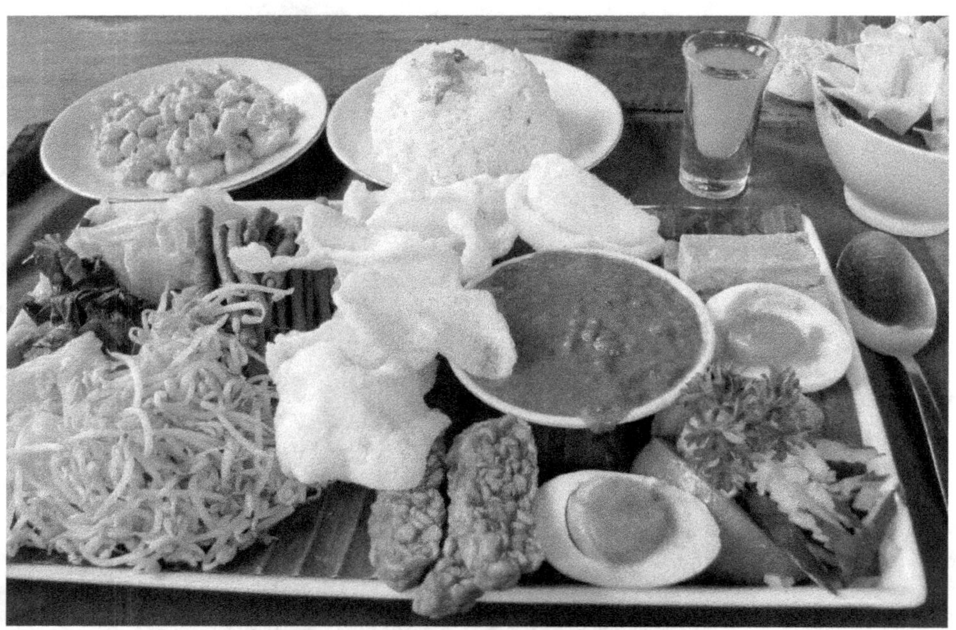

Easy to fill up on local dishes like gado gado

Peeking inside the oversized grand entrances of residential compounds during festival time, I found women on mats with tiny staplers creating flowers out of strips of dried leaves while children pulled at sarongs on grandmothers, stirring woks of fried rice.

Mothers, fathers, children, and all sorts of relatives make up the families living in separate structures, all within one walled compound.

Sleeping, kitchen, and storage areas have their own walled-in area, though some are open and without walls.

Most compounds have an elaborate carved structure with open sides where the older folks spend most of their time.

As families age, they want to spend more time near the *sanggah,* or walled-in area, containing the shrines for prayer and offerings.

When they die, their spirits will come to live in the compound's *sanggah.*

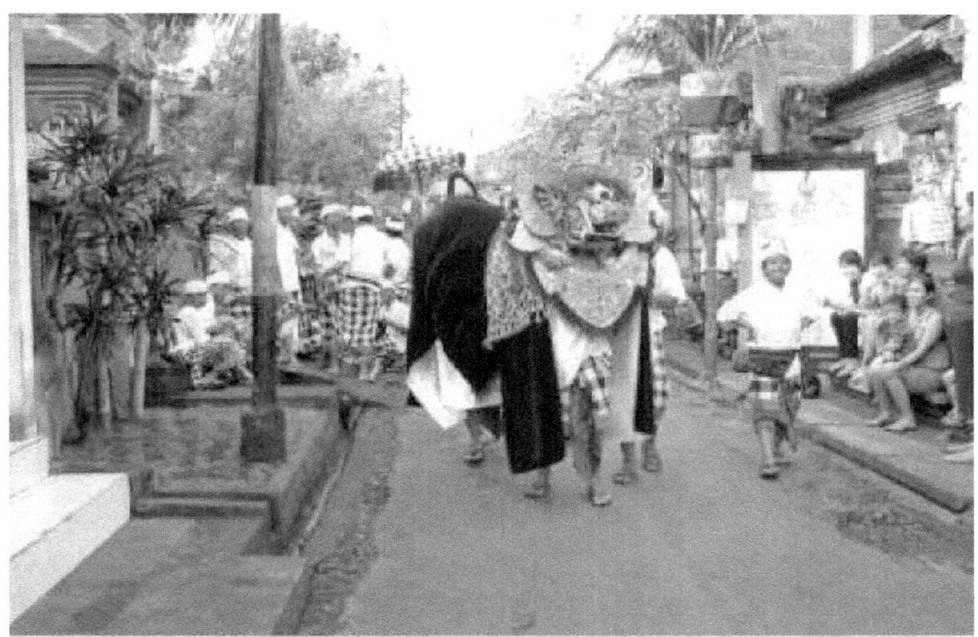

Children carrying heavy puppets entertaining neighborhoods

***

Groups of children, some with musical instruments and others under a ten-foot-long dragon puppet, walk the streets, stopping to entertain families.

Often, while you walk through neighborhoods, families will motion for you to join in the entertainment.

Children hear the traditional sound and come running outside their compound into the streets as the groups approach.

Small coins reward the children entertaining while little observers sit on rocks outlining the compound, watching in amazement at the scary, sometimes laughing, creatures jiggling their backbones or jerking their long dangling tongues up and down.

A Halloween without the candy!

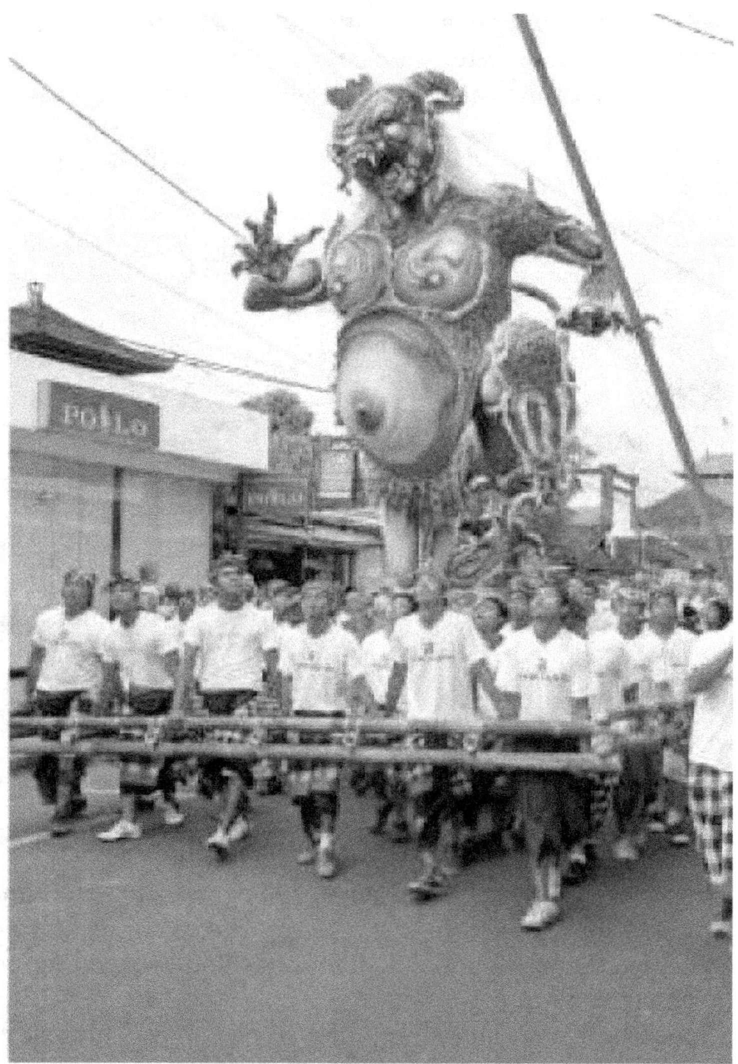

Bamboo poles lift the electrical wires

Imagine an international airport shutting down for an entire day while an island of people remained inside their homes for twenty-four hours. Westerners open their New Year with loud celebration. In contrast, the Balinese begin their New Year in silence.

The event, called Nyepi, starts with preparations days in advance for the Ogoh Ogoh parade and the building of effigies, representing evil spirits from traditional Balinese folklore.

These demons battle each other at sunset while parading down main streets on the evening before Nyepi begins. This visual highlight stands in stark contrast to the twenty-four-hour period of silence, beginning at six the next morning.

People arise early, take a bath, eat a small meal followed by twenty-four hours of no cooking, lights, fires, noise, working, or even love making. Some go a little further and remain silent with complete fasting. Waking on New Year's Day must feel like living a dream.

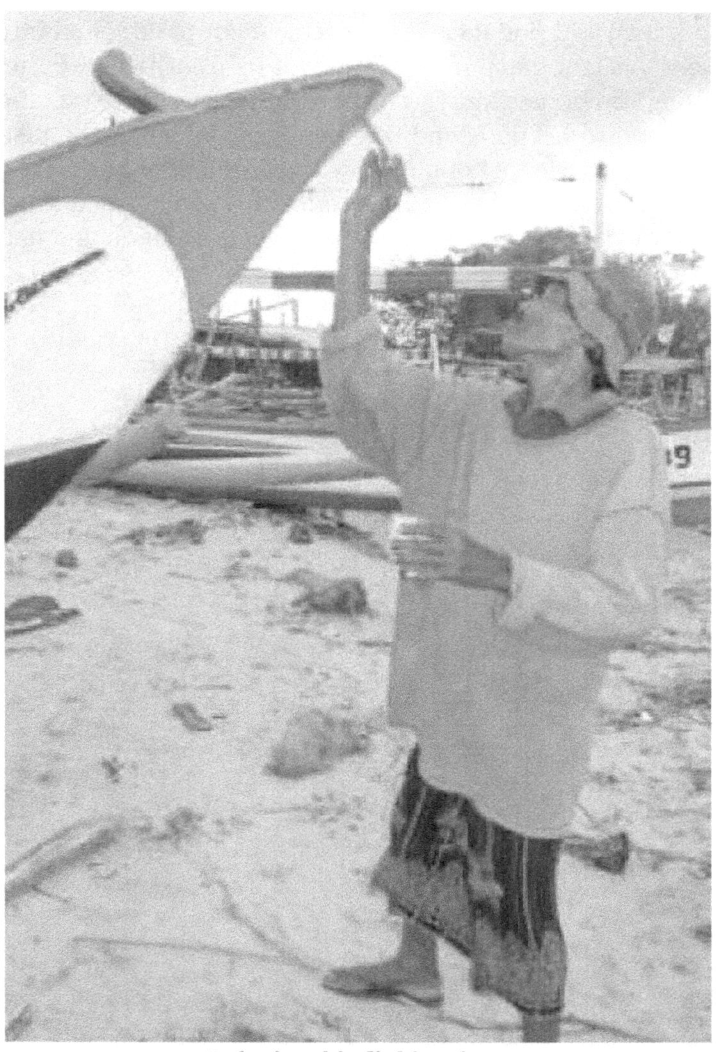

Painting his fishing boat

The *Pecalangs,* or traditional Balinese security men, control the streets by stopping any activities disrupting Nyepi. Hotel guests may not venture outside the hotels, and many hotels minimize the lights and sounds inside the complex as well as provide food for the day. Many hotels are simply family compounds with rooms made into guest quarters for rent. These types of guesthouses offer no restaurant or food service except on Nyepi when guests are required to remain inside the compound. On that day, the guests are included in the family mealtimes.

The Balinese believe if they trace back what they have done in the past, both evil and good, they will find it easier to decide what to do for a better life in the upcoming year. A silent and pure environment helps achieve a better introspection for decisions on values like forgiveness, kindness, patience, and love.

On this otherwise hectic island, the sounds echoing in the distance might originate from an occasional baby crying, dog barking, or birds, competing with insects and frogs. The Balinese believe--with this symbolic control over themselves and their world--they will start their new year clean and new.

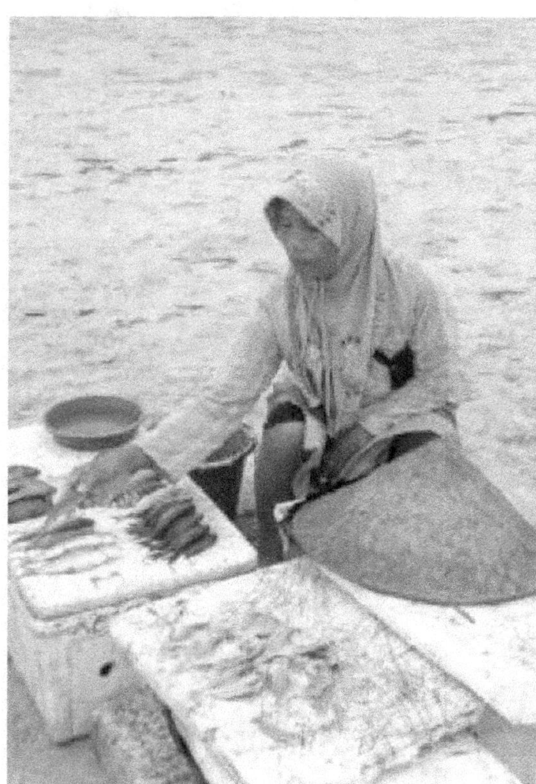

The day's catch for sale

Sizzling aromas from neighboring woks, colors in vivid sarongs, sparkling beaches, and magical dances come to mind with thoughts of Bali.

However, for me, the definition of Bali remains in the magic the people maintain with their devotion to traditions.

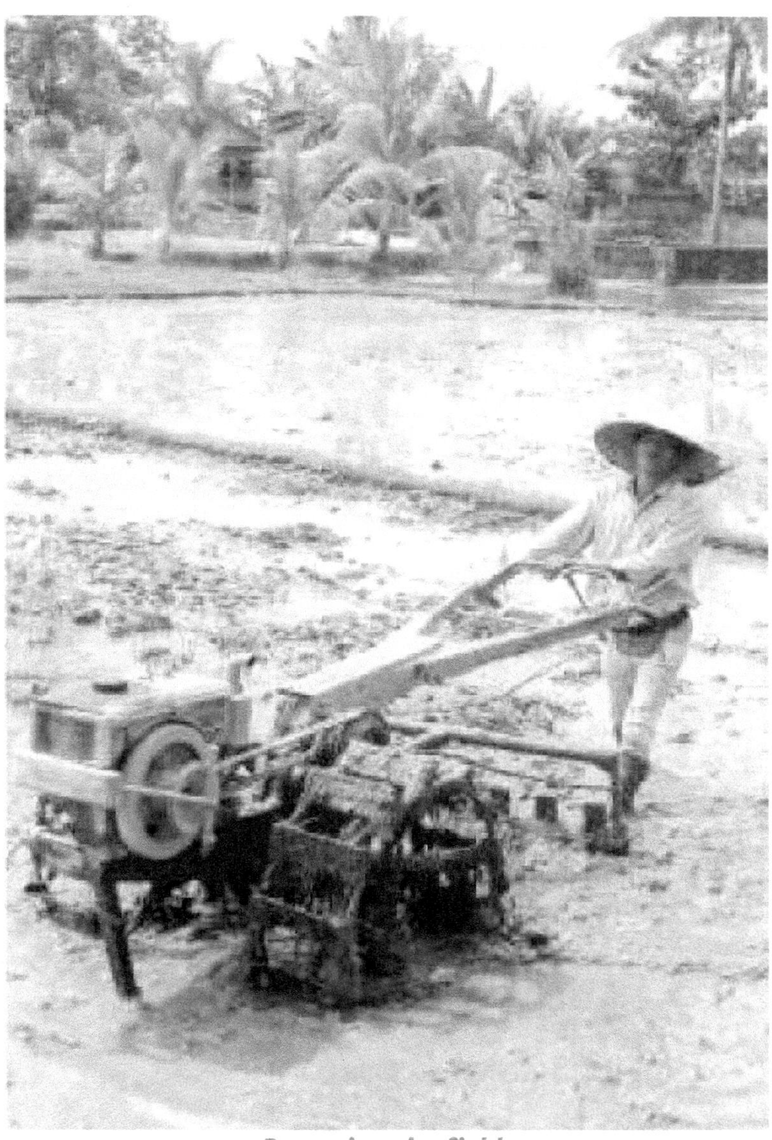

Preparing rice fields

Warm sprinkles washed the taxi, waiting for my departure to the airport. The gracious owner of my small hotel took my hand and with a warm smile said, "We cry because you leave." Such beautiful sentiments speak of the heart of the Balinese culture.

CHAPTER FIVE

Burma-the Temple's Emptiness That Fills the Mind

"Life shrinks or expands in proportion to one's courage." Anais Nin

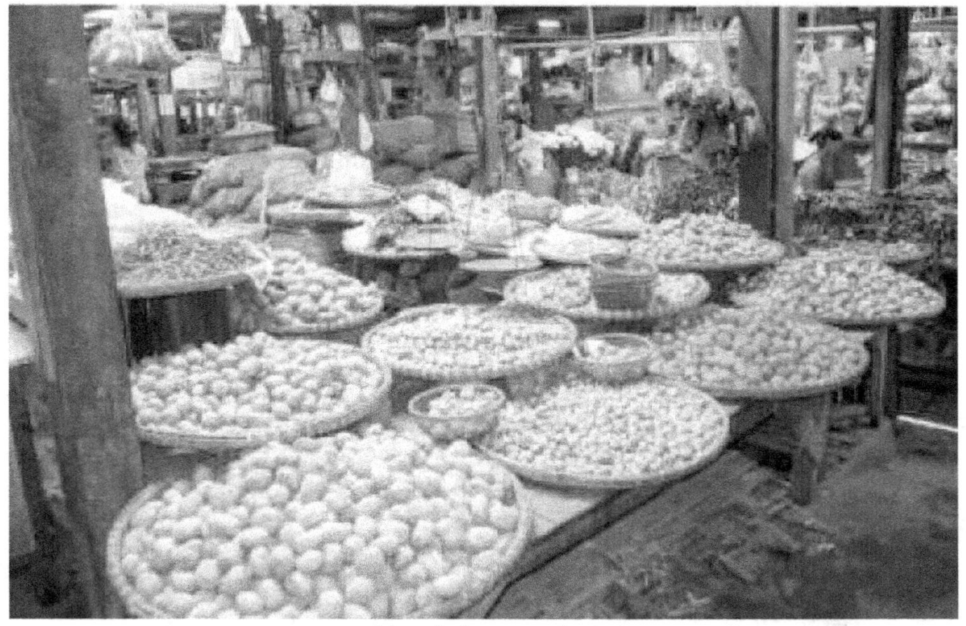

Mandalay market

The donut holes burned my fingers. The oily funnel-shaped paper wrapper slipped to the ground, freeing the fried dough to roll under the market-woman's feet.

With an ear-to-ear smile, she prepared another paper cone of pastry. I pointed to my camera.

She nodded, taking a practiced pose of looking down, hiding our sociable encounter.

What a perfect scenario to describe Burma.

Initial smiles fade, dissolved by the obscure chemistry of the Burmese government's perplexing authority, seeping into the soul of its people.

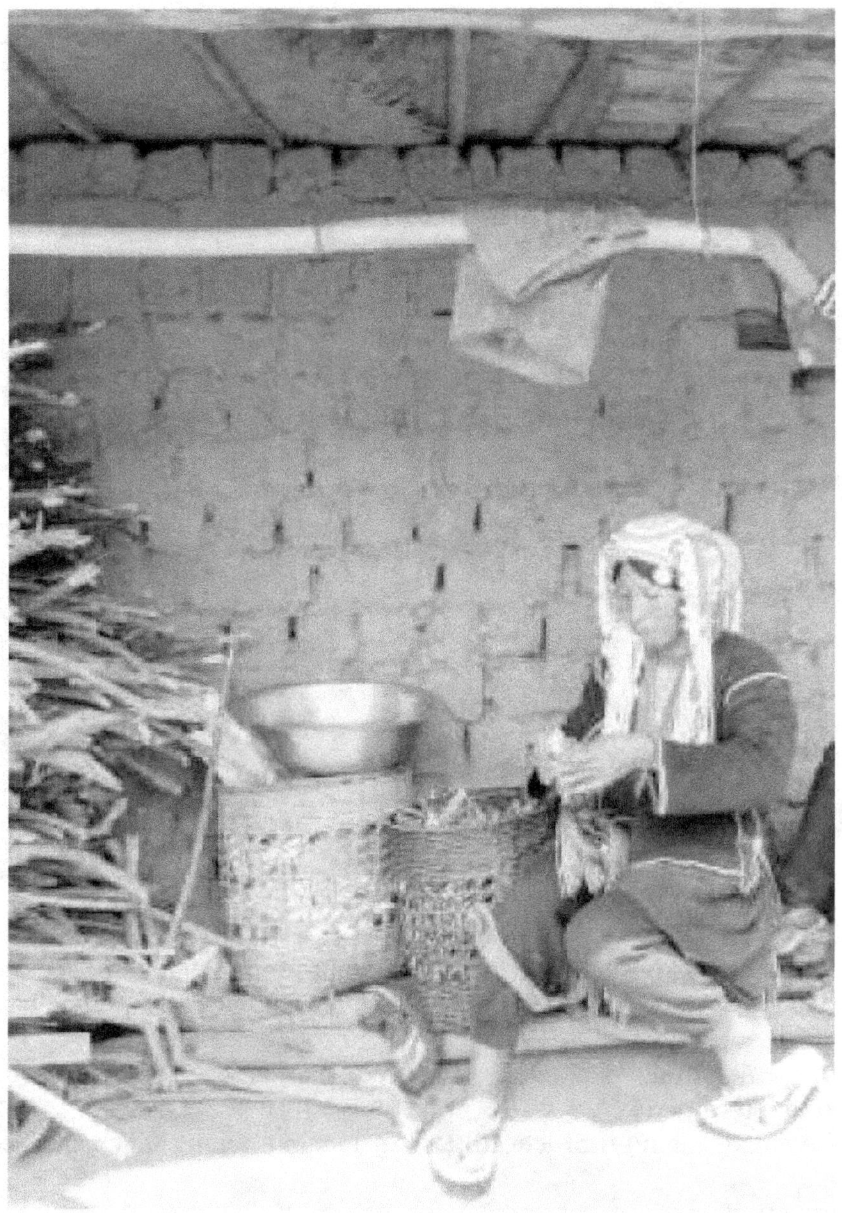

Ahka woman cleaning vegetables in Kyaing Teng

Unlike ordinary tourist maps, Burma maps show more colorful details for the veins of travel. Clouds of green conceal parts of the country, off limits to foreigners, with roads radiating from cities marked in colors, indicating "unapproachable without a government permit." Until 1988, Burma remained a closed nation to tourists.

The UN recognized the 1989 name change from Burma to Myanmar. The United States, UK, and Canada have been slow to recognize the new name and often continue to refer to the country as Burma.

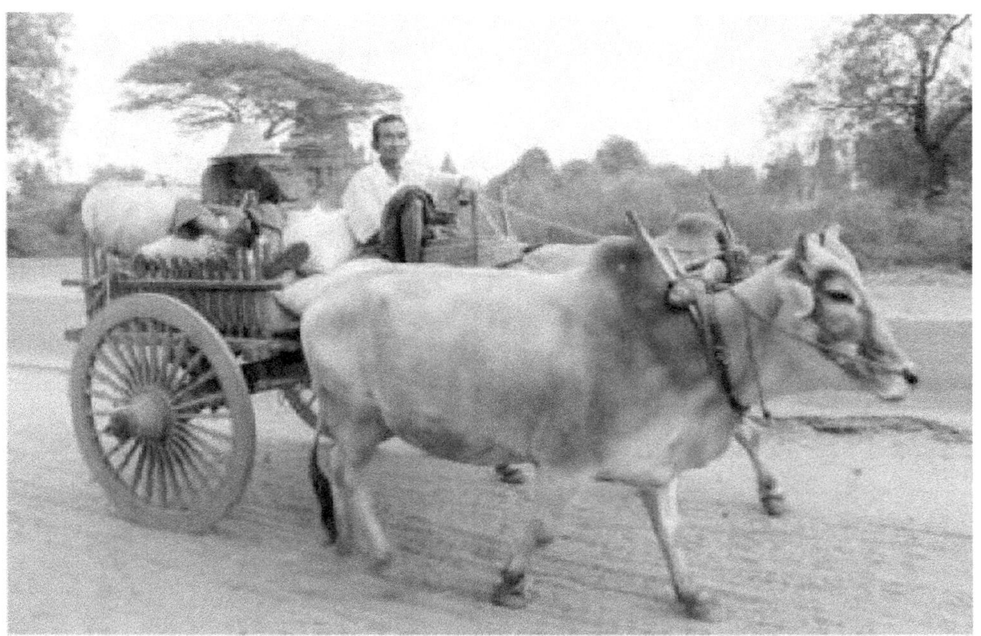

Home from market in Bagan

Your first impressions of this country will calm your anxieties. The locals welcome visitors, and thousands of pagodas thrill the eye.

The world has touched the country with gentle hands.

In the year 2002, no public access to computers existed, and businesses had e-mails monitored. General Ne Win seized power in 1962, closing any window of opportunity for travel to the country until 1988.

Kipling's reaction to the beauty of Burmese women haunted me as I read it. Burma, India, and Laos remained on my wish list as thoughts of time standing still came to mind.

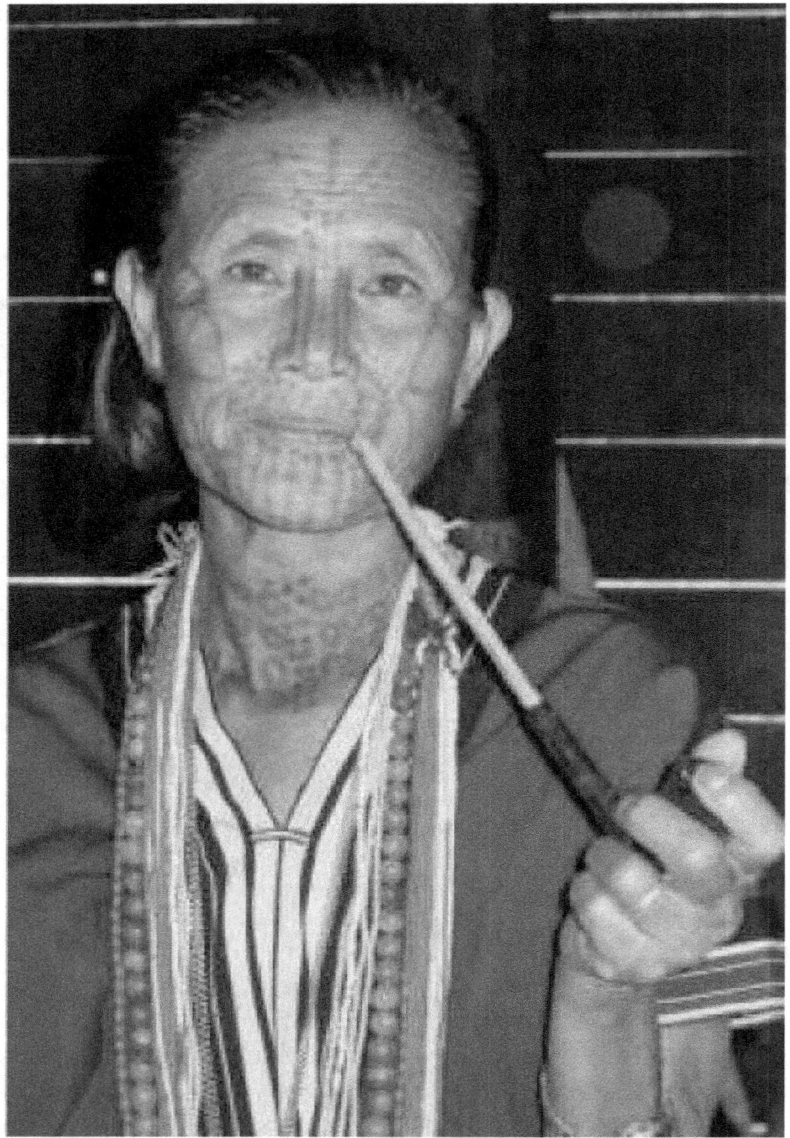

Chin woman, tattooed, living in Aye village

Rudyard Kipling, twenty-four years old in the year 1908, stopped at the port of Rangoon in a cargo ship, transporting him from Calcutta to Japan. His poem, "*Mandalay,*" written there, achieved world fame with the song, "Road to Mandalay."

He said, "She shall look all the world between the eyes, in honesty and good fellowship, and I will teach her not to defile her pretty mouth with chopped tobacco in a cabbage leaf, but to inhale good cigarettes of Egypt's best brand."

My spending a month in a remote place to explore vanishing ethnic villages left those at home nervous. I wanted to write home.

A local contact found a business with internet service, explaining he could sneak me in after hours to send a message. My message reassured my friends and family of my safety but warned them not to expect any more messages due to the government monitoring of all correspondence leaving the country.

My message never reached home. Recently the country has lifted many of these restrictions.

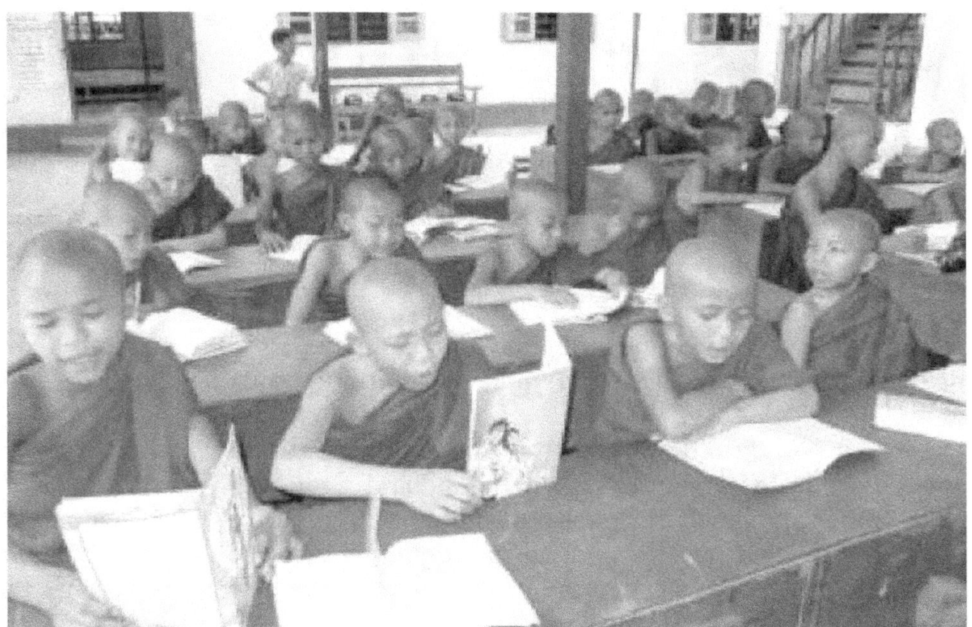

Reciting lessons at a Buddhist orphanage in Yangon

A ten-year-old novice hid smiles with his hand when I kneeled to share photos of my son with him.

The dark Myanmar youth gazed at pictures of my boy's curly blonde hair as he conquered small hills on his dirt bike back home.

I asked permission for a photo, and he nodded but lost his smile.

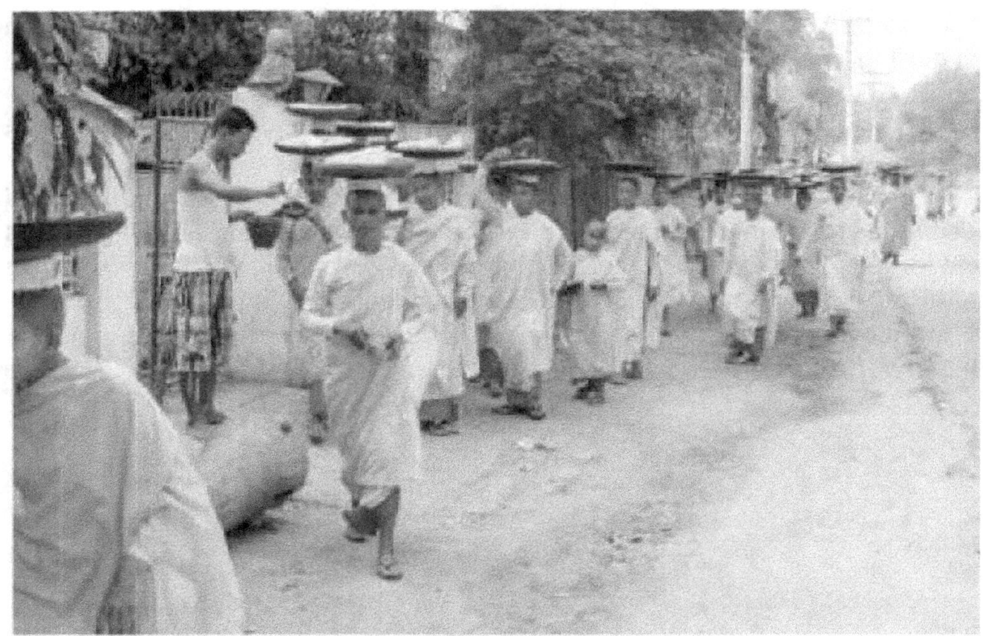

Nuns receiving alms in Mindat

The traditional custom suggests every Burmese Buddhist male between the ages of seven and thirteen spend time in a monastery as a novice. Considered the most significant day in a boy's life, his novitiation calls for grand celebrations.

A festive parade with the boy dressed as a prince sitting on someone's shoulders ends at the local monastery with the shaving of the boy's head. Then, wearing the robes of a monk, he takes the vows and honors of a son of Buddha.

This ceremony begins his *shinpyu,* or religious education, and earns his family's community pride, given when a son wears the monk's robe and carries the alms bowl.

Men return to the monastery after age twenty for three months, most often during the rainy season, changing their title from *Samanera* to *Hpongyi*.

The vows adhered to include a prohibition against intoxication, killing, lying, stealing, wearing jewelry or perfume, sleeping on beds off the floor, accepting money for personal use, and eating food after noon. These vows are not enforced after leaving the monastery.

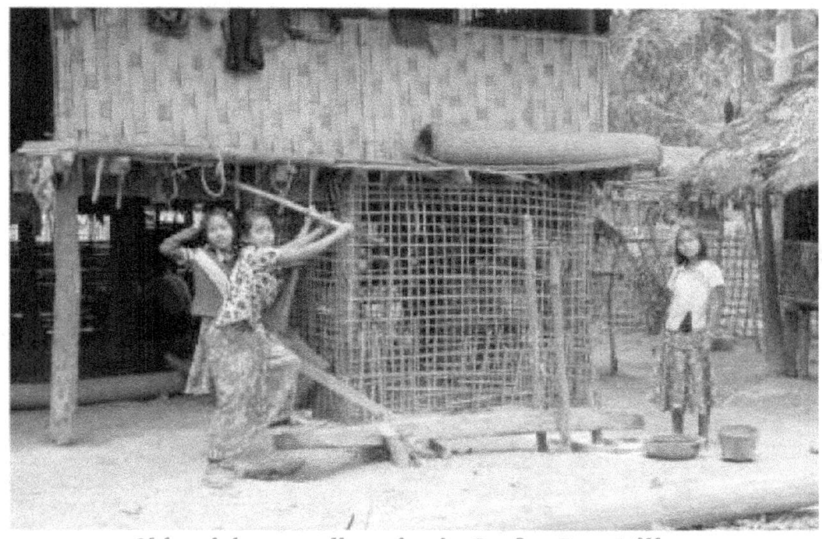

Chin girls pounding rice in On for Row Village

In the larger cities, a visitor could awaken at dawn and view hundreds of monks walking the streets with their alms bowls. Locals stand outside their homes and businesses with little offerings of food and water to place in the bowls.

The mountainous backdrop of rural Burma with thousands of gold spires, and the mark of a pagoda create picturesque hiking opportunities as you pass ancient villages, standing still in time, impervious to the intrusion of a modern world.

Villagers handloom the traditional garments they wear except for those of a few young children, running around in shorts or long pants left by missionary groups.

Charmed by a ride on an oxen cart to a small village, I wanted to focus on the children, waving and laughing along the way. My camera took priority with my attention on children clearing garden plots and young men cutting bamboo.

The village chief, always proud to have guests, welcomed me with open arms. I felt uncomfortable accepting his invitation to share dinner and sleep in his long wooden hut on stilts.

Nevertheless, his wife moved several textile pallets to one side of the room, leaving a space for an extra one. A line of ragged rope dropped from the ceiling to reveal a mosquito net, which covered my new bed for the night.

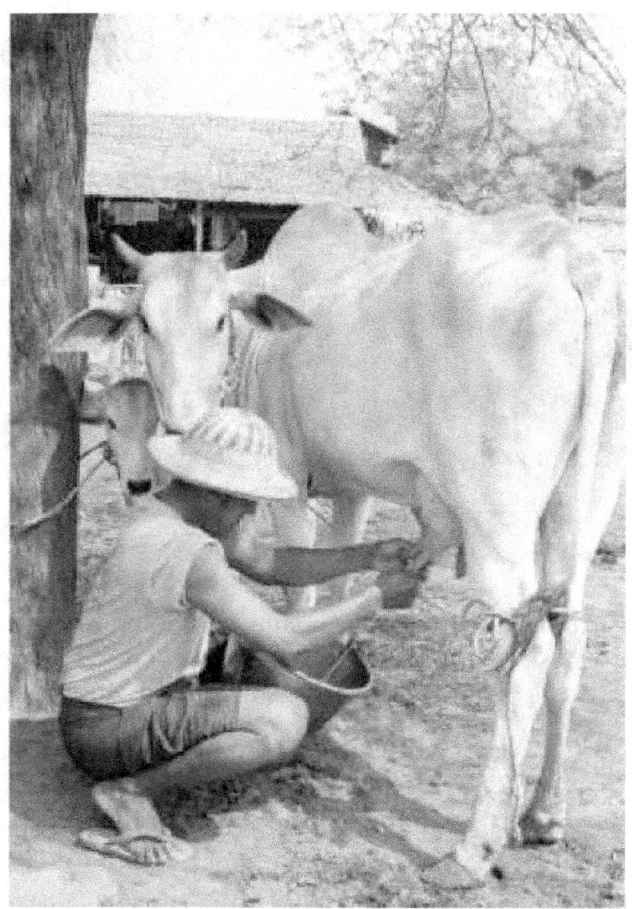

Yekyi man

Walking into remote villages, I found children not accustomed to cameras. After taking a few digital images and showing them to the children, I received a surprise from the adults of the village. Jealous of the attention, the adults would touch my shoulders, back up, and pose.

Smiling cheeks of women and children cracked with the *thanaka,* or pastry cream, used for sun protection and better skin health.

The pale-yellow powder, mixed with water, comes from grinding bark and roots of certain trees on *kyauk pyin,* or stone slabs.

For two thousand years, women have used the sandalwood-scented paste, forming designs on the face and arms.

Women believe it makes them beautiful, giving them a pale appearance while controlling the oil content of the skin.

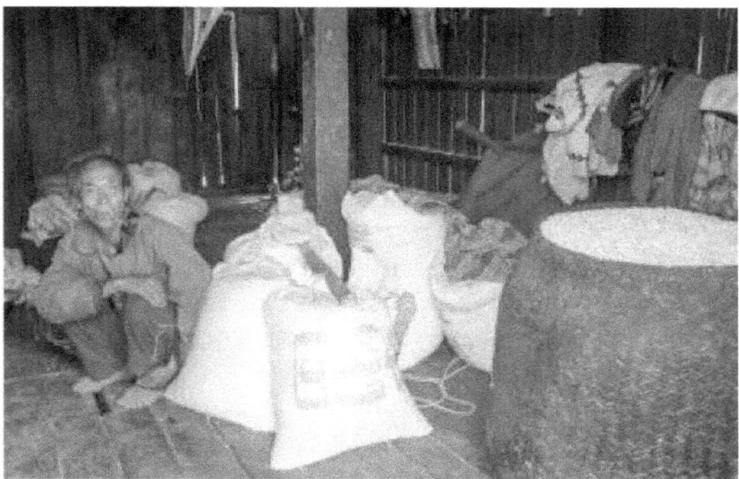

Chin man proud of his corn crop in Mashi You Village

An older man waved from his stilted hut window. I walked up the narrow log ladder to find a man in his nineties, putting on a traditional ethnic hat and shirt.

By gesture, he invited me to come inside, posed, and stood rigid against the wall so that I could snap a photograph of him. He smiled, no doubt his biggest smile in a decade, when he saw his image. The digital monitor hid the red-stained teeth so common among the locals. The stain accumulates from chewing betel nuts. I am not sure if he had ever seen his own photograph.

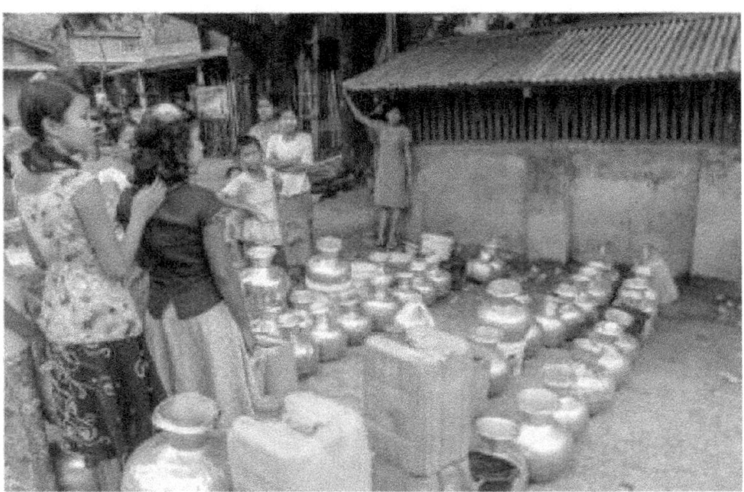

Mrauk generators run twice daily for filling water jugs

Giving gifts to villagers creates a dilemma. I don't want to introduce western ways, which tend to change their ways of living.

However, I did want to thank them for their kind offers of a room, some food, and, of course, their friendship.

This trip, I brought a few dozen pencils and notebooks and asked the Village Chief to give them to the local schoolteacher and not mention them as a gift from visitors.

I don't know if he understood as I used hand motions to point to myself and shook my head side-to-side. I felt the pencils and paper could help the schoolchildren but did not want them to start expecting gifts from strangers.

The quiet and serenity of the country village sets a mood that always brings internal peace to visitor and villager alike.

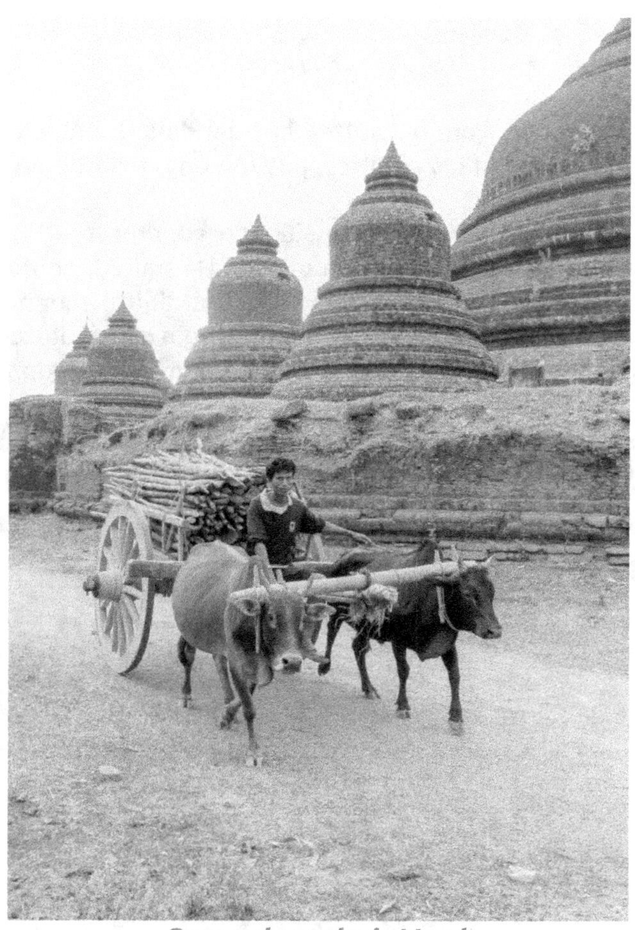

Oxen and pagodas in Mrauk

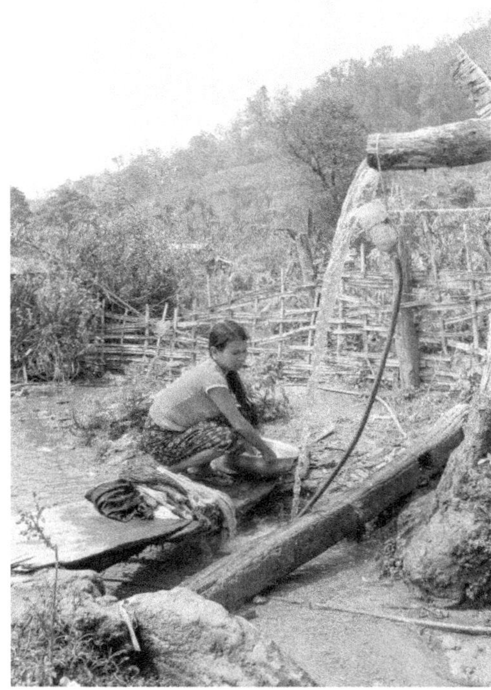

Palaung washing clothes in Pen Tha Pye Village

Ox carts of every size passed me on the walk down from the shark-tooth hills. Onions spilled out of the fat rice sacks as the cart's wooden wheels fought with jungle growth, creeping across the dirt path. Alongside the more traveled roads, villagers stacked sacks of corn, beans, onions, rice, and piles of wood or bamboo.

Large trucks lumbered by and picked up these items for export to other countries or the larger city markets. Two hours after I caught a ride with a private car and driver, the driver slowed to a sleepy pace. Alongside the road, rusty fifty-gallon oil drums showered fiery crimson sparks over the heads of old men stuffing firewood underneath. Young women walked with perfect posture, balancing cradles of cloth filled with hand-cut stones on their heads. They used stones to fill the holes in the road. Teenagers filled metal buckets with hot tar and handed them to women and men resurfacing the road.

Mothers ignored small children, climbing piles of rocks or dodging oxen carts, bicycles, and motor scooters. The lack of machinery caused me to ask my driver why families worked on the road by hand. He said, "The government requires all the villagers nearby to refrain from any personal work so that they could help on the roads needing resurfacing, until completed. All members of a village must help, including children."

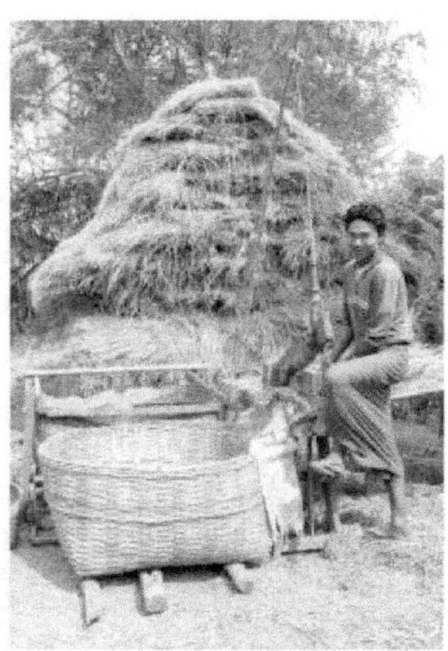

Yekyi cutting wheat

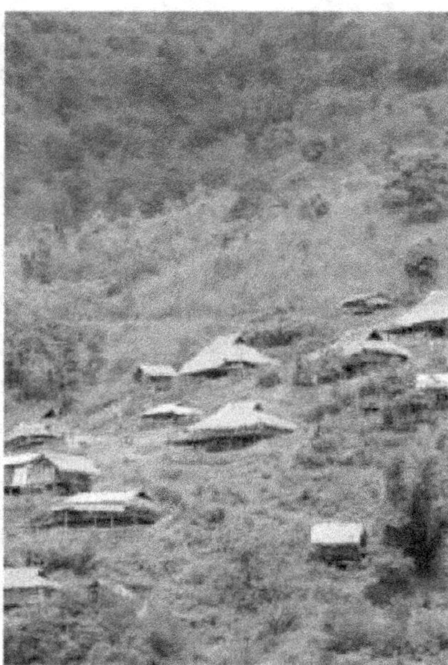

Ahka village

The sight of green, floating gardens filled the windows of the car driving from the airport in Heho to Lake Inle. Fruits, vegetables and tubs of fresh fish crowded roadside markets, a vast difference from the forested village markets of the Akha tribes outside of Kengtung. Vivid colors from melons, tomatoes, beans, and flowers, in every rainbow hue, called for a stop. Surely, the Golden Island Cottages would prepare any vegetables for my dinner and leftovers for theirs. In two weeks, I had not seen such a bounty of tempting fresh foods, all within reach.

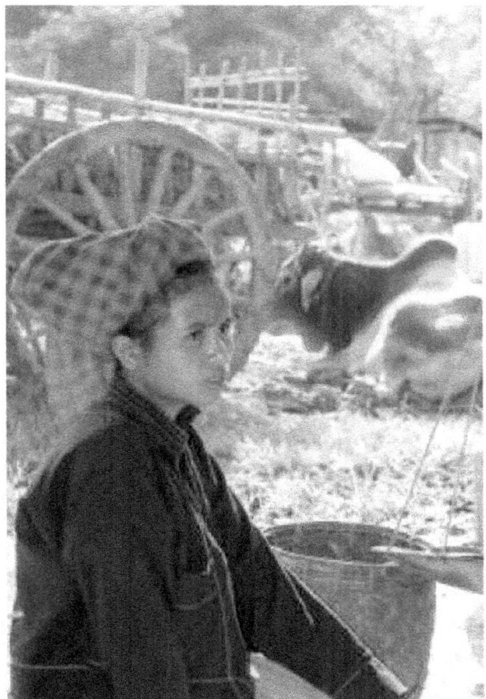

PaO resting at the market

The PaO tribe owns the hotel where I stayed, a place consisting of individual bamboo cottages on stilts, with private balconies, in the middle of the lake. The PaO take turns working at the hotel and returning to their villages for fishing and gardening responsibilities. A small canoe rested on the shore waiting for the arrival of guests. The real treat began when a group of employees, playing instruments, drifted to the hotel steps in the canoe. The staff's enthusiasm coaxed out my smiles and conversation.

Serendipity existed in the midst of those cottages. Unplanned discoveries happened all day as I sat on the balcony watching the lives of the Intha people in full view. Sunset provided me with a visual state of happiness unlike any other place I have traveled. Fishermen crisscrossed through the sun's rays, their conical hats on fire from the bright pinks and reds of the evening. Because the water gardens and silting crowded the banks of the lake, leaving the shallow waters muddy, women paddled further out into the lake in order to refill their jugs with cleaner water.

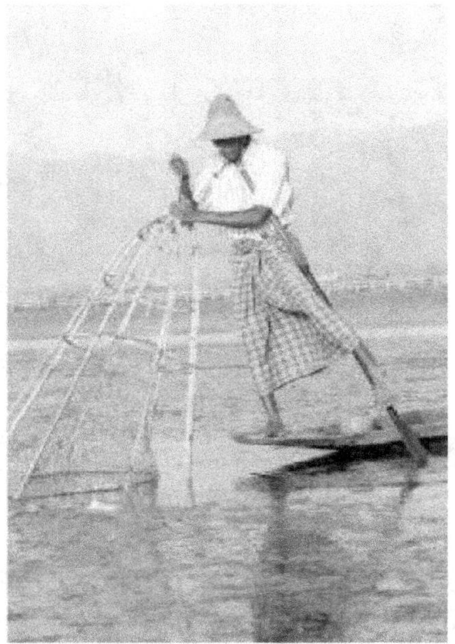

Intha leg rower with fishing net on Inle Lake

Due to the natural conditions of the lake, the fishermen devised a traditional way of rowing their flat-bottomed teak boats. Reeds and floating weeds infested the shallow water, making fishing difficult for the fishermen while sitting. The distinctive style of rowing involves standing on one leg and balancing the other around the oar. While standing, the rower had a better view of the water. With hands freed from holding the oars, the anglers lowered the conical-shaped nets with heavy bamboo frames. Locals say the age of the ruins of Kekku began before the sixteenth century. A Westerner first saw the ruins in 1996. A monk from the nearby village of Naung Hke engraved a stone, counting the number of pagodas as over twenty-four-hundred. A PaO tribal man, named Kyi, who spoke a little English, graciously offered me the rare opportunity for getting to know his people. He suggested we take a day to go into some of the off-limit areas of Burma in his small canoe, exactly the kind of experience I look for in a trip.

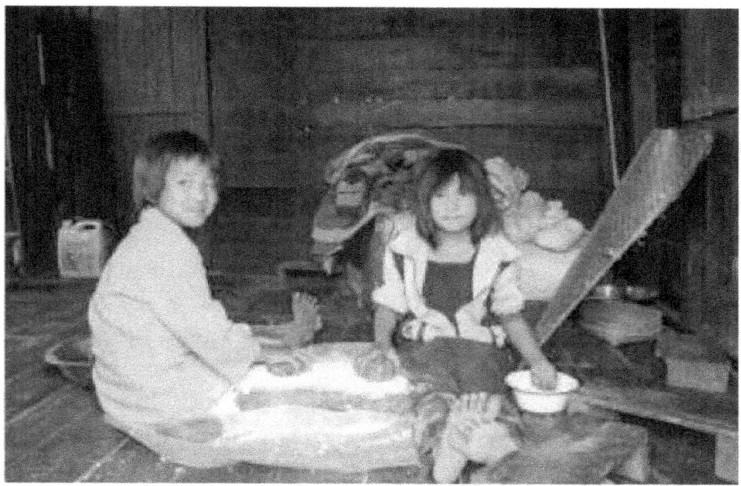

Chin girls smashing corn, one seed at a time

I asked, "How can we legally travel into the non-touristy areas?"

"I know many military who watch the bridges over the canals to small villages," he replied. "They will allow me to communicate with radios as we cross into their territory and pass freely with my friend."

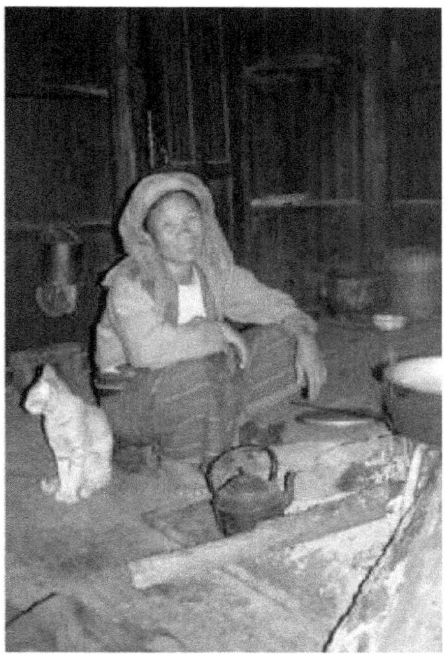

Palaung woman cooking

Canoeing before dawn scared me, as I knew the dangers of traveling into an off-limit area might include arrest if caught by the military.

My naiveté sometimes surprised me when I completely trusted people like the hotel owner, telling me it was safe to go back into prohibited areas.

Voices traveled across the water, and I remembered reading about a floating market in the area. People in large and small canoes gathered in groups, encouraging bartering back and forth.

I hope that the ripples from our boat didn't cause any pinched fingers for those steadying their neighbor's boat.

Containers of fermented rice, flopping fish, bundles of flowers, and piles of lacquer-ware balanced in the wobbly boats.

My friend Kyi paddled under a bridge while checking in with a man, peering over the railing, waving us forward. Around the bend, lives cloaked in secrecy maintained their primitive ways of living.

Women lined the water's edge scrubbing, dipping, and wringing clothing clean.

Twenty children waved us toward them, wanting us to stop. They giggled and pulled us toward a stilted hut with a notched, log ladder to climb. Their tiny bare toes scrambled up the steps like those of little monkeys. My clunky tennis shoes barely took hold.

Aware of the strangers entering the hut, a perceptive man offered drinking water, while scooting children out of the way. With care, I placed my feet between laps of children holding other children.

The thought never occurred to me that I could not understand the words of the story the aged man told so well, using eye contact and drawing pictures with his hands.

Leaving only a smile as a thank you, I hoped they knew how much I enjoyed their entertainment.

I crossed my fingers, hoping I would not fall as I descended the skimpy, narrow, vertical ladder, not designed for tall, lanky Westerners.

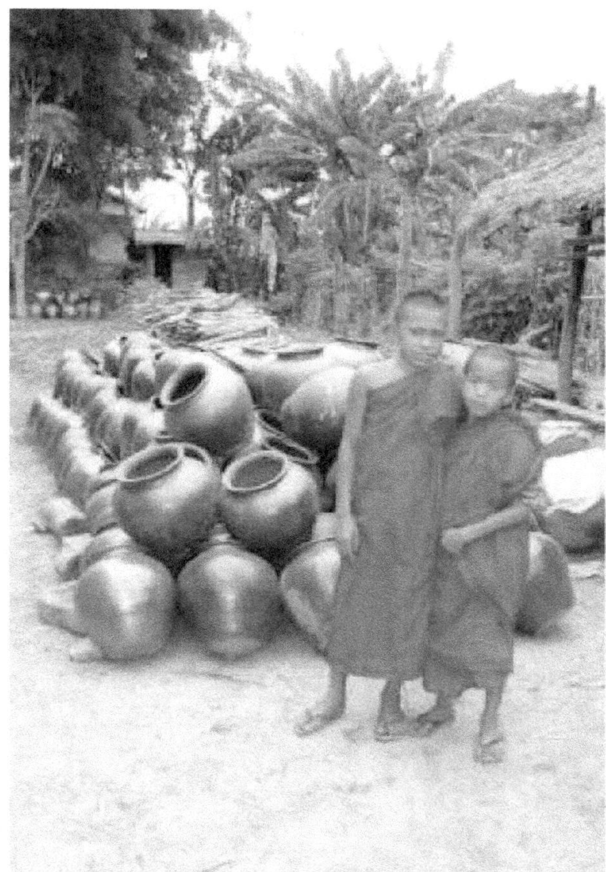

Novice monks in pottery village on Inle Lake

Two boys dressed in burgundy robes pointed down a little path. Deep ruts in the path made it hard to find a foothold. Ahead, a hole in the ground the size of a hut surprised me. Smoke escaped from a chimney over what looked like an oven, sitting deep in the hole. A man, so thin I could see the shape of his bones, looked up and smiled He pointed to my left side with a skeleton-like finger.

In the distance, I noticed the stacked piles of pottery. One of the novice monks told Kyi the story of the pots. Locals buy the pots to give as gifts to couples getting married. The children, finished with their story, circled around me with curiosity. I took a few photos to remind me of the genuine kindness they had all shared, and we left for the boat.

Almonds covered the ground in square patches, some on tarps and others lying on bare ground. Loud noises came from a hut close to the water. Inside, a large ox, tied to some kind of contraption, pulled a log in circles. The log crushed the almonds on the ground, extracting the oil.

A lone figure, with knees pulled tight to his chest, blocked the light coming in from the single window. He lifted a handful of the nuts.

His expressionless face changed with the 500-kyat banknote I left in his hand after gently tilting his palm and depositing the almonds into mine.

His lips did not smile, but his eyes glistened from a sliver of sunlight when he turned toward me. A single tear dropped to his bare chest. He reached for my hand again and squeezed. I suspected he did not get much attention from the young energetic children coaxing the buffalo to grind the nuts.

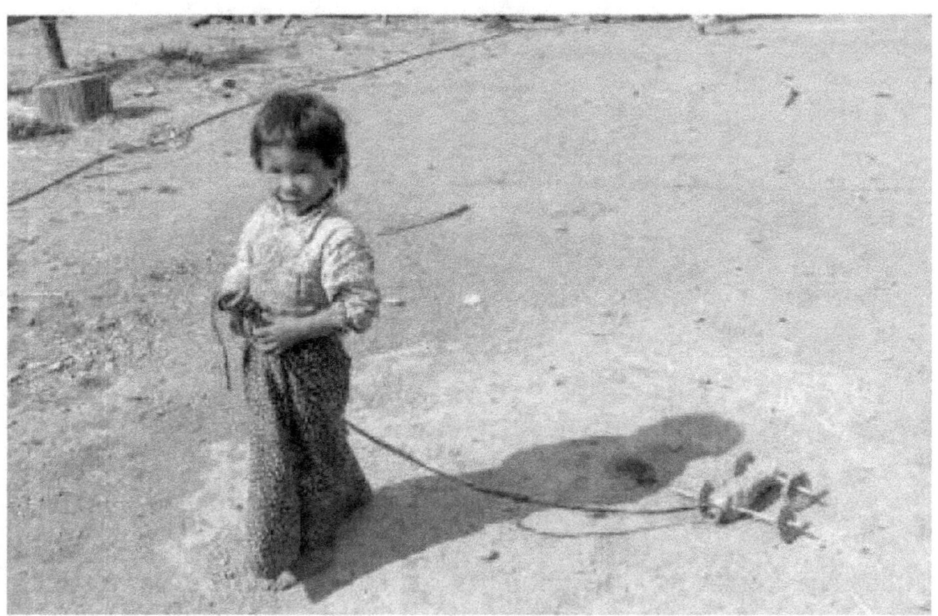

Chin playing with toy car in Htet Shwe Village

Back in the boat, we passed small pagodas crumbled along the water's shoreline. Children splashed us if the canoe got close and interfered with their games.

Mothers washing toddlers stopped long enough to catch a glimpse of the stranger yelling min ga la ba, or hello. My respect for these people grew by the hour. They made a living by growing almonds and trading for the things that they needed to supplement their sustenance.

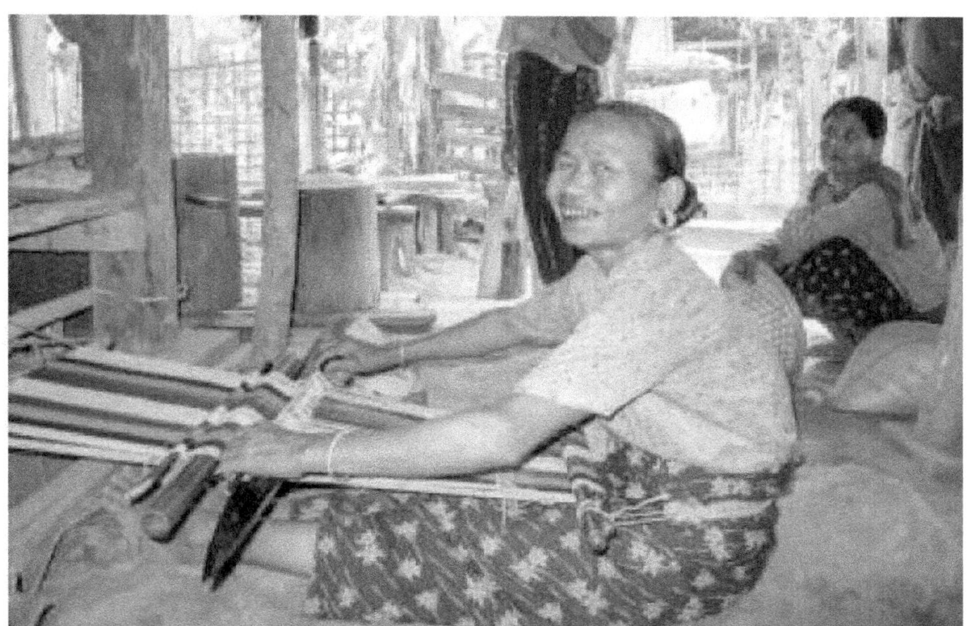

Chin weaving in a small village outside of Mrauk

A blurred template of wood canoes and paddles filled a small cove off our water path.

At least a hundred boats rocked and banged in rhythm from the movement of our incoming boat. Each boat owner needed to step from one to the next to get to shore. I wore a *longyi,* or traditional apparel, like all Burmese men and women wear.

The longyi looks like a sarong tied at the waist in various knots, depending on social status. Several times during the day, both men and women retied their knots, after squatting alongside the road to pee. Sports require the male to bring the back fabric up through the legs to tuck into the tight waistline.

A PaO from the hotel wrapped a *longyi* around my waist as I left in the morning, knowing I would feel more comfortable with my legs covered. Exposed legs, and even a bare shoulder, draw attention.

As I followed the others from boat to boat in order to reach the dock, the loose fabric of my *longyi* caught on something on one of the last canoes tied to land, causing me to stumble. I almost lost the fabric covering.

Several PaO turned to help hold the fabric up. The grown women laughed like little girls, wrapping the fabric around my waist and tying it to itself once more.

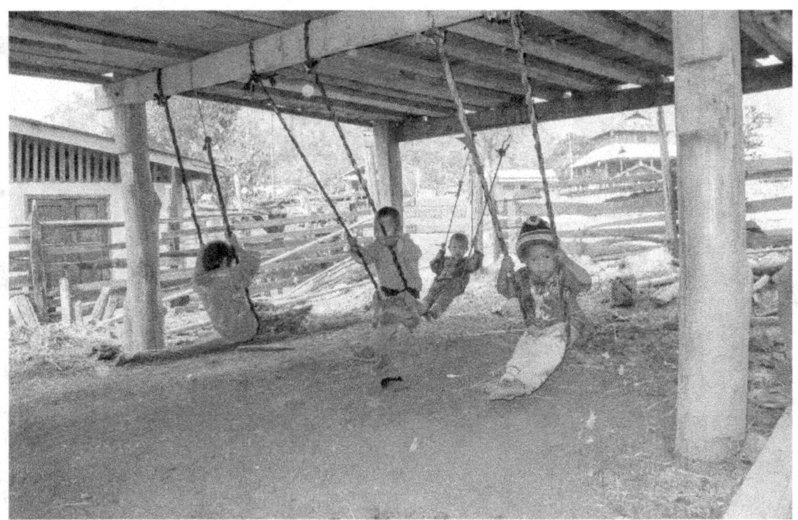

Palaung children under home swinging

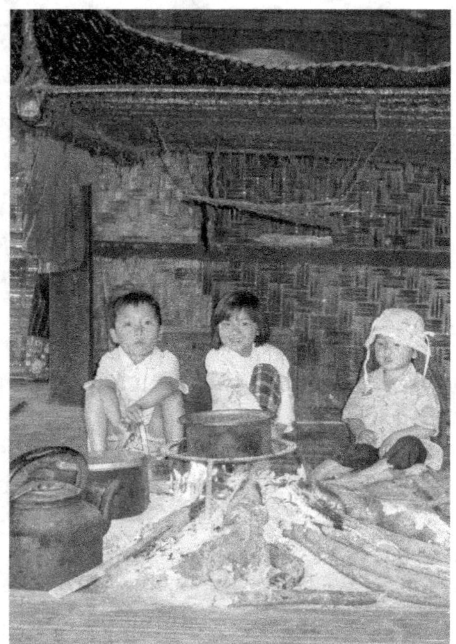

Outside Putao

All kinds of items, hoping for a buyer, lay on the ground. A thin man, resting on gnarled knees, looked hopeful for a sale when I slowed in front of his little packets of herbs and roots and magic potions

Illustrations of health disorders covered each packet. Pictures showed a bruise on an arm, a swollen ankle, a pregnant belly, a bone broken in half, and a handful of other ailments, all curable. I wandered in all directions for hours watching the interaction between friends and neighbors, bargaining over a pinch of a special spice or a day's catch of fish.

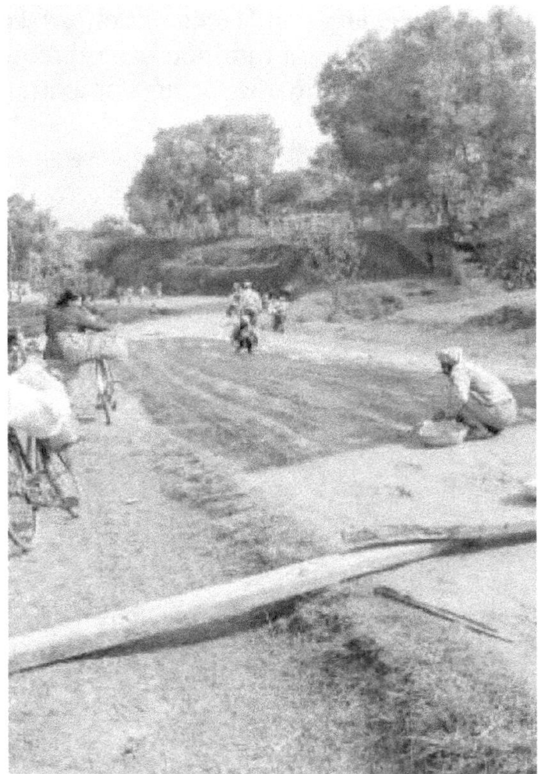

Putao women cutting rock, heating asphalt

The sociable calling back and forth between these people while trying to maneuver oxen carts squeezed together, or as families worked at setting their boats free, created a wave of laughter among them, without any sign of frustration. For centuries, the PaO have followed the rules of the market, resulting in their peaceful contentment.

Across the lake from my cottage, the canoe skimmed the water "sidewalks" around two-story homes balanced on stilts. A tour of two of the buildings allowed me access to weaving factories. Eight-foot tall, ancient-looking looms blended in against the walls.

Spindles of bright-colored silk threads crowded warping frames and old-fashioned spinning tools. Inle Lake residents have developed a method of spinning the filaments inside the stems of the lotus plant into threads.

The long hours of pulling the plants apart, cleaning, softening, dyeing, spinning, and weaving create wrinkles in the faces of the old women and increased prices for the finished products. After browsing the tiny shop, filled with hundred-dollar scarves and placemats that I could not afford, I decided to return to the cottages before the thunderstorm that had been threatening all afternoon finally opened the sky with lightning and torrents of warm rain.

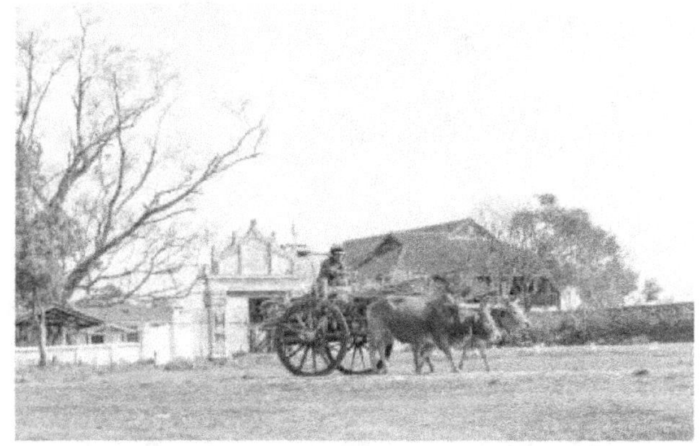

Oxen cart, heading home from fields of Putao

The manager of the Golden Island Cottages wanted to see me before I left the next morning. In his little gift store, consisting of shelves filled with woven garments, he chose an earth-colored jacket tied with a ribbon and presented it to me to show his gratitude of friendship.

Khaki and browns filled my wardrobe because these did not show dirt and wear from the dusty roads of travel. The jacket fit my long arms, but the manager looked puzzled. He jerked a pile of *longyi* to the counter and pointed to them, indicating that I should select one.

I had barely pulled my hand from the light purple one before the manager unfolded the fabric. A PaO girl wearing the traditional black pants and jacket walked around the counter and tied the fabric around my waist.

They refused the money I offered for the items. However, my promise to come back soon met with their approval.

Despite the military administration, meeting the people of Asia's most secret country will convince the visitor to make every effort to understand Burmese tradition. An era of increased access and encouragement of tourism has already begun.

CHAPTER SIX

Ecuador: Suspicions Were our Traitors

The mind sees this forest better than the eye. The mind is not deceived by what merely shows. H. M. Tomlinson

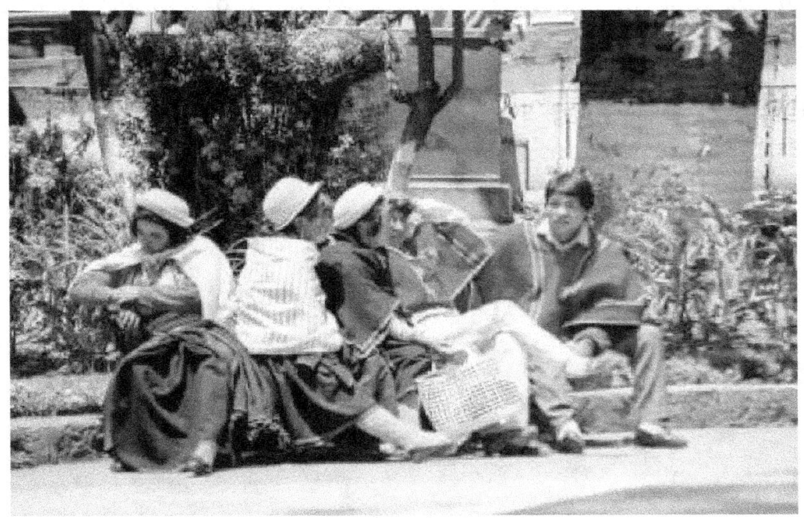

Relaxing at the bus stop

The trip ahead did not seem real. Have you ever thought about the anxieties that build in anticipation of a new beginning? So much to do in preparation for my journey ahead with a teenager, while leaving behind children and a husband needing clean clothes, prearranged entertainment, and food ready for the microwave.

Allie, my seven-year-old daughter, suggested opposite direction vacations for the "lounge-in-the-pool/water-ski" family members versus the "adventure-into-the-jungle" members. Her father jumped on the idea, as he could take those not ready for the jungle, including himself, to the Lake of the Ozarks for some sailing and ski ball games. Katherine, my thirteen-year-old, thirsty for adventure, couldn't wait through the planning stages for the Amazon jungle trek.

I'll never forget little Allie on my lap, saying she wanted to go to the Amazon, not even knowing what this place had in store. Brennan, older and wiser at the age of ten, happened to mention all the shots necessary for such a trip. That did it for Allie! She had never been fond of shots and decided she would be happier with her father. She proceeded to jump from my lap to her dad's, a much more secure corner for this discussion.

The journey I was about to take with Katherine began with tremendous anticipation, but I could not help feeling the heavy weight of the fear of the unknown in my back pocket.

Anxious for a positive answer, I whispered to my daughter while boarding the plane, "Do you regret our decision?"

With a gentle grasp of my hand, Katherine smiled and said, simply, "No."

My thirteen-year-old daughter's confidence amazed me as we embarked on a three-week journey into the wilds of the Amazon jungle.

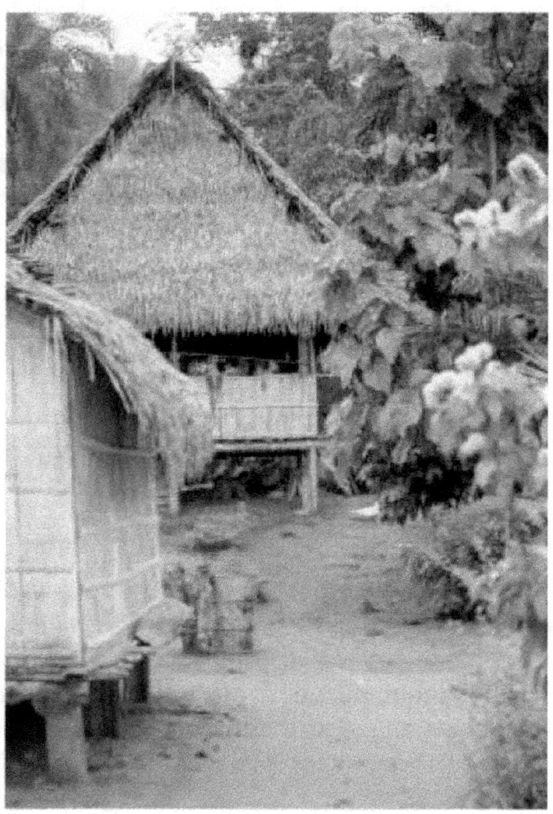

Home in the Amazon

The fifty-foot canoe forged through the downpour, not caring that passengers, luggage, and food got drenched. Huddled together for warmth, Katherine and I sat motionless, sharing a tarp with numerous wood crates packed with camping gear and food. Our safety net, Louis Garcia, had our lives in his hands. Louis knew the ins-and-outs of jungle life from studying for his role as a medicine man, and he came recommended by the South American Explorers Club.

The canoe jerked to a stop on the muddy shoreline. I could hear foreign voices, undecipherable in the distance. After we removed the rain-soaked tarp from over our heads, Katherine and I noticed the angry sky had gone quite dark. People stood on the banks of the river, pulling the canoe forward in the mud.

Out of nowhere, Katherine said, "I'm freezing cold and wet but not sad."

"Why would you feel sad?" I asked.

"Racing down the river in a fifty-foot canoe, trusting our boat driver in the dark, and fearing the unknown, maybe?" Katherine smiled as her slender, ice-cold fingers squeezed my hand.

Our brand-new boots sloshed through the mud while we climbed a steep embankment. A Quechua home on stilts graced the river with candles, and steaming hot chocolate and tea waited for us. As we wiggled out of wet clothes and slipped into dry ones without baring skin, I recalled my sailing coach, summing it all up as "time on the water."

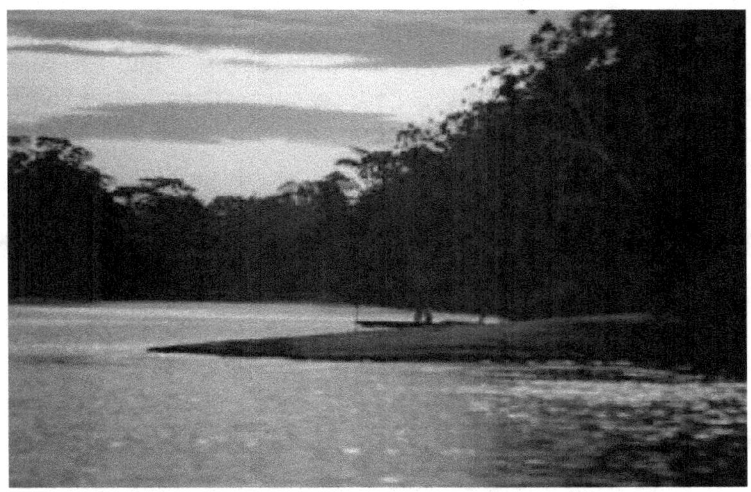

Sunset in the Amazon

At lunchtime, we'd eaten hot pasta with lentils, peas, corn, potatoes, tuna, bread, and dripping orange slices over huge banana leaf placemats; could our dinner menu match that? I thought the chances were good.

Alfonzo, a wizard in the jungle kitchen, created miracles from boxes and vegetables tumbling out of overstuffed rice sacks.

The next morning, we hopped a ride on a canoe, and Alfonzo boarded with his pots, knives, butane stove, food supplies, and our gear. Our guide Luis guessed at our boot sizes as he handed each of the five in our group a pair of tall-to-the-knee rubber boots. Snakes, tarantulas, and army ants prefer to meet with exposed legs and ankles.

With machete in hand, Luis pointed to the tagua nut tree as Davel, a second guide, grabbed a vine, leaped forward and came back toward the group hanging from the end of it, yelling with laughter. Everyone except me grabbed a vine for some fun.

Logs provided us with steppingstones over swampy areas. A careful sense of awareness guided my steps. With a lake ahead, peeling off rain jackets and sticky, hot, rubber boots felt almost as refreshing as the jump into the warm water.

The guides reminded us that piranhas love open wounds and have sharp teeth. Luis painted red designs on our faces like those of Indian warriors. I never understood why! Everyone covered his or her body head-to-toe with soap before springing into the water. Shampoo floated around us as we splashed and kicked in the cool, refreshing water.

Luis pointed to a rubber tree next to the new Quechua home for the night. He made a four-inch incision in the trunk and collected the white sap that oozed onto a leaf. Next, he held the leaf over a flame for a few minutes to let it "cook." After it had bubbled and solidified a few seconds, he rolled up the solid rubber into a rubber band, stretchy and strong. He explained the twenty-foot tree might make three rubber tires.

Our second morning under the mosquito-net-covered straw mat, I smelled pancakes in the jungle! I roused Katherine, motionless with sleep, next to me. "Smell the hot chocolate!" I cried excitedly.

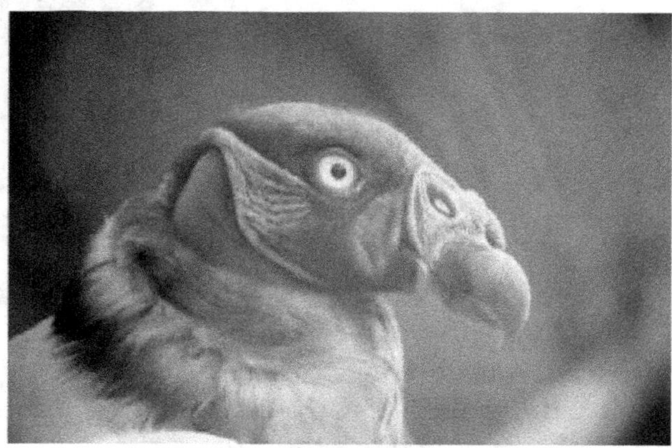

Weird jungle bird

We threw off the netting and followed our noses! Fried cornmeal pancakes with cheese filling oozed enticingly under fried bananas coated in cream cheese! Our guides filled our plastic plates with the wonderful meal, and Katherine and I sat down and laid our plates on the banana leaf tablecloth. The tagua nut button Davel carved out of one of the handfuls of nuts, gathered the day before, hung around my neck on a bark string, swinging gently while I ate.

"A tagua nut becomes hard as a rock as soon as it's exposed to the air and might last forever," Davel had told me.

Threatening skies did not slow the process of our preparations, including the tugging on of rubber boots before a trip to the jungle open-air toilet. After walking for a couple of hours, Luis zeroed in on a line of army ants exploding from leaf litter, covering the jungle floor. The blind ants attack anything in their path with claw-shaped jaws, armed with long knifelike teeth. After Luis had summarized the ant's ability to paralyze a horse in four hours or kill a small child, I looked at a twenty-two-year-old-girl from California (part of our group) who defied all of Luis's rules. She walked barefoot in the jungle!

The ant's teeth serve to help worker ants attach themselves during an attack. To demonstrate, Luis picked one up and let it bite him to show how the pincers simulate stitching up a wound. The bite drew blood, but the skin pulled back together tight. He carried the ant back to its group where he had picked it up.

The Quechua used some of the trees on the trek for medicinal purposes. One tree had bark the Indians would eat for hangovers or malaria as it contained quinine. Small termites by the hundreds covered a small tree. Luis relayed the story of Indians getting naked, hugging the tree for a minute or so to allow the termites to crawl all over their bodies. They would rub the termites into their skin, killing them, which allowed an umbrella of protection from mosquitoes.

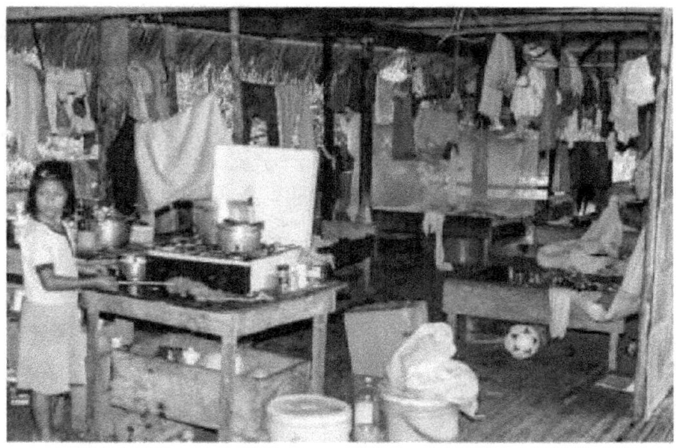

Traditional Quichuan home in the jungle

I cringed, adding, "I'd rather use mosquito repellent."

Davel's job included making everyone laugh as well as following our group to protect us. At one point someone noticed him missing, so we stopped to wait for him to catch up.

While we waited, Luis showed how to use a slab of dead palm branch covered in a white fungus as a tablet to write messages or draw images. After another half-hour trek, Luis found a tree with claw-like buttresses used for emergency messages like a telephone in the jungle. Various numbers of knocks hit against it with a machete meant various things; the echo sounded for about three kilometers. Luis pounded on the trunk, hoping to signal Davel.

Davel appeared, laughing. "You took the wrong turn, and the canoe waits an hour upstream."

Davel ran back to bring it close to the group and saved the day.

***

Covered in mud, I rang the bell on the wrought iron gate at the place where we would stay, embarrassed by not having clean clothes or shoes to wear after returning from a few weeks in the Amazon with Katherine. The front door opened, and it was obvious that the owner was surprised by our appearance.

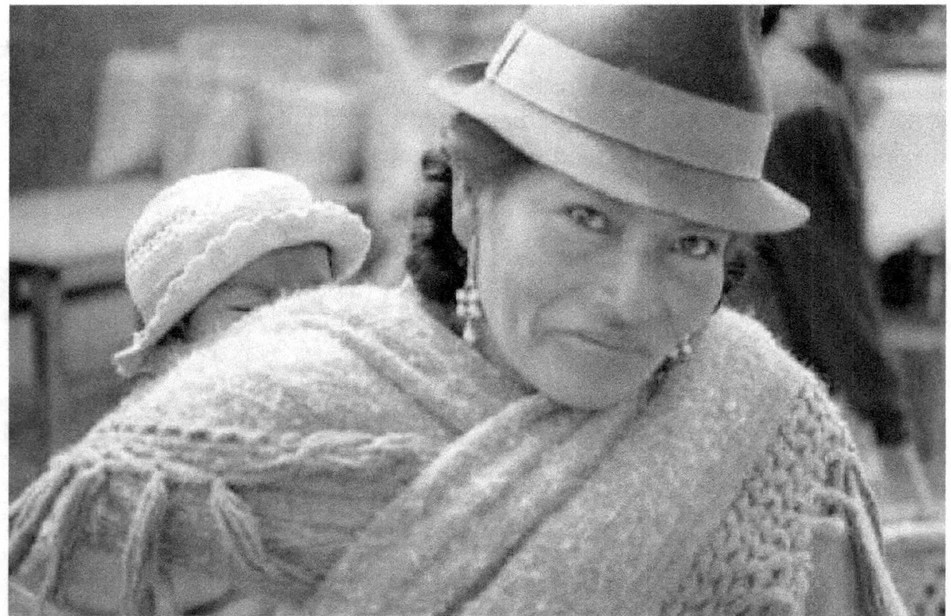

Otavolo market

"We trekked in the jungle," I told the woman, by way of explaining our filthy clothing and dirty hair.

She said nothing, perhaps did not speak English, but she unlatched the gate and motioned for us to follow her up the stairs.

"A shower, clean sheets, and an ad on the wall for Pizza Hut delivery!" I cried elatedly to Katherine.

Two hours later, we laughed at the piles of mud-covered boots and clothes. The pizza arrived by motorcycle with the familiar Pizza Hut logo on the box and on the delivery boy's shirt. I paid the boy quickly, impatient to get back inside, the smell of the cheesy pizza amplifying my appetite. I wanted to devour the pizza right there on the sidewalk. A full night's rest would follow our dinner, and then Katherine and I would be off to the Galapagos to find a boat for a week of cruising to the islands and talking with the wildlife.

Smelly and noisy Guayaquil felt uncomfortable even for the few hours it took to get to the train station.

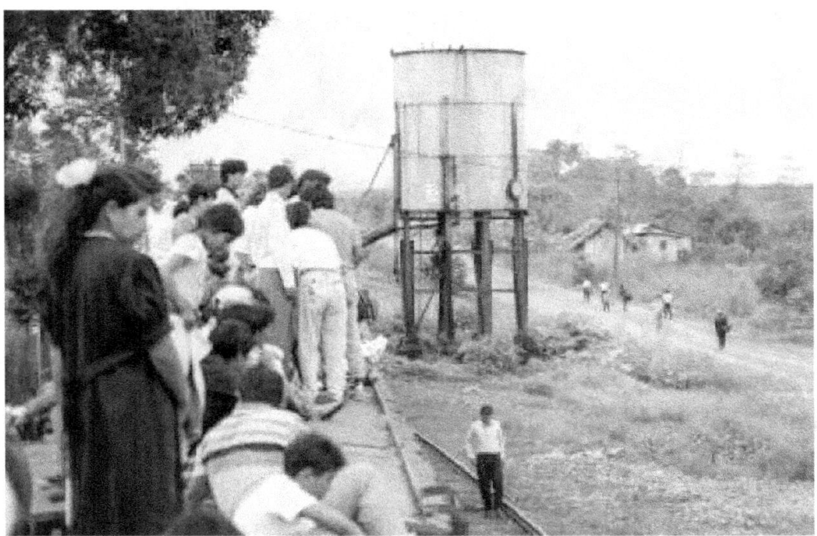

Riding on the roof of the train out of Guayaquil

"Let me hand my backpack to you once you find a handrail on top of the train," I told Katherine as she maneuvered the vertical step to the train roof.

The curved metal roof felt cool to the touch, thank goodness. Several men speaking in Spanish stood to open more room for our bags while pointing to a place we could sit. Gawking and whispers broke out around us. Daring to look over the edge of the roof, I spied a group of local women selling *cangil,* or popcorn; wrapped pieces of *hornado,* or pork; cone shapes of paper filled with sweetened *humitas,* or corn dumplings; and corn husks filled with *mote,* or hominy. I had visions of this old train rattling and vibrating my daughter and me right off the edge of the roof. The engine chugged a few feet forward, and steam burned my eyes.

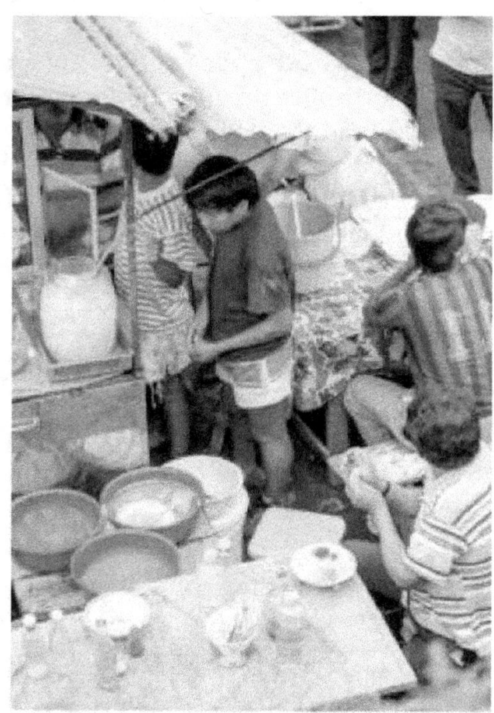

Looking down at sellers from the roof of the train

I could hear the final pleas for last-minute sales as the women ran from train aisles to open doors, exposing the safety net of stationary sidewalks leading home.

"Koy, koy, kan khil, kan khil," shouted the women even as they leaped from the moving train.

Roasted *cuy,* or guinea pig, pronounced "koy," a favorite of the Andean highlands, crowded tree branch skewers. Corn, or, as Ecuadorians would call it, *cangil*, pronounced "kan khil," is a longtime staple of Ecuador. Cangil found its way into numerous food dishes, containing flavors limited only by the imagination of the cook. The corn spilled over funnel-shaped squares of paper as the women below us called out to last-minute buyers.

Little villages along the tracks called for stops to load new passengers, giving the rooftop riders a rare view, looking down into the crowd.

A young boy about ten sat down next to us and talked with my daughter, who could understand and speak basic freshmen-year Spanish. The train crossed a rickety section of track and derailed.

The young boy hurried down the train steps into the sugar cane field adjacent to the tracks. He came back, handing up fistfuls of sugar cane to eager hands, reaching for the sweet treat. Never having held or tasted raw sugar cane, I waited for the boy to start eating it so I could see how it was done. After peeling off the outer layer, he began chewing on the fibrous cane.

"I think the boy said he lived on the train roof, hoping for donations of food, as he had no family and would like to come and live with us," Katherine explained to me wistfully.

"We can't adopt this little orphan," I told my sweet, sensitive Katherine gently. "To get a visa and passport without paperwork is impossible.

Please convey to him as well as you can that we would have loved to have him in our family, and your brother, Brennan, is the same age."

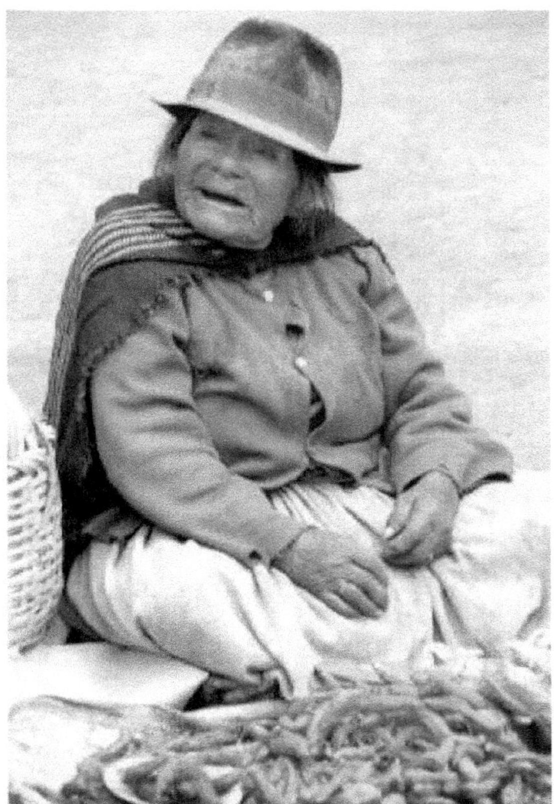

Selling peppers along the roadside

The train jerked forward, regained the rails, and abruptly stopped in the middle of nowhere. Then it moved backwards. "We just passed that group of children, waving." I looked to Katherine for an explanation.

The little orphan understood my questioning look and did a motion of back and forth with his hands. Later I learned the train, in order to descend the steep mountain, does a series of switchbacks. The train goes forward. The tracks switch and the train goes backwards in a seesaw pattern. El Nino had damaged the section of track we traveled, but the run continues with the reputation as one of the most dangerous train rides in the world. It rumbles from Riobamba while another trip leaves from Quito. Both trains now offer cushions for rent for a dollar.

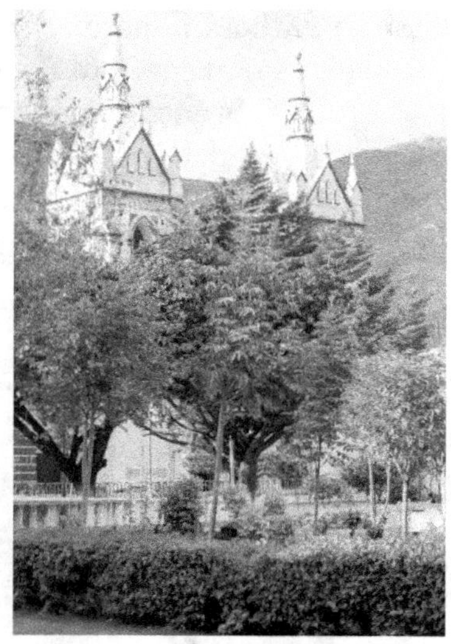

Banos

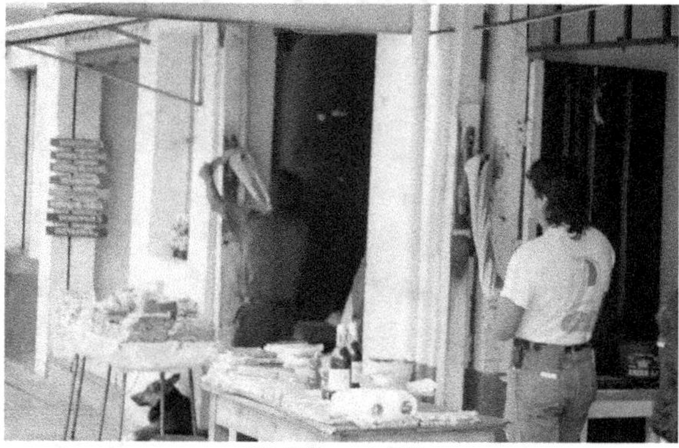

Pulling taffy

When we reached Banos, energy from samples of homemade taffy sparked our enthusiasm for a day of wandering the streets and joining numerous sightseeing treks. Banos is a town located in a region called the "Avenue of the Volcanoes." Shadowed by the oft-erupting Tungurahua volcano, Banos struggles with the clutches of weekend visitors, turning the hot mineral pools into crowded bathtubs. A few modern conveniences confirmed my decision to spend a few days here with Katherine, sleeping late, and getting acquainted with the local cultures, as well as experiencing some horseback riding along narrow, sandy volcano trails. Even the garbage truck in this quaint little Andean town is special; it plays music while it drives around town.

Sugar cane exported by the ton sits close by the town of Banos, known for its taffy. Taffy making begins with the cut and crushed sugar cane juice going through a boiling process. When it is cool, the *panela,* or sugar cane, is scooped into buckets, poured into molds, wrapped in plastic, and sold to markets throughout the country. However, in Banos the hardened *panela* goes through a second boiling for thirty minutes before it is placed on hooks located on doorframes of mom-and-pop shops up and down the streets. Stretching the panela, folding it over, pulling it and repeating the process goes on for thirty minutes. The *melcocheros,* or young boys, slap the *melcocha,* or taffy, while pounding it on the worn doorways, trying to release the air bubbles and sugar crystals. Ribbons of fruit flavorings and nuts add interest to the molded confection. Caution! The sticky candy loves loose fillings.

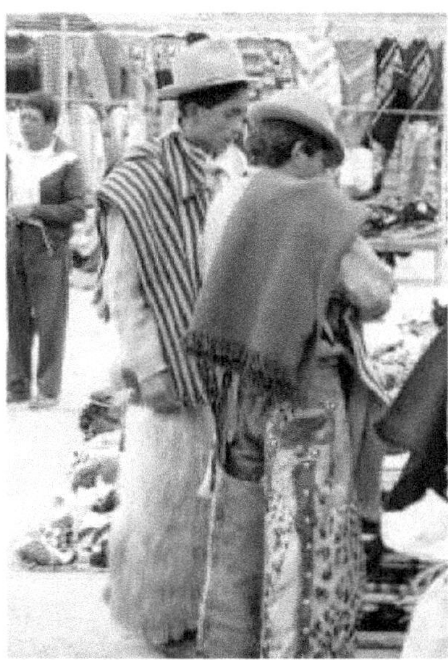

Surprised to see cowboys at the market

Caballos con Cristian offered popular horseback tours ($18 for a three-hour trip). Halfway up the volcano, we stopped for a swim in a hot pool to soothe our sore muscles. We watched as city folk hung on to their mounts for dear life as their horses galloped on their familiar paths, sometimes too close to the edge of the mountain, tensing both the riders' muscles and horses' reins.

Back in Banos, temporary booths outside the church sell religious souvenirs and balloons. A train, shaped like a caterpillar on wheels, whistles to the city, where children wear inflatable rings and adults chew the local taffy, all still dripping wet from dips in the hot springs. Busy sidewalk cafes blast disco music for tired hikers, rafters, and bikers.

The least expensive transportation, the bus or sometimes a van called a bus, offers interaction with locals while we find the next destination on a map. Buses fill with everything accompanying people on their way to fields or markets or shops.

Handmade baskets, larger than a laundry basket, transport a hundred ears of corn one day, and some hand-woven textiles to tempt foreign visitors the next. Last-minute passengers take plastic stools into the aisles or stand crunched between upside-down baskets covering chickens, bundled babies on mothers' backs poking over laps, and potatoes, spilling out of sacks with each bump in the road.

Otavolo, a quick two-hour drive north from Quito, has the reputation for the best market in Latin America with textiles commanding the most attention.

Villages around Otovalo work as cooperatives, each excelling in one art or craft. Wood carvers and furniture designers work in studios along the main street of San Antonio de Ibarra, selling choice carved pieces from wood.

Leather workers in the village of Cotacachi design quality leather clothing, handbags, luggage, and saddles. In Peguche, traditional weaving continues on looms creating shawls, wall hangings, and rugs at a fraction of the cost back home in the states.

The Otovalo market, a feast for any age, tempts with items such as toys, jewelry, handmade clothing, and unusual art on display. Bargaining opens communication between shopper and seller.

Shopkeepers offer better deals when business slows. Careful attention to detail keeps the shopper's instincts sharp, helping him avoid those occasional mass-produced products.

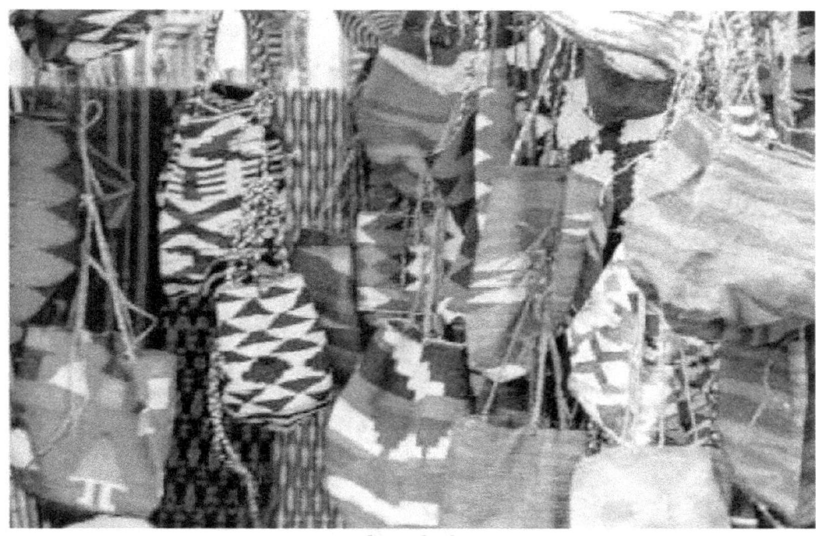

Handmade bags

Ready for some downtime after an intense jungle trek, Katherine and I chose the market town of Otovalo for a few days' visit. Cool air from the mountain chills the air at night, and my research described hotel rooms as void of heaters. Our hotel of choice, the Ali Shundhau, had a room for the first night.

I grabbed Katherine's arm and squeezed, saying, "The room has heated blankets, hot showers, and did you hear the hippie-looking owner say he had an obsession for safe food and water for guests?"

Scrutinizing every morsel for weeks on end to avoid food-borne illnesses seems like an endless responsibility. Breakfast at the Ali Shundhau started with hot cinnamon oatmeal with slices of papaya, pear, and pineapple artfully placed around the bowl. The second course came minutes later. Toasted, cinnamon, raisin bread, filled a basket under tubs of homemade fruit jams. Stuffed, we had little room for the breakfast dessert served last. However, we found room for our favorite: French toast with raspberry syrup.

With much hesitation, I agreed to the (advertised) two-hour horseback ride, now five hours. All ten riders appeared inexperienced, but after a few town streets, the horses began galloping along mountain paths, some so narrow I had to close my eyes and let the horse use his own judgment. Riding at full speed, with one hand around the reins and the other in the air, I felt a taste of extraordinary freedom. Our horses jumped streams and gullies near corners of bluffs as if they knew they would not brush up against the rock walls. Indian villages, and sometimes a single hut, sat off the slippery, sandy paths. The tranquility of the secluded village life stood in strange contrast to the fury of each horse's pace. The energy streaming from the horses' exuberance rattled our spirits inside out. Katherine felt tired, but my exhaustion could wait until bedtime. One more village to explore before dinner, I told myself. I knew the answer before asking about walking the three kilometers to the Village of Peguche to see weavers working on Spanish treadle and back strap looms.

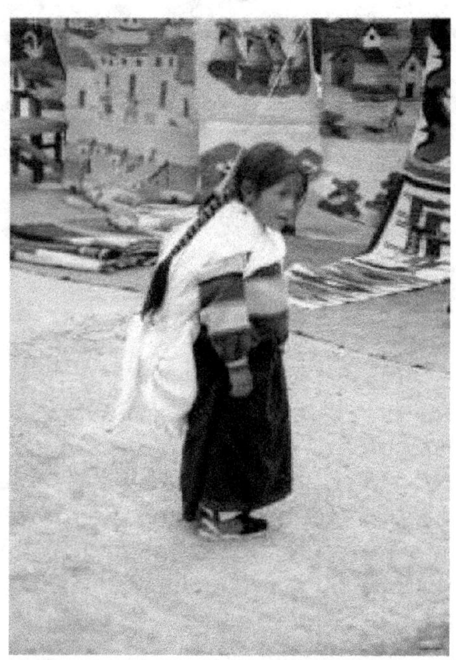

Young girl, carrying brother while & watching father's textiles

My obsession for textiles carried over into my developing the craft of weaving for a few small consignment shops and my own use. Before leaving Ecuador, I wanted to watch the famous traditional weaver, Jose Cotacachi, at work in his studio. Jose based his exclusive designs on prehistoric cultures such as the Nasca and Inca.

"Near the central plaza, to the right and behind the church," I explained to the taxi driver and held up the map with the village name in Spanish.

Seeing the inside of his working studio, I asked Jose, "How could anyone choose a wall hanging? Each one has a unique story to tell."

Trying to find the legendary Las Cascadas de Peguche waterfall took twenty minutes instead of the ten the townspeople reported. A woman, washing laundry, did not like me taking her photo and began yelling and did not stop even after I gave her 500 *sucres,* worth about $.50. Back at our new hotel, the Hotel

Cacique, we watched Spanish-dubbed English television in color. We were exhausted, having enjoyed a full evening of entertainment during dinner at our first hotel, then packing up and coming here. A steaming-hot broccoli-and-cheese casserole warmed me instantly. Katherine tried a submarine sandwich while eight boys about thirteen years old played all sizes of panpipes. I wanted Katherine to get up and join in, as she played the flute in school and could pick up the Ecuadorian flute with ease.

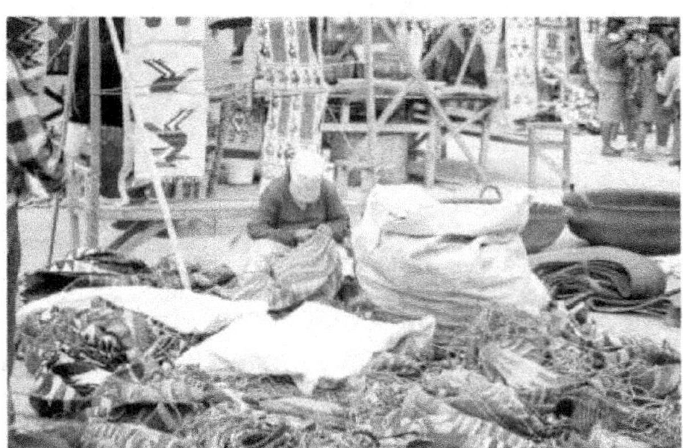

Stitching fiber baskets

By the time the sun came up, the mountains cast shadows over the animal market, alive with grunting pigs, crowing roosters not happy about the cages over their heads, and an occasional calf, hollering for momma. Women stationed themselves in between this chaotic unfolding of bargaining and selling.

Dark skirts, layered over yards and yards of white, complemented embroidered tops, wound with hand-woven, bright-colored bands around the waist.

Strands of gold and coral necklaces interrupted the women's task of measuring piles of potatoes on a hand-held brass scale as the beautiful jewelry intertwined among the vegetables in the measuring process. Lacy white sleeves fluttered about as the women worked, arranging peppers in rows.

A woman pulled me to the side of the aisle with her eyes and a generous smile. She wanted me to buy a handmade band several feet long, showing me several intricate woven designs. I walked close to her makeshift table of wood planks, balanced over five-gallon buckets stacked double high. Her fingers made a twirling motion, wanting me to turn around and sit down on an overturned bucket. After pulling my long hair back tight into a ponytail, she selected a band that she had caught me looking at more than once.

She wrapped the bright band around the ponytail, making my hairstyle mimic hers.

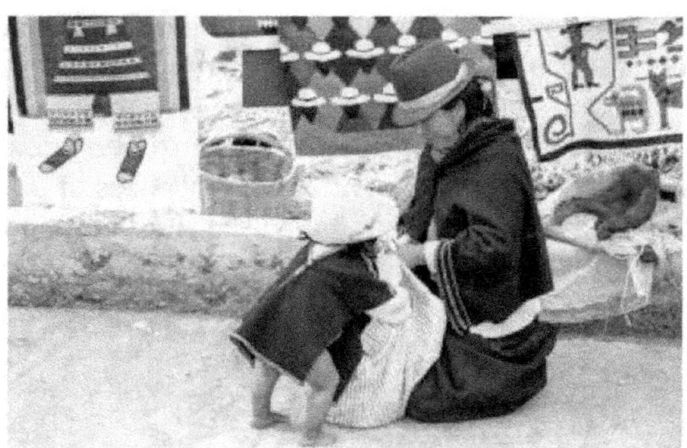

Helping mother unpack her textiles

Tired of cattle bumping into our sides and the barnyard smells of the animal market, we opted for more cinnamon oatmeal at the hotel, while waiting for the Poncho Plaza to open and for bargaining to begin.

Bargaining, a part of the purchasing process, requires practice and confidence.

If not sure about dickering over a price, you should rehearse a technique in the hotel room. Experience has taught me to offer fifty percent of the asking price or even less.

In Timbuktu, Mali, starting the bargaining process must always lead to a sale. Never ask the price or enter into bargaining unless serious about purchasing the item, no matter the cost.

Practice bargaining with a friend by making disbelieving faces, and always reject the first few prices.

Definitely, practice walking away.

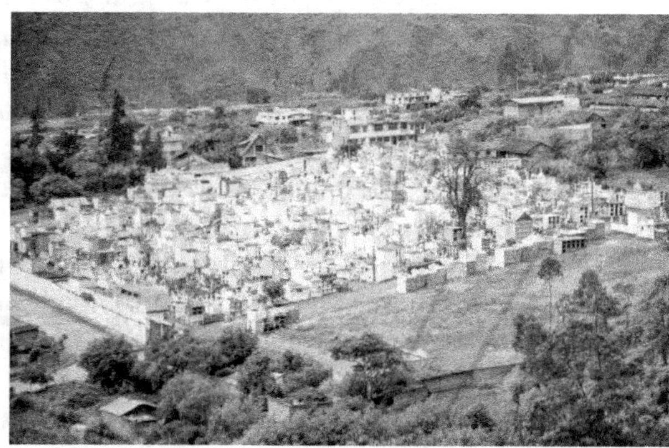

Cemetery of Banos

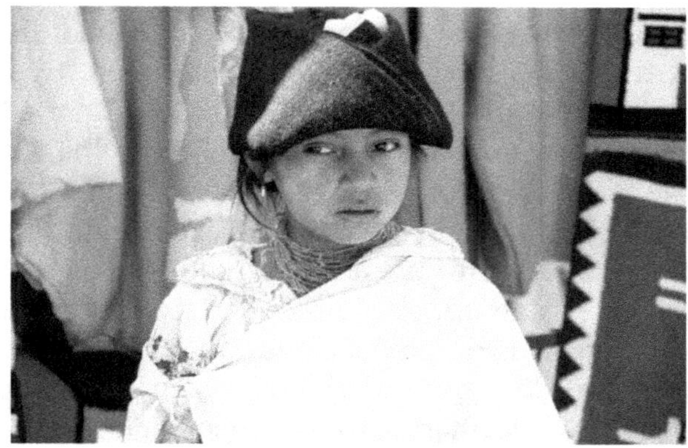

More textiles for sale

Otovaleños wear clothing distinctive to their area. Men wear the famous Panama hats, made in Ecuador.

Otovalo's beauty exists in its people, the indigenous Otovaleños.

Morning sun creates a blinding maze of color over one of the most spectacular markets in Latin America. It offers extravagant shopping opportunities with cultural significance.

Andean pipe music competes with Quichua, the native tongue, heard throughout the market. Skinned calf heads and armadillo-shell guitars balance on racks.

Dark blue ponchos, hiding long hair in braids, adorn men, wearing white trousers and claiming the benefits of health remedies in little jars and the magic of herbal soaps.

Glistening handmade saddles perfume the air while shopping bags overflow with bargains of a lifetime: the wonders of intricate, hand-woven garments.

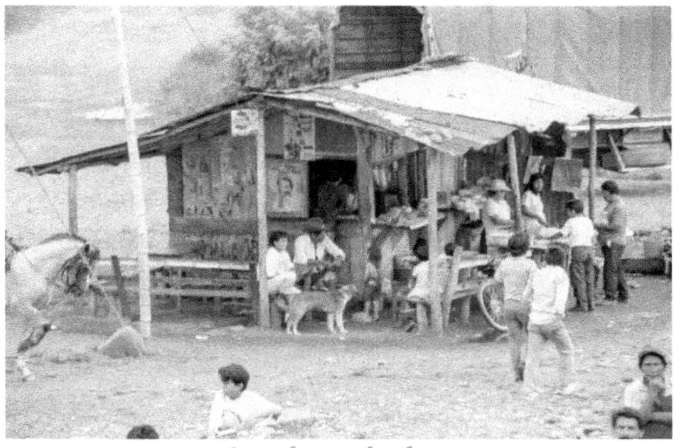

Local snack shop

Friends, curious neighbors, and my mother have asked, "How can you really do this trekking-through-a-jungle trip?" And the next most-asked question from family and friends is "Why?" I have explained that I wanted the challenge of traveling as a homemaker alone with my daughter in the wild. I needed to get in touch with my inner voice (or maybe to experience the solitude of nature). I felt a push toward satisfying my internal and external discontent.

Life itself seems like a trip. What would you trade for these experiences? Iguanas climbed over Katherine's feet during breakfast on the patio of a restaurant on Galapagos Island. While a tarantula climbed up my leg toward my chest, Luis said, "If you scream or sweat, he'll acknowledge your nervousness with a bite." Katherine picked up enough Spanish to communicate with an orphan on the roof of a train. Katherine and I both learned the meaning of trust between mother and daughter. We also welcomed the strangers who came into our lives uninvited, but we allowed to stay.

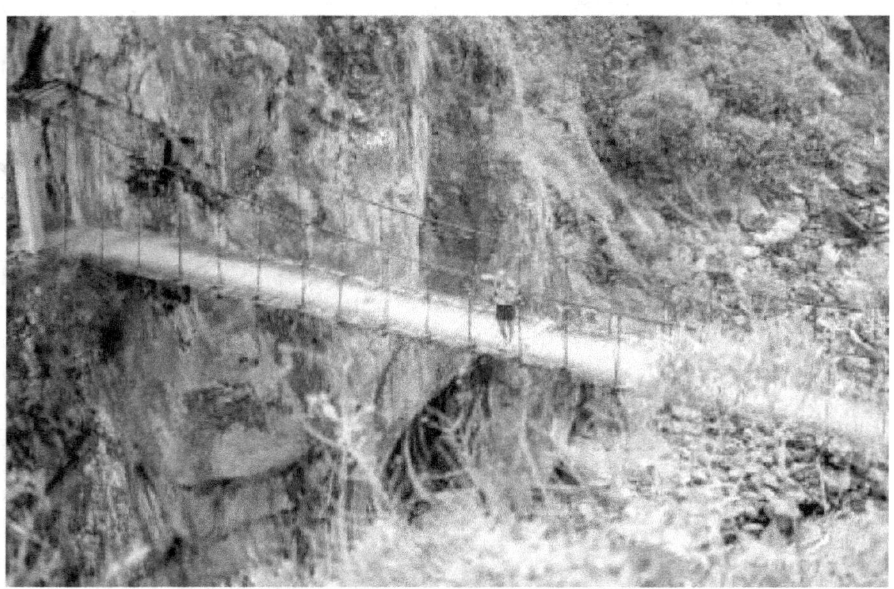

Katherine crossing suspension bridge

Ecuador let us borrow its people, wildlife, and nature long enough to teach us lessons of contentment and grace.

CHAPTER SEVEN

India: Complexity Meets Simplicity

"So far as I am able to judge, nothing has been left undone, either by man or nature, to make India the most extraordinary country that the sun visits on his rounds. Nothing seems to have been forgotten, nothing overlooked."
Mark Twain.

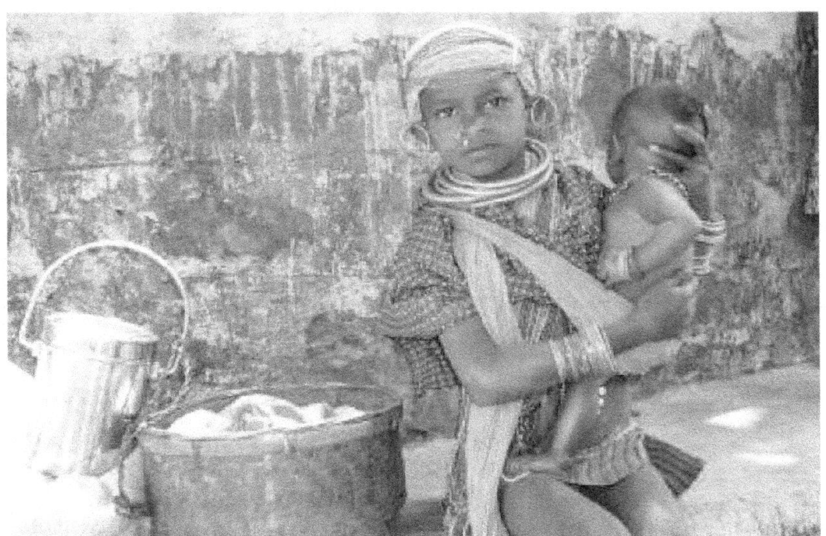

Bonda girl, babysitting and selling food

Travel virgins, inquisitives, or globetrotters succumb to the magnetism India exhales. Discover the authentic India through your mind's eye. The maze of sensory overload when you arrive weighs heavy on the heart. Outside layers of sights and sounds flirt with the senses, hoping to satisfy your expectations.

Take giant steps to find the essence of India, buried in the richness of India's soul: the people. No other country in the world offers such a delectable palette: a melting pot of religions, cultures, and languages brought together by traders, pioneers, and soldiers for the last five thousand years.

Escape a life sentence of boredom; join me in the labyrinth of alleyways painted with the sparkles, reflecting from mirrored baubles of Gujarati and Rajasthani women and Tibetans, standing guard in street-stall doorways.

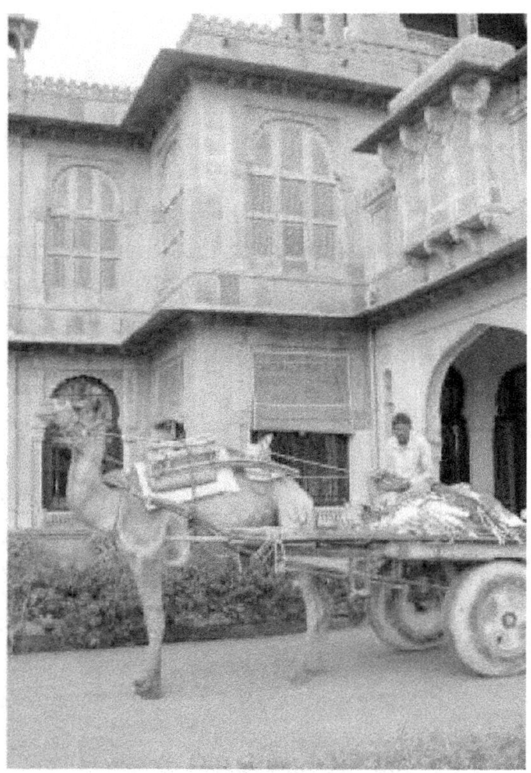

Transportation by camel

Landscapes, dotted with the powerful depth of vision transmitted in variations of extravagant architecture accent the scent of incense, spices, and poverty, as well as the sounds of claustrophobically dense cities. Colors more brilliant than any rainbow and tastes and textures of exotic foods combine to embroider the lush texture of India.

The appalling poverty, in the shadows of extreme wealth, a reality living out of sight, commands a balancing act. It contrasts with the mystical charisma of historical forts, mosques, temples, gardens, and unique lifestyles. Tractors, pedestrians, camels pulling carts, luxury cars, and cycles by the hundreds orchestrate intersections in near-perfect rhythm. Soon after agents stamp your passport, pollution levels thicker than maple syrup, and spaces, too small to turn sideways, disorient you. Cows, water buffalo, camels, and dogs all roam without fear of confrontation in cities and add to the chaotic frustration. The definition of culture shock for India appears in no dictionary.

Soon after arriving in Delhi, travelers must pass the test of extremes by proving their ability to embrace differences. An unlimited level of patience, an intense curiosity, and an adventuresome nature will encourage your exploration of India's cultures.

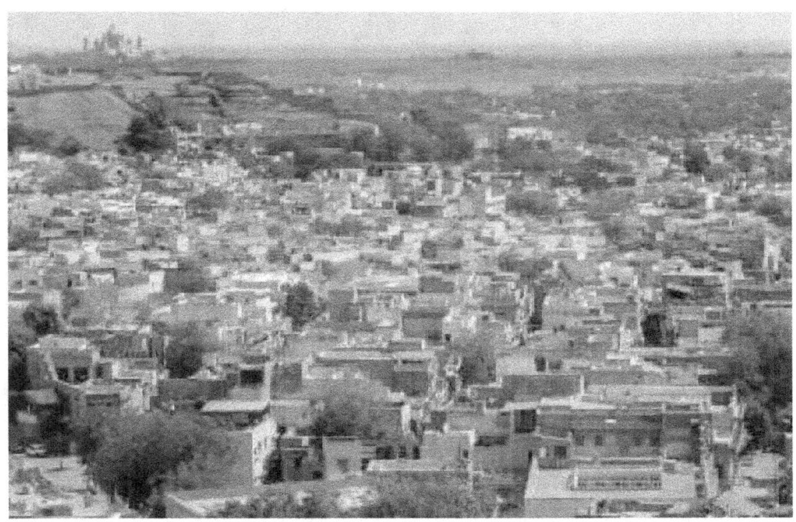

Jodhpur's blue city

Rajasthan's vitality lies in its people, living in a kaleidoscope of temples, forts, and palaces, adding color with indigo turbans, brilliant saris, all overlaid by a rich history. Hundreds of temples casting lifelong shadows, paint a historical mural, circling Pushkar.

The fall Camel Fair, an important pilgrimage for tens of thousands of Hindu pilgrims, provides an annual event for worshiping during the full moon. The ritual dip in the holy waters of Lake Pushkar climaxes the five-day wonder of camel racing, magic shows, jugglers, musicians, snake charmers, and locals bartering over cattle, goats and camels. Pushkar's domes look like onions, surrounding the many temples.

The disharmony of chanting, gongs, bells, and drums rattle the town's speakers. Pilgrims bathe in the sacred holy lake, said to have appeared when Brahma dropped a lotus flower from the heavens.

Priests stand on the bathing *ghats,* or stairs, leading to the lake, offering flowers to visitors who throw them into the lake while reciting prayers for good luck.

Camel treks, led by men wearing crimson-colored turbans and balloon-legged pants, cost about $15 a day. A camel trek to Jodhpur takes about seven days.

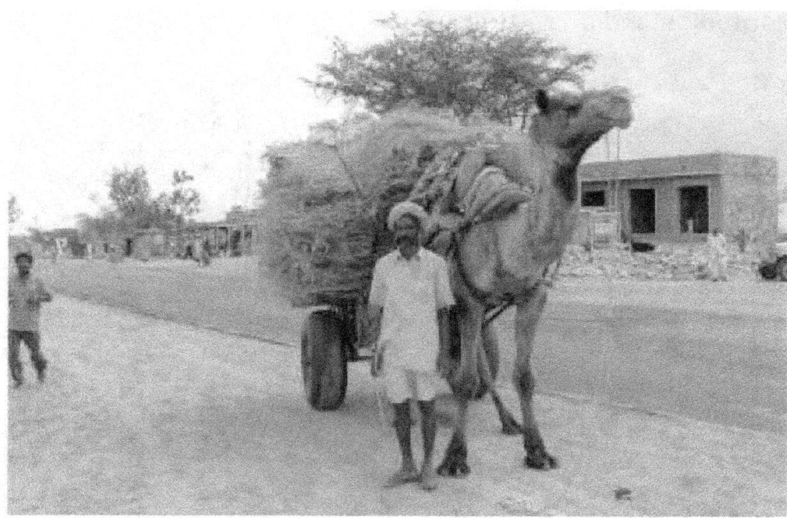

One of India's many modes of transportation

An eight-year-old boy, both proud tour guide and entertainer, shared a small palace, running from room to room pointing to details in architecture. Seeing his image on my digital screen brought a wide grin and his gestures for participation on his drum. Embarrassed giggles filled the minutes. I tried to ask questions using my hands, but my young friend never understood my pantomime. All it served to do was interrupt his playtime.

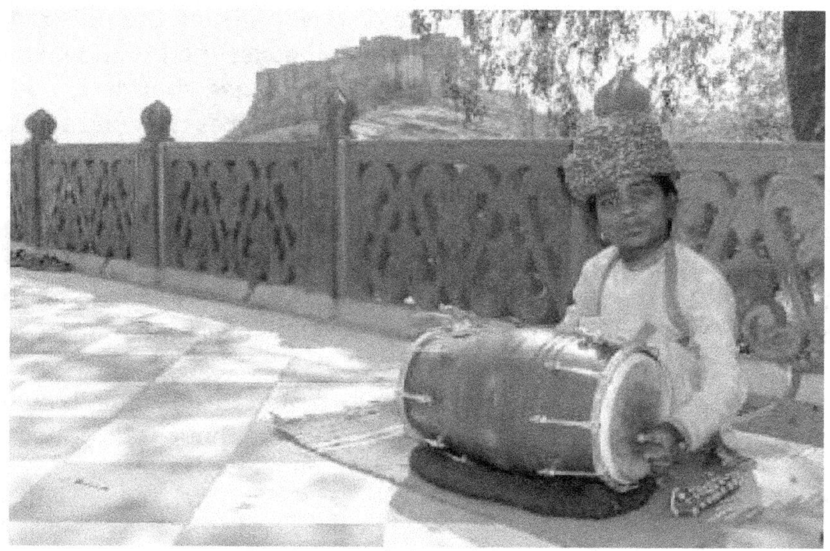

Entertaining visitors

Jodhpur displays a frontier personality, offering choices of temples, palaces, and perhaps the most majestic fort of Rajasthan, the Mehrangarh Fort.

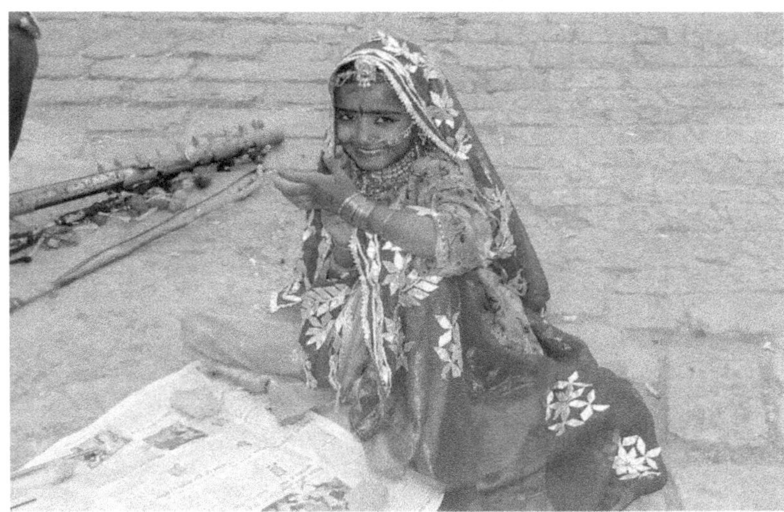

Rajasthan girl, living in the fort

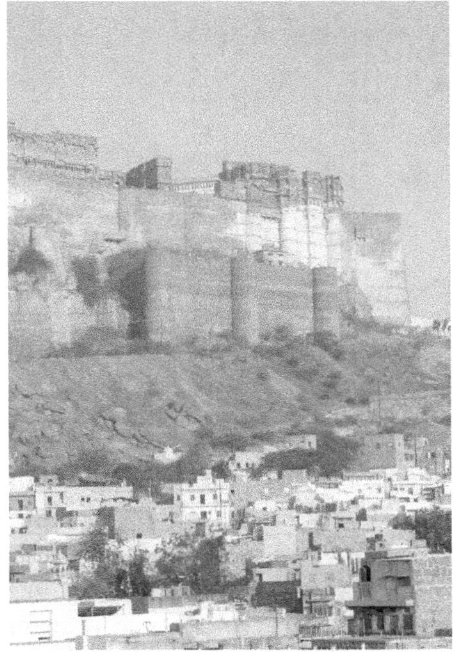

Jodhpur's Mehrangarh Fort

Standing four hundred feet above the horizon of Jodhpur, the fort commands attention, showing an unconquerable attitude.

Red sandstone construction began in 1459, and Maharajah Singh completed the fort during his lifetime (1638-78).

Because of its mountainous proportions, Rudyard Kipling called it "the work of giants."

The families living within the fort exhibit smiles, hoping for business in their restaurants and shops where they sell silver jewelry, woolen shawls, silk saris, antiques, and more antiques.

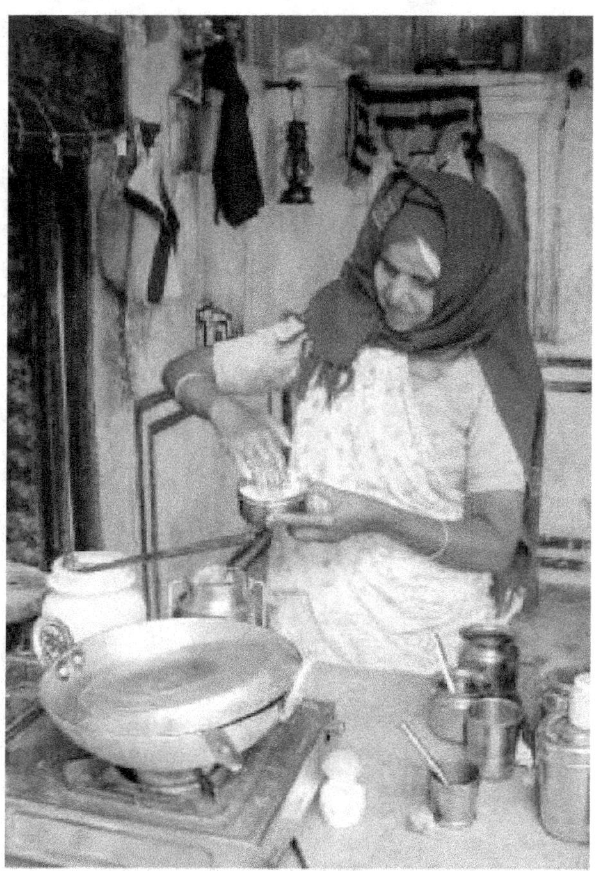

Pancakes, prepared in the fort

Hidden pathways reveal families living as their ancestors taught them. The shawl-covered woman, preparing pancakes of flour and goat milk, motioned for me to stand behind her table.

Sticky white fingers removed yards and yards of a fabric apron, shook the flour dust free, tied the garment around my waist, and pushed my fingers into the midget-sized bowl of gooey dough.

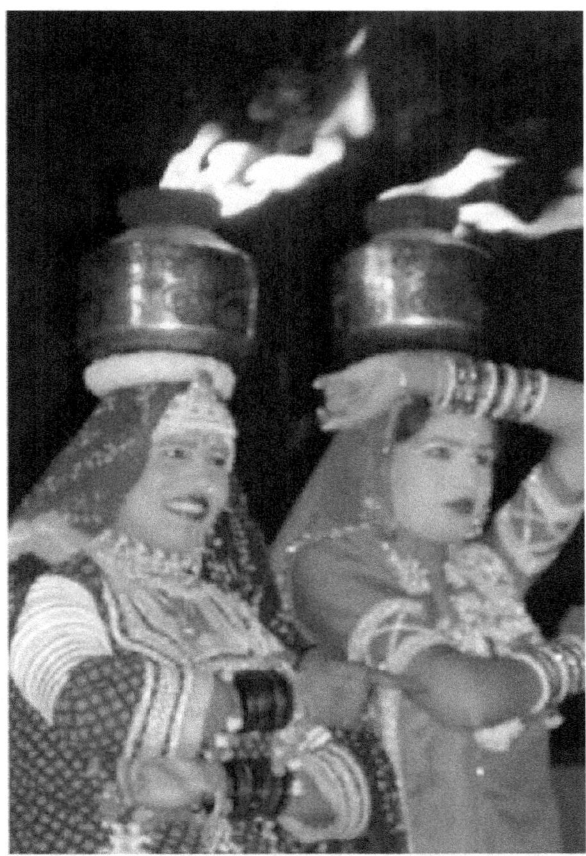

Dancing for locals

Inside the fort, discover a playground of alleyways breathing the traditional rhythms of Indian life. Stumble along the cobblestone paths to find pockets of gardens or dome-shaped ovens made of clay. Crumbling stones create fences for babysitting goats or chickens. Children decorate their mud pies with bits of straw or dried flower petals. On the stone walls of the fort, place a hand in the imprint left by concubines and widows, sacrificing themselves on the funeral bonfires of deceased spouses. The riding pants called jodhpurs originated here. Rooftops and walls of homes painted in blue create the masquerade of Jodhpur, known as the blue city.

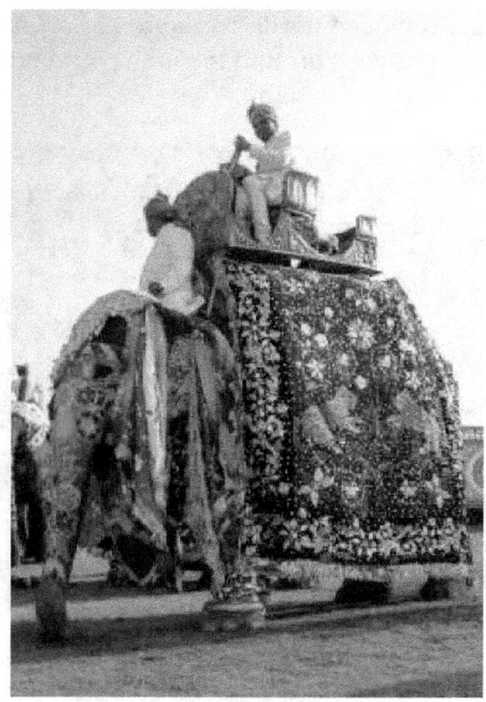

Mahouts, or elephant handlers

Jaipur, the capital of Rajasthan, presents the unique Elephant Festival held each year in March during the festival of Holi. Although all of northern India celebrates the Festival of Holi, Jaipur adds the charm of the Elephant Festival.

Locals spread words of caution on the day of Holi. Clouds of colored water or powder (flour mixed with dyes) fill the streets. People walk around covered in bright purples and pinks, head to toe. Even those passing on motorcycles must protect themselves from the shower or else leave the area on their bikes completely covered in cherry and violet hues. The night before Holi, sky-reaching bonfires light up the sky, symbolizing the elimination of the evil demon Holika.

Singing folk dancers follow horses, elephants, and chariots hauling canons to begin the procession around the polo field, called the Grounds of Chaugan. Musical instruments like the *bankiya,* or trumpet, mimic folk tunes. The female elephants wear layers of embroidered silk and satin brocaded fabrics. Brilliant colors camouflage the saggy wrinkles, enlisting painted designs, jingling baubles, and hundreds of strands of beads. The *mahout,* or keeper of each elephant, uses exceptional care in decorating his animal, hoping to win the coveted prize from the best-decorated elephant contest.

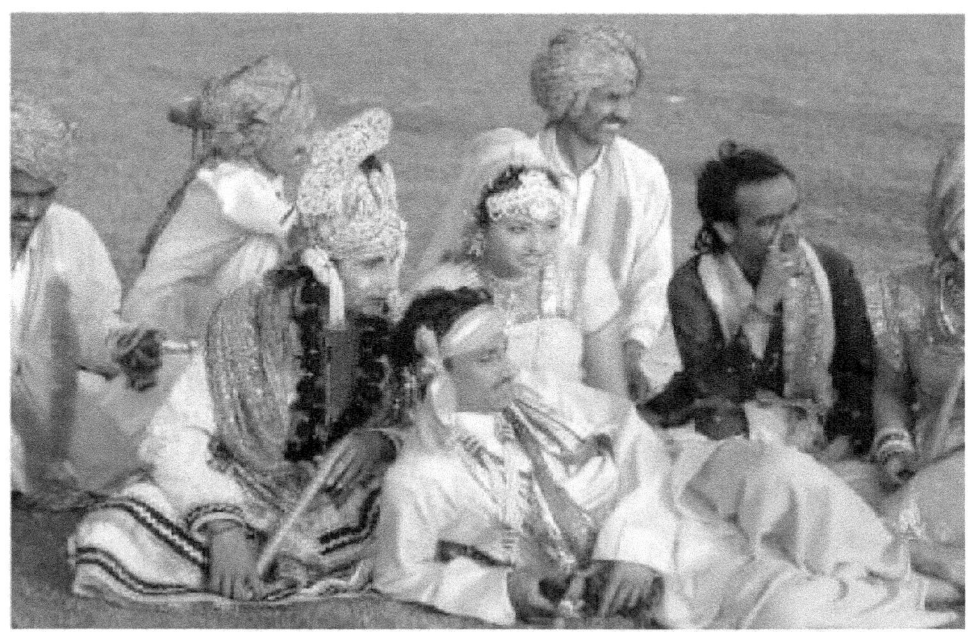

Folksingers, watching Elephant Festival, Jaipur

Shouts echo from mahouts atop dozens of elephants; so tired are they of standing in line.

Camels bellow with irritation, joining the cacophony. The walls, surrounding the festival grounds, separate the event from real life, where I found activity in every direction.

Fathers paint the naked bodies of their young sons white, and they attach puffs of cotton to the wet paint.

Ten feet away handfuls of twinkling glitter fall to the ground, missing the camel as he jerks upward to stand.

A young boy asks for a picture of himself and his two camels.

I negotiate every step to avoid groups of children, practicing a dance while regally costumed, independent horses entertain.

No break time for my shutter button until the camera demands fresh batteries!

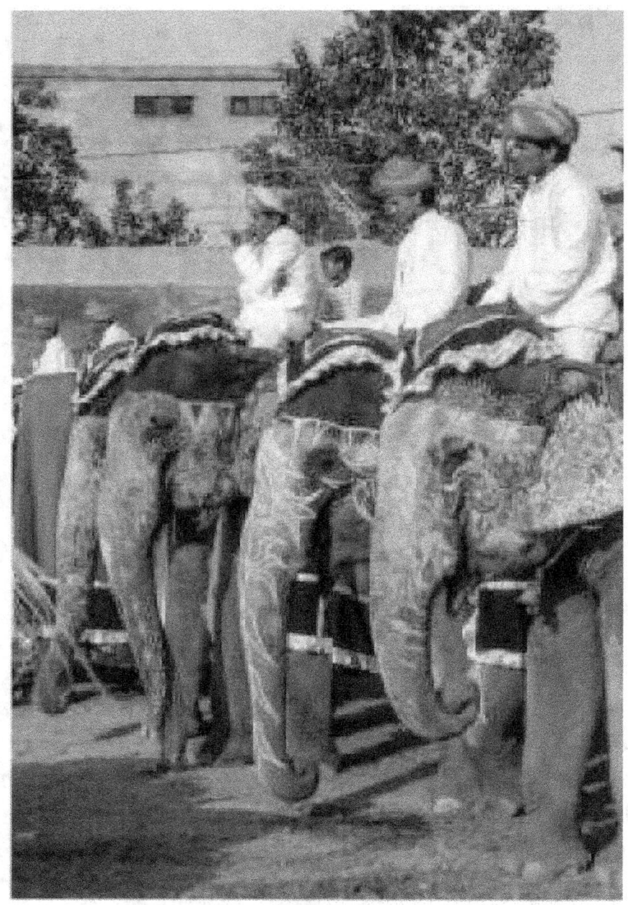

Waiting for the parade

The graceful elephants move in procession, holding the audience spellbound. After the procession, they play a game of tug-of-war against long lines of men, standing on the grass in the arena.

Crowds cheer the elephants, waiting to see the most gifted elephant win a race and afterwards play polo. Male polo players in the royal game of polo wear long saffron sashes tied to scarlet turbans. They use long sticks, reaching the ground from atop the elephants' backs, and a plastic football, as they try to score points for their team.

When the games end, tourists come down from the grandstands, mount the elephants, and participate in the fun by throwing colored powder on other players, riding elephants. Over past centuries, the elephant provided the Imperial Mount for royal families, nobles, and kings.

The age-old tradition of performing elephants attracts tourists for its historical significance.

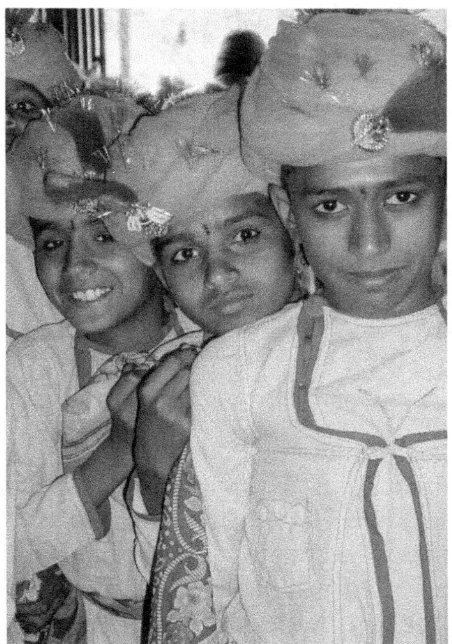

Performers at festival

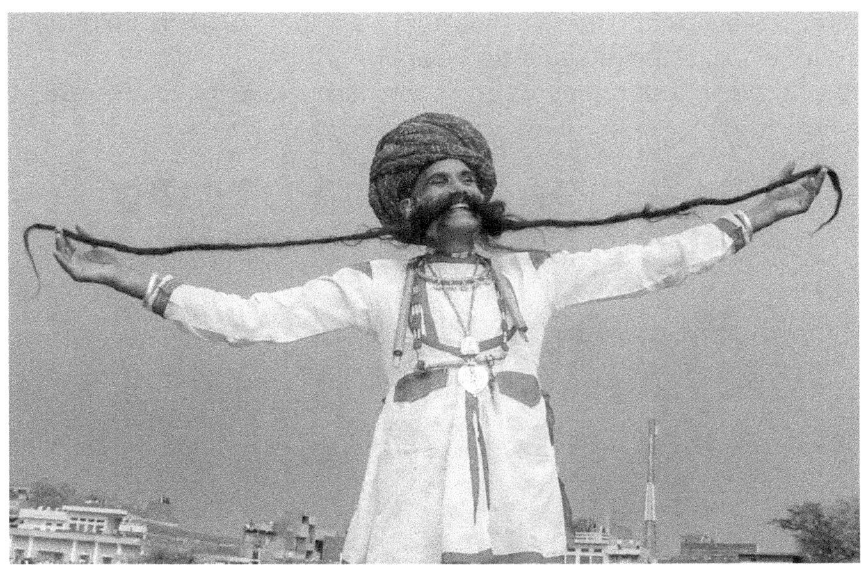

Proud citizen with three-foot mustache

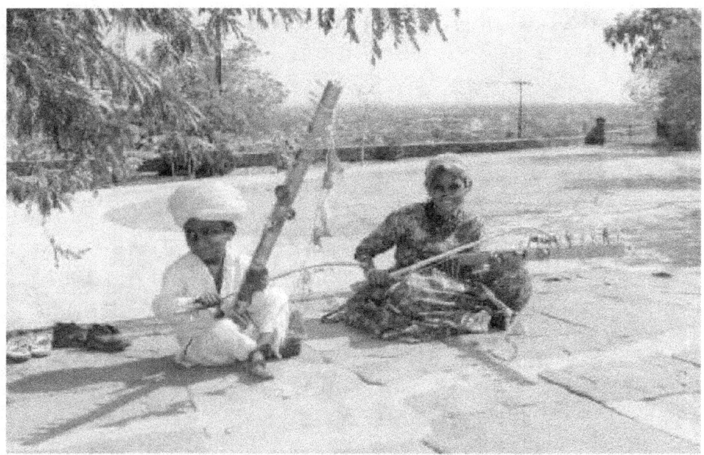

Girl danced after playing her instrument

Other famous sights include the Pink City, a section of Jaipur where streets divide the area into rectangles that house various arts and local crafts. Bathe in the pools inside the golden Temple located in Aritsar.

One of the ancient eight wonders of the world, the Taj Mahal, built of white marble in 1630, resides in Agra, India. Tagore, the Indian poet, described the Taj Mahal as a "Tear on the face of eternity."

The Emperor Shah Jah built the Taj Mahal as a symbol of love for a favorite queen named Mumtax, who died giving birth to their fourteenth child.

In meticulous detail, twenty thousand hard-labor workers built the symmetrical shrine over a twenty-two-year period.

The Taj Mahal has a reputation as the most exquisite, well-preserved tomb in the world.

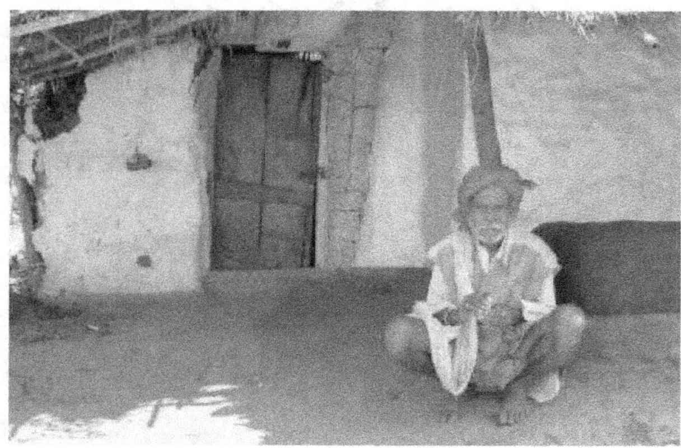

Friendly local

"Not a piece of architecture, as other buildings are, but the proud passion of an emperor's love wrought in living stones." Sir Edwin Arnold

Southern India offers a different view of India, off the tourist track, where rural charms live and breathe. A place that feels a world away, Orissa, lies south of Kolkata (Calcutta) on the east coast. Bhubaneswar makes a great base for tours down to Jeypore and Koraput to visit the Bonda, Kondh, and Gadaba indigenous tribal people.

Orissa feeds the spirit a banquet of visual excitement. The Bonda, also called the naked people, live in inaccessible hill regions that offer preservation of ancient customs and an escape from modern civilizations.

Farmers harvest rice, using handmade tools, or plow fields employing buffalo carts built decades ago. Earth-toned homes sculpted of mud and sand cluster inside virgin jungle growth.

At a village center sits the Sindibar, built on a platform and used for gatherings. A house-god protects the interior of each house.

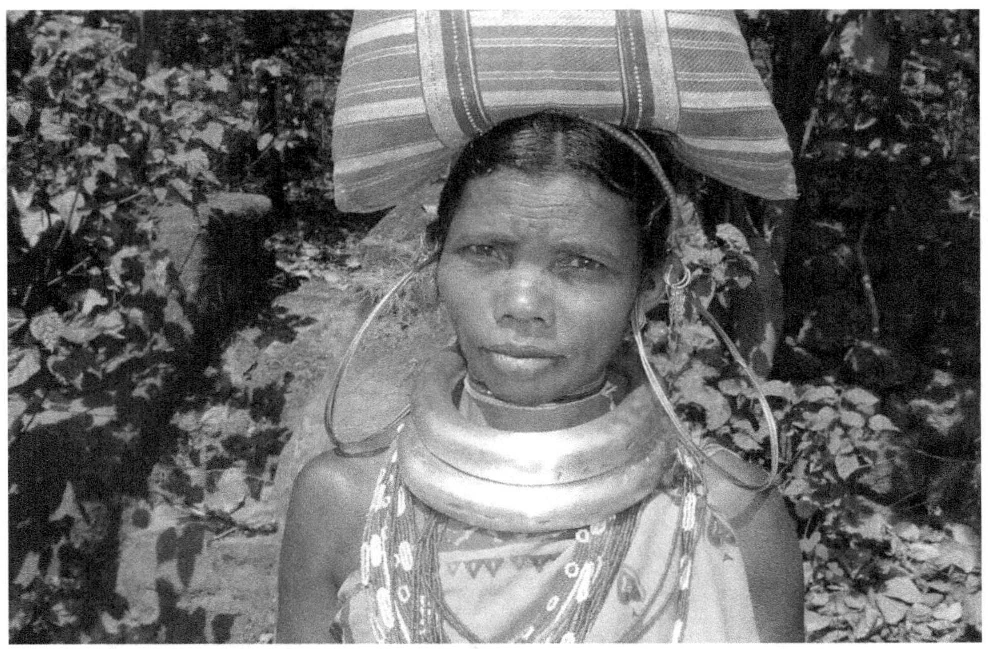

Gadaba woman in Orissa

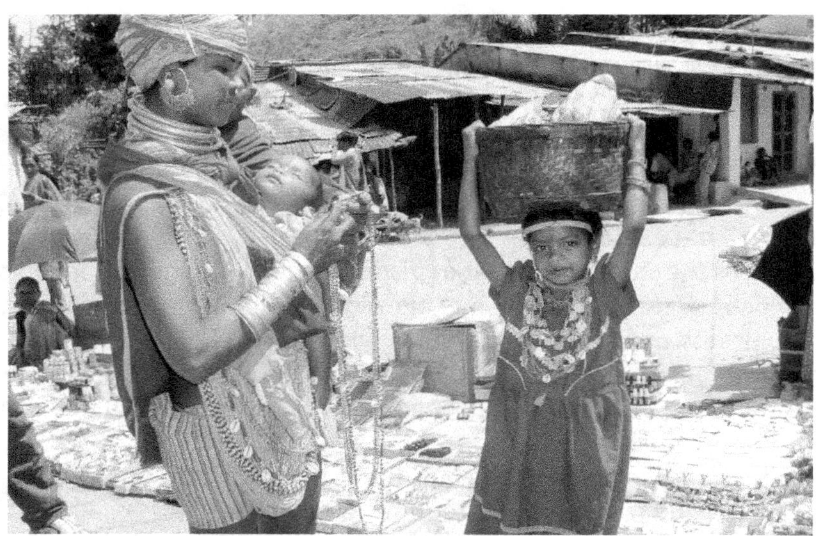

Bonda shopping in Orissa market

Walking the rural areas transported me back one hundred years in time. Sweaty men, dressed in loincloths, scaled tree-branch ladders to reach rooftops. Misshapen dead tree limbs, laid to rest in the openings of the roofs, created a base for bundles of dried grass or sheets of tin, if available. Women and children sat on stones and unused logs, and offered me gourds of brown river-water to drink. Careful of my health, I declined and said, "Namaste."

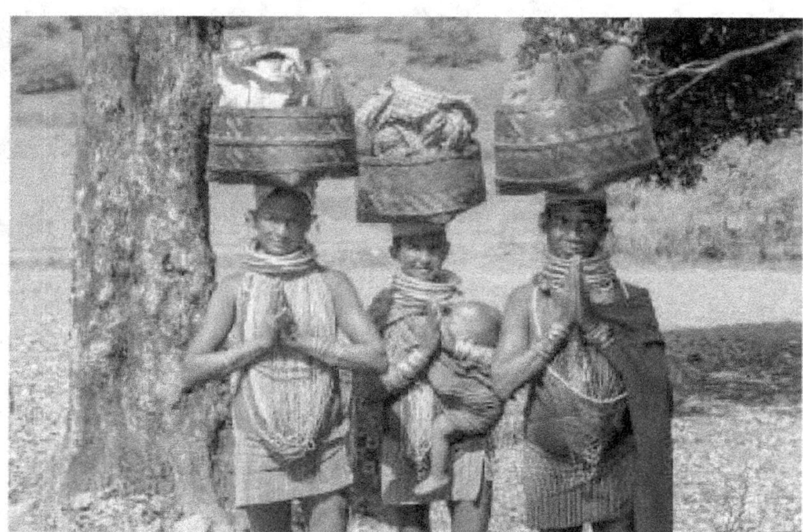

Offering Namaste

"Namaste" describes a custom where hands come together at the palms in front of the heart with head slightly bowed. "Namaste" means, "I bow to you," and speaking it to another allows individuals to come together in a place of connection and timelessness. The word also translates to a respectful greeting and a thank you.

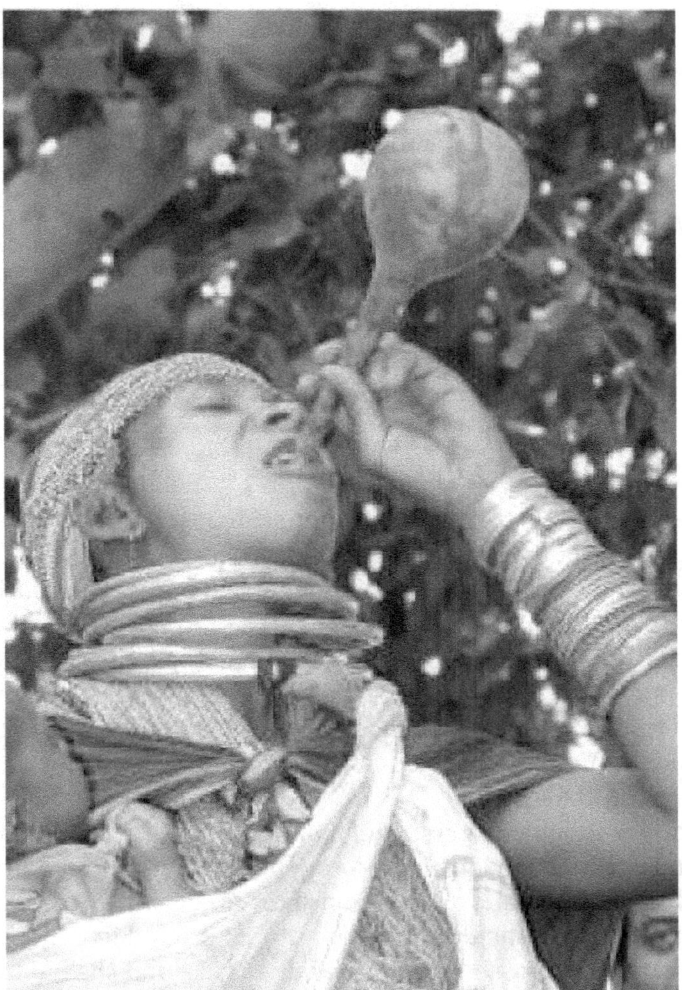

Bonda, drinking salap while walking to market

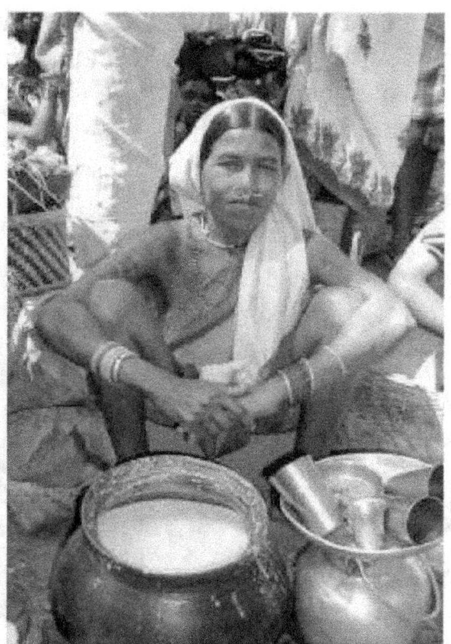

Selling salap liquor in Orissa market

My guide, a staff member of the Jeypore Hotel, found a driver whose looks matched the classy older car he drove. Dirt roads and a morning departure guaranteed me encounters with Bonda villagers trekking rugged paths for miles, leaving before sunlight on market days.

The anticipation of meeting extraordinary people built my excitement and apprehension as I recalled their reputation for wild, ferocious attitudes.

Several trees shading the road made a natural rest stop for families and our car. The driver motioned me to leave the car, ignoring the trickles of nervous sweat wetting my cheeks.

Small groups of women circled me, while touching my skin and long brown hair. A teenage girl reached into one of my many overstuffed pants pockets to bring out a fistful of batteries and memory cards.

After a quick glance, she dropped them to the ground like they were poison. An older woman embarrassed her with harsh words, and she hid herself behind the vehicle.

The guide, talking a mile a minute, pointed to jewelry, beads, and baskets of vegetables. His explanations overflowed the palm of my hand as I scribbled notes even on my fingers with a red ink pen.

My camera had the capability to take videos, but I did not think to capture his stories live. Instead, I wrote in shorthand on my palms while he chattered on, and unfortunately, those stories got lost in the day's sweat.

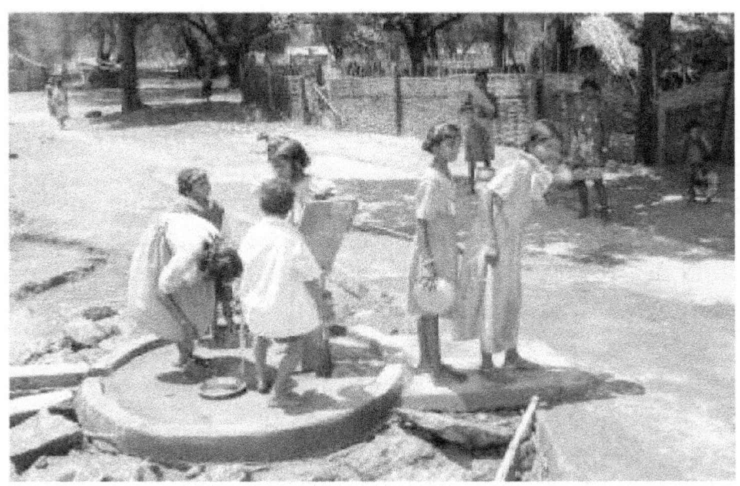

Schoolchildren, getting a drink during break

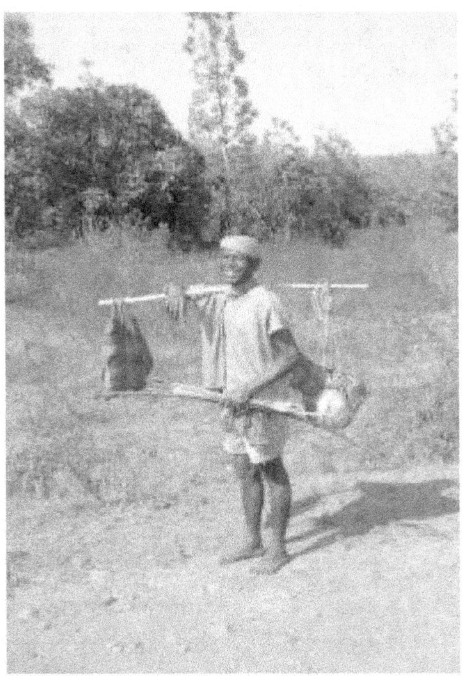

Bonda wanting to sell handmade bows and arrows

Thick aluminum necklaces rested above the voluminous strands of beads, hiding the women's bare breasts. Bright contrasting yarns complemented the local *kerang,* or colorful cloth fibers from native trees, woven on crude looms to fashion loincloths.

Strands of beads or woven palm fiber wrapped around the women's shaved heads. The Gadaba women wear a long strip of bright kerang around their waists and another across the chest, and they love chunky brass and aluminum ornaments to decorate their bodies. The unmarried girls sleep in dormitories, called *Selani dingo.* The boys sleep in *Ingersin* dormitories.

A custom exists to pay a bride price for a wife. Ensuring social acceptance and a prestigious method of marriage requires negotiation. Families regulate marriages and ask for steep bride prices, whether the marriage originates by capture, exchange, or mutual consent.

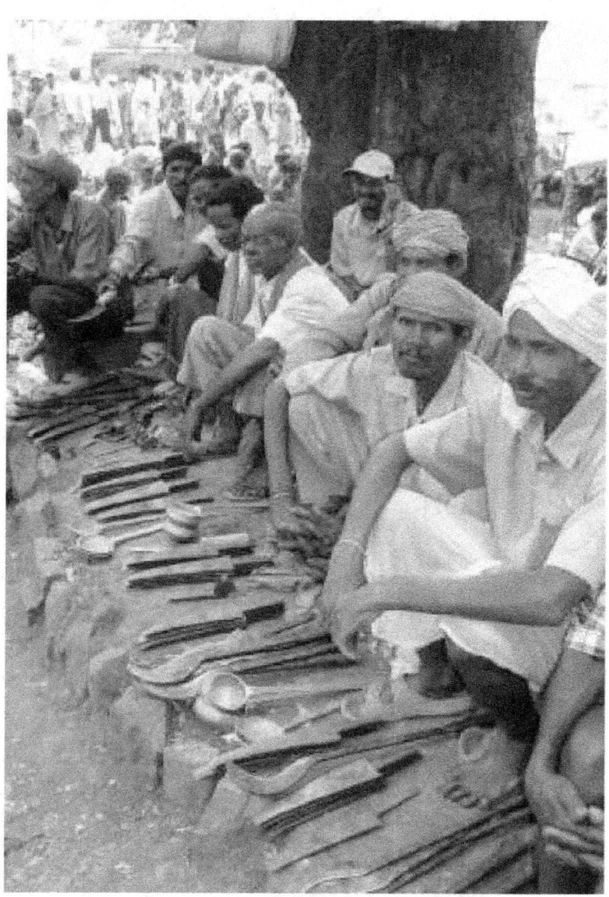

Handmade tools for sale in market

Village markets, the local heartbeat of a culture, persuade onlookers to stop and peruse the goods on display.

Villagers walk for miles from every direction, providing the market with a variety of foods and products for sale.

Well-behaved children sit beside mothers under umbrellas of blue tarps tied to trees.

The tangled mess of sellers and buyers intrigued me for hours, but I needed some quiet time and remembered my wandering tendencies in the past have opened new doors.

Three girls passed the time playing cards not too far from the last row of the market. After watching the game for a few minutes, I understood the rules and gestures. They invited me to join. Explanations were beyond translation.

I kept up, although laughter ruled and there was no real belief in any of us that I could possibly win the game.

The girls waved and beckoned as I stood pondering my guide's suspicions of my whereabouts.

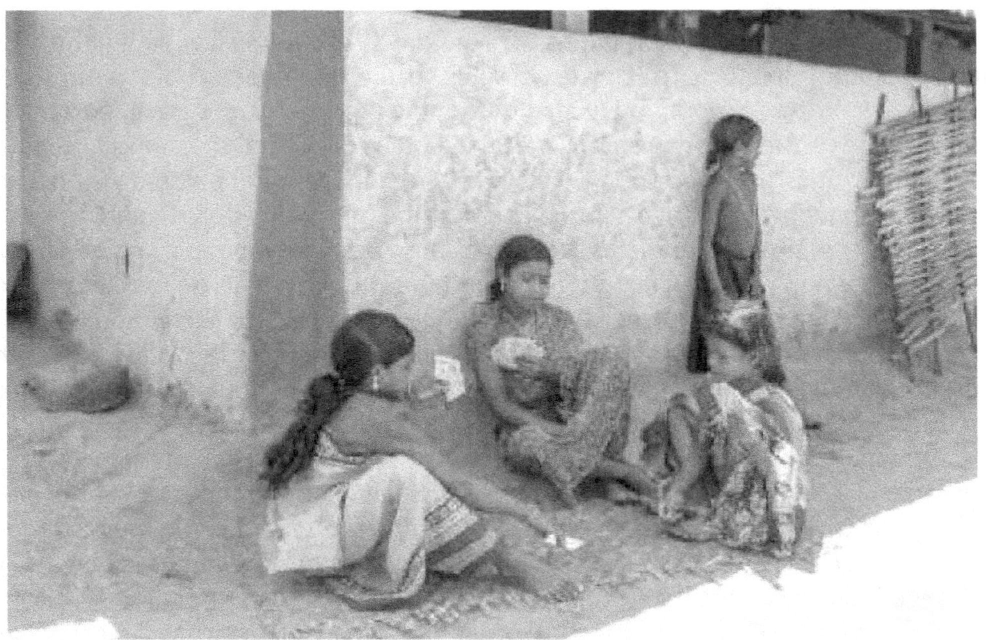

Playing cards in the shade

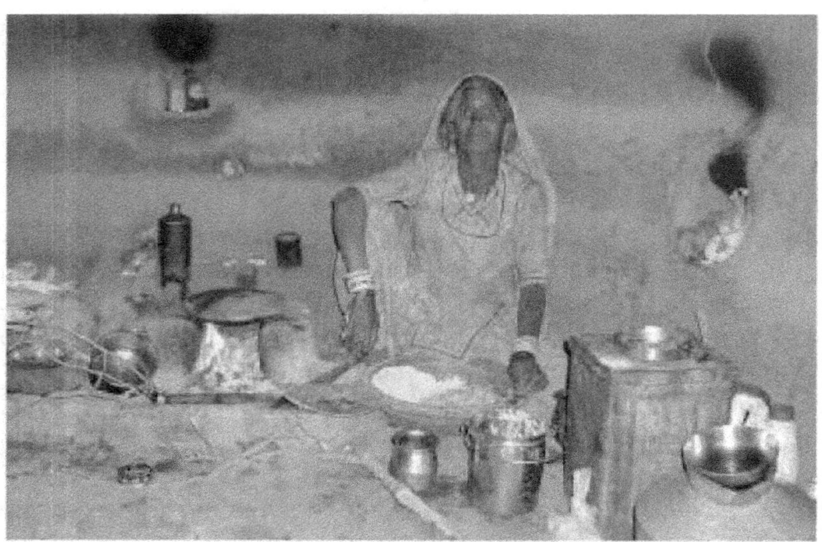

Cooking inside village hut

Local Bonda and Gadaba ignite the Onukudelli tribal market selling or bartering small parcels of fruit or vegetables, crude handmade tools, palm fiber baskets, and the aluminum jewelry, adorning every woman's neck, ears, and wrists. The consumption of salap, the local liquor, energized the market all day.

Salap comes from the sap of a palm tree, and each man owns the rights to the sap from one tree. They tap the liquid in the morning before leaving for the fields. Left to ferment for a few hours, the salap becomes a potent and addictive liquor. Men and women alike drink the frothy, sour potion. At the markets, huge gourds of salap line the rutted paths. A villager might hope to barter homegrown vegetables or handmade tools for enough basic essentials for the following week or, in other words, make the equivalent of one dollar. Community markets offer a constant assault on the senses.

Discovering winding passageways in a fort or taking photos of temples built of love may satisfy your travel passions. However, the memories of people met along the way will pull at your heartstrings for a lifetime. Visiting India creates profound changes to your soul and brings to life the old saying, "You can't change India; India changes you."

The majority of people I encountered in India insist on sharing their meager quantities of food with travelers, whose lucky souls arrive as strangers but leave as friends. A kaleidoscope of these memories will challenge the flexibility of your spirit if you ever decide to visit here. Experiencing India changes attitudes. Consequently, the visitor gets a better appreciation of the grand diversity in the world. Enjoy India while there and bring back a treasure trove of amazement. Allowing India inside your heart alters your perspective, forever.

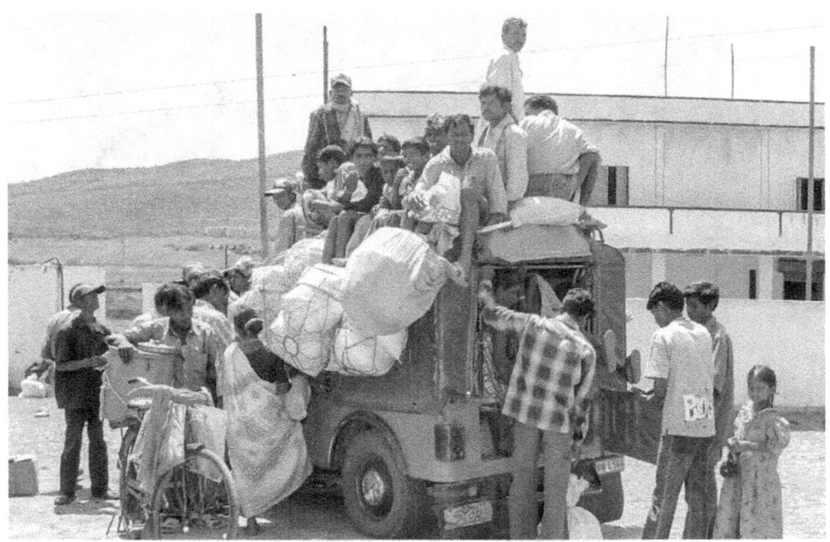

Making the most of transportation

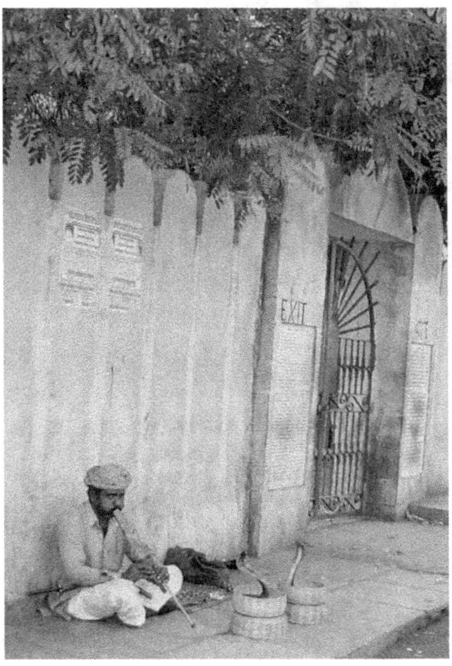

Snake charmer

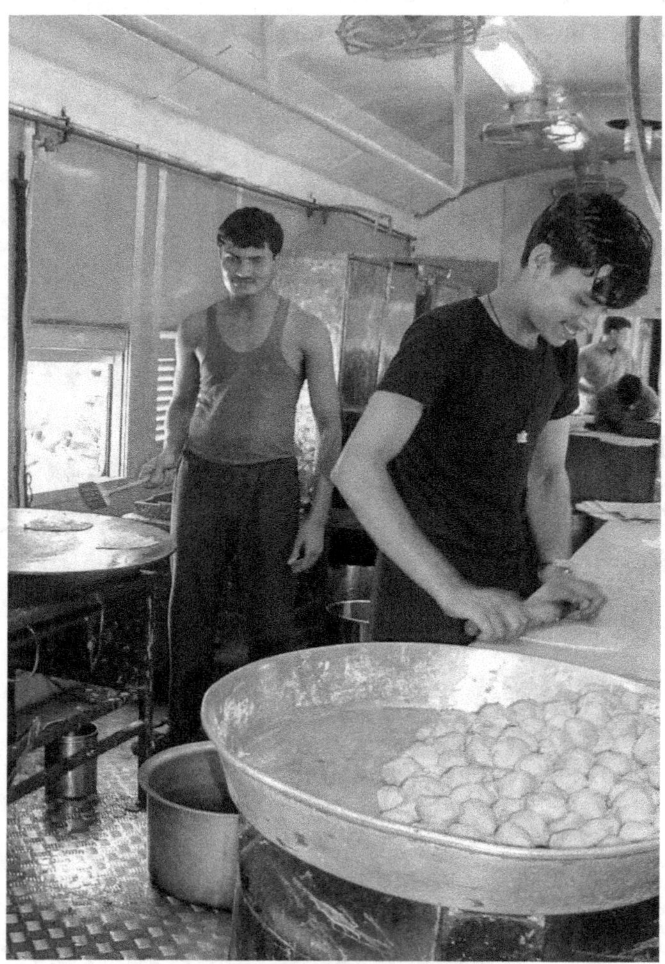

Cooking on the train

CHAPTER EIGHT

Morocco: Accidental Fortunate Discoveries

"It takes as much energy to wish as it does to plan." Eleanor Roosevelt

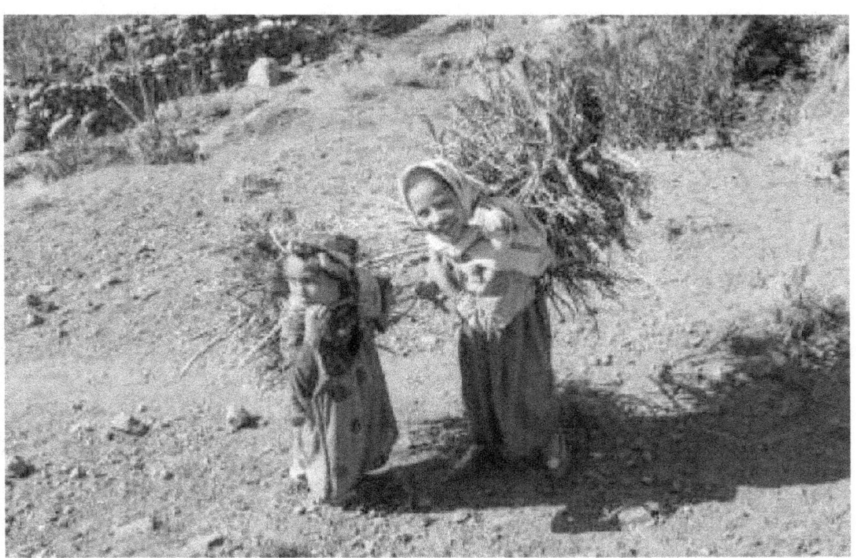

From a distance, these children looked like ants

Oncoming traffic signaled us to pull off the road. The marshmallow sand of the road shoulders tempted the tires of our car to sink deep.

Great time for some stretching, I thought, after hunting in several bags for water. The shiny bottles I pulled from my pack caught the attention of black spots, moving down the hillside opposite the road.

Those tiny spots turned into children, doubled over with heads low to the ground and carrying stacks of firewood taller than their little bodies.

Three adorable girls, about eight years old, came rushing toward the car begging for food or water.

My camera captured their smiles and heavy loads, and I thanked them with a few small coins.

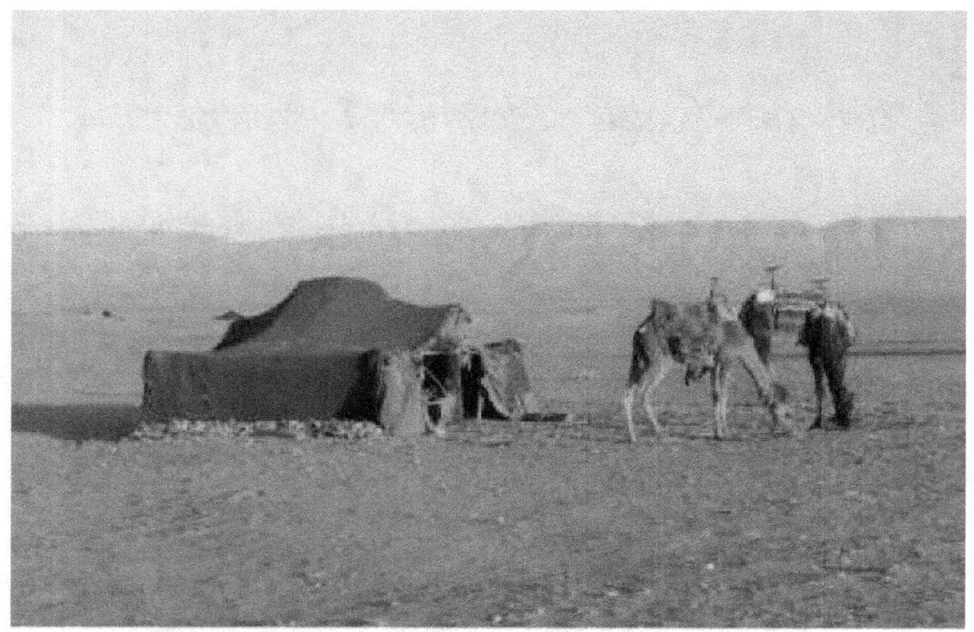

Camel treks for the Erg Chebbi, drifting sand dunes that change color

An older boy ran past us, out of nowhere, grabbing the coins from one of the girl's hands. She cried while she struggled to get the wood off her back and onto the ground.

I made the mistake of opening the car door, exposing all kinds of potential gifts to the crying little girl. A package of crackers and two water bottles calmed her, but a few more coins dried the tears.

I wanted to hold the little girl tight to me, offer her safety, and protect her somehow from her harsh environment.

While the girl drank the water before the bully came back, I attempted to lift the bundle of sticks she had dropped.

I fell down, causing hilarious laughter to erupt from the children and the guides, and I could not stand up under the weight, let alone carry the load back to the village.

Undersized donkeys with loads double their size passed the car as my driver coaxed the girl to stand back. She reached her little hands into the vehicle for a loose bag sitting on the floor.

With regret, I shook my head while touching her shoulders with a gentle push, indicating I wanted to close the door.

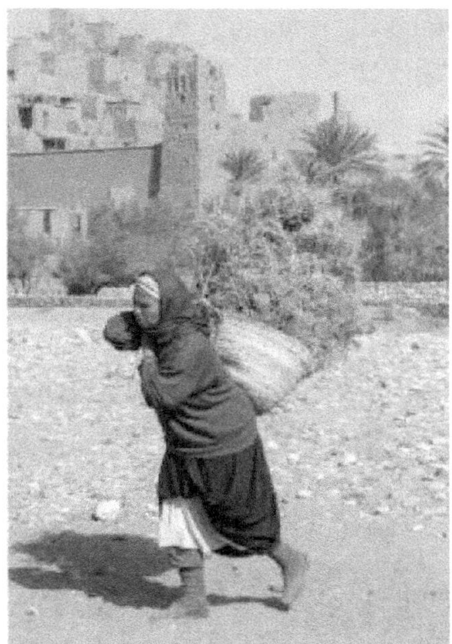

Passing the most-filmed Kasbah

In the High Atlas Mountains of central Morocco lies the Vallee des Roses, better known as the Valley of a Thousand Kasbahs.

The impenetrable hedgerows of wild roses lined the roads with see-through thorny winter brush. Snow-white blossoms of almond trees bandaged square plots of baby green sprigs of wheat.

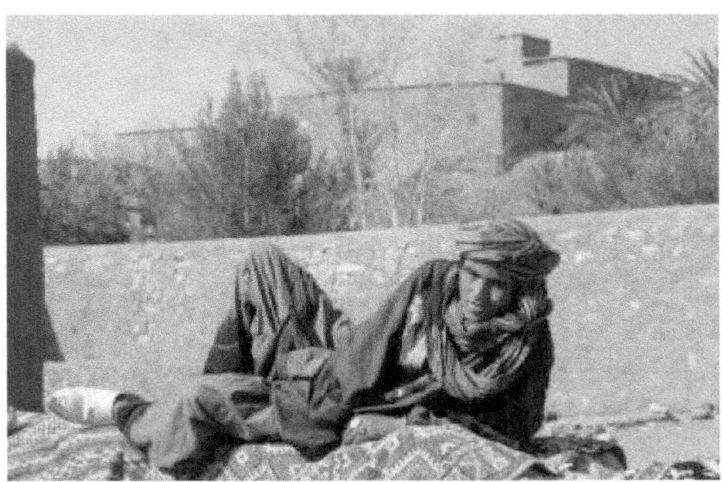

Tuareq with the UNESCO protected Kasbah

Crumbling kasbahs along the roadways remind me of the ancient camel caravan routes through Morocco and most of Africa.

Known as the door to the desert, Quarzazate resided as the powerful base for southern trade routes.

Two famous kasbahs, Taourirt Kasbah and Ait Benhaddou, open their gates for visitors.

Kasbahs, built of straw and mud, sit high on a hilltop and boast high walls and few windows.

Powerful leaders used kasbahs as a place of defense and refuge when a city came under siege.

Magnificent architectural gems, these fairy tale creations display towers and ramparts, covered with Berber symbols.

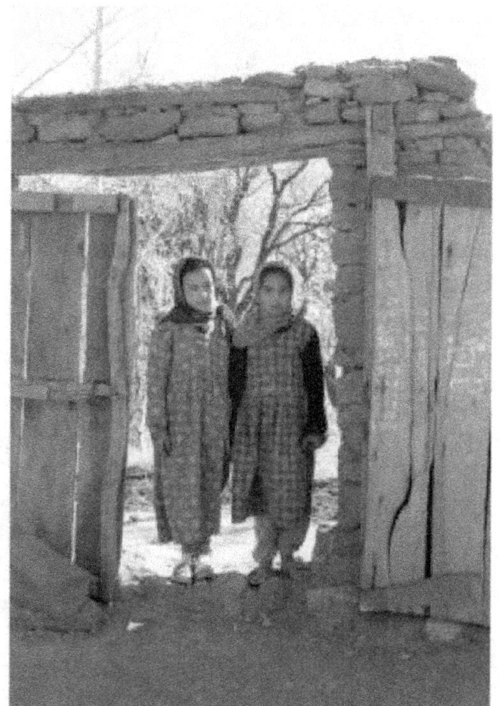

Village girls outside Taourirt Kasbah in mellah, or Jewish quarters

Ait Benhaddou Kasbah housed over 1000 members of families and slaves in more than 300 living quarters. Attached earthen shelters for ceremonies, stables, granaries, bathhouses, and military headquarters border the soaring maze of passageways. As you ascend the labyrinth, you pass children tending goats or dipping crusty breads in oil. Colossal pillars, made from canyon wall, support the bright tiled and vaulted ceilings of Taourirt Kasbah. Branches from the overhanging stork nests atop the towers clutter the inside courtyards. Ornately carved wooden doors and iron window coverings contrast beautifully with the magnificently tiled walls surrounding the luxurious interior decorations of their day. Artists used natural dyes like blue indigo, red henna, mint green, and yellow saffron for tile making.

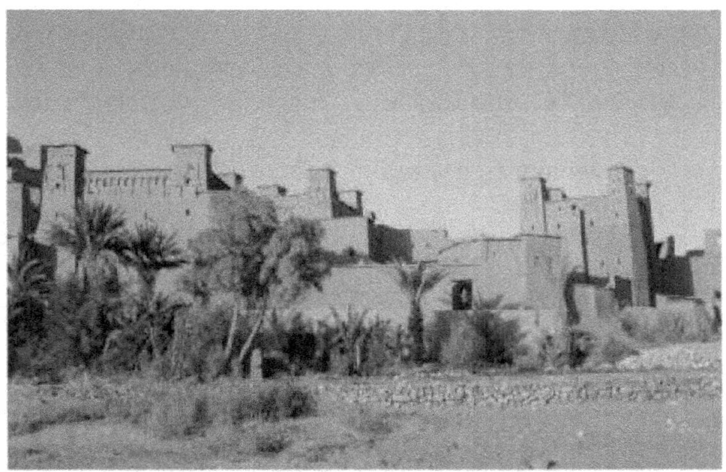

The exotic Ait Benhaddou Kasbah

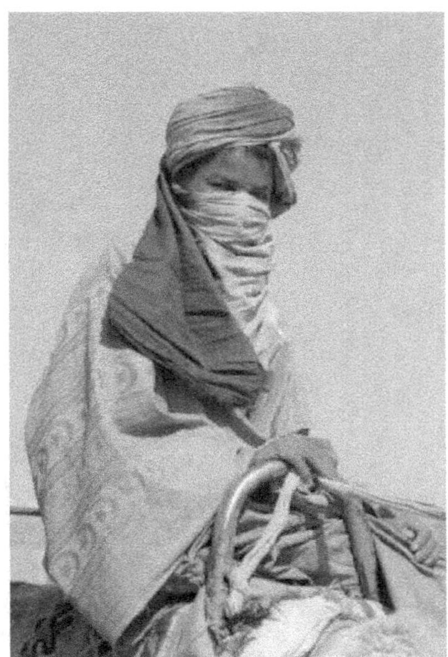

Berber, dressed in his djellaba, resting on his camel

With our boots removed and pants rolled up, we crossed the shallow river to reach the Ait Benhaddou Kasbah. So powerful and majestic, the Kasbah gives Morocco its fame, and many filmmakers have used the Kasbah as a backdrop to movies set in Morocco. (*Kundun*, and *Gladiator*).

Proudly, my guide explained the rebuilding of the main gate after the plane crashed through it during the making of the movie, *Jewel of the Nile*. Within minutes of entering the towering fortress, the twisting and turning chambers excited yet confused me.

Once filled with hundreds of families, goats and donkeys, the Kasbah now houses about ten families, not concerned by the lack of electricity or running water.

More modern conveniences, in the village across the river, have enticed other families to leave the Kasbah.

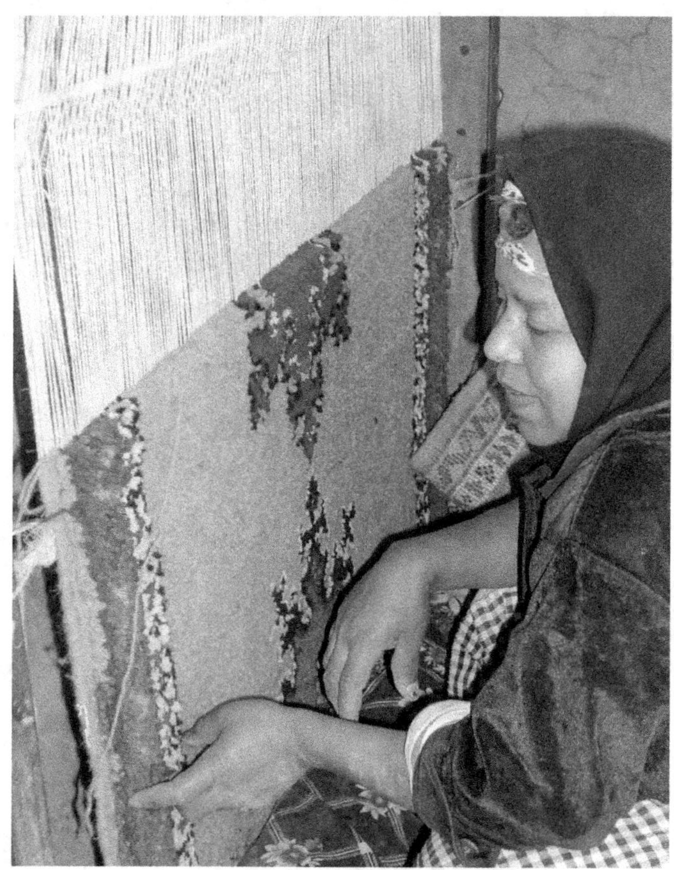

Weaving inside the fort

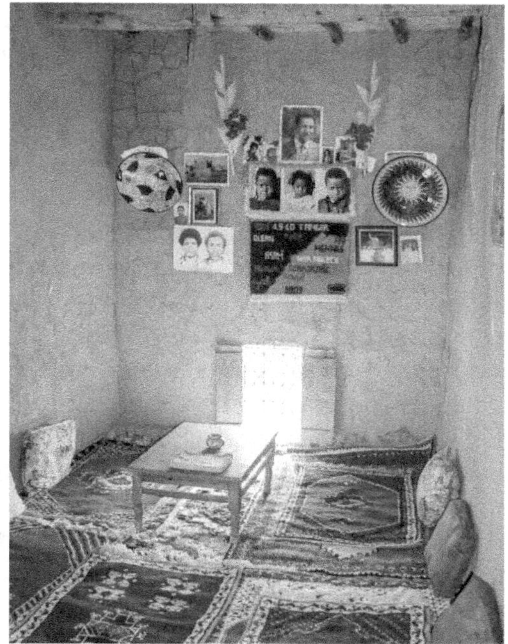

Living quarters inside Ait Benhaddou

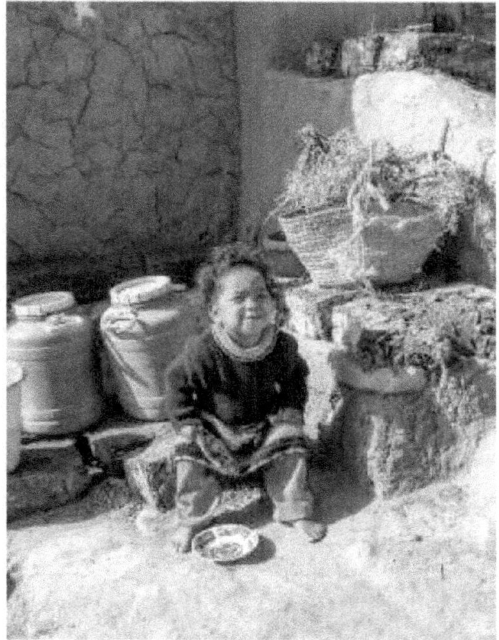

Breakfast time

A sweet woman motioned for me to enter her home after I stumbled into a courtyard where a small girl sat eating her flatbread breakfast.

The mother, proud to show off her collection of handmade pottery, talked rapidly, assuming I understood the Berber words she spoke. Berber is not like Arabic. For instance, "hello" in Berber sounds like "*ago,*" while, in Arabic, you hear "*salama lekum.*"

"Thank you," in Berber: "*saha*", and in Arabic: "*shukran.*"

After a few *sahas,* and enough shutter clicks to fill an album with photos of the little girl, who seemed immune to the stranger from the faraway land capturing all her mother's attention, I moved on. A tiny stable housed a group of bleating goats, trying to jump over the mud walls. An old man with only one eye crouched in a corner as if guarding the handmade carpet draped over the wall behind him. He covered his face when I pointed to my camera. I respected his shyness and moved on. Hours of getting lost felt good, and I somehow reached the top of the Kasbah and observed two boys kicking a wadded cloth ball into a group of squawking chickens. The sun warmed the red color of the walls and highlighted the entrance to the grounds several stories below the roof.

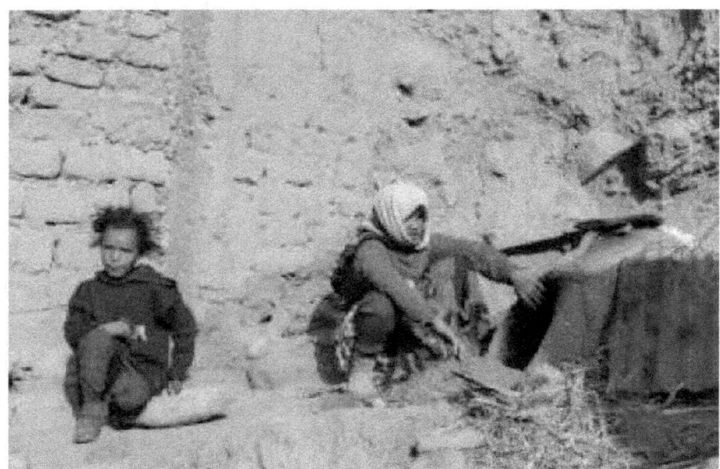

Cleaning the fire pit in the Ait Benhaddou Kasbah

Outside, a Tuareq man, sitting high on his white camel, posed for one of those exotic pictures everyone dreams of taking. Bored, or hoping for a nice tip, he sat there, dressed in typical indigo-dyed blues, with just his eyes exposed to sunlight.

This fairy tale land inspires exotic dreams of kings and carriages. My driver here in Morocco was a man by the name of Omar. He refreshed my memory of the long journey to find the camel camp, after I found our car hidden behind a small group of camels. Two women with tattooed foreheads and chins held the camels steady. Omar explained the significance of the tattoos. Some of the Berber women, like the Bedouin tribes, wear forehead tattoos, representing their tribe, with chin tattoos, indicating their name.

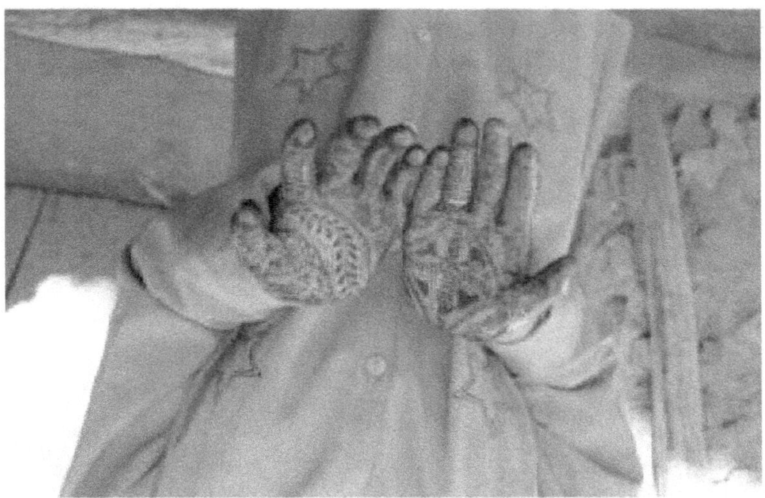

The veiled girl tattooed her hands to impress her new fiancé.

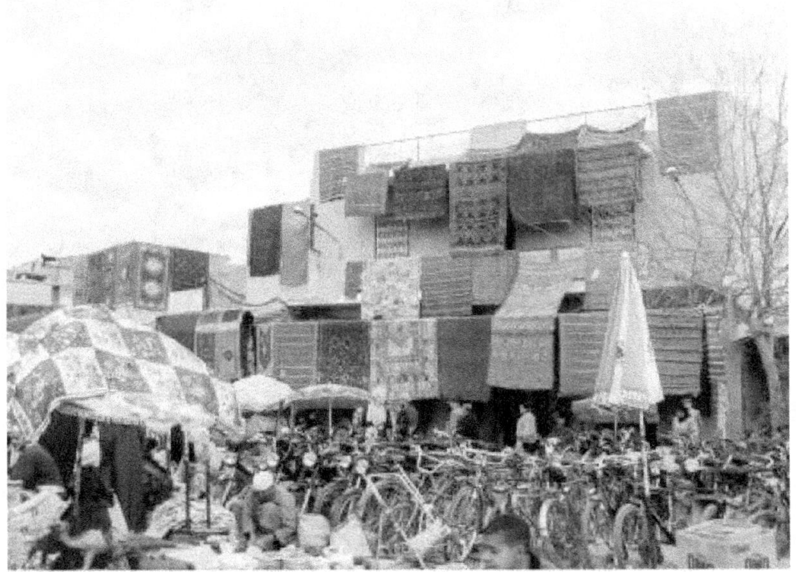

Rugs for sale

Geometrically designed carpets hung from windowsills, bringing the Berber mud villages to life. Trucks, swarming with people barely able to hold onto the sides, bounced on and off the shoulder of the road, not wanting to slow for passing cars.

The road ahead framed the snow-capped High Atlas, leaving behind the oasis-like palmeries (date palms along the river valleys). Tarps rested under olive trees, ready to save those olives falling ahead of picking season.

Women suspended their scrubbing and beating of dirty laundry to stare at the car, slowing along the roadway above the river.

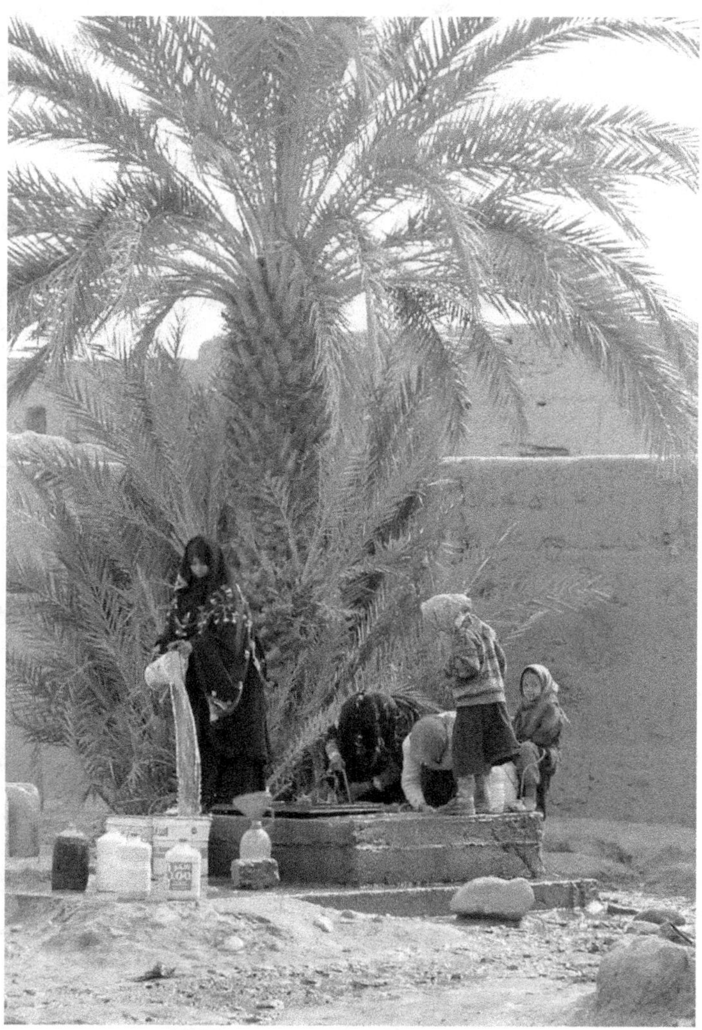

Filling water jugs at the well

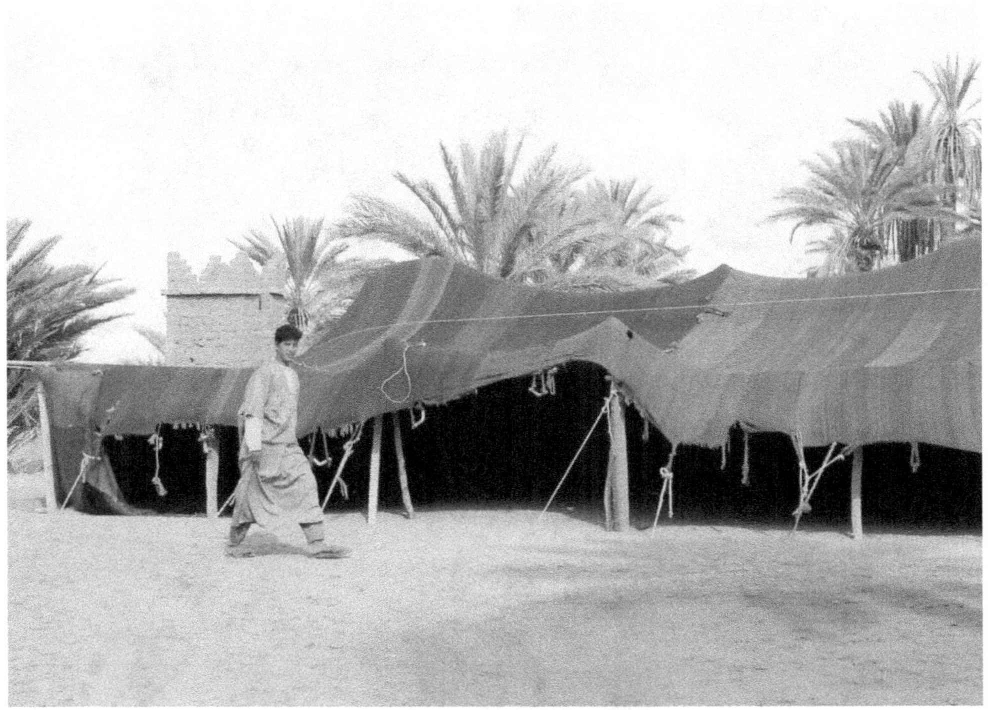

Berber wearing his djellaba

"We wear white in summer," a Bedouin guide explained in his language, and Omar translated.

He wrapped yards and yards of cheesecloth-like itchy fabric around my head and face, leaving only my eyes exposed.

Women believe in hijab, which means they feel the need to cover their bodies to conceal any signs of their shape or gracefulness.

Men and women wear *djellabas*, or long and loose robes.

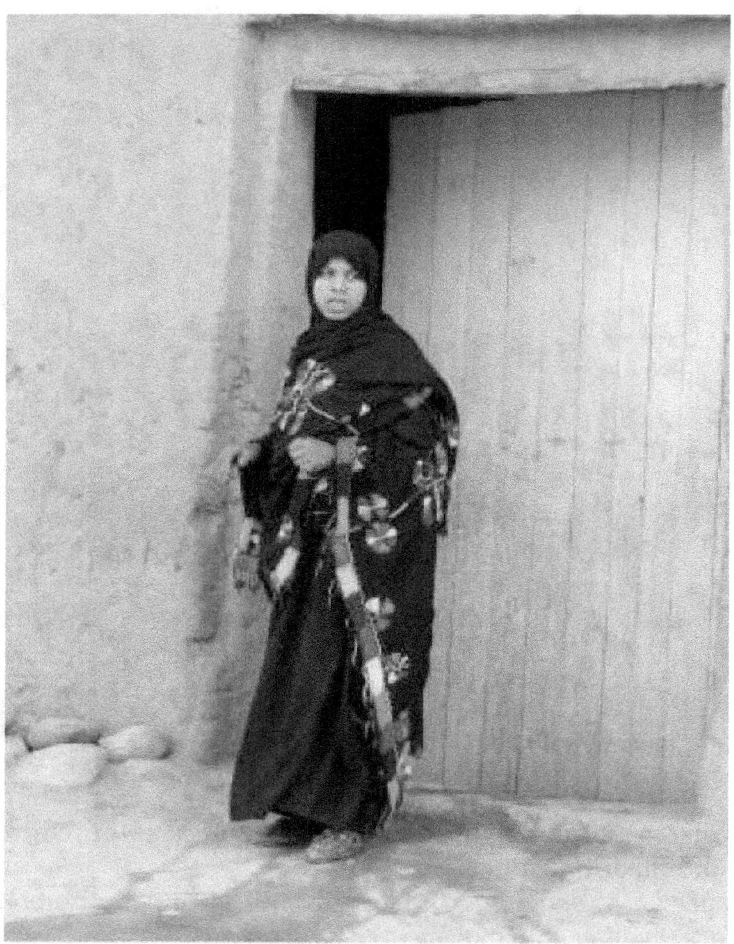

Woman in hijab

Maneuvering the sculpted rock formations of the arid plateaus changed as the caravan approached Merzouga.

The camels lumbered toward the Bedouin camp up and over massive desert sand dunes, shaped by wind. The Sahara crowned my expectations with gratified silence.

A huge tent welcomed our group, tired from the constant irritation of red sand finding its way under our sunglasses.

Even the kids (baby goats, not children) stopped their incessant bleating.

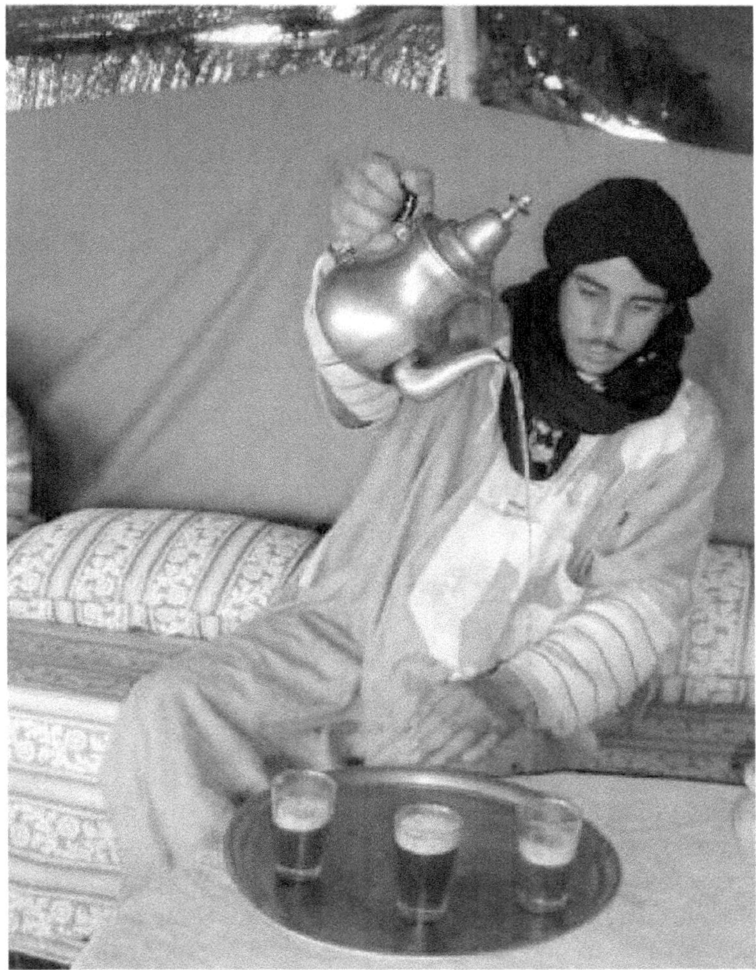

Serving tea in the desert

Tea time. Sweetened mint tea, an integral part of the culture, sounded refreshing even though served hot.

The serving of tea becomes a ceremony in itself. The tea server pours the brew from a distance of sometimes a foot or higher above the cups.

Omar explained, "In the Berber culture, it is said that if a man likes a woman, he asks her to make him tea. If she does not like the man, she will use salt instead of sugar. Otherwise, she makes the tea very sweet."

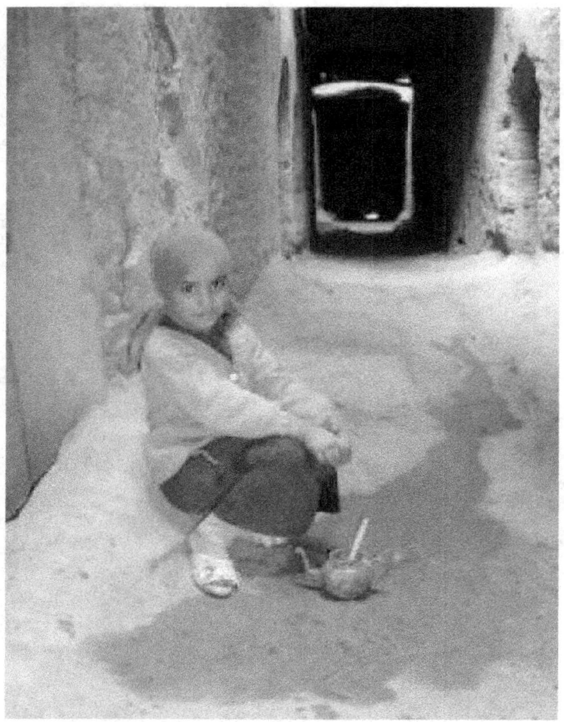

Enjoying a private tea party

Menus in Morocco limit themselves to three dishes: tagine (stew made with chicken or lamb), couscous with chicken, or kebabs of chicken or lamb.

French fries find their way to every plate. The traditional table in a Moroccan home sits low around the knees. Communal eating is done with the hands. Everyone eats from the same dish and washes their hands at the table. The left hand passes dishes or breaks bread to help scoop up food. Napkins clean the mouth, never the hands.

The name tagine, the typical national dish of Morocco, shares the same name as the clay cooking pot.

The base unit, circular and flat, fits under the dome-shaped cover that rests on top of the base. The shape of the cover enables the condensation to slip down into the bottom of pot, adding moisture back to the food. The slow-cooked meals made with the tagine produce tender meats from the all-day process.

The medley of ingredients such as apples, pears, olives, dates, nuts, lemon, and honey added to a tagine pot blend together and excite the palate. If taste buds still sleep, add the complexity of saffron, ginger, cinnamon, cumin, and paprika. They say that for every month of the year, a tree provides fruit for the tagine pot.

The morning call to prayer, a nice reminder of unfamiliar surroundings, started the day. The smell of fresh pastries lured my hungry body to the rooftop restaurant, overlooking the city of Marrakesh, awakening below.

The market opened like a riddle. Artisans, motor scooters, donkey carts, and monkey wranglers cluttered every inch of space with chaotic activity.

Hundreds of Marrakesh shopkeepers opened stalls down narrow arteries, exposing $1500 "real" silver necklaces and even single cigarettes for sale.

Sausage makers filled casings with meat, tied them like cigars and hung them for display and a quick sale. Women stood in silence as they spread butter on square folds of dough to ensure flakiness for their *warka,* or paper-thin dough similar to Greek phyllo.

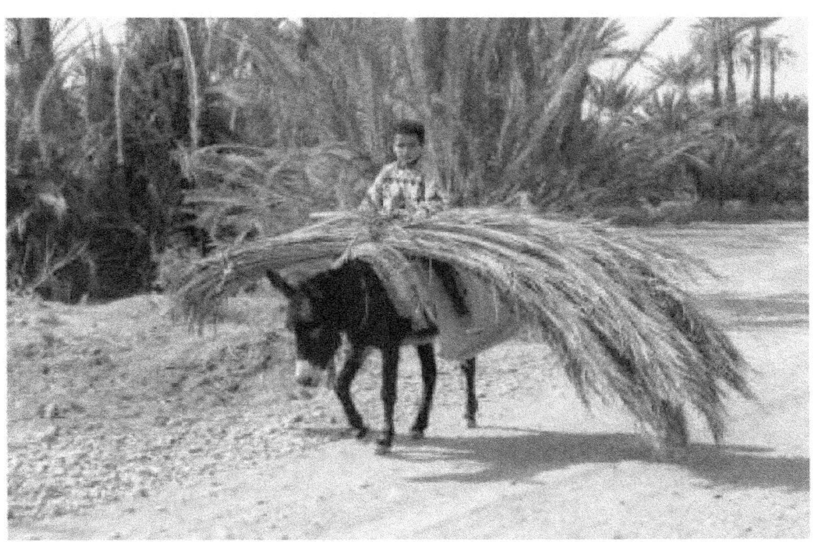

Long day of working in the fields

Mohammed suggested trying *a hammam,* or bathing house. "Get to know our people and customs. You will meet many women. Some will speak English and invite you to dinner. Before going, shop the market across the road from the hammam. Buy some *sabon,* or black olive oil soap, and *rhassoul,* or lava clay, to scrub the skin. And don't forget to buy a little bucket to scoop the water over your body."

My white skin captured the attention of every woman in the room. Rules to remember included no total nudity and do not waste the water. Dressed in underwear, a young woman took me under her wing and showed me the procedures of the bathing ritual. We started in a warm room, each carrying two buckets of water: one for use with soap and the other for rinsing. Next came the hot room, allowing one's pores to open for deep cleaning, and then the warm room again for more scrubbing. Then there was the final rinse, followed by sitting in the cold room to close the pores.

The women offered me tea and a massage, which I declined, but later I learned this customary offer happened every day, with expectations of getting one in return. The social function of the hammam brings people together (most often the traditional woman who seldom leaves her house) for debating the latest gossip and neighborhood news.

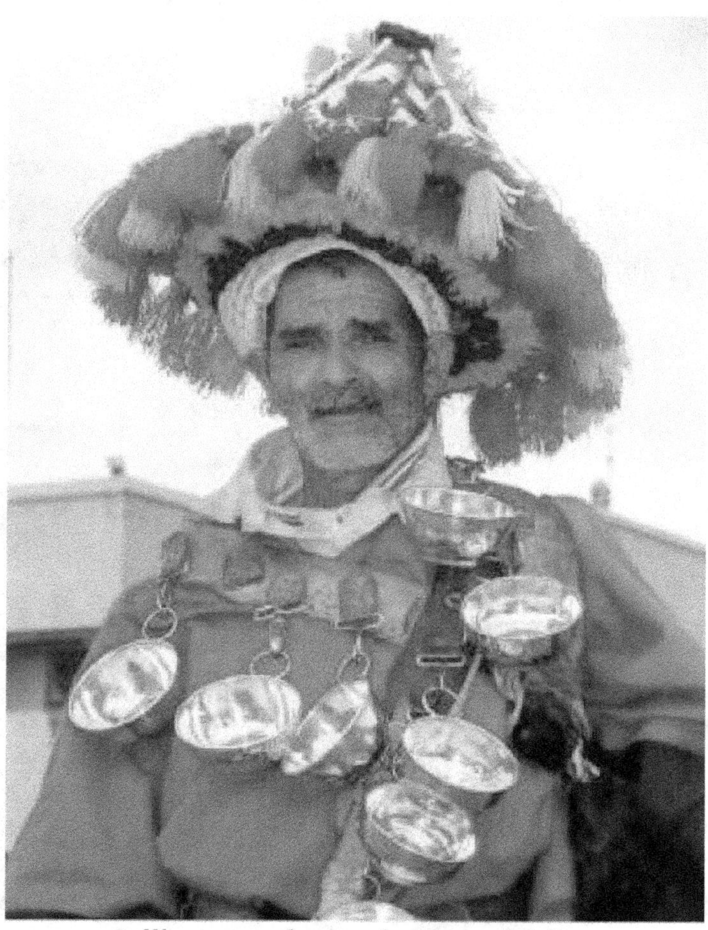

Selling cups of water in Djemaa el-Fna

I left the hammam and found myself peering into the thick forest of awnings, displaying every palette color.

I felt intimidated by the alleyways and empathized with jungle undergrowth that always seemed to be screaming for more space to breathe. The shady walk brought forth goose bumps on my squeaky-clean skin, as I pondered the effects of declining dinner from my new hammam friend.

After rounding the first corner, I knew I'd need a ball of string to help me find my way back. I felt the helplessness of knowing only English.

Stalls started to come to life, and ladies begged for henna tattoo business next to a round man, holding giant pliers that he would use to pull the next painful tooth.

The food market bustled from the morning frenzy. Smells clashed, giving me the urge to search for nose plugs. Milky eyes stared into nowhere, dead and unseeing: double stacks of sheep heads.

Buying in the *souks,* or markets, begins with expected bargaining, about fifty percent off the initial asking price.

Inspection of the possessions and dress of the potential client might set the asking price quite high if expensive jewelry and cameras hang on necks. Prices change throughout the day, depending on the business of the vendor and his success at selling.

The more the seller sells, the higher the price. A little experience and bargaining become a natural part of buying.

Sellers appreciate clients willing to negotiate with patience. An interest in the artisanship attracts the seller's attention and starts the process with his or her opening price.

A little body language like shrugging the shoulders with a few words of "way too much" gives the seller an indication of your interest, along with the signal that he needs to drop his price. His response will include lowering the price by a small percentage and asking you to counter-offer.

Shake your head, and put the item down, which will encourage the seller to take an active part in making the sale.

At that point, offer fifty percent of the asking price, or less, if you assess the situation as one where you see few shoppers and perhaps no sales.

The seller will try to embarrass you with an offer of less than your price.

The tried and true reasons for lowering the price come into play now, which might lead to some interesting conversation.

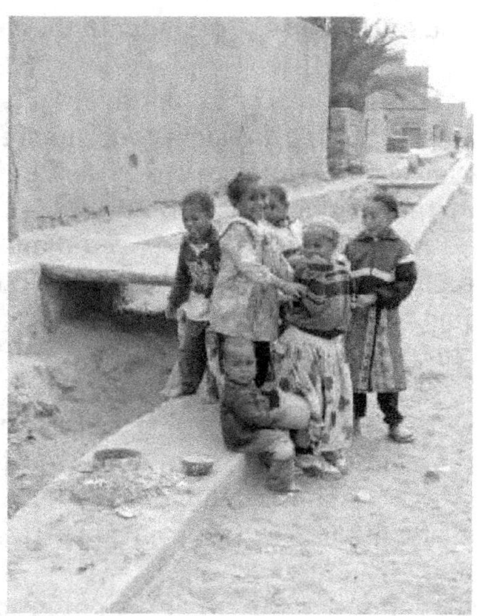

Playing in the sand

Explain that another vendor offered the item for less money or that you don't need the item. The seller may or may not reduce the price again, so walk away no matter how much you want the object.

The bidding often moves toward a lower amount in a series of steps. Not close to fifty percent off? Walk away, and before you reach the door, the seller may accept.

Never bid on items unwanted, and avoid the use of credit cards in markets. Use confidence, and say no and walk away if the bidding becomes stagnant. Use sound judgment when answering questions about your travel plans, where you stay, and what other purchases cost.

If a vendor turns aggressive or lacks interest in an offer, move on. The same item sits under the next awning with a seller anxious for their first sale of the day, called their "good luck sale," bringing luck for the future business of the day.

A handshake, thank you, and little gestures of tapping the item against other products make that first buy almost an adventure in itself.

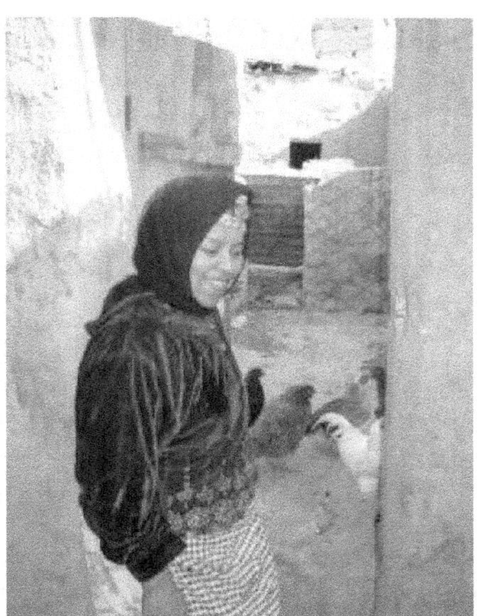

Chickens in one of the mud cubicles of the fort.

For hundreds of years, the livelihood of Marrakesh has focused on the Djemaa El-Fna Market.

The character of the market builds, starting at dawn, and turns into chaos by dark. Masses of people bridge the open gaps between entertainment and food.

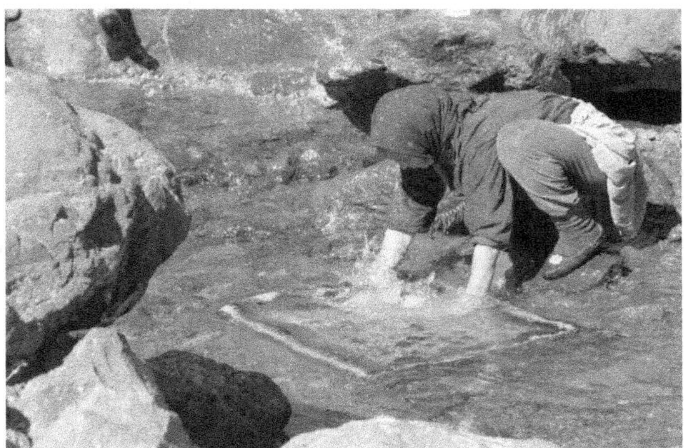

Rock boulders provide a warm spot to dry laundry

Women grab at the hands of prospective customers, offering a henna tattoo sample, shoving worn-out design books at anyone showing any sign of slowing down. Monkeys crawl on the heads of their owners, showing photos of tourists with the chained creatures on their shoulders. Snake charmers shout for payment if one stops too long to watch the cobra rise out of its basket.

If you see a circle of people surrounding the storyteller, it means he has started his story, and a few coins from you might encourage him to tell the ending.

Boiled sheep's heads with eyes intact, witches' pots of bubbling snails, and trays of fried fish cause steam to cloud the strings of lights powered by annoyingly loud generators.

Waiters shout, "Better than McDonald's," and point to confined stools pushed under wobbly tables.

Fortunetellers accost anyone giving them eye contact. An old woman lies horizontal in a dentist's chair, preparing for pliers to enter her mouth. Children hand the waterman a coin for a drink and use one of the dangling brass cups on his belt as he pours from his container of water.

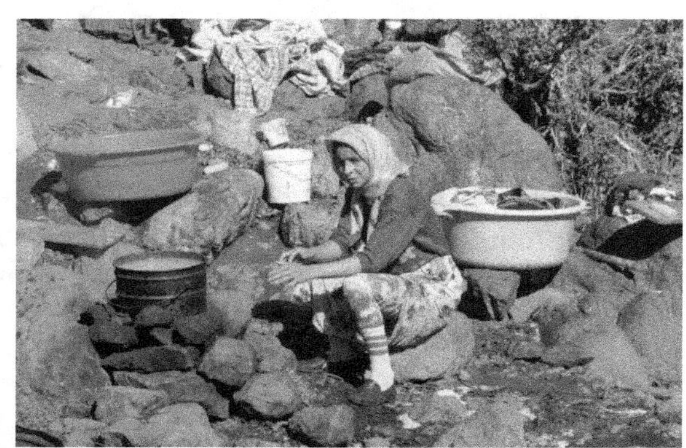

Small fires warm icy river water for laundry day

The claustrophobic crowds and multitude of shops and streets make it impossible to remember how to find your hotel. Motorbikes, crisscrossing between groups, contribute to the confusion you feel as you try to get your bearings.

Instead of attempting to find my way back to the hotel alone, I hailed a taxi and got a ride back. Not having to deal with unfamiliar streets, I was able to allow the memory of the hypnotic market to sink in.

We season our travels of the diverse cultures of Morocco with differences. At the journey's end, the involvement, although cushioned, brings out the similarities of people around the world. Time seems to move like unhurried snails on the road to a thousand kasbahs. Maybe the people perform a trick with their fairy tale traditions.

CHAPTER NINE

Panama: Unconditional Hospitality

"If you reject the food, ignore the customs, fear the religion, and avoid the people, you might better stay home." James Michener.

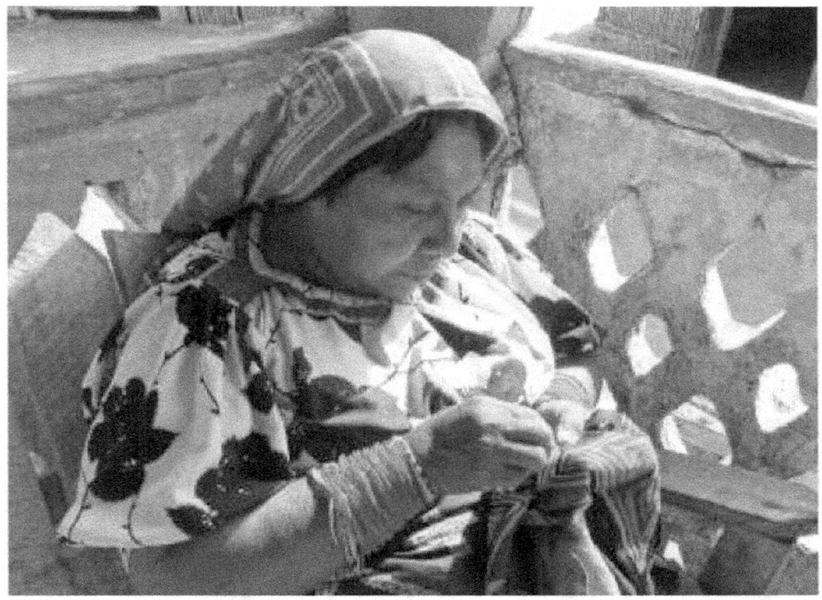

Kuna, stitching elaborate embroidery

Seeing the imagination and artistry used on the *Diablo Rojos,* or red devils (buses so named for their numerous traffic accidents) felt like striking a vein of gold upon my arrival at the new Allbrook Mall and bus terminal.

A bus driver here, licensed for one or more bus routes, purchases his own bus. Often an operator will hire several driver/conductor teams each maintaining with great pride their own old U.S. school bus. While trying to find my bus, I marveled at elaborate, painted murals of wild animals, aliens, or pirate ships, wrapping the sides of the buses like kids' birthday presents.

Mountain scenes and landscapes to dream about ran across the top of the front windows with wild letters describing the final destinations underneath. Hood ornaments ranged from naked women to rearing horses, bracing themselves along the front edge while pink fins stood erect on the roofs. Exaggerated

Felix-the-Cat drawings or slogans like "Toxic Shock" filled every crack and crevice. Brilliant neon lights wrapped around the back windows blinded drivers following behind. The sun played games on the massive chrome exhaust pipes running up the backsides to the roofs of the buses.

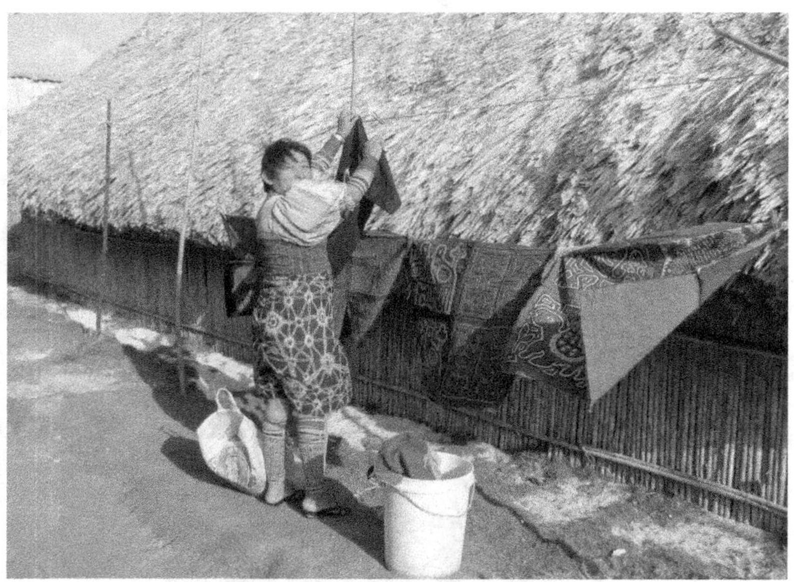

Hanging molas for sale

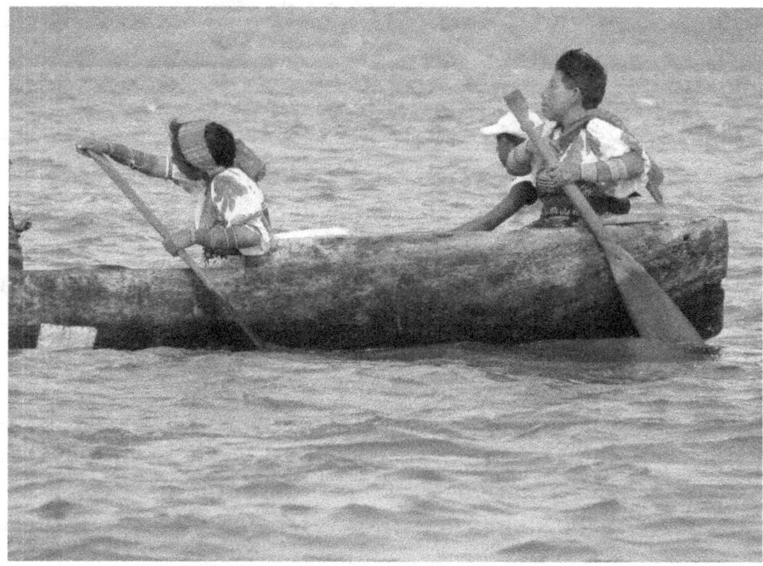

Dugouts offer the only transportation between islands

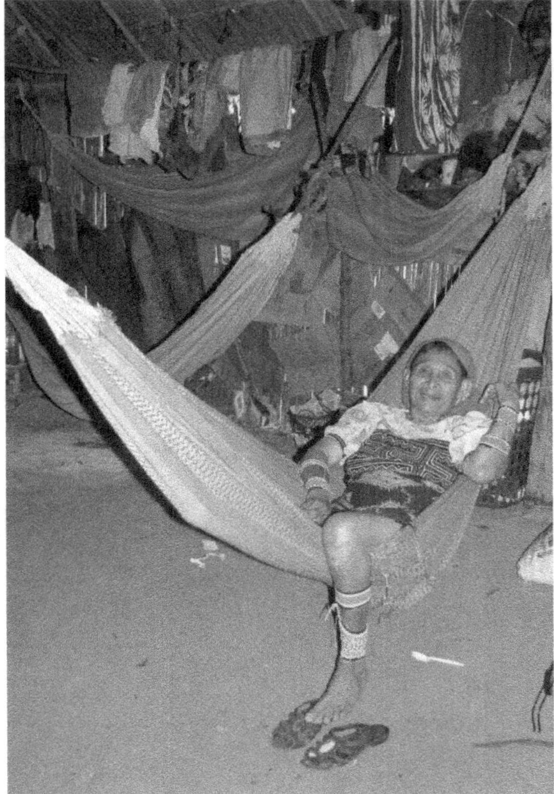

Afternoon naptime

Inside the buses, feather boas draped across the dashboards and around photos of Jesus or new babies. Pairs of baby shoes crowded dozens of strands of Christmas lights. Dangling pieces of glass prisms sent rainbows to every passenger. Signs in Spanish hung above the driver's head with blessings for a safe journey. Bus drivers needed those signs. They all acted like trainees for a NASCAR racetrack!

While manipulating the manual door openers, searching for CDs, changing money, and giving directions, our driver's hand rested on the horn as he swerved around other vehicles, zipped in and out of lanes, and swooped across the road to pick up new passengers.

The co-pilot, or passenger-hustler, hung out the door with a foot and hand wrapped around a metal bar and used the other hand to wave and shout to anyone standing close to the road. He used his boundless, youthful energy to stuff everything from baskets of chickens to people into every available place on the bus.

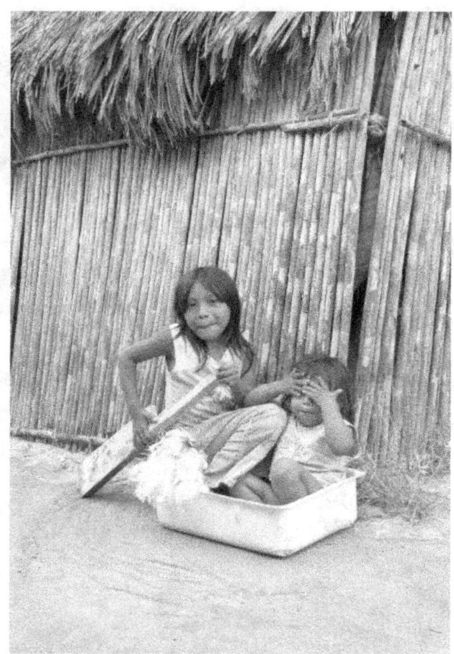

Paddling a pretend boat

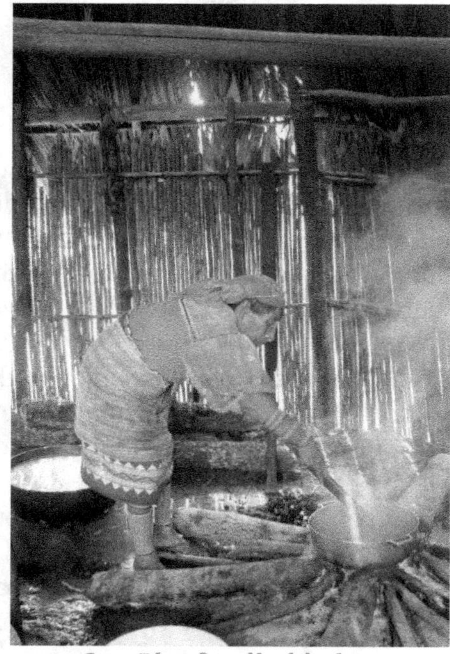

San Blas family kitchen

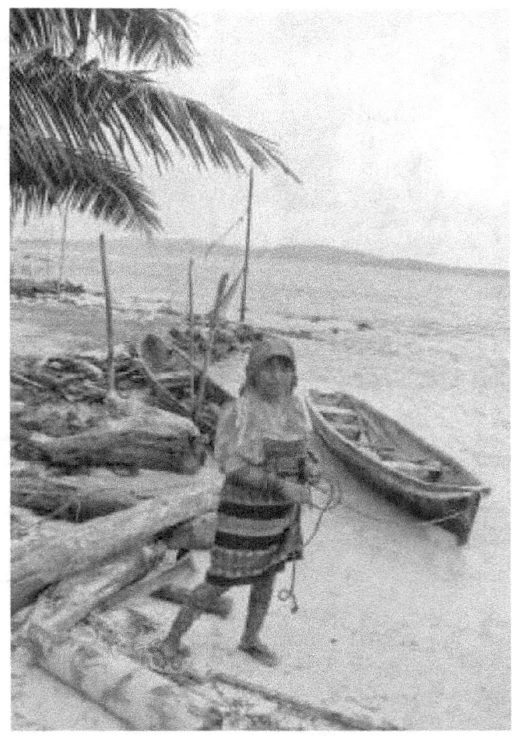

Preparing for high tide

"The desire for safety stands against every great and noble enterprise." Tacitus.

Apprehension oozed from my senses as I boarded my red devil, knowing that by day's end, I would reach the borderline of the Darien Gap, the end of the earth for Panama.

Seeing a television monitor hanging to the right of the driver's head meant one horrible thing: The captured audience was forced to listen to music or movies so loud that even the goats tied on the outside roof wanted to dance!

The bus driver kept the temperature *mucho frio,* or very cold, in order to remain awake (I guess).

This made the stops to stretch legs, and to find disgusting outhouses for toilet breaks, challenging. This was worse for me because I wore a tight-wound sarong and sweatshirt.

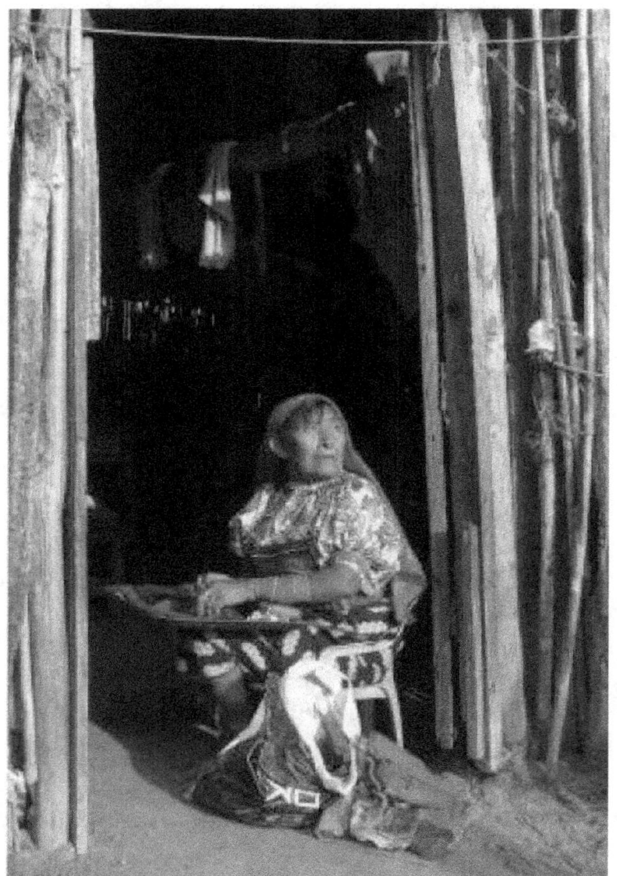

Her embroidery reflected her imagination

Soda pop transferred to plastic bags, with the sides tied around a straw, saved buyers from paying a deposit on glass bottles.

Next to me, a young mother tried to funnel orange soda pop into her baby's bottle, but with the bus driver, swerving our vehicle all over the road, she was not able to do such a great job of it.

The orange, bubbling liquid felt cold as it dripped on my tennis shoes. Weaving in and out of the steady red of brake lights, the driver tested the tempting shoulder of the road, affording him the opportunity to veer back into traffic without notice or regard.

Although, at times the road narrowed to a single lane drivers ignored common rules of courtesy and safety, creating six lanes, sometimes all going the same direction.

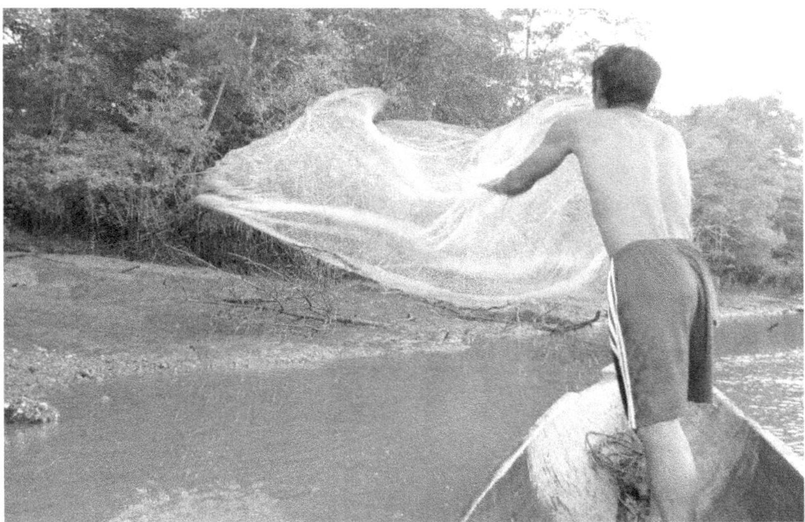

Fish provide much needed protein

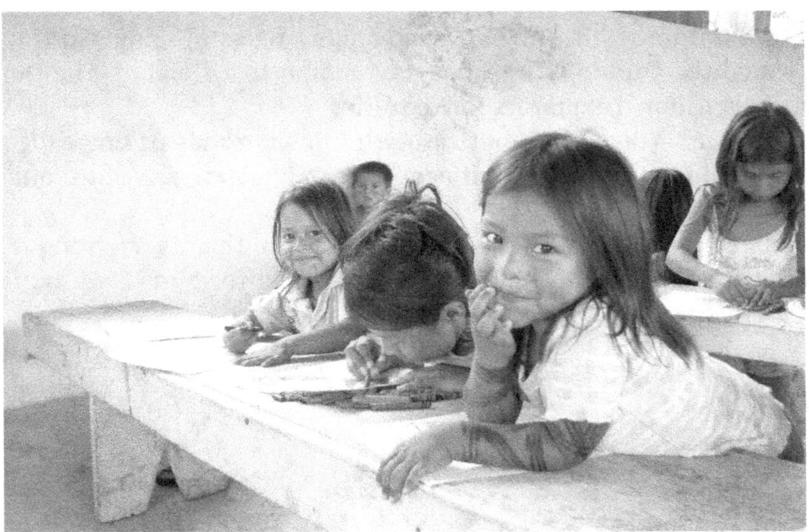

Coloring in school

Across the aisle, a young boy held a shoebox, like a treasure chest of gold, never setting it down the entire trip. Inside, a bird protested the claustrophobic quarters with non-stop, irritating chirping.

Six hours later, road dust floated into windows duct-taped open. The bus station for Meteti, the last decent town before the end of the road in the Darien

Gap, consisted of small *chivas,* or pickup trucks, working their way in circles with drivers yelling out their routes.

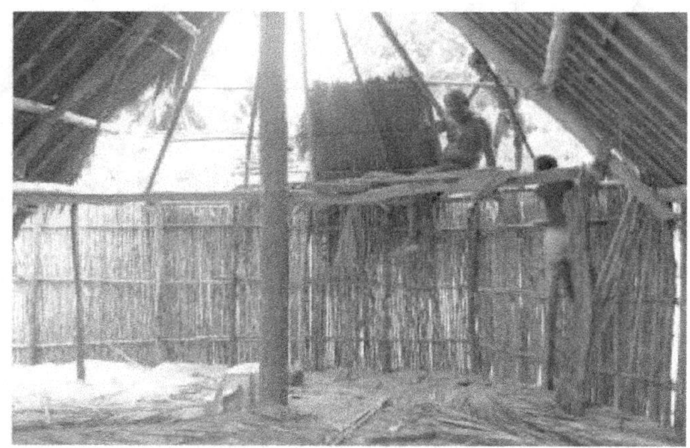

Son, helping dad rebuild roof

Wild and untamed, the ten thousand square miles of undeveloped, steamy jungle, called the Darien Gap, connects Panama to Colombia. The Darien has voraciously consumed explorers for centuries.

Harsh and assertive, the jungle growth inhibits roads or any other type of civilization, but it encourages fugitives, drug smugglers, guerrillas, and jaguars like a magnet.

This gap creates a land bridge between two continents, creating a mixing-ground for animals of both Americas and a funnel for birds that migrate over the land between them.

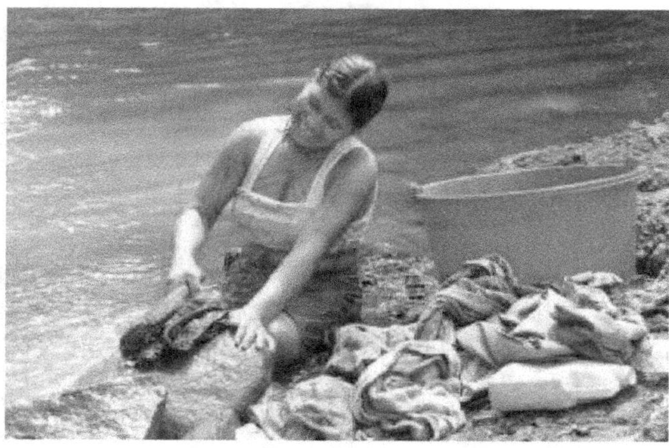

Pounding clothing clean

The Chocó Indians, now known as the Embera and Wounaan, number close to 17,000, having survived smallpox and other diseases the Spaniards brought over.

They live deep in the heart of the Darien, close to river basins, very much the same as their ancestors lived during the days of Christopher Columbus, guarding generations of secrets.

Both tribes have similar lifestyles, painting their upper bodies with *Jagua*, a dye coming from a local fruit that lasts about a month before needing reapplication.

These tribes have made significant contributions to humankind's pharmaceutical medicine chest.

Because of these tribes and their botanical skills from living in the forest, scientists and researchers gain knowledge indispensable to people in today's world.

The modern birth control pill comes from the Central America yam.

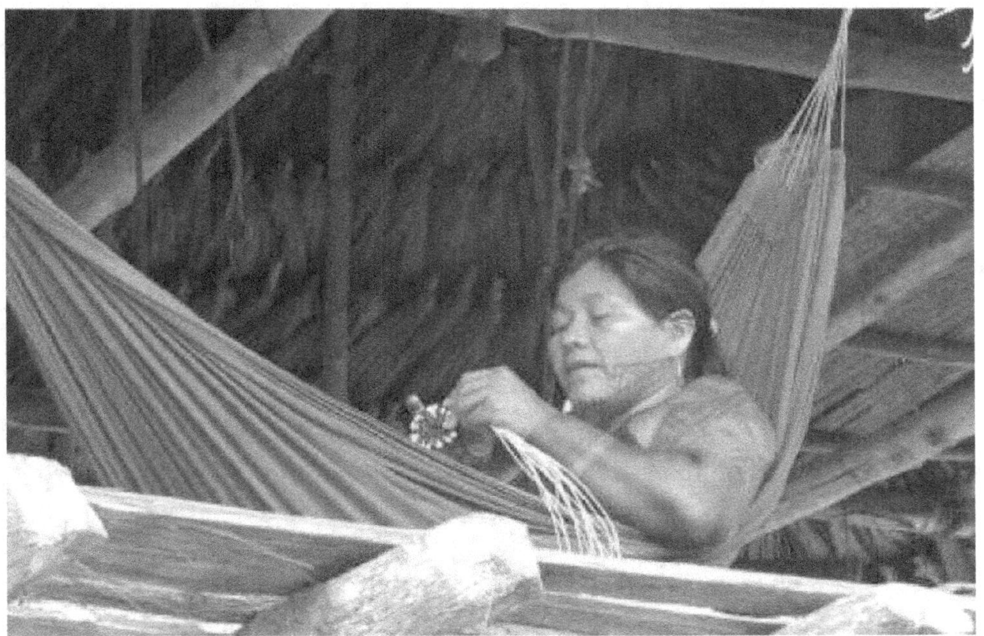

Elaborate basket making

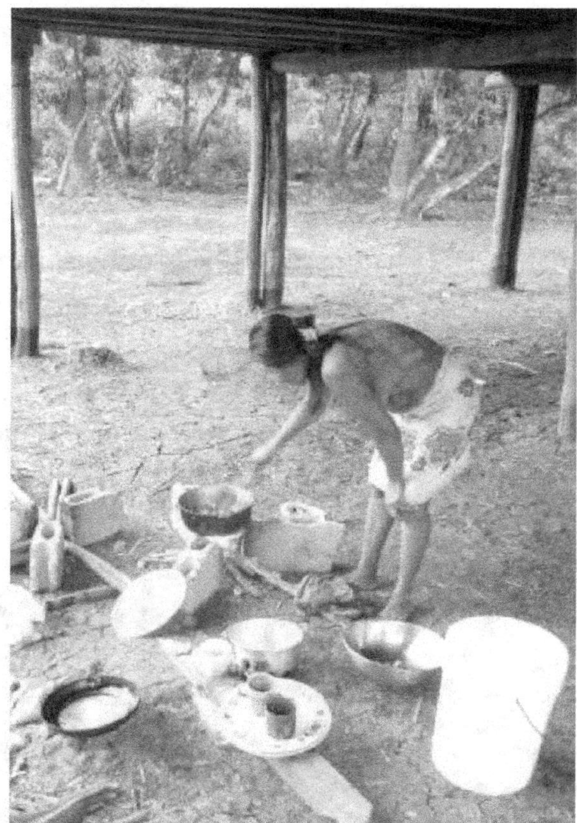

Building a fire for dinner

Regarded as master artisans, the Embera weave incredible baskets valued at thousands of dollars on display in museums and galleries worldwide.

Their imagination, inspired by the exotic plants and animals of the rainforest, runs wild, especially with their carvings made out of tagua nuts or vegetable ivory.

Natural dyes (like red from the achiote and orange from seedpods) color the figures and baskets.

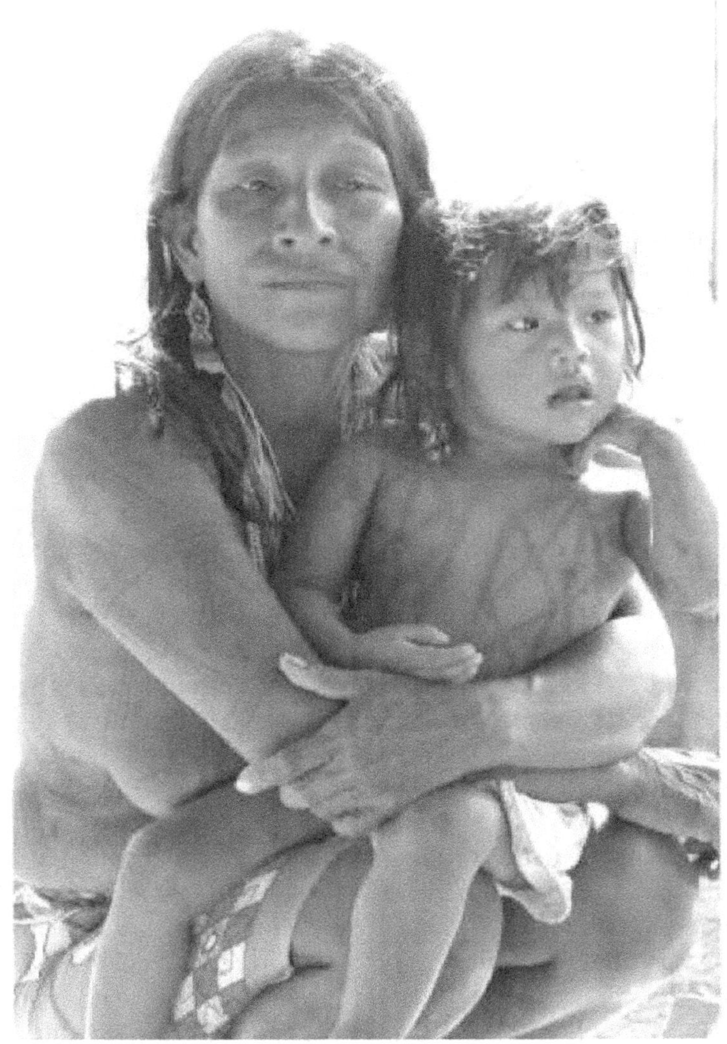

Tattooed bodies of the Darien

Embera teach their young sons the skill of woodcarving to fashion canoes, paddles, furniture, and weapons like blowguns to use with the poison gathered from the tiny orange-and-green tree frog.

A man, dressed in camouflage with a few badges on his shirt, waved for me to follow him. He carried a fat notebook of bent pages and wrote notes as we walked across the street to a rickety structure shaded by its tin roof. "Pas-saporte," insisted another man, sitting at a table with lips matching the curve in his eyebrows. He saw the passport and questioned, "Americano?"

I nodded and listened as the two conversed in Spanish back and forth in argumentative tones. After a half hour of captivity, Sad Face flopped a registry book in front of me with a pencil. The camouflaged man swatted at flies on the hunt for lunch. I gave them a gracious smile, much more than they deserved, considering their strange and lackluster attitude. A wood sign, declaring the town's name, Meteti, squeaked on its hinges.

Now, for about a dollar, we tried to find a pickup truck to Puerto Quimba, a small port on the Rio Iglesias River, and to catch a boat, for double that amount, to La Palma. Nineteen kilometers later, I found myself renting a boat. The sun, hot on my skin, told me the day offered plenty of time for the boat trip and for my introduction to the mangroves and river life in the Darien. Although La Palma holds the title of capital for the largest province in Panama, its police station, airstrip, hospital, restaurants, and few hotels fill one street.

La Palma sits at the mouth of the Golfo de San Miguel, the actual site where the first European, Balboa, discovered the Pacific Ocean. Unless a visitor speaks fluent Spanish, traveling upriver to share the world of the Embera tribes necessitates hiring a guide and/or boat driver.

Casa Ramady offered an adequate twenty-five-dollar-a-night room with a balcony view that outweighed in aesthetics the inconvenience of the cold showers. A cold marinated *ceviche,* or raw fish stew, sat behind a counter in the reception area and smelled so strong I started digging for protein bars in my pack for dinner.

We arranged for the boat to take us to the mouth of the Rio Sambu through the son of the hotel owner, who knew a friend of a friend for a "cheap" price. The crew exchanged their fast boat for a small dugout canoe in order to reach the primitive, isolated Embera *comarcas,* or traditional regions, upriver on the Rio Sambu. People or goods entering this far-removed place arrive according to the timing of the next boat on the river, their commercial highway. The Embera leaders in Puerto Indio, located across a shaky bridge from the tiny town of Sambu, approve travel into the comarcas. Strict regulations, requiring registration fees for future travels, govern the area.

Not far upriver from Sambu, the Village of Caresia, an authentic Embera village, sat two kilometers from the river. The boat beached on the shallow rock ledge of the river, and the guide pointed in the direction of a sandy path, smelling of horses. A yellow-and-blue macaw squawked as the sound of my feet cracking branches interrupted his noontime siesta. The impenetrable jungle acts as a funnel for migratory birds from both north and south. Tall rubber boots protected my feet and legs from poisonous snakes, roots from unruly jungle growth, and slimy streams. Long pants and sleeves, sticky from sweat, clung to my skin like a tight bathing suit. A hallway enclosed with dripping leaves circled past a waterfall.

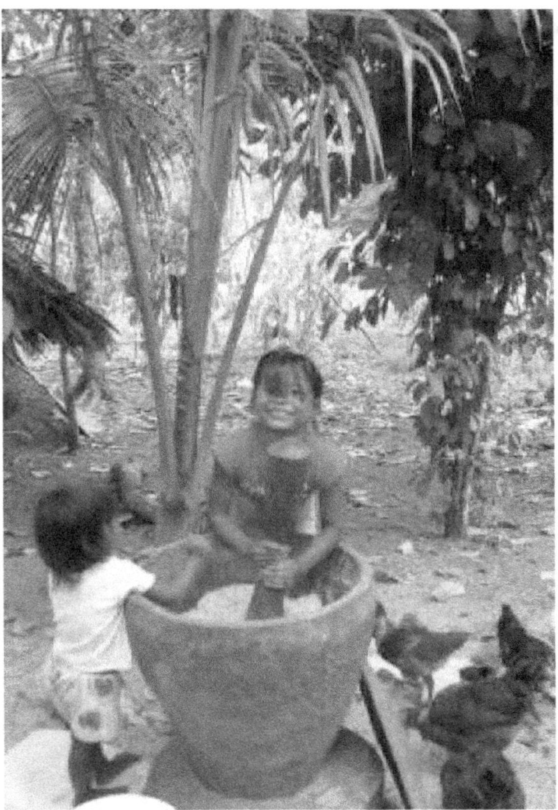

Crushing grain

A warm welcome greeted me as I passed by little thatched roofs, covering open-aired huts on stilts. Villagers smiled and sometimes waved me inside, wanting to share a hammock or offering to "tattoo" my face or arms with their homemade dyes.

Children took my hands and pulled me forward, wanting me to run to the next hut or down an embankment to see several women beating clothing on rocks. I have never understood how beating fabric on rocks helps get the articles clean!

Children jumped off the top of the small hill into the river, squealing and splashing, their mothers unresponsive to their antics.

Not too far from the river, villagers invited me inside their hut by climbing a narrow tree branch ladder. Its notched steps led to the interior of their hut about ten feet off the ground. Weaving a basket, a woman lay in a hammock swinging as she hummed.

"May I take a picture?" My words evaporated quickly.

Embera gibberish bounced off the wide palm leaves of the hut. Modern researchers reduced the language to written form.

A teenage girl came close, pointed to my camera, nodded her head up and down, and ran to the back of the thirty-foot-long, open hut.

Her clothing, a short piece of fabric wrapped around her waist, was not appropriate for modeling for the camera. A handful of plastic necklaces caught a sliver of sun as I searched for the exact spot to reflect its light back into the room.

The girl slipped a tee shirt, belonging to her ten-year-old brother, snuggly over her bare breasts. The strands of beads clashed with the huge, green, alien face on the shirt. River water washings had caused the green, rubbery edges of the design to work free. I wanted to pull some of those loose ends, which reminded me of peeling sunburn!

She combed her hair with a hand-carved wooden comb and smeared red achiote paste on her lips

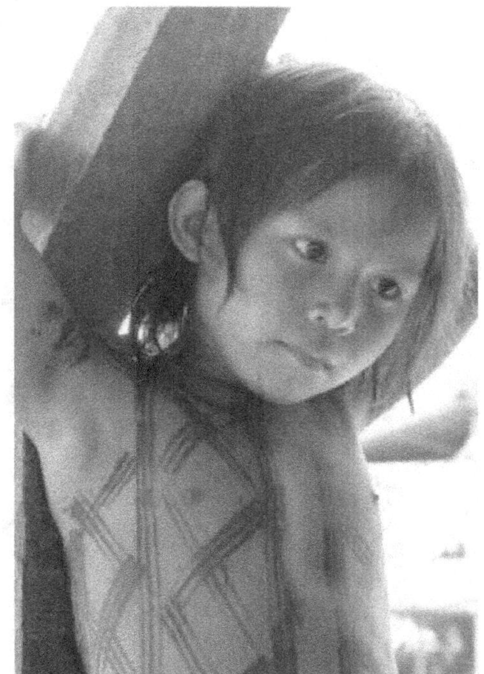

Natural dye tattoos wear off after a month

She stood straight as a board, without expression, a few feet in front of me, wanting her picture taken.

However, her excitement exceeded the noise level of the rest of the group as she viewed herself, perfectly manicured, on the back of the digital camera screen. Lacking a sense of pride in their culture's traditions, most teenagers envy the presence of modern toys, hanging around tourists' necks or hugging tourists' ears.

Prayer flags (a hundred pieces of colored fabric, flapping in every direction) filled the hut. Without closets or shelves, every article owned by the family had a place on a sharp piece of bamboo stuck in some crack, draped on a line, or piled on pillows in hammocks. The girl's sister, or maybe daughter, about three years old, kneeled at a plastic pot full of dishes and water.

While trying to pay attention to the teenage girl, begging for communication from me, I noticed this little girl washing the dishes with a rag and stacking them every which way on the floor to dry. The brother handed me his puppy. He must have thought that I loved dogs because I spent time talking puppy talk with the dog when I walked past the house earlier.

I started a game I liked to play with children of any culture, using my hands and a takeoff of "Simon Says." Children pick up the idea of copying my motions and listen when I say, "Stop," in their language.

The mother's nimble fingers never ceased weaving, as she watched the interaction between the present and the past that took place before her.

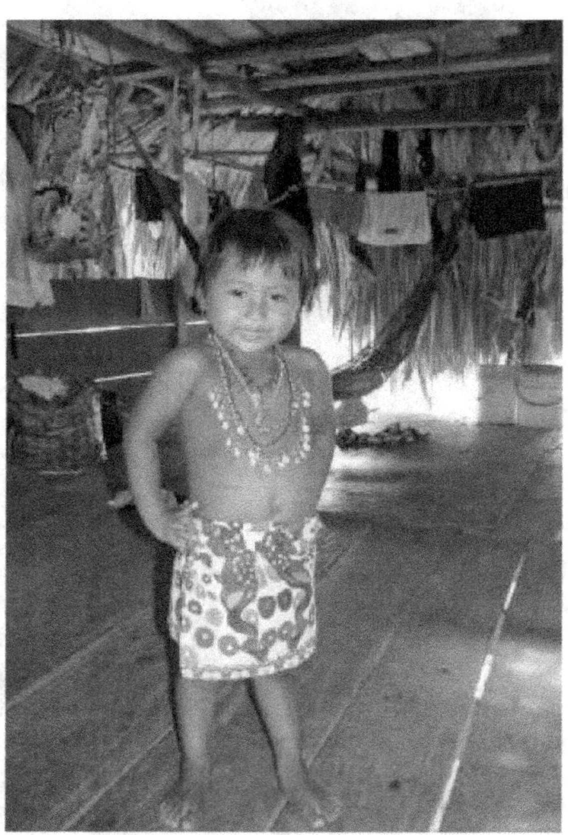

Dressing up for the camera

After the open reception to village life in Cesarios, my excitement swelled, thinking about spending a few days in just one village and taking the time to get to know a few families. Two hours upriver, the Village of Churoco (the name I recalled) sank into darkness while my two boat drivers assured me in soft, untranslatable words that we could get there before dark. My empty stomach reminded me that along with welcoming smiles I needed food. With every new group of shapes on the horizon, I expected to turn toward the shore, secure the boat, and find families wanting to share their hut for a few days. The Darien opened the door to one of the last wild frontiers, punctuated with tears of fears and joy. Several hours passed as tree shapes against the night sky changed from interesting to ugly, frightening black ghosts. How would the boatmen ever find a village without cell phones or landmark signs in this sinister gloom?

Shaking from wet spray and the cold mist, hovering over the water, I tried to control my imagination, running wild with thoughts of crocodiles lining up for their dinner after the boatmen lost their balance, causing the boat to capsize.

What if the boat hit a log in this angry darkness? Would I make it to shore where machine-gun-toting guerillas stood? If Robert Pelton, author of "The World's Most Dangerous Places," experienced kidnapping in the Darien, why not me? Calm down. Take deep breaths.

Through a wet, thick fog, a blurry shoreline appeared, illuminated by a fire pit. The distinct smell of food cooking awakened my senses. I sat up straight and braced my feet against the wood sides of the boat, waiting for the boat to hit land.

Scratch-thump! The boat slid into shore. Three cheers to the boatmen! A few huts stood naked against the black jungle, and it wrapped them in silence for the night.

Women, their naked breasts tattooed, presented me with a huge bowl of cooked vegetables and rice as I stepped onto shore.

The wood-floored hut with thatched roof gave me a new appreciation for home sweet home.

Still too nervous for sleep, I wrote by candlelight about some of my unforgettable experiences downriver, like the walk through a forest of decayed buttress trees, protecting millions of tiny crabs, making their way to the mouth of the river.

"To strive, to seek, to find, and not to yield." Tennyson's words sheltered me, along with a mosquito net for the protection of my sweet blood. Fear allowed my watchful eyes to remain on the lookout for movement, perhaps from a wild rodent with a sweet tooth.

My dried fruits soothed my soul when the trail led to a dead end. I have had rats and mice eat huge holes in my canvass luggage to sample my protein bars in countries like Burma and Papua New Guinea.

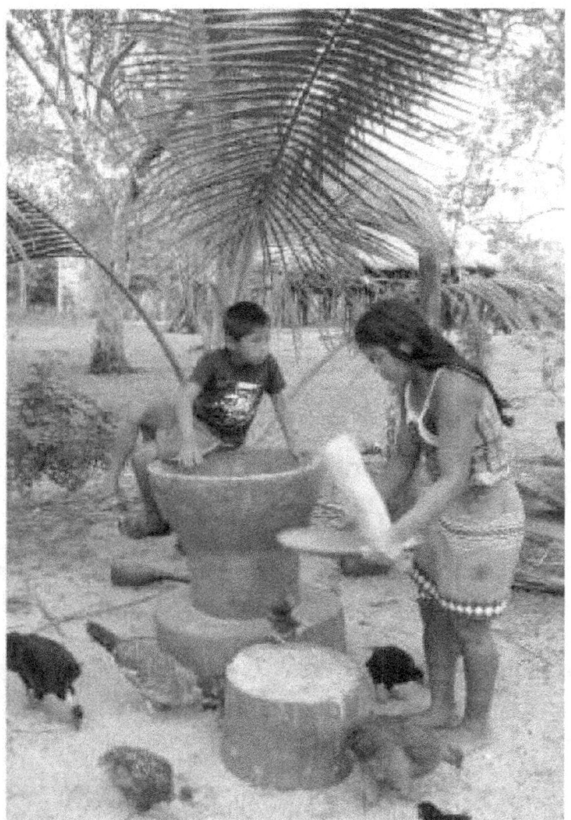

Sifting rice kernels

Hearty explorers bathed in the virgin waters of the Sambu River. A bucket of river water met my needs quite nicely. Suspicious eyes disappeared after the first day of my wandering the village. River-fishing walks to visit neighboring families, and an invitation to meet the local medicine man for explanations of medicinal plants and their uses, gave me opportunities to understand the pride these Embera people felt.

The huts, open on several sides, offered me hours of entertainment. Young men, carving the tagua nut with slivers of bamboo or crude knives, sat with crossed legs.

Their creations detailed parrots, turtles, monkeys, and other rainforest creatures painted in severe fuchsia with lime green wings or tails.

The color combinations needed help. I pointed to a white nut and then to a toucan, hoping one young man would understand my wish to buy a non-painted carving. His big brown eyes went back to carving. A group of watchful men gathered under the same roof of a hut in the center of the village.

A couple worked on shapes of horses using Cocobolo wood. *Trupa* palm oil finished the carvings beautifully. The profitable craft of basket-making filled the days of most Embera women.

Children made games in which one could strip the youngest leaves off the stems of palms while mothers prepared natural dyes using roots and plants. *Naguala,* sometimes called the Panama hat palm, provided a flexible inner coil. The basket-makers came up with original designs, planned as they wove, without the help of computer-generated programs, pencil, or paper. A couple of exquisite baskets bordered the edge of an open-air hut. I had to pinch myself when I was told the price was two thousand dollars!

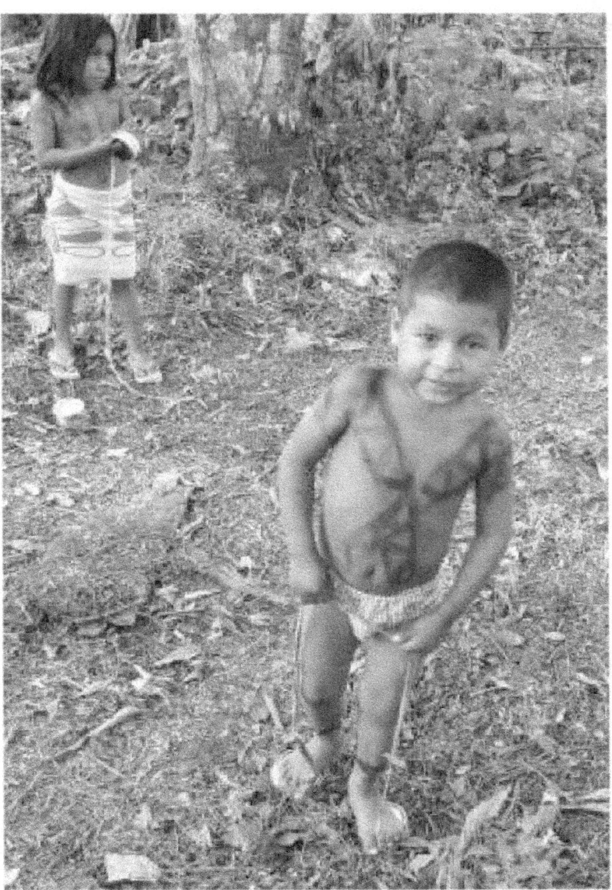

Walking on tin cans looped with string

A group of little girls grabbed my hand, wanting me to watch them play a "London Bridge is Falling Down" game. They all fell to the ground, giggling when they would encircle a child, and then jump up to start again. Two girls had strips of fabric they used like wings when floating around the others.

Looking for an outhouse meant sharpening my sense of smell while walking behind huts. The one in view had legs showing under the half door.

No problem. I decided to wait my turn as a photo opportunity unveiled itself behind me. Several children balanced their tiny bare feet on top of tin cans, holding on to ropes tied through openings in the sides of the cans.

The littlest of the group kept falling off, but the bigger ones reached down, retied the rope, and encouraged her to get back on.

What an imagination these children conjured up from basic articles of trash! Spending time with the Embera stirs a deep compassion for their ability to pass on to future generations their beautiful culture.

Their respect for the environment that sustains them inspires their lives. Mother Nature guides the Emberas as a best friend and teacher. The Embera satisfied my yearning for exposure to a simple way of living within the wilds of a jungle.

CHAPTER TEN

China: Disappointment Scarcely Acknowledged

"Most travel, & certainly the rewarding kind, involves the kindness of strangers, putting yourself in the hands of people you don't know and trusting them with your life. The risky suspension of disbelief is often an experience freighted with anxiety. But what are the alternatives? Often, there are none"
Paul Theroux

Subject: Arrival in Hong Kong 8:24 p.m.
Hi all,

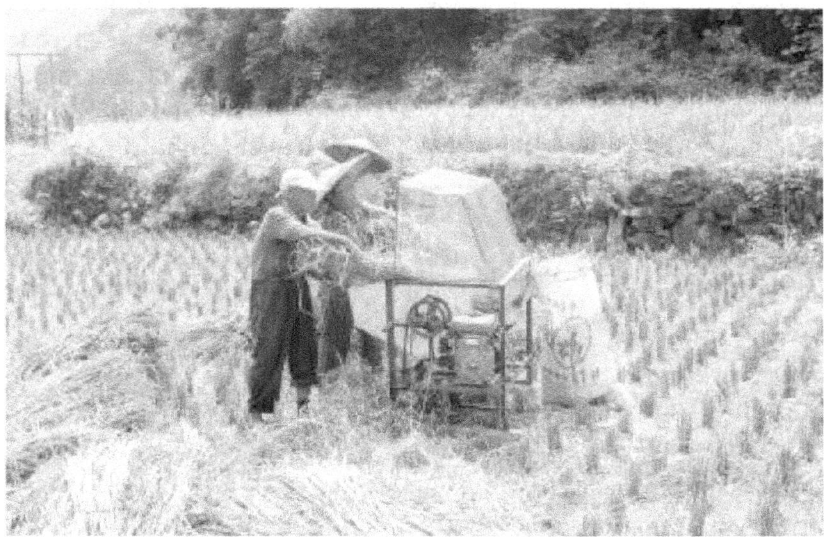

Mechanical threshing separates grain from rice straw in Lijiang

Arrived safely, after sixteen hours in the air, five movies, and three meals. Very comfortable flight, and time passed so fast it almost scares me. After checking with a few hotel booths still open, I found that the fast train into Hong Kong/Kowloon for a cheap hotel would cost about $60 round trip, and the cheapest hotel might cost around $50. Opted for a first-class lounge with private room, luxurious feather bed, and shower. The walls made of silk fabrics and some with slits of bamboo invited my touch. Little slippers wrapped in plastic waited for tiny feet to enjoy. All the food and internet I could scarf down

before flight time for a little less than hassling with figuring out the way to find a hotel after getting off the
train, at midnight at that! I had tea sandwiches, fresh fruit, soft drinks and cookies before bed and woke to a hot breakfast of Chinese sausages, poached eggs, lettuce salad, and handfuls of butter cookies! Maybe my last "real" food for a while!

Leave this morning for Shangri La, China, the last outpost before Tibet, so I'll experience high altitude about 12,000' and temps a little chilly, in the fifties maybe. Tibet has a reputation as one of the most beautiful places in the world, but the Tibetans don't like tourists and make it difficult to travel within their country by imposing huge fees for travel. One has to hire a guide or stay with a group, which averages about $300 a day per person. Not sure how I'll do in that high altitude so never wanted to experiment.

I will get to see the lifestyle of Tibetans, as it is different from that of the rural Chinese on the rest of my itinerary. It's a four-day bus or two-day train ride to Shangri La so opted for a flight instead to save time for more travel.

Hong Kong has a high cost of living, and I don't see how the common person can afford to live here. I managed to pack most of my own food somehow in carry-on luggage so I will not have to worry about asking if the soup contains cat, rat or dog.

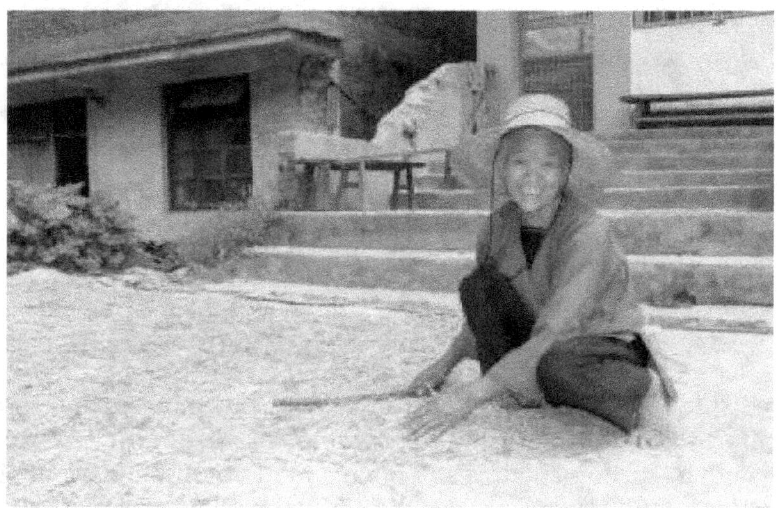

Beating rice kernels off rice stems-PingBu Village

I'm sending this to friends who may wonder what I'm doing. Let me know if you'd like off this list.

James Hilton wrote the book, *Lost Horizon*, in 1937, calling his happy isolated town, Shangri La. Hilton wrote his book based on stories he read by Joseph Rock, an explorer of the southwestern provinces of China. The Chinese government renamed the town of Zongdian to Shangri La based on claims from the book. The monastery in the book sits on the outskirts of Shangri La. If anyone wants to see the movie, most libraries carry it. It's in black and white, and they omitted some of the pieces when they tried to put it together, so some spots include still shots of the actors where they filled in the missing spots.

The movie tells the story of a group of people whose plane crashes in the mountains of Tibet. Groups of Sherpas meet the plane and transport them to this paradise they call Shangri La, which seems like an oasis of beauty, with sunshiny days and warm people so content the group becomes startled and envious. Worth watching!

I anticipate, with excitement, the journey ahead, while I ask myself at the same time, "How in the world did I get here and why?" Just one other "tourist" on my flight from Los Angeles, so I know that the trip offers a unique opportunity that most don't take advantage of. About flight time for sure now, so better click send. I do not want to lose this "connection" with all my friends, so until next time.... Warm regards to all, jackie/mom

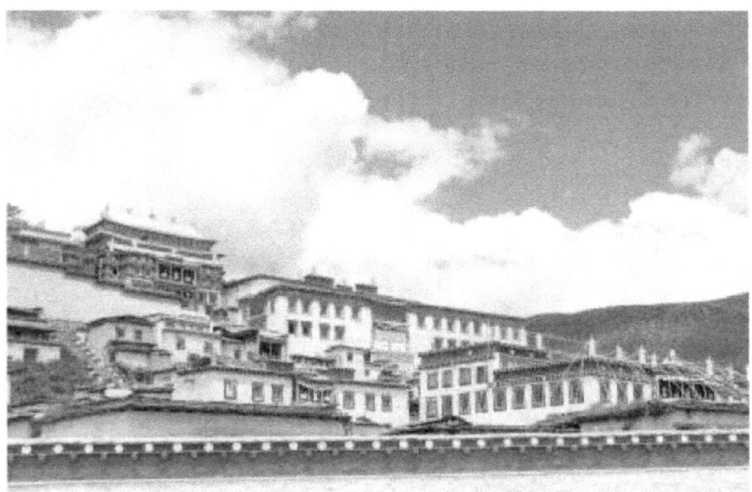

300-year-old Ganden Sumtseling Gompa Monastery: 600 monks

Subject: Shangri La 7:31 a.m.

Hi all,

Spent the day in one of the most remarkable places I have ever experienced. Arrived in Shangri La late last night, and the taxi driver had to make two stops to ask for directions to my little budget guesthouse ($12). The helpful owner offered all kinds of info on how to see via bicycle the local Tibetan farmers with their yaks a few miles from here.

The cool weather? Well, the pilot announced the temperature at fifty-nine degrees, but I know he meant thirty-nine! Lucky me, however, the owner said the beds had electric blankets.

Not sure if the roosters would win a popularity contest by crowing at 3:00 a.m. or the dogs, by barking for attention all night long. Hot scrambled eggs and blueberry tea started the day before the journey to the huge monastery, housing 600 monks in the mountains.

Not long after finding the bus stop, I smiled as bus #3 arrived, heading to the Ganden Sumtseling Gompa Monastery this morning.

Little alleyways and open doors invited me to wander in on a whim for a taste of monk living. Dark orange robes with bald heads showed up every so often between stone walls, peering out of windows, or sometimes walking past! On two occasions, I received blessings from the eldest of the monks with a hand-made string necklace tied around my neck and later a hand-carved beaded bracelet slipped over my wrist.

Painted walls told of the lifestyle of the Tibetans in every nook and cranny. Ribbons, silk sashes, and braided ropes wrapped photos and paintings by the hundreds. Candles and incense filled every building.

Bowls of sacred water for sprinkling on carved objects sat next to containers of small soft rocks to scoop up and drop with care over miniature silver temples for good luck.

Ornate gold-leaf statues guarded every empty space.

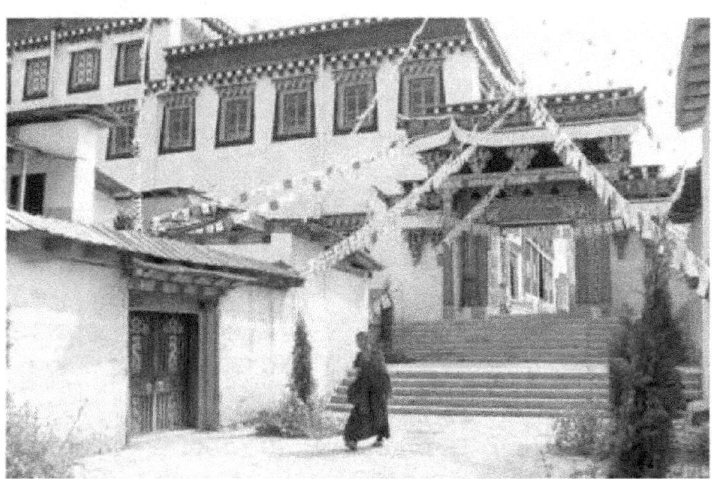

Prayer flags flutter in the Ganden Sumtseling Gompa Monastery

Words can't describe the feelings that fill your every sense as monks chant or swirl prayer wheels or giggle with each other behind closed curtains, acting their age, as some appear very young.

My hotel owner said this place compares to Tibet, more so than Tibet itself. The people here live the active, traditional Tibetan lifestyle, unguarded and more content than the people dealing with the weather and natural hardships high in the mountains.

Most women here wear the beautiful pink or red padded headdresses and have light skin and faces that are flatter than the traditional Chinese. They're very easy to recognize.

I've learned a few words already in Tibetan. *Thoo jaychay* means thank you and *tashi dele* means hello. I'm still practicing the pronunciation.

Tomorrow I'll ride a bike into the countryside for a glimpse into the past. I'm told I'll see yaks and common Tibetan farmers, as well as other sights of this time-forgotten culture.

Have to close for now and catch up on journaling.

Warm regards to all, jackie/mom

Subject: Shangri La 6:31 a.m.

Hello all,

While I enjoyed some muesli, fried eggs and blueberry tea for breakfast, a woman in her forties joined me.

I first apologized for our wet tablecloth as I poured boiling water in a cup with EmergenC, vitamin C powder, which fizzed all over the table.

What a story she had to tell. While biking alone into Tibet, she met dogs that attacked her after going over the pass, and she had to catch a bus and come back down the pass to Shangri La.

I can't even imagine having the courage to bike into Tibet alone on such hilly, narrow roads.

Her explanation of always going uphill convinced me to turn away from the idea of joining her!

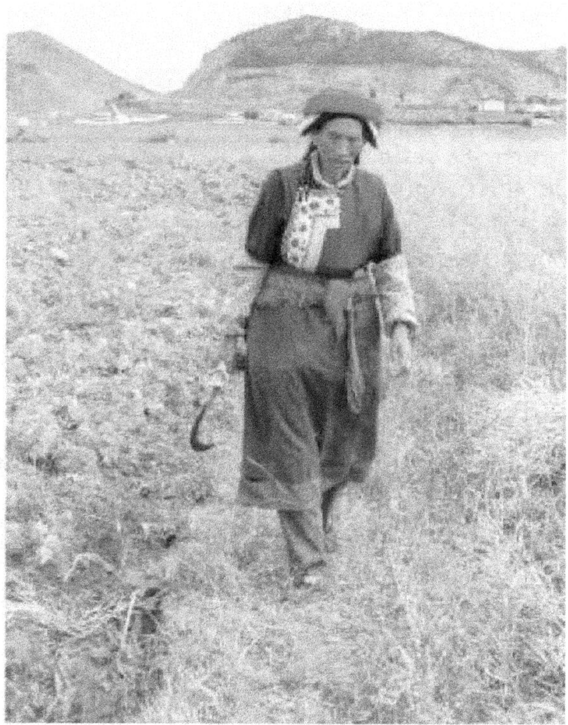

Tibetan cutting yak grass in Shangri La

Okay, so now comes the tricky part of the day. Figuring out how to get into the countryside, and to experience the real Tibetan way of living offered my first challenge of the day.

Long story, but the driver I decided to hire instead of taking a local bus, charged me ten times the local price and dropped me at a tourist spot complete with a cable car for viewing some "Blue Moon Valley" for $30! I decided that to see the countryside I needed to get out in it.

I had him drop me when we passed a herd of yak grazing along the road. Huge brass bells hung from the necks of every yak. The large beasts searched for that perfect patch of green, while their bells orchestrated a melody, fit for heaven. Another kilometer of walking and Tibetan life began to breathe right before me.

A young woman high on wood vertical rails stood waiting for her husband to throw to her bunches of winter grass for storage. Her husband, standing in his tractor-trailer, eyed me with caution as I inched my way forward, missing piles of yak dung, puddles of mud and tall weeds.

Within range of hearing, I said often, *"ni hao, ni hao,"* meaning hello, and their apprehension turned to smiles. The man nodded before I could even point to the camera.

A few pics and *shay shay* for thanks and their waves gave me the incentive to move on for more of the same. Oops, can't remember, but I think "thank you" sounded like *jei jei*.

The vertical racks looked empty heading into the countryside, so seeing them filled for the winter storage of grass for the yaks answered my questions concerning a use for weird-looking rails fifteen feet off the ground.

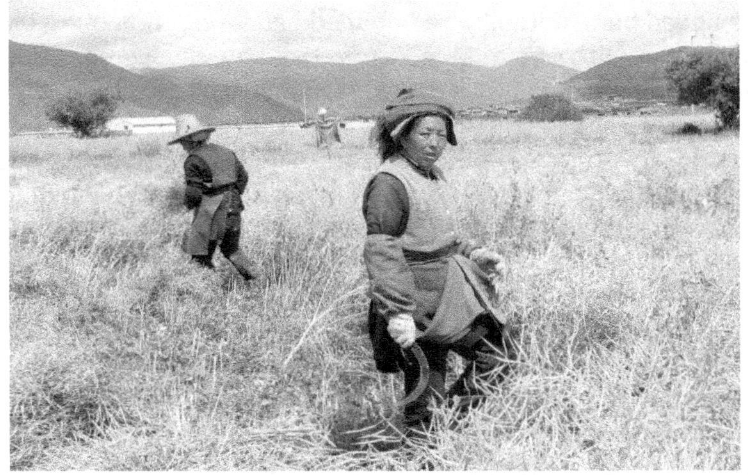

Tibetans, working fields outside Shangri La

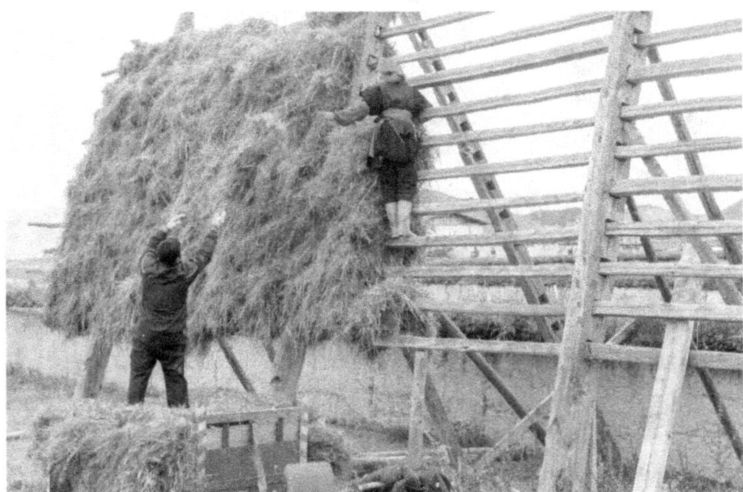

Tibetans, storing winter yak grass Shangri La

A few more kilometers and fields of scarecrows caught my attention, as the women bent at the waist with sickles, cutting grass, looked more like mounds of weeds, topped with red flowers. The bodies without heads shouted phrases back and forth until my approach changed their posture to upright, almost fearful, frozen stances. Waiting for a change in my activity, their stares led me to adopt a slow walk past them, as Tibetans don't like their pictures taken.

Again, "knee how" broke the ice, and they began their rhythmic motion of bending, cutting, standing, piling mounds, and bending again. One woman opted for a break, pausing to remove her gloves and tall rubber boots, followed by digging deep into her apron for an apple.

She removed her traditional red padded headdress, revealing two more layers of fabric, wet with sweat. Men, across the way, moved yaks to greener pastures by yanking the long ropes tied to prevent them from roaming too far from home.

Sticky and sweaty despite the high-altitude weather, I decided to try a local "bus" for the return to the hotel to reclaim my luggage stored behind a counter. A local bus made the ride to the town bus station easy and cheap. The bus station, unlike most remote stations, offered a clean and safe environment for the wait for my four-hour bus ride to Lijiang, my next stop on this incredible journey. Starting above the tree line, the bus meandered its way down alongside a roaring river, threading itself through the dark green of a million trees, gardens, and hillside rice terraces. I send good health wishes to everyone. Please touch base with me often. I like a reminder of the familiar in my life. Take sweet care,
jackie/mom

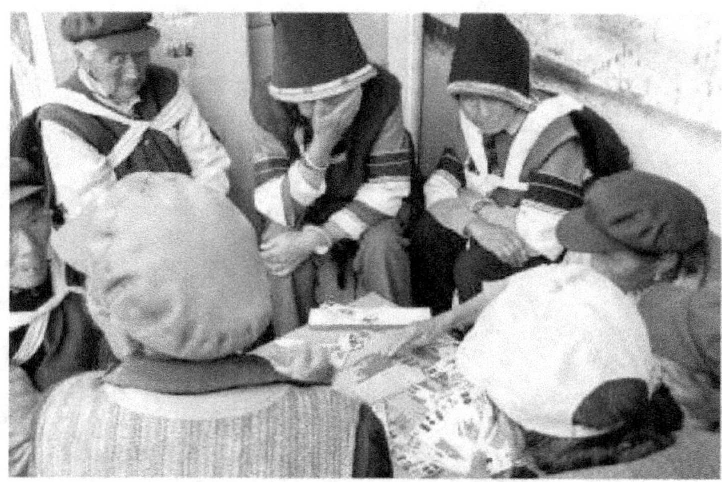

Playing cards on a Baisha street corner

Subject: Lijiang 4:32 p.m.

Hi All:

Rain, rain, go away...great day for catching up but bad news from the train station as I can't get a train to Kunming at all and sure don't like the idea of an eleven-hour bus ride, although it has advantages as it is a sleeper bus with beds. After that, I take a long journey to Guillen and not sure as of yet if I can even get there via train but will try to figure that out. Every time I get my shoes out in the sun for about thirty minutes, the rains start again, and they get even wetter! Yikes, what's a girl to do?

Will spend most of the day catching up on writing in my journal. The house girl at this place gave me a pear, so I brought it back to my room and peeled it with my own knife. It tasted delicious. Mamma's Guesthouse staff kept giving me fruit. I do not know why, as the girl from Germany had greater hunger needs than I did (she came in late last night) and hadn't eaten any fruit on her trip. I gave her the banana the staff had given me and told her I'd give her an apple later today. I have to give this woman from Germany so much credit for spending several weeks biking all alone in China. And I thought I was gutsy?

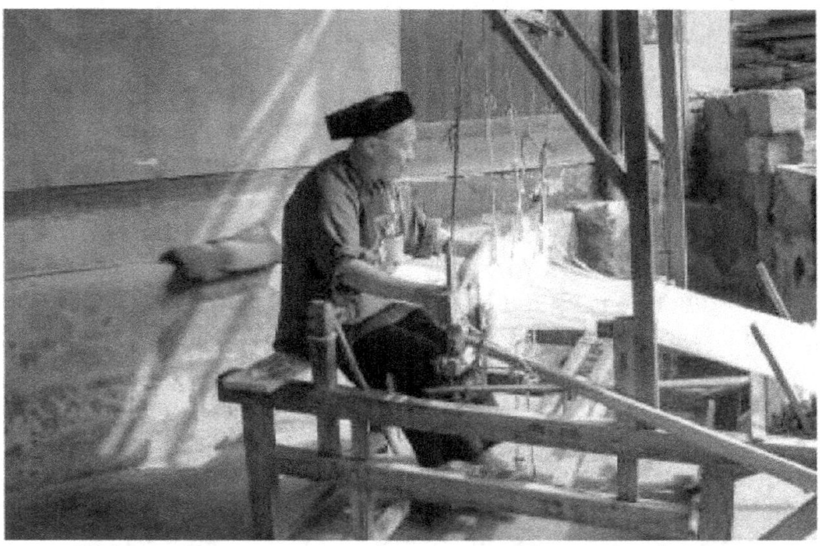

Hidden alleyways reveal century-old weaving looms

She leaves tomorrow. The noise bothers her. They put her in the other guesthouse beside this one, with groups of young backpackers who make noise all night long. I sleep alone in this place as the rooms cost a few dollars more, and the backpackers can't afford the expense here, so yippee! I can sleep at night.

I have a scenic balcony and a daily pot of hot water for my tea right outside my door. A miniature table with child-sized chairs looks down into a courtyard with plants and vines. Cats balance like tightrope walkers across the tops of the tile roofs.

Budget guesthouses or hotels offer a unique experience. I try to spend less than ten dollars for a room, which gives me privacy and often a private bathroom but no hot water, although I do have it here at Mama's Guesthouse. The dorm rooms cost only around three dollars, but noise and lack of privacy keep me from saving money at my age. The camaraderie from sharing stories, telling when and where not to go, eat, sleep and best of all, favorite places not to miss, becomes a significant advantage of a guesthouse or budget hotel. I see people younger than thirty, but, for some reason, they do not mind sharing and communicating with an old woman like me. If you spend a few days in a place, you get familiar with people and their stories and begin to share more and more. Anyone speaking a little English becomes friendship material immediately.

Internet at one time equaled luxury. However, now almost all budget hotels have free Wi-Fi in all rooms and a few computers in the lobby for use. Internet cafes are filled with locals playing games and talking on Skype across the world to travelers turned friends.

In thinking about the magic of this place, I guess I'd have to say that it's more the surprise that catches me off guard that makes it magic. A man comes up from behind, pulling a heavy cart by hand and stops as he passes me. The cart carries round cylinders of charcoal. He loads them into his arms and carries them into a retail store.

Evidence of a difficult life shows in his hardened face and calloused hands. Stories fill an old woman's face as she squats, waiting to sell the last of her gigantic sunflower heads filled with seeds.

Tomorrow I may or may not leave this place called Lijiang. It takes ten days in advance to get tickets for the train to Kunming, the next stop on my way to the Village of Guillin, which serves as a steppingstone into more remote villages.

Someone asked me in an email why I didn't go buy some warm clothes and shoes, since mine got wet in all the rain the last two days. Two reasons, but for sure, Chinese clothing sizes fit short people with small feet.

I stand tall with big feet, and their pants hit my shins and the tops end below the elbows. Sure, I save a little money, but more important, the challenge of roughing it tests me and helps me find out a little more about myself.

I may have mentioned this before, but when someone questioned my reasons for desiring remote travel, I had to reply that a trip like this rewards me in so many ways but exhausts me, as well.

I always look out for my safety and try to keep as clean as possible with constant hand washing or sanitizing. So, the issue for tomorrow? Can I figure out a way to move on to my next destination?

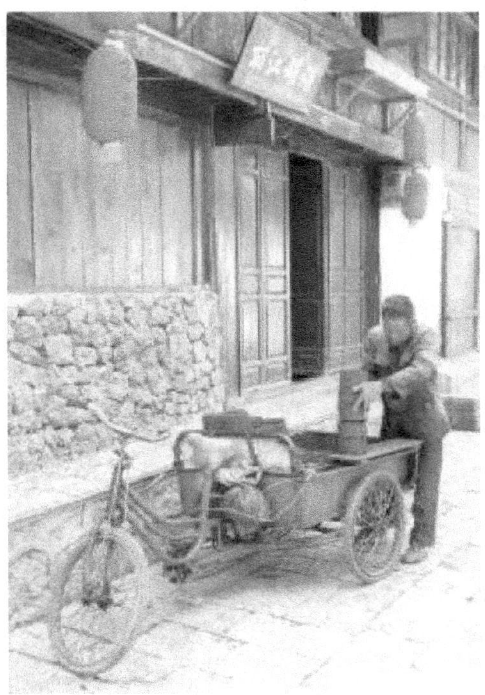

Delivering sold handmade charcoal cylinders in Lijiang

Nighttime here/morning there, so morning to all, jackie/mom

subject: kunming 10:00 a.m.

hello again. survived the eleven-hour bus ride without any regrets. no snorers, no spitters, and no playing of loud chinese movies, a situation typical in foreign countries. didn't sleep as the lumpy bed measured five-feet long and one-foot wide. the driver hurried no doubt, as the five o'clock arrival in kunming became a little intimidating in a dark bus station, filled with chinese hovering around the door openings.

this computer quarrels with me with the usage of capital letters so the need to type fast means no capitals. sorry. my train doesn't leave till seven tonight so figured i would find a cheap, budget hotel for the day and to shower and regroup. remembered a brochure i picked up in lijiang about this place and showed the taxi driver. good thing, as all these brochures now have the words, take me to...in chinese and she knew where to take me. the cloudland hotel room should cost about 100 rmb or yuang, but she gave it to me for fifty, or about eight dollars and a bargain at that.

all along one side of the guesthouse, stone walls surround little nooks and crannies used for sitting areas, computer geeks needing plugins, and book readers, looking for some peace and quiet.

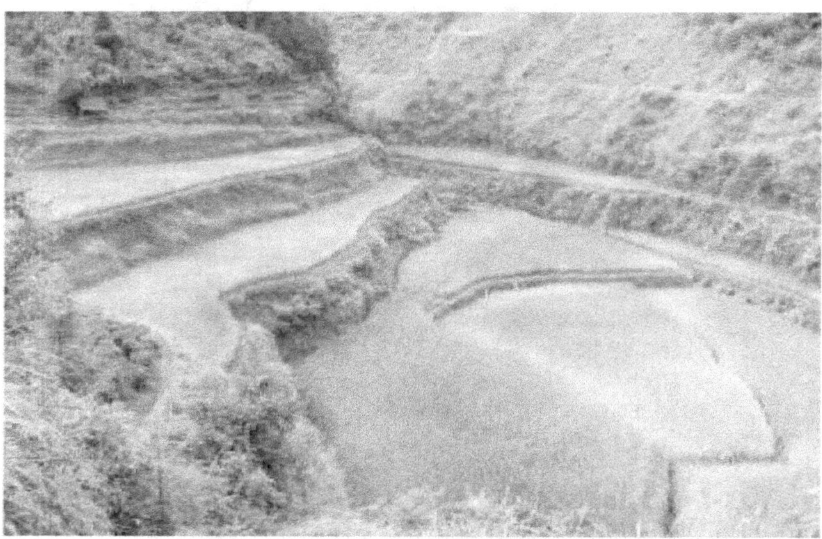

Tea fields outside of PingBu

one room offered magazines, newspapers, duds, and books to swap or borrow, and in the very middle, i discovered a little cafe with the works. music playing in the background sounded like a female singer that i have heard everywhere i go and will try to find her cd. cappuccino, tuna, pizza, or whatever else you could dream up as well as hot soups, chicken sandwiches, and a huge breakfast menu stared me in the face. a short hour nap refreshed me enough to savor the most delicious eggs since leaving home and homemade cookies after the oatmeal and fruit.

i can't describe eggs in foreign countries. for years, i tried to come up with a name for them, as they differ from anything we know back home. they fry eggs hard, in inches of pig fat or some kind of greasy liquid, with edges so crisp they can't cut them. no matter what country, they look the same, but here today, they came out perfectly, over easy, and tasty.

outside the window sit twenty chinese, playing some tile game on square tables, laughing or humming and shuffling the tiles and starting over again. took a walk and found some locals playing unfamiliar instruments in the park. another park looked like a new york flea market selling everything from tribal, ethnic shoes to toothbrushes in piles that overflowed tables. new age drinking straws for drinking yak milk out of bottles came in bright colors.

found a dud store selling duds for one dollar, and we'll see if they work or not as it becomes a guessing game. two foreign films caught my attention as foreign films can turn into real gems.

meeting westerners comes as a part of the art of travel, i suppose, as you should have an outgoing nature, which i do not. however, as an experienced traveler, i've found qualities such as curiosity help in my case, plus i like the role of a good listener, as some have so much to share, if you know the right questions to ask. met an eighty-two-year-old woman yesterday in lijiang, traveling from her home base in new zealand, where she settled after scoping out the world. she took the same route as I did and for sure forgot her diet as she consumed a plate-sized banana pancake in less time than it takes my herbal tea to brew (maybe ninety seconds).

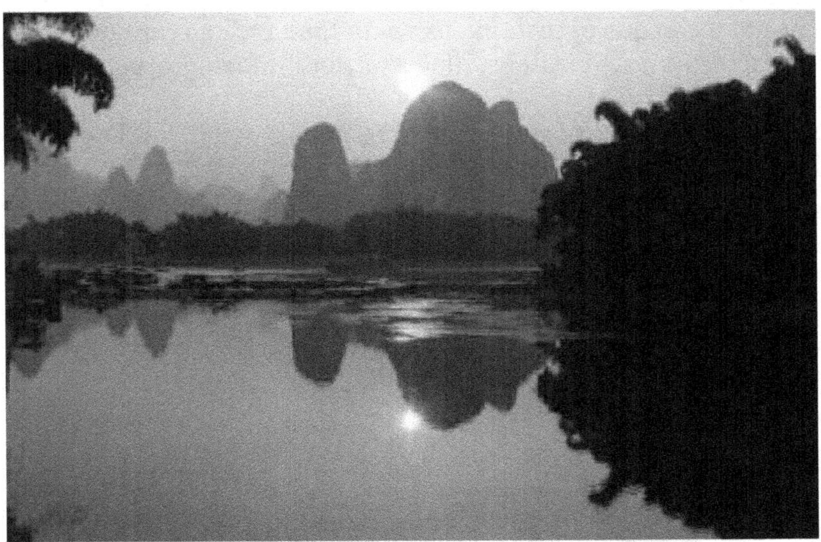

Karst peaks on Li river in Xingping.

Different computer, thank goodness. The guesthouses I write about fascinate me. I cannot describe the feeling of renting one, but several friends have inquired about them and what kinds of people use them. People from all walks of life use budget guesthouses.

Here in China I see Israelis, Germans and a few Europeans. Never ever do you meet someone from the States, ever!

People use these places to chill for a few days and wash clothes by hand, so they hang all over the place on stair rails and door openings and windowsills. I search for new ideas from other travelers who have traveled where I might want to go.

Owners design facilities for the young and restless as info and pictures about strenuous treks and other such physical adventures hang on walls. This place has an interesting wall with frequent questions asked, and answers, from the simple of how to find something by bus, to where to buy fresh fruit. In the bigger cities, you may even find someone who speaks a little English. Where I will travel from tonight forward, I expect little, if anything, to look familiar, as far as food or language goes.

I may head out now to find some DVDs as they cost under a dollar, and I love to add to my collection of foreign movies, which don't get to stores in the states. I'll sleep on a train for the night and go on to Yangshao on the Li River, a place mystical and shrouded in huge lime karsts with peaks so pointed they look like they touch the stars.

My main goal, and hope I don't jinx myself, is to witness some fishermen using the old technique of catching fish with their trained cormorants. We'll see. Picture postcard ancient villages line the river, making a bike trek the most memorable ever.

May skip several days before I find a computer again, but I never know, as I said the same thing last night, and here I sit.

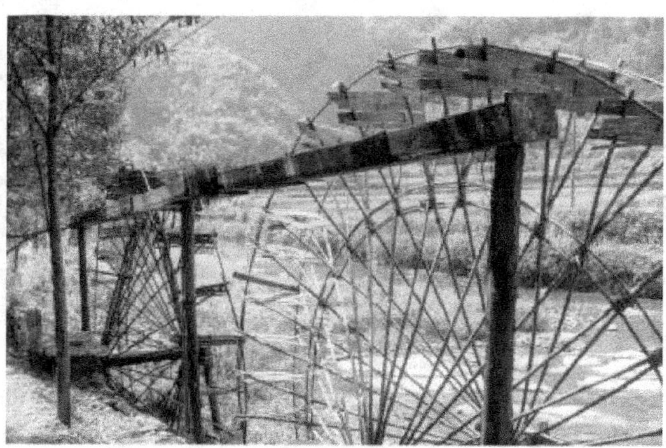

Water wheels irrigate the rice paddies

Take care to all and thanks for your words of wisdom and positive thoughts as I need them. I wish you could hear and experience this incredible culture.

Sometimes it can feel lonely, and reaching out to make a connection might not happen for a few days so email makes up for that. jackie/mom.

P.S. If you write, know I enjoy your notes. I have limited time for responding, and I will catch up when I return home.

Subject: Yangshao 9:00 p.m.

Hello to all,

Survived the train, and, of course, paid for a four-person, first class private room and received a six-person open room with my "bunk" on the top of two others. Well over six feet to climb, and the thought of 18 hours in that bed? Yikes! Met some interesting travelers, one a young man about 32 who teaches English in the school in Yangshao, my next stop.

He told me that he earns about $600 a month, with free room, and all the food he can eat, plus free beer, and loves the job. He said one can volunteer for a day or month and get the same deal, but if you teach you can stay a month or a year or whatever, as they value English-speaking teachers and, no, you don't need experience as a teacher.

He told me about many opportunities in different fields that have the same cultural interaction with the people, and they pay you to help them out. Slept okay between the rocking and rolling and having to get up once to "try" the squatting WC, or water closet (toilet), a hole in the floor.

I would like to see any one of you squatting to use the toilet on a moving train as it suddenly jerks backwards and you try to keep yourself from falling into the "hole." The flush connects with a lever that opens another lever to the ground below the train. Sure wouldn't want to walk the train tracks in China!

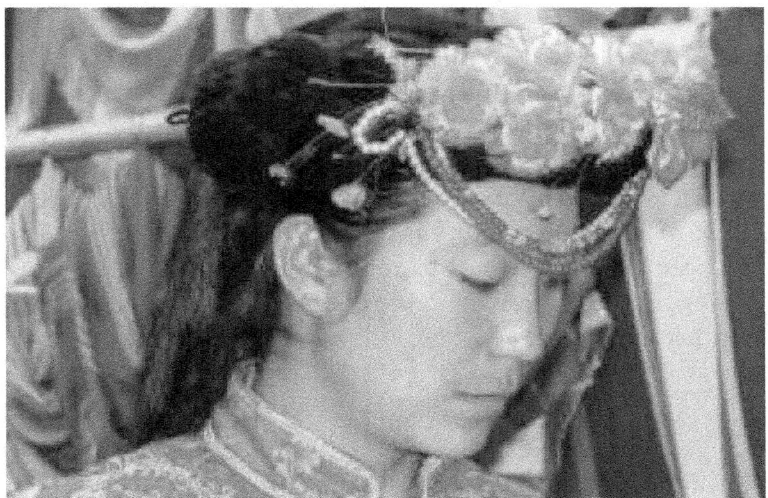

Lijiang weaver in traditional clothing

It's about 9 p.m., and I will stay at the Bamboo House Hotel and Cafe for the night. Did not stay in Guillin at all. Went straight from train to bus to Yangshao, and found the guesthouse within two minutes.

Got scammed, however, as I looked like a white-skinned tourist, I guess, and a lady hollered Yangshao as I exited the train station after standing in line for about thirty minutes, checking on train schedules for next week. I said yes, and she rushed me toward a bus pulling out, and I boarded quickly.

She boarded with me and asked for fifty RMB, about $7, and I didn't question it until I started thinking about other bus trips that lasted four hours and cost about a dollar, while this one took just one hour! Sure enough, she earned plenty of pay for her day.

Hmmm, yummy fried egg sandwich with tomato and cheese on wonderful homemade whole wheat bread for dinner. Room way too expensive at 100 RMB (about $14), and way too hot and tired to rethink my plans, so I stayed.

Oh my gosh, they have homemade whole wheat bread here and homemade banana bread, plus free internet, as well.

Temps here feel like over a hundred. I am wet to the bone from walking from taxi to the hotel, and I stand about two blocks from Li River, yeah! One room looked out from the top floor and had a view of the river, but they wanted 180 RMB, about $25 or more, and on the seventh floor. In this humidity, I don't want to do that to myself. Would rather spend the energy on biking tomorrow.

I planned to see the cormorant fishermen tonight. When I got there, they offered a real touristy thing they had set up.

They had put huge floodlights and birds on the bamboo, and a ninety-seven-year-old man with a pointed, white beard sat beside them, with seats on the raft behind him.

I want to see the real thing, not something set up for tourists. The cormorants learn, as babies, to give the fish they catch to their owners, but for safety's sake, the owner ties string around their necks to prevent them from swallowing the fish.

Legend says the owner takes the string off after they dive seven times so they can enjoy some fish for their hard work.

Woke for a sunrise photo of the towering limestone karst peaks, jutting their way out of the ground, surrounding the villages in this area.

I rented a bike for the day, and a bridge proved an ideal choice for the first shot, as the reflection on the water looked incredible.

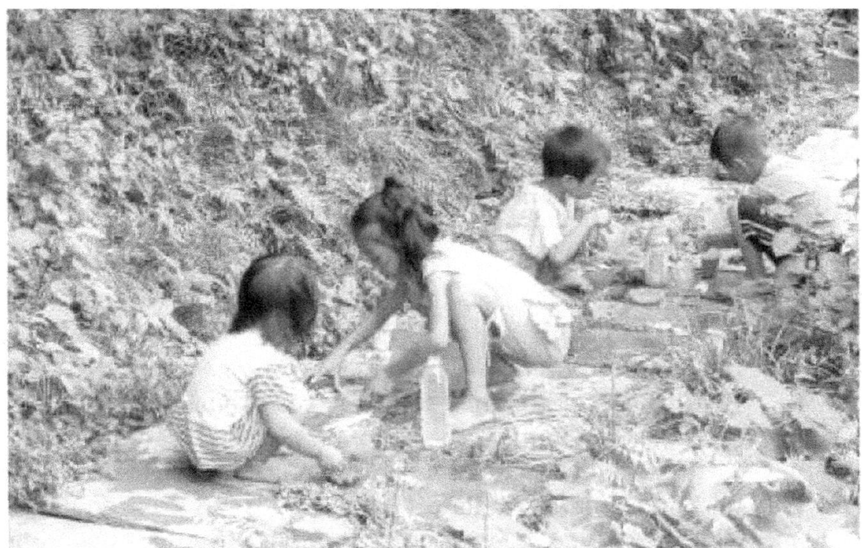

Kids are still making mud pies in Chengyang

Headed out, after a huge breakfast of muesli, banana, yogurt and eggs, for what I thought might include the rural village of 600-year-old Baisha, but first the Dragon's Backbone Bridge. May not do a good job of interpreting the map but had brought lots of sunscreen. However, no traffic, no people for over an hour and a half, meant lost! According to the map, the river on my right should sit on my left.

Back to town to sort out my plans and to cool off as sweat soaked my clothing. With about 15 miles behind me, I tried not to feel sorry for myself, thinking I needed a rest. I did get to see rural China with its farming communities, and women walking with four-foot bamboo poles across their backs, balancing buckets or baskets overflowing with veggies or stacks of firewood. Children built mud houses topped with flags of leaves.

This time I stopped every mile to ask, "Is this the road to Baisha?" Research suggested visiting Baisha, close to the famous bridge. Never found Baisha, close to Lijiang, last week in the pouring rain, so hope my luck has changed.

In many third/fourth-world countries, they build the walls around hotels and homes with cement, topped with slices of jagged glass to keep trespassers at a distance.

The irregular points of the karsts, standing guard behind villages, reminded me of those broken-glass-topped walls.

A white cat zigzagged across my path for good fortune. Cool sprinkles won the race with the warmth of the sun's rays for a few minutes, giving me a much-needed break.

Never having pedaled a bike more than a mile, I felt grateful for the more than “ten-mile, soaked-to-the-skin exercise” last week trying to find Baisha. The hotel clerk said a max of one-hour ride, and so far, more than that passed rather slowly.

A woman appeared beside me on a bike and asked the same question I had heard all day long, "Bamboo?" (Meaning, do you want to take a bamboo raft ride on the river?) Wrong question, as I sat on a bike. I said no thank you and prioritized the idea of rearranging my bottom on this teeny narrow bike seat.

Pedaling past gardens with funny-looking scarecrows shadowed by sky-scrapers of green peaks helped me forget the aches and stiffness in my muscles.

The map showed the paved road becoming a "country road," meaning a four-inch wide dirt-and-rock meandering path crossing close to front doors, chicken coops, women sorting red hot peppers in piles bigger than my bedroom, and men selling some yellow and purple round things, floating in basins of water.

Slender blades of rice plants, dressed in full green, waved as the wheels squeaked over rocks and pieces of roots.

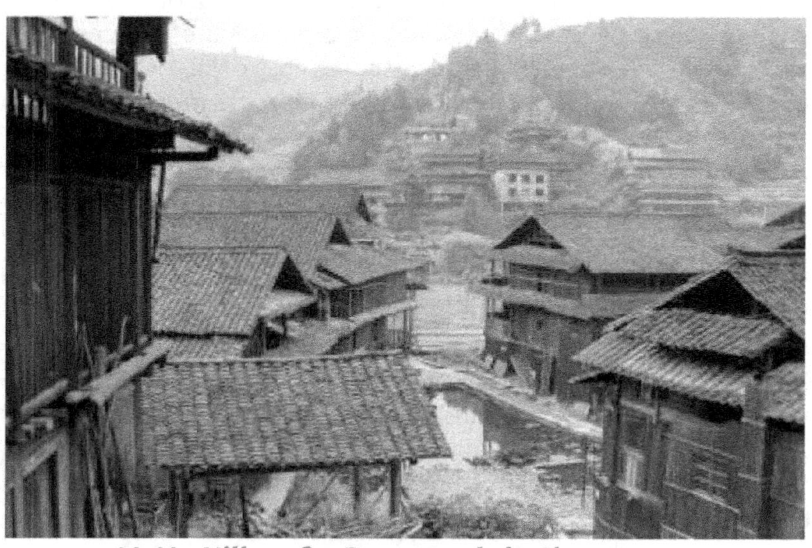

Ma'An Village for Dong people in Chengyang

Around a bend, an old woman switched a leafless tree branch over the back of a water buffalo and disappeared before I could access my camera bag.

A fork in the road ahead. Looking to the right, I saw that bamboo lady, saying, "Dragon's Bridge," and I turned to bicycle onward. Anticipation for crossing the Dragon's Backbone Bridge kept my legs from resting as the one-thousand-year-old bridge with its walls slanting inward and stone steps worn to different heights. This is where the name Dragon's Backbone originated and it seemed like a perfect photo opportunity.

Riding another thirty minutes, I came to another fork close to the river. Two men approached me and said, "Look for the red arrow on the tree." Well, I never found the arrow after another half hour of intense sun and riding, but out of nowhere, the bamboo angel (not sure if she was real) appeared far ahead of me. She pointed down a narrow footpath and disappeared! Off and on, a few couples passed me so I felt maybe I had not gone astray. Then the path opened to a wide gravel road with not a foreigner in sight. The heat melted my energy faster than I could reach deep inside, find a positive thought for encouragement, and use it!

I wear nylon clothes when traveling as they dry fast when washed in a sink basin. Having a carry-on for a month-long sojourn, I don't have a problem with clothing.

Needless to say, my clothes dripped, not quite as fast as the sweat trails from my forehead, all the way to my waist pouch hiding my money and passport. I stopped for a water break, and past a small hill stood my bamboo angel pointing forward. By now, I didn't question her judgment, be she either real or ghostly, as I'd lost my way in rural China and could never have found a path in any direction to anywhere now.

By the time I had biked to where I thought her arm pointed, the one opening in the vast rice paddies looked like a tiny rutted gap, wide enough for a bike tire. The challenge of that rice field felt better than the simple alternative of staying on that dusty road going who knows where? Crossing narrow stone bridges took precise balance as did leaning in the opposite direction of thorn bushes, growing wild in the soggy ditches.

A wrinkled mass of skin stared at me as I pushed hard to reach the top of a "small" hill, and she yanked forward a thick rope tied around the massive water buffalo following her. The woman looked at me, as if I'd arrived as an exotic alien in her rice field, but the buffalo kept chomping. The sides of his belly left traces of mud on my nylon legs, as he tried to share the path with my bike.

A man ahead, wearing a paper emergency room mask, carried a garden sprayer similar to one I use in my own yard to spray weeds. The sprayer blasted chemicals as he wet both sides of the path in front of him. Guess I assumed all rice grew organically without pesticides or fertilizers.

Maybe a river created the opening I could see ahead, threading itself past squatty, whitewashed houses. Peeking around the last house, I could barely distinguish the bamboo angel waving me forward.

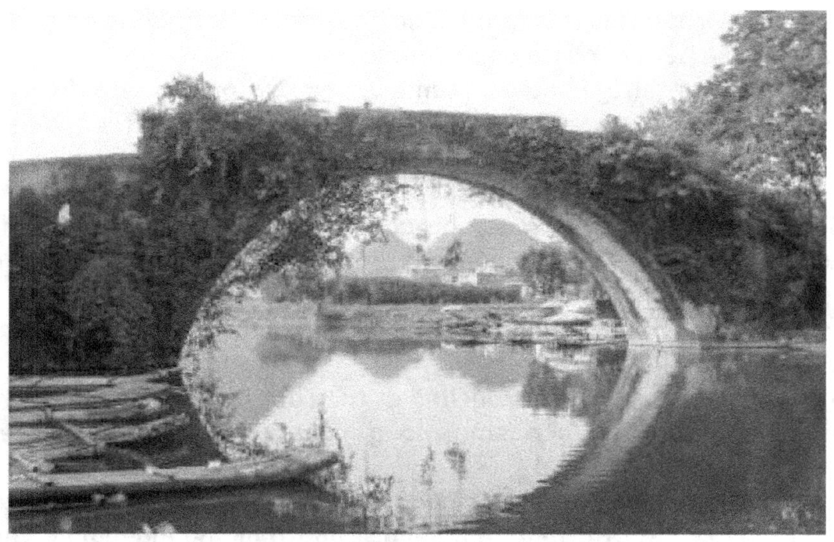

Dragon's Backbone Bridge in Baisha

I made my way to the small village and streets filled with intrusive honking and the familiar "hello" from every child on the block, smiling when I returned their greeting with hello. Finally, the proud bridge, guarding both sides of the river, sat waiting for one more person to climb over her back. Vines hung graciously, almost trying to hide the uneven surfaces.

The Dragon's Backbone Bridge filled the camera's viewfinder with fragments of history. Without the bamboo angel, I never would have found it.

I searched the area for that lady, and, sure enough, over in the far corner of the bridge, she sat with a group of women and smiled when I caught her attention. I never did figure out why she led me there because I had given her no incentive to do so!

I have never ridden as I did today, and the heat suffocated me at times. I have never drunk so much water either! When I felt tired and didn't think I could make it to the end of the road, I remembered someone once saying that sometimes you need to reach deep inside and find that which will give you light at the end of the tunnel and help you make it there.

On to Baisha, a few miles up the road, to find a small guesthouse for overnight and some discovery the next day. I need these trips to remind me of where

I belong in the world. Back to Yangshao for the next adventure: to find Yingping on the Yulong River.

I'm excited to get out into the countryside tomorrow as I will see the real China, I think, and I'm ready for that. I saw buffalo, pulling carts across the river tonight and can't wait to see that up close. I took a few pics of the unique karst peaks (limestone-jagged peaks surrounding the entire village here). Hope I can figure out a way to send some pics before I leave this area.

Think I'll head out for another walk tonight as the town feels safe, and I'd like to get a little more exercise in before bed so I can sleep well. I spent the night on a bus two nights ago, and on a train last night, and didn't sleep well either night.

It's so hard for me to share what I feel while here. I miss my little house on the lake back home in Florida and the simplicity of that way of living, but I love everything here so much.

I often think that life passes me by in that house. I wake up. It's Friday morning again, and each week it seems all of sudden I realize, wow, it's Friday again already, and what did I accomplish this last week?

Here, I feel each day I accomplish some incredible feat, something so wild, unusual, and memorable that it doesn't compare to life back home. It's not that I want to travel every day of my life. It's that I need this challenge and satisfaction in my life.

The Chinese people have customs strange and difficult to understand. Their weird language takes years to read and understand.

I have written a few characters to show to bus drivers and ticket takers and don't have a clue as to how to understand it all. One character can have fifteen meanings, and you add that to another and now you have a word.

I've met a few people who have lived in China a while and shared their thoughts of the Chinese.

It seems they lack the emotion and passion for life, children, and each other and concentrate more on making a success of their lives.

Whether selling junk gifts in market stalls or slinging a long piece of bamboo on their shoulders to balance two baskets full of enough fruit to feed a zoo full of hungry creatures, they work hard and often smile but have little incentive to care, I'm told, about each other.

Life involves security and making sure someone provides for you as you age.

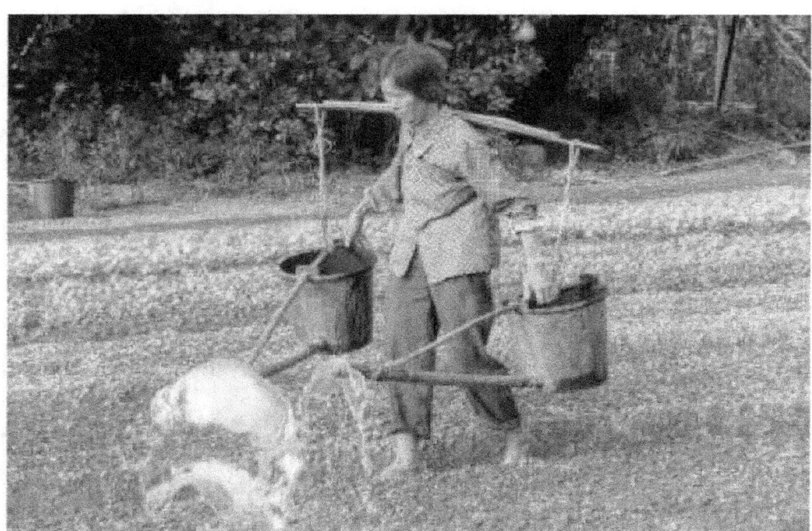

Watering garden in Xingping

Again, to all who write personal notes, I appreciate them so much and have read each one. I do not have time to respond but know that I do care. Thanks again for all your positive thoughts as they help me get through the day. My time in a place where sometimes days go by without hearing English wears me down. I don't depend on myself for entertainment in our take-for-granted life-style. Best, jackie/mom

Subject: On to Xingping 5:00 p.m.

Hello everyone,

I remember in the Sahara Desert I felt so hot I could think only about water. I took a small sip and let it stay in my mouth for as long as I could. Xingping offered a different version of hot: the kind that gets under your clothes and drenches them through and through. Eyes burned and lips tasted of salt. The bottom edge of my nylon Capri pants dripped sweat down my legs. The Li River slithered between high peaks of limestone like a snake searching for a place to hide. Boats lined the riverbanks, waiting for a tourist or two to give in to the bamboo ladies' shouts, offering the best deal.

I knew the guidebook said foreigners could not ride on the local boats for safety reasons, but what could they say to me anyway if I tried? I walked right down into the middle of this old beat-up, barely-floating, boat filled with locals chatting away until I intruded into their world. I smiled with a "knee how," and the crowd ignored me. I had hoped the boat went up or downriver. Instead, the ferry just crossed the river. One RMB ($.30) and I decided to figure out a cheaper way to get out on the river rather than paying the 200 RMB the bamboo ladies wanted. Found a lady downstream and bargained with her for an hour ride to Yanxi for eighty RMB ($10.30).

Water buffalo bathed in the cool water so close to my bamboo boat I thought they might tip it over. Women washed clothing, and men bathed without a care if others watched or not. The tips of mountains sticking out from the ground became the main attraction, however, and lining both sides of the river, they took the lead for any beauty contest of the day.

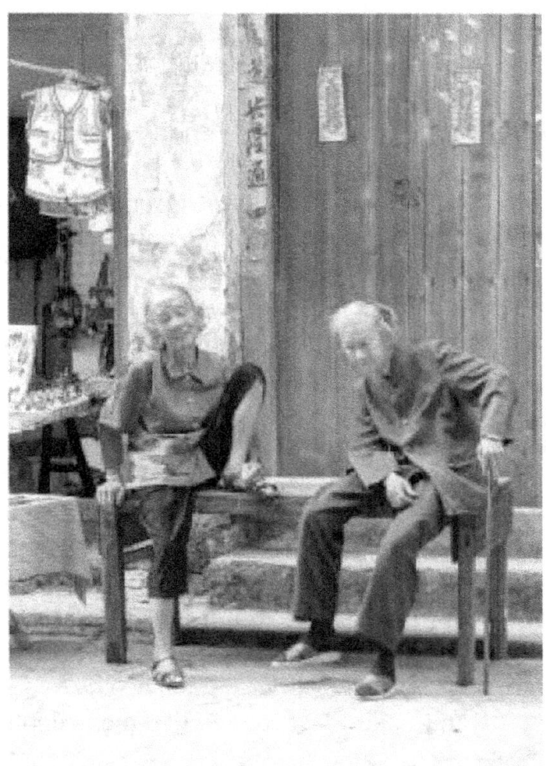

Chatting in Xingping

Sunrise the next morning came too early, making a waste of setting alarms as it turned out hazy, and restaurants didn't open until eight-thirty! Met an Australian lady, while lost in the maze of cobblestone streets and narrow pathways. She heard me ask a group of young people whether they spoke English as I looked for a place to have breakfast.

What a find! Jean moved here a short time ago, opened a small art gallery across from an old temple, and invited me to see "how" she lived. Trillions of cobwebs and dust covered two floors of basic wooden walls and ceilings, but she made it intriguing, telling me how she lived here in this small village. She outlined all her costs and problems as well as the opportunities she experienced. By the time I finished eggs and a banana, I thought about another shower. Checkout time approached, so I opted to hop the bus back to Yangshao for some relief from this heat.

Found an old man, who would take me out to see some cormorant fishing late in the evening. I knew the method had changed since his ancestors had taught him, but the idea interested me all the same. The black cormorants have long necks, an easy handle for the fisherman to grab after they surface with a fish in their mouth. The rope tied around their necks keeps the bird from swallowing the fish. The fisherman scoops the bird back onto the boat. After squeezing the neck and claiming the fish, the fisherman throws the bird back into the water. Then the process repeats.

Darkness fell, and I found it hard to photograph the scene. The real photo I wanted with the fisherman on the old bamboo boat disappeared. Modern boats, old and dirty but with motors, replaced the slow, less efficient, bamboo boats.

After showing me his “tricks,” he pulled ashore, pointed to my camera, and took a picture of me holding one of his cormorants. Quite a day!

The food here looks horrible, unrecognizable most of the time, and is cooked swimming in oil. I knew that when I came, so brought a lot to eat, like foil packs of tuna, assortments of nuts, dried fruits, and protein bars. Oh, and my favorite, packets of peanut butter.

But, China exists on rice and noodles. Have not seen much bread except at that one hotel in Yangshao with the homemade whole wheat bread. So how do you eat peanut butter without bread? On stale crackers covered in salt?

I always pig out when I get home, thinking that I feel deprived or starved and deserve pizza and donuts.

Did try Madowell’s, as they call it here, and the chicken sandwich contained some dark brown stuff with skin that looked like a chicken's skin, but the meat attached to it had fat and gristle.

Not sure where they got that chicken? But I couldn't eat it! Miss you all, love jackie/mom

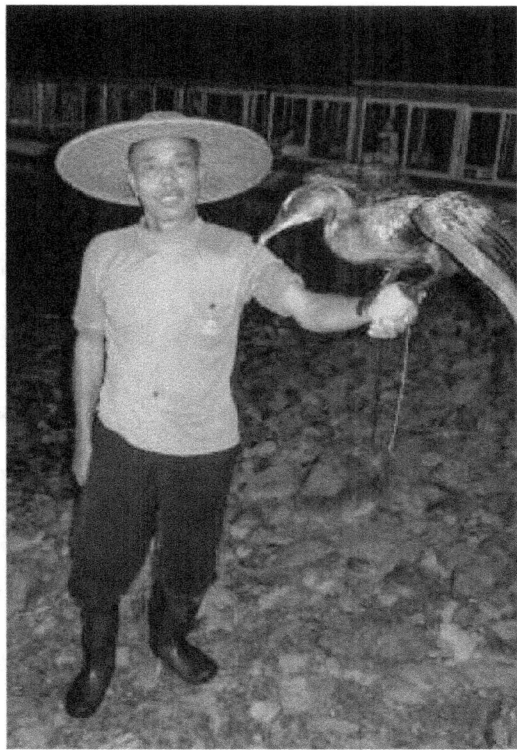

Cormorant fisherman on Li River

Subject: Sanjiang to Ma'an 5:00 p.m.

Hello all,

Six hours to Sanjiang. Two from Yangshao to Guilin, but the buses gave me a glimpse of the locals, interacting with each other. Patience becomes the watchword when trucks block the road for an hour and dust begins to settle on your skin.

Found a driver who knew the route to the Village of Ma'an and even to the covered Chengyang Wind and Rain Bridge.

Unfortunately, the driver let me off right in front of the ticket taker for tourists to see the bridge. I tried to explain that I wanted to cross the bridge to get to a hotel.

At last, I gave in to the expensive visitor fee. If the driver had dropped me at the end of the block, I could have walked across the bridge without hassle. It's morning for you, and I just had some dinner.

Believe me, the food does taste horrible. I had some eggplant, mushrooms, and cucumbers stir-fried in heavy oil mixed in with the tuna I brought, but I sure miss real meals! I had an amazing day, and the internet will not cooperate at all, as it keeps going down and just now started working again.

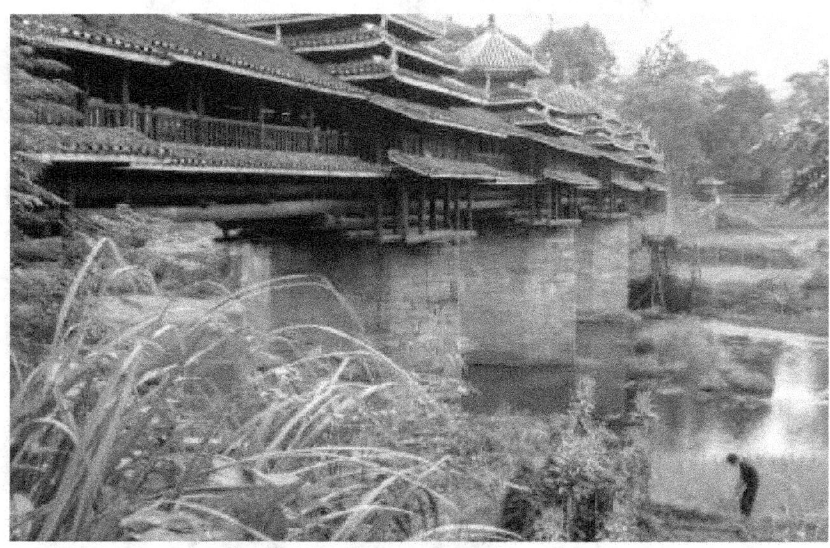

Wind and Rain Bridge Chengyang/Sanjiang [No nails]

I found out the wooden beds have a cotton mattress pad over them, which my hotel last night forgot to give me, as I saw them in some of the rooms when I left. They didn't have change and said, no matter, pay later, so I left without paying the six bucks!

This new hotel did not have a good fan, but does have the mattress pads, so who knows if I'll sleep?

I loved this day more than any other. I walked and walked, in and out of villages, and had a map in Chinese so had to stop often for directions. Stopped to watch three waterwheels used to irrigate the rice paddies.

I didn't think too much about the protein bar lunch, as the water fell from the spokes of the waterwheels into bamboo chutes working their way into the paddy fields. Amazing people, always smiling and saying, "knee how" no matter how young or old. A friendly area of Dong people.

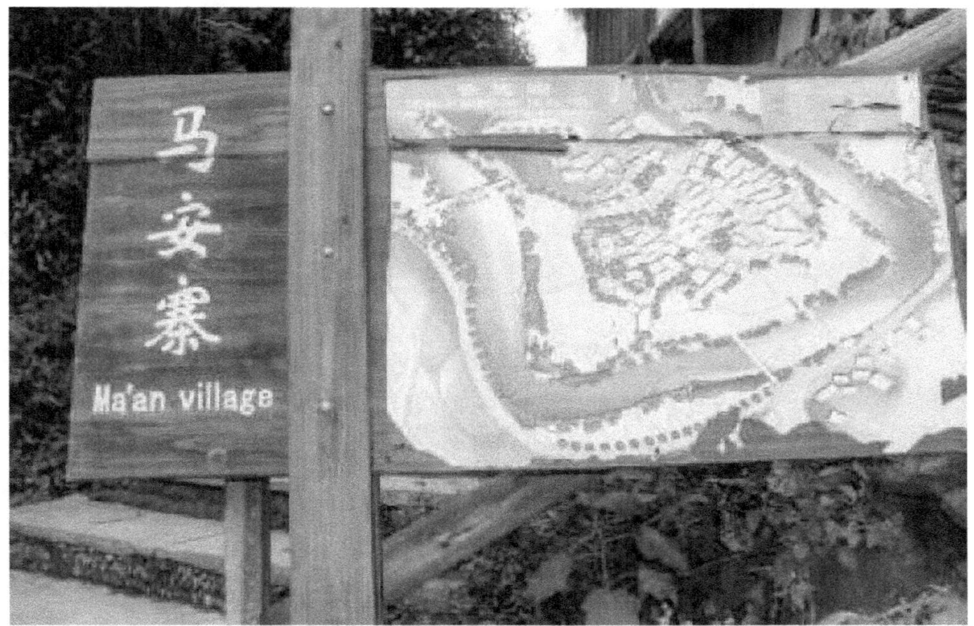

Ma'anVillage map in Chengyang

My morning walk started after I enjoyed some eggs mixed with tomatoes and white bread toast.

The Village of Ma'an reminded me of irregular chunks of chocolate fudge sitting on top of each other, melting. Each several-story home towered over the next with uneven paths winding around and down to little streams hiding under thick brush.

A giant's maze, not for viewing at night. Surprises ready for the release of the shutter button waited under little bridges, at the end of walkways, or inside windows with cautious eyes peering out.

Children played in the mud close to the river, making a mud pie village of twigs and leaves. Each Dong village had its own drum tower, a pagoda-shaped building with a drum made of cow skin hanging on a tower.

Some of the bridges had drums sitting at the entrance and exit, used to call for assistance in accidents or to gather people together for meetings.

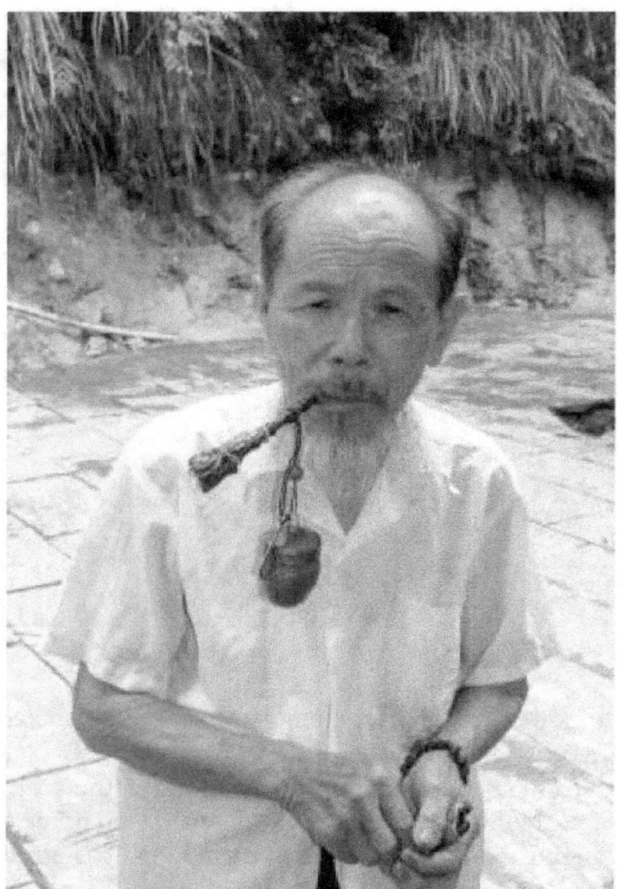

Dong man, smoking

The Oriental man, who lives in our memory banks when we think of rural China, smoked opium in his intricate pipe and greeted me with caution as I came off the bridge.

Innocent and natural in his homemade clothing, long, tapered white beard, and lack of hurry, he knew my ways threatened his without my knowing anything about him. My brief encounter with him paralleled my views of China. My ideas and knowledge felt shallow and stagnant. He breathed life into my day.

The stone walkway across the river looked safe, despite a sign in English stating no crossing here. Thinking it better to cross here, and not lose my sense of direction into the next Village of Ping Zhai, I found the same crazy quilt pattern of houses at every level with walkways in all directions. I stopped for directions often, and knowing the name of the next village always helped. A Dong tribal man passed with a bundle of firewood on his back. His pace never slowed.

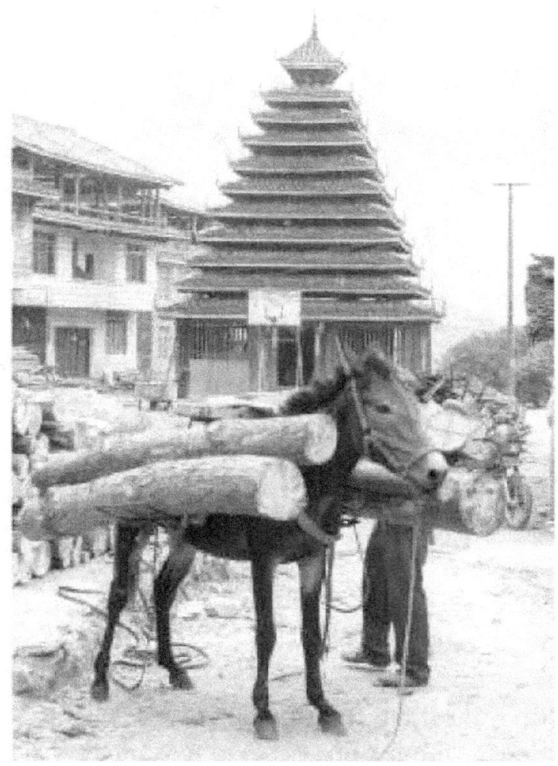

Carrying logs down the mountain from PingBu

I realized more people crowded the tiny dirt pathways. Maybe a sign of a market nearby. Vehicles honking, and diesel trucks shifting gears, signaled a road (maybe the one I wanted), going to the Village of PingBu, high in the mountains. I passed the typical market and took my chances on a local bus (for a few coins) heading uphill. The driver understood my pronunciation and nodded. A stop for some bottled water might help me get back down the mountain without becoming lost if I took off in the countryside. Donkeys laden with logs worked up and down the worn paths. In the background, the village's drum tower stood watch with its artistic carved birds and symbols. My walk ended at a dead end, and I knew I wanted to go south and downhill, but how to find a path puzzled me. I turned to see a woman sitting on the ground beating a stalk of rice on a tarp and then piling the few kernels together to the side. I watched her for a few minutes, and she gave in to a smile.

Hours of walking and I saw rice terraces and rows of tea bushes ready for harvest. Although lost in China's beautiful countryside, with a few hours to spare before dark, I knew I had time to return.

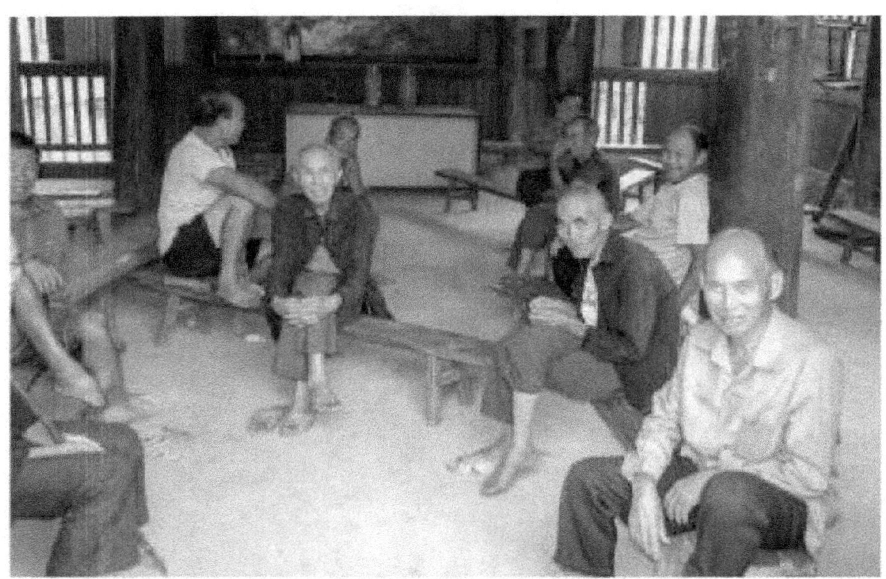

Men, gathering in the drum tower, wore yellow shoes in JiChang

Shapes of rooflines mixed with the mountainside forest, but the road kept on winding for at least an hour until the appearance of the village square of JiChang almost scared me. The peacefulness of the walk traded places with the evening activities. The older men of the village sat in a circle in the drum tower, discussing the latest news and decisions. Children ran around the square with ice cream dripping on them and the ground. Some played a game with paper money and dice next to the little grocery store. I pointed to myself and to the little lanes, heading off the square, and a few women nodded with smiles. I hungered for a more simplistic life, but seeing the girl about eight years old wash her hair alone in the stream made me realize the independence that goes along with it. With it now almost dark, and hours from my guest-house, I asked a group of men, talking and laughing at the side of the square, about transportation. A van and a motorcycle sat there, and maybe I could ask for a ride back down the mountainside for a dollar. Nobody seemed to understand my motions of myself, vehicle and down the road while waving the money. A man stood and opened the car door for me and slipped behind the wheel. He didn't want money. In the end, he smiled and drove away.

Here, I send a few more pics to share, and more notes in a few days about my trekking today into the rural China I came to see. Unique villages off the beaten path with courteous smiles nodding with "knee how" (hello) as they pass. Take sweet care, jackie/mom

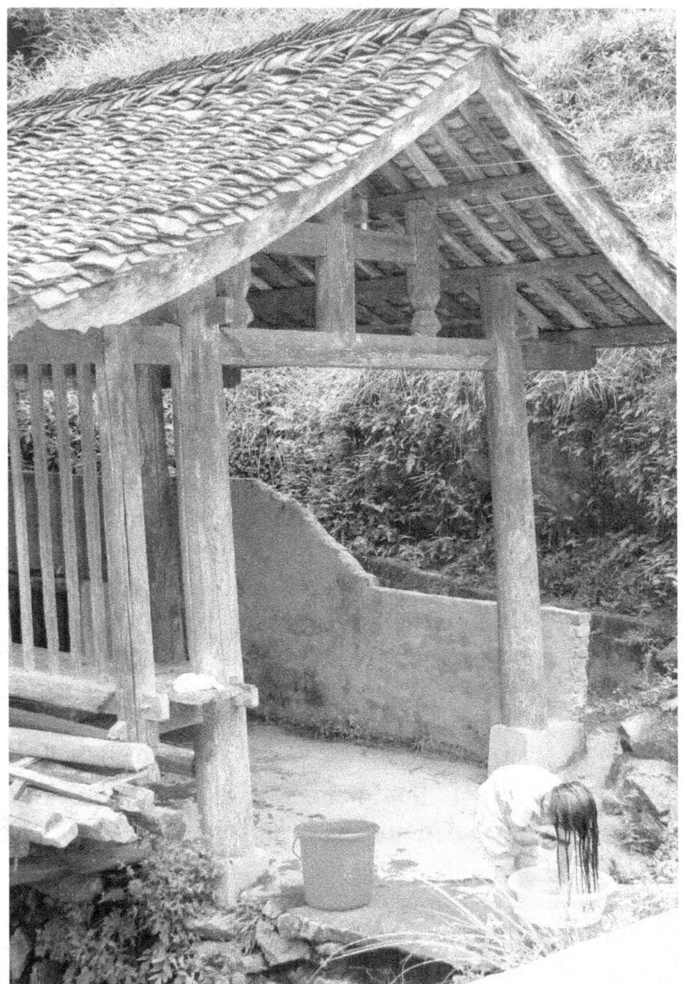

Eight-year-old Dong girl washes hair, alone at river in JiChang

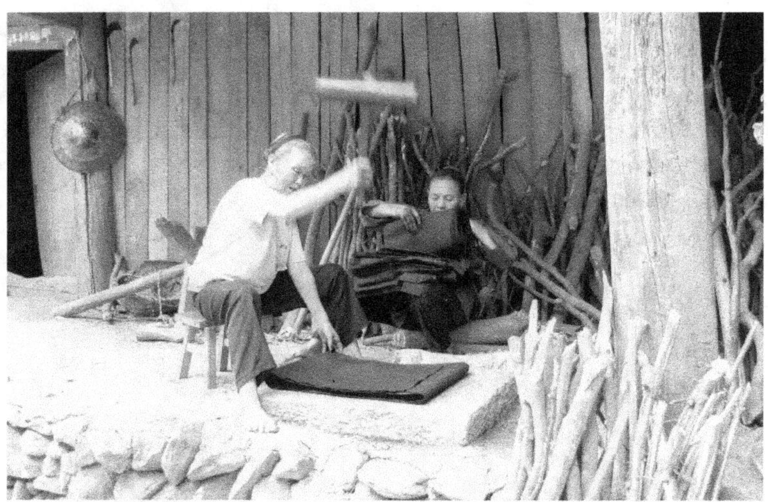

PingBu women, beating indigo-dyed Liangbu cloth

Subject: Sanjiang to DeHang 6:10 a.m.

Dear friends/family,

I know I overlooked writing about some stories and have some worthwhile ones to share, but I left the beaten track and found dark age-old and slow computers with Chinese keyboards, difficult to type fast as I often do when writing a story. I do have some down time at the end of my trip, as I couldn't get a train back towards Hong Kong and had to schedule a day in advance, so maybe I can catch up.

Had a frightening night the night before last. Arrived in Sanjiang to take a train or bus to Jishou, farther north. The bus station attendant said no buses, which shocked me, as buses sat squeezed into every corner of the lot. So I made it to the train station and found the schedule in Chinese and the doors all locked until midnight that night, the departure time for the train. I spent about an hour going through my notes and found the characters for the town I wanted to visit. Found a room that none of you would even believe a human could stay in, but my weary bones needed to sit down as I had about twelve hours until train time.

Long story short. At 11:00 p.m., the station opened with one man running the show. No tickets onto the train available! No English spoken by anyone present. I pondered my situation as I was thirty miles from any town, and found a locked and closed hotel, with hordes of young men hanging around the station. This town had no taxis. I kept going in to the ticket taker and showing him different destinations on my map. He looked at me, clueless, but kept writing on a paper the train time of 00:19. Finally, after about an hour of worrying and stressing,

I remembered a town just north of Sanjiang and thought if I could just get on the train, maybe I could somehow stay on the train all the way.

Well, it worked, and, no, I don't believe in luck. Luck equals determination and perseverance. I found a huge amount of both that night.

Sardines might have had it easier than I during that train ride, as people laid on top of each other, in aisles and even on tops of chair backs! Six hours and I would make my final destination if I could somehow avoid the conductor.

A young couple graciously squeezed me in-between them, and there we sat, looking at each other for six hours. The conductor came by once, and I pretended to sleep, but I would have given him fifty bucks to let me stay. My ticket cost a whole $2.25!

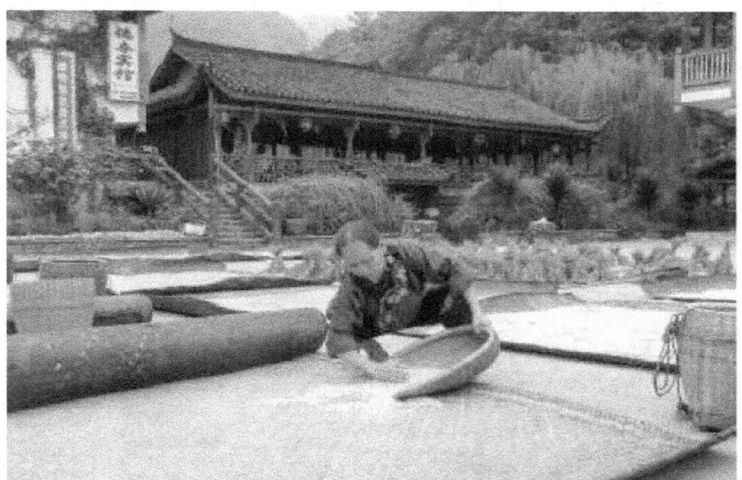

Spreading rice to dry in DeHang

I just discovered Dehang, China, a remarkable place. I have taken more pictures here in one day than during my entire three-week journey thus far! The people live a true rural, farm lifestyle here. Amazing. So much to write, I can't begin right now. I climbed for eight hours today in pursuit of a waterfall and "heaven-questioning platform."

Well, I found the waterfall and felt satisfied knowing I made it. Guess I don't get to ask about "heaven," as I never found that area! I became curious about people living under Communist rule, now that I have so many villages to compare. This place differs from any village I have visited. The people have no incentives to move forward with their lives. Great in many ways, yet keeping their village clean and safe includes change and planning for the future, which they ignore. I suspect a food kitchen here, as I have seen most of the villagers coming into this one building and leaving with a bowl of food and chopsticks. AND speaking of chopsticks, you would think that by now I could say that I have mastered them! No way. Not even close. I can't say rice scoops up easily.

Katherine and I, about fifteen years ago, traveling in the dark, deep jungles of New Guinea, living with remote Stone Age people, sometimes ate a bowl of white rice a day. Katherine, fourteen, swore she (I joined in) would never eat white rice again, ever! But, after the eggs they serve here in this country, I have given in to rice. Not bad with eggs! Really!!

Last night I found a computer, allowing me to watch a movie. I bought about fifty DVDs for less than half a dollar each in Yangshao and chose *Amelia* to watch. Some thoughts from that movie struck home with me: "Who wants a life imprisoned in safety? Flying lets me move in three dimensions." Hmmm, describes how I feel about travel. I recommend the movie to all!

Amelia said, "Everyone has oceans to fly if they have the heart for it! Is it reckless, maybe? What do dreams know of boundaries?"

And finally, the best I could want for everyone to feel: "The world has changed me!"

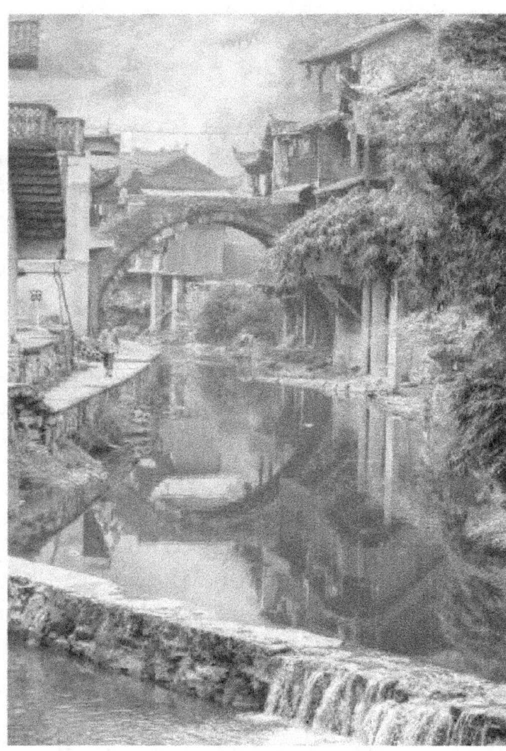

DeHang beauty

Sometimes I get lazy back home.

My day climbing steep rocks proved I had abilities greater than I gave myself credit for.

I passed men, cutting bamboo for various uses, women, washing the roots of plants for cooking, men, smoking under stands of mountain bamboo chatting, and men with sickles cutting old rice plants down and inserting handfuls in some wood machine that had a cylinder inside with nails protruding.

That machine spit the loose hulls and broken pieces of branches out of one end, and the solid pieces of rice kernels into piles on the other end as the owner turned the cylinder by hand.

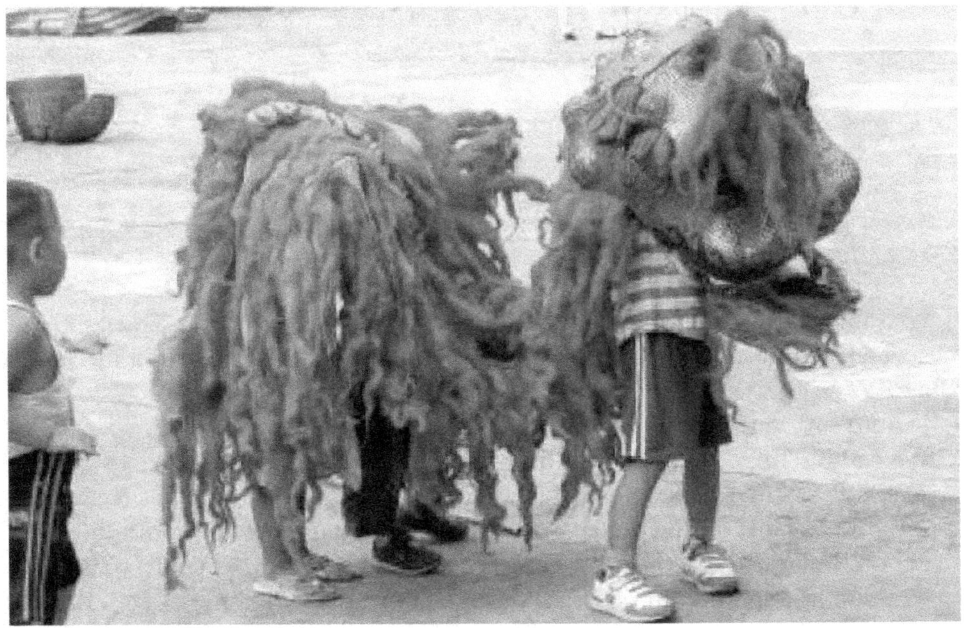

Children, wearing the dragon puppet, scare elders

Grasshoppers played hopscotch on ancient stone rocks, disregarding the sound of footsteps, soon to ruin their game!

Sprinkles cooled me for the trip back.

I stashed the camera, so all I had left involved my sore feet, my thoughts, and visions of an imaginary salad and broccoli-cheddar soup at Panera's!

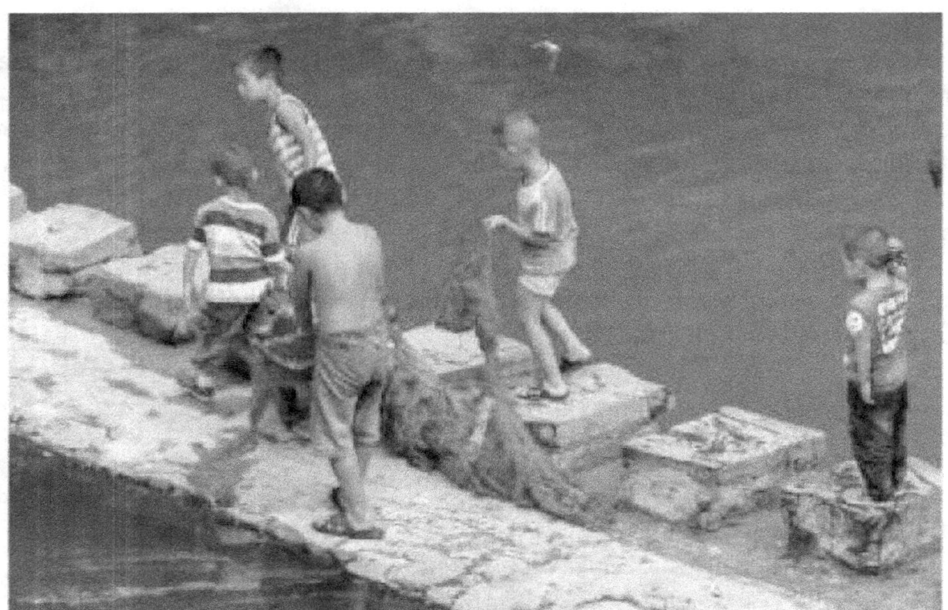

Children, salvaging the dragon puppet after playing in water

Last night I felt sad about a situation that at first excited me. From my hotel of sorts (no hot water, towels, soap, toilet paper, air conditioning, food or cleaning services),

I could see some children playing with a dragon. It stood about six feet long with a hollow head, allowing a human to put his own head inside.

The kids would lift up the back and tail part and put them over their heads, and about six children would run or walk around yelling and laughing.

I could imagine how many old stories that dragon puppet could tell.

I enjoyed the entertainment. Walking back to the room, I took another path over stepping stones that crossed the river outside my hotel and two little boys about seven had taken the dragon to the river and tried to "ride" it in the water! It had beautiful heavy paper painted with sequins and glitter.

The fabric for the body contained wool. Decades, if not centuries old, this represented the history of this village and now lay ruined by these children who didn't have a clue as to what they had just lost.

The dragon sank! Promise to catch up later. Best to all, and thanks for all your wonderful notes, positive thoughts, and beautiful words of wisdom! Love, jackie/mom

Subject: Fenghuang 6:00 a.m.

Dear family/friends,

Never trust a guidebook, as they always make a place like Fenghuang sound enticing and delicious! Ancient, charming, walled-in city on the river with crumbling houses, rooftops carved with fish and birds, and bridges older than time itself. Well, if you could see the houses and

rooftops, fine, but the tourist sites distract from any so-called ancient sites, including the bridges, which have souvenir stalls all the way from one end to the next!

Fenghuang refers to the Chinese word for the mythical phoenix, which represents long life and good luck. The legend came after two birds found the village so beautiful after flying over it. Gondolas pass by my balcony every few minutes, filled with Chinese tourists toting cameras and more cameras. I opted to stay the night, exhausted from the heat and walking the uneven cobblestones, pulling my supposed carry-on luggage. Thanks, Eddie Bauer. I love you, but you made your carry-on too lopsided, and it keeps falling to one side!

I liked the room, the best yet and of course, the most expensive ($26), but typical Chinese, almost Japanese-style with mattresses on the floor, and glass walls from bath to outside balcony with little short stools and chairs meant for toddlers! A real live computer sits on a table, and I connected to the internet immediately.

First time I have ever seen that in my life. Will relax and head back for Dehang tomorrow to see more of rural China, the last of my visit to this country, I would guess!

Fenghuang, my dream village, turned into a tourist mecca since my original research of online photos and recorded stories. I saved two extra days to spend here, roaming the dozens of stone lanes winding up and down the hills with crowded wooden houses on either side. The chaos of the area centered on the river. Hundreds of tourists focused their activities in the area around the river. What a claustrophobic jungle. The restaurant, recommended by the hotel owner, had a line waiting outside next to the cages of guinea pigs, cuscus, and rats running in circles.

This town has everything for sale one can imagine. Combs made from yak bones, and costumes from centuries past to try on. Then you walk to the internet a block away and pay for your printed pics! Saw shops selling herbs and roots and age-old remedies for every ache and pain imagined, tanks of fish, ducks, plates, and bowls of strange slimy creatures moving about, cheap trinkets next to expensive clothing Signs advertising pizza and spaghetti line the crooked alleyways and riverfront walks while the huge, pink stone wall stands guard over the city.

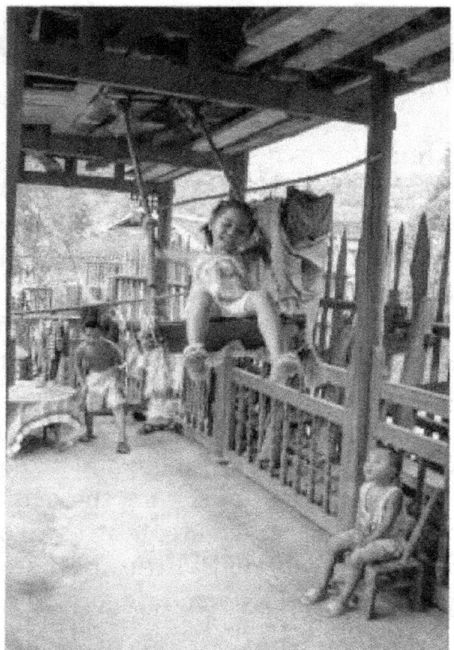

Swinging under a house in DeHang

Tried to find some soda water today as I found a brand in Yangshao. Nothing like ice-cold soda water to quench your thirst when you don't drink sugar or caffeine drinks. None around and sure makes me miss ice!

Evening almost here and a beautiful custom takes place on the water close to the steppingstones across the river at dusk.

They light little candles and place them on paper leaves to float them down the river until they burn out or sink in the waves after the villagers make a wish.

Back to the countryside to find some water buffalo to photo. I want to understand more about rice cultivation, as the processes they go through by hand mystify me.

I don't look forward to more tuna fish and protein bars, but what's a girl to do?

Time for some dinner. I hope to find some veggies so the tuna will not threaten me for the next few days back in Dehang! Best to all and thanks again for your messages; will write to each of you when I return, jackie/mom

Subject: DeHang to Jishou 9:23 p.m.

Hello all,

A tossed salad of ethnic minority groups lives in China's rural villages.

Yunnan province, the area I left behind a few days ago, kept the fish, eels, frogs, or crabs alive and well for someone's dinner. Raw meat of "who knows what," chopped into unrecognizable parts, sat in plastic trays with utility lights hanging inches above.

Men pushed plastic bags of DVDs for a dollar in your face (watch out if you buy one or more, as that opens the door for you to see their special buy of the day, a "real Rolex watch"). I left the hordes of tourists behind in Fenghuang.

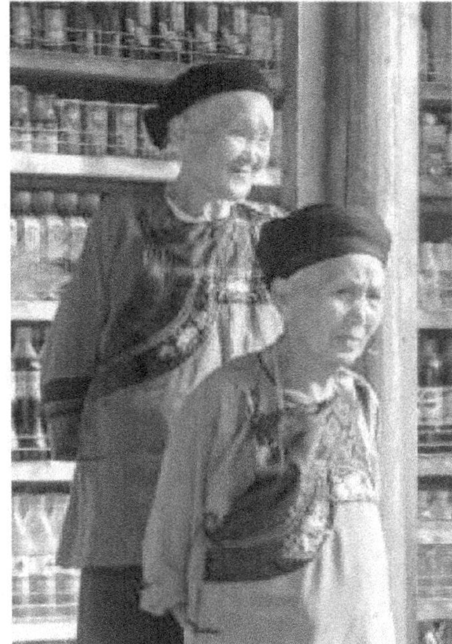

Local DeHang women watch a festival

My DeHang hotel overlooks the town square, perfect for spying on the local happenings! Overgrown with moss, a river separates me from the heart of the village. Steppingstones to the right allow quick access to cross, but the main artery flows over a stone-covered bridge to my left. After washing buckets of yesterday's dirty laundry, both men and women hang sheets, shirts, pants, and even winter jackets in sunny spots on the bridge overhang.

Men cut bamboo with sickles into strips for weaving baskets used to carry products from markets.

Old men, tired of living, watch the passersby, wondering what type of world they will leave their children. A man walks under the bridge. His legs, wrapped in algae, stirred the clear water to murky as he reached for trash with tongs similar to those sold on the shopping channel for people in wheelchairs, who need to pick up dropped items.

About 500' farther down a stone lane, I found the Jie Len Bridge, a special lookout spot as it connects the backsides of the village, which hug the gigantic peaks of the karsts, shadowing the village no matter where the sun tries to sneak in a few rays of light. In the northern horizon, the sun traverses the sky at an angle, which gave me three sunsets in one night!

Below the bridge, on top of the bridge, and on the roof, I photographed the sun sinking between vertical crevices of different peaks. No matter how many people have discovered DeHang, you feel like you discovered it yourself. The mists greet one head-on as you start on the day's agenda. Short sleeves and sunscreen do not fit the climate, as the dampness almost chills. The Miao people practice skilled embroidery but love their silver ornaments, as well.

The women wear clothing with bright, embroidered, flower motifs along the pants legs and shirt tops.

Shops, some with cement floors, and others, hard-packed dirt, sell "silver" buffalo key chains and bracelets.

I've lost track of time, and it's beginning to get dark, so I need to rush back to my hotel, as the steep, stone steps back become treacherous without use of a flashlight.

I have gotten lost so many times in these back alleyways; my landmarks consist of daytime remembrances!

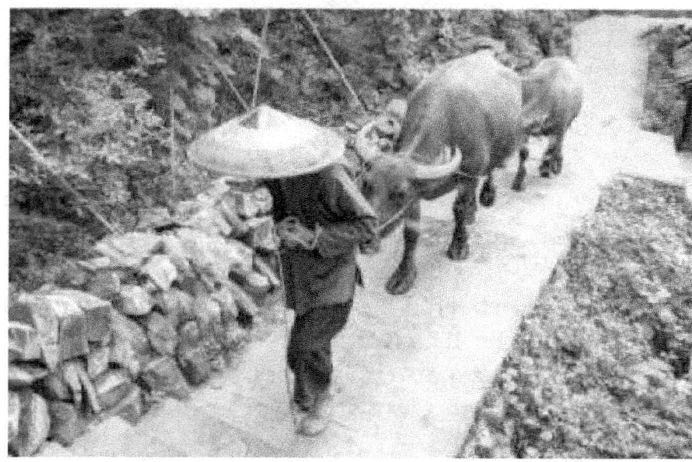

Leading buffalo home for the night

Packed up a small bag of stuff I don't need, including leftover unopened food for an old man, living across the river from my hotel, in a little hut. He talked on and on when I took it over, as he had no idea why I came onto his property.

I leave tomorrow morning for my journey back. I take a bus to Jishou and a six-hour train to Changsha. From there, I spend the night and all next day until midnight when I board a train to Shenzhen, China across the border from Hong Kong, which will involve a fourteen-hour train trip, I think. I'll have all day in Hong Kong till my 8:00 p.m. flight back to LA and will arrive at 8:00 p.m., same time I left on the same day. Spend the night in LA, leave the next morning at 8:45 a.m., and arrive back in Orlando.

I'm so tired of tuna fish; I hope I will not burn out on fish altogether! Today shall become a wonderful day for reflection and much-needed rest before the long journey back.

The time in Changsha could challenge my patience, as it's a dirty, huge factory town with nothing to offer the traveler. I may try to sneak into the Crown Plaza hotel for a meal or two. The hotels there cost too much, and to pay a couple hundred dollars for a room seems wasteful at this point!

More later when I have time.

Best and take care, jackie/mom

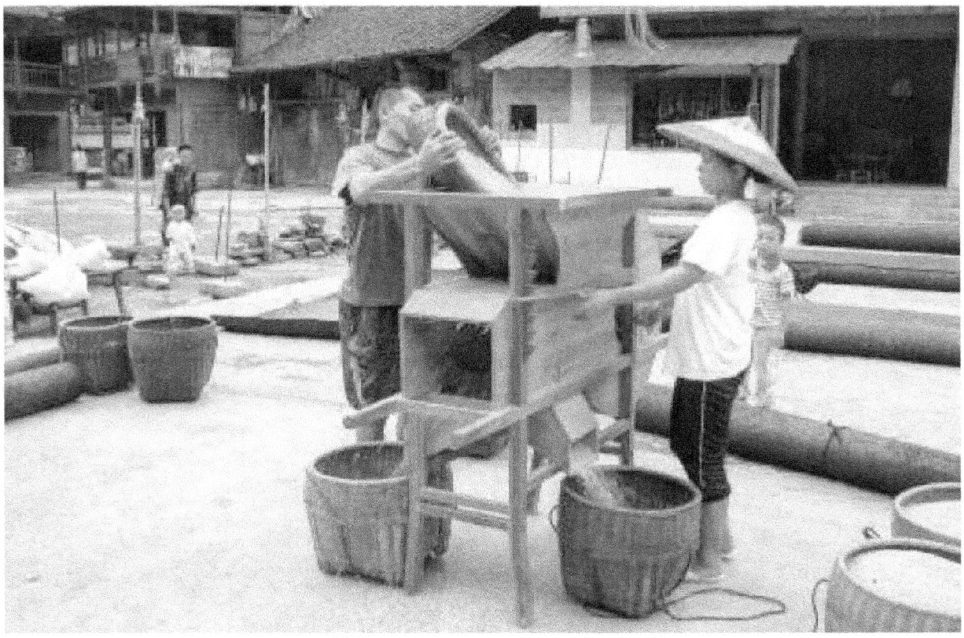

Milling rice removes the hull

Subject: Waiting in Changsda to come home 9:15 a.m.

Hi everyone:

A strange and fast last 24 hours for me. Took the train for eight hours from Jishou to Changsda. Found a hotel IN the train station, lowlife, but seemed clean and safe but not cheap at $18 for the night. I will stay here 'till midnight tonight, after coming in last night at 6:00 p.m., so will pay for two nights, as I have had my fill of hanging out in train stations in hard seats with no fans, etc. In addition, my room has a coffee pot, and I can make hot tea and eat my snacks on a comfy bed in privacy, which I need after my travels.

Thanks for all the support and kind words. Traveling alone has its moments, and sometimes I wonder why I do this. Now I can ask myself what I loved/hated the most and come up with some great answers.

I learned a lot about myself, and that in the end satisfies me. A sedate lifestyle is appealing, since I've moved around a lot, and the confusion of trains, planes and buses becomes a hectic lifestyle after a while.

Not sure how I did this trip. In reality, I would not recommend it to anyone, man or woman. The trip developed into something more difficult than I ever imagined. Just found out my daughter Katherine passed the VT bar exam, so I feel super happy for her.

I leave tonight on my long train ride back toward Hong Kong, first Shenzwen, and after that, I cross the border from China by train, probably, but would prefer a ferry, as one of my most memorable sights must include the junk boats in Hong Kong harbor.

I would love to take a photo of hundreds of them and enlarge and frame it for my lake room but won't have time for that tomorrow as I arrive late afternoon, and my flight leaves at 8:00 p.m. I have experienced a trip of a lifetime. Take sweet care, jackie/mom

CHAPTER ELEVEN

Sulawesi- Devotion Beneath the Surface

"For an immeasurable time, one went somewhere extraordinary and loved extraordinary things. One has been a traveler; and it is not a traveler's feet which ache." JH Patterson

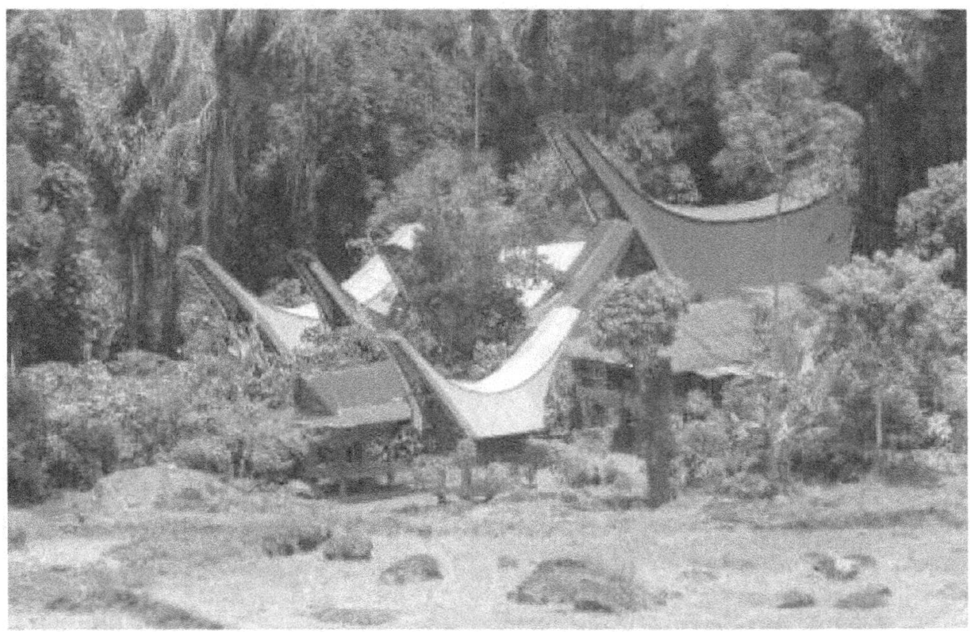

Tana Toroja homes in the valley

"Tell me about the most unusual thing you have ever eaten?" I asked a German woman, standing next to me, absorbing this incredible sight.

"Monkey, snake, bugs, worms, rats, cuscus and dogs seem normal in Fourth-World countries," she said as she scrunched up her nose and eyes while she answered. "But the worst-tasting animal ever is cat!"

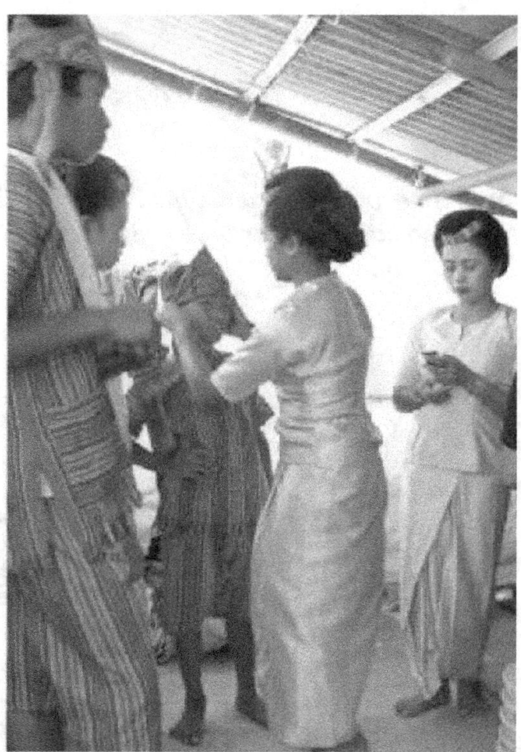

Tana Torojan costumes

The driver suggested I buy cigarettes for my hostess-gift. The cashier wrapped the carton in brown paper and tied it with string. Nonsmokers feel uneasy giving this gift.

The driver explained, "Friends will envy a gift of store-bought cigarettes, considered a real luxury. Everyone smokes here in the mountains of Sulawesi."

Pigs squealing in the distance gave my driver a direction to follow. A few people, both in front of us and following, confirmed the driver's thoughts of a funeral ceremony, taking place in some village close to the road closing ahead.

The driver accompanied me to the main structure for proper introductions to the deceased man's wife, which would allow me to wander the compound as part of the extended family. After I had offered the wrapped gift to women serving tea and biscuits, I followed the driver's motions of sitting Indian-style inside the makeshift funeral structure.

Now an official friend of the family, I felt comfortable enough to walk the village and enter the traditional longhouse, built on poles to house the coffin, left here for the last two years.

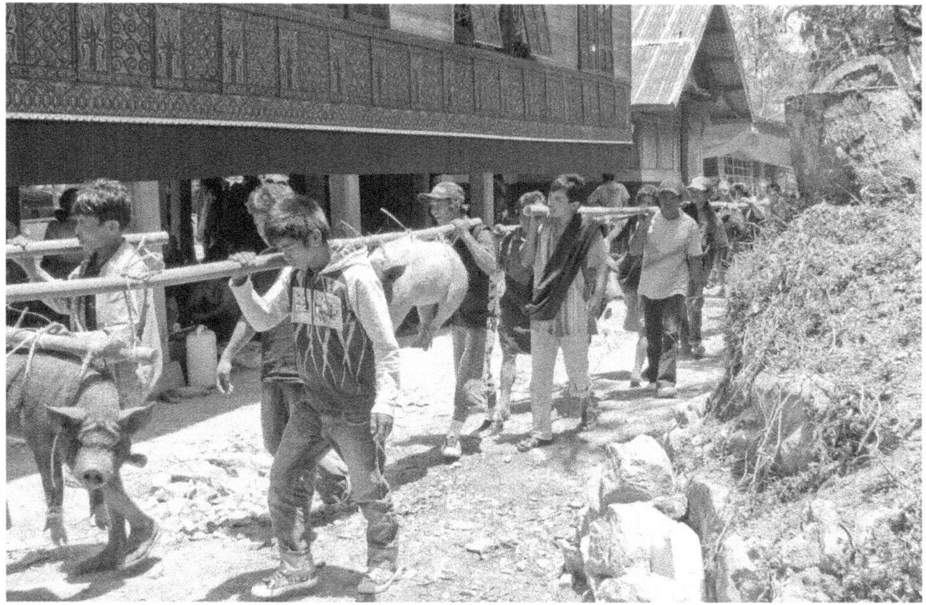

Parade with gifts

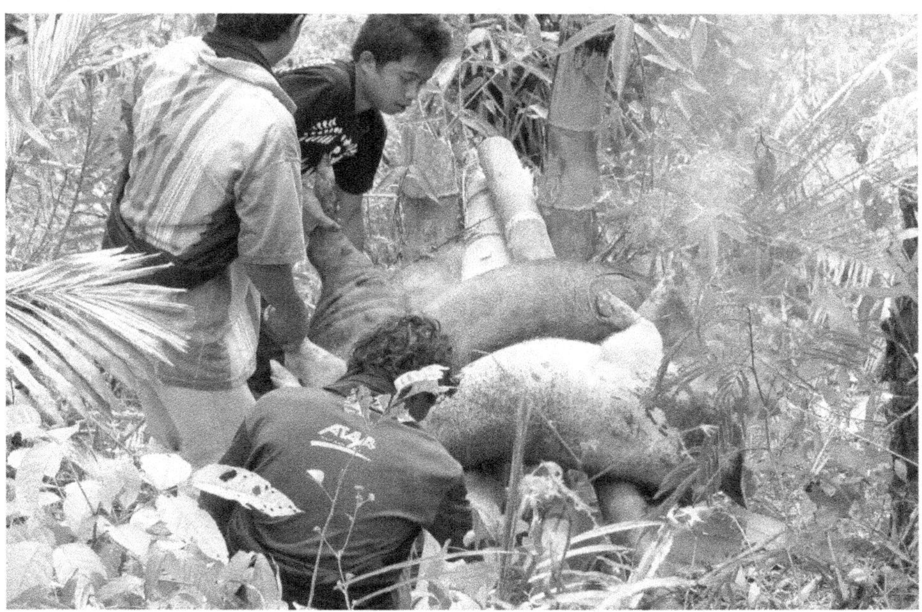

Roasting the slaughtered pigs

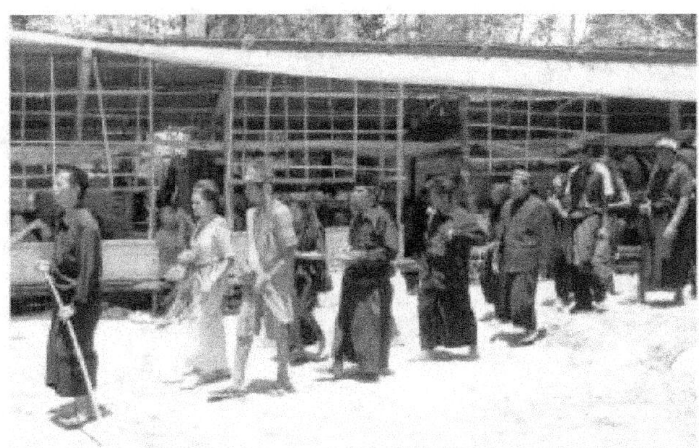

Funeral procession with family and friends

I watched the funeral ceremony all day. Whining pigs tied upside down on lengths of bamboo weighed heavy on the shoulders of men who struggled to get to the main ceremonial arena of the compound. Relatives encouraged me to take pictures of the coffin. The deceased, still part of the village, occupied a room alone. Makeshift structures circled this area for visiting relatives, friends and neighbors, some walking for days to attend. About twenty-five people, including children, watched in silence as four boys laid the pigs one by one on piles of banana leaves, sacrificed them with a knife, and cut them into small pieces.

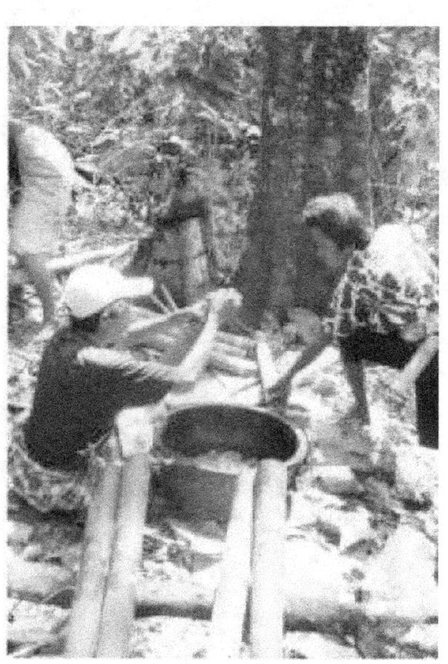

Stuffing bamboo with raw pork

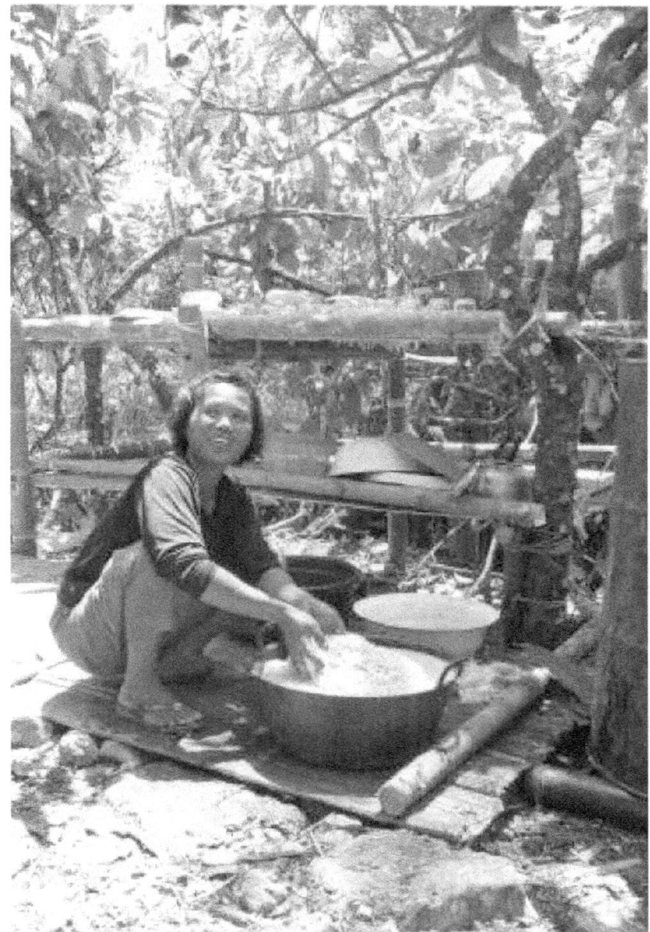

Preparing rice to feed hundreds of funeral guests

Sweat dripped onto the bloody hands of the young men, boys, and women stuffing the fresh cut pork into segments of bamboo.

The fire pit sent flames and sparks flying high after its feast of pig-fat dripping from the bamboo. Women picked up the hot bamboo with edges of sarongs and served hundreds of people sitting, walking, or standing in the longhouse.

The squealing in the distance seemed nonstop. I headed closer to the source of the commotion.

Several men towed pigs, feet first, toward the front of a line where two men made the deadly cut behind the ear. The noise bothered me, so my movie video (not for the faint-hearted) ended abruptly.

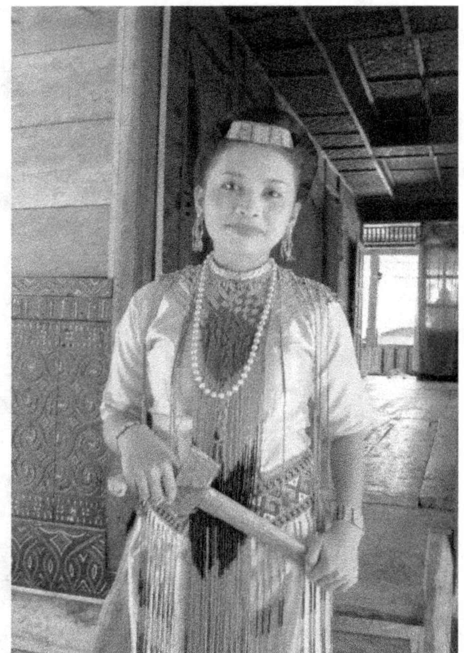

Tana Torojan in traditional dress

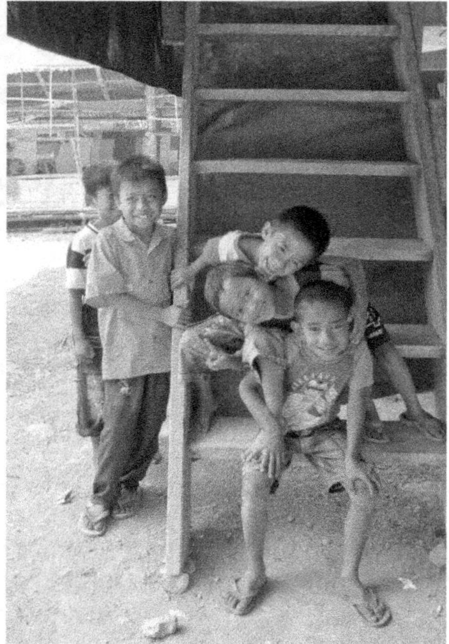

Children, playing on steps to home

Two parades began from opposite directions, each with family, neighbors and friends from afar.

The teasing and laughter of a group of young people, dressed in bright yellow traditional clothing, contrasted with the silent parade.

Funerals bring people together from distant villages, giving them an opportunity to arrange marriages, talk about business ideas, and establish bonds with relatives and friends.

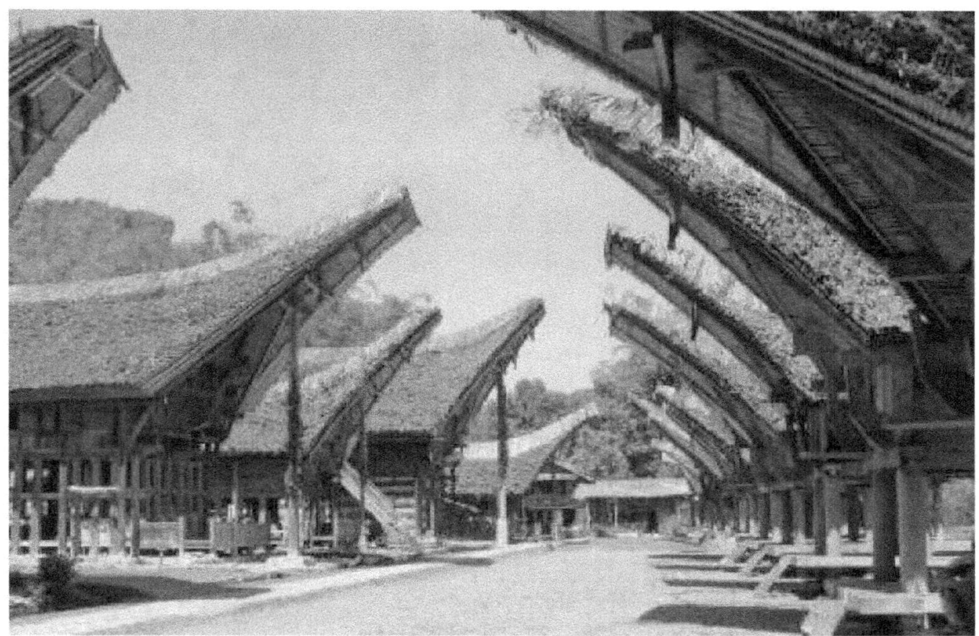

Tana Toroja homes

Pots two feet in diameter filled with raw rice sat waiting for their turn over the fire.

Women rinsed hundreds of plates and cups clean in a small stream behind the bamboo-slatted structures.

Young girls, bored from the monotony of carrying dishes back and forth, refused to smile.

Nobody seemed to care that the German woman and I watched and photographed them with looks of surprise at their customs.

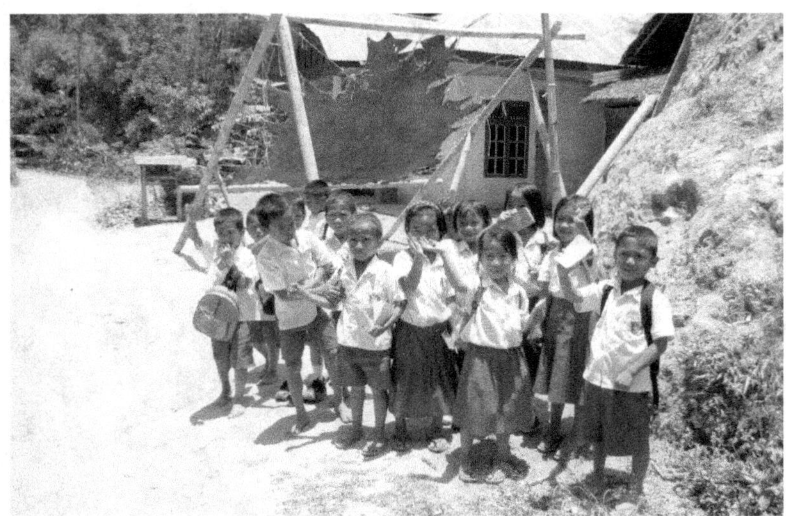

Schoolchildren

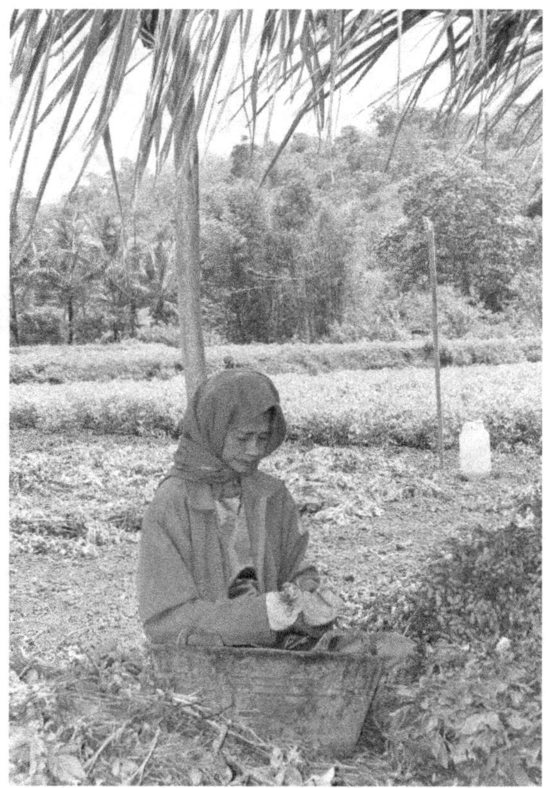

Cleaning peanuts

Immersion into the Toroja culture begins as you reach the jagged ridges, stretching over misty valleys drenched in history.

Red roofs of odd boat-shaped houses pierce thickets of bamboo and become a familiar sight on the seven-hour drive from the capital city, Makassar.

The most notable customs focus on elaborate funeral rituals, which take place up to ten years after some relative dies.

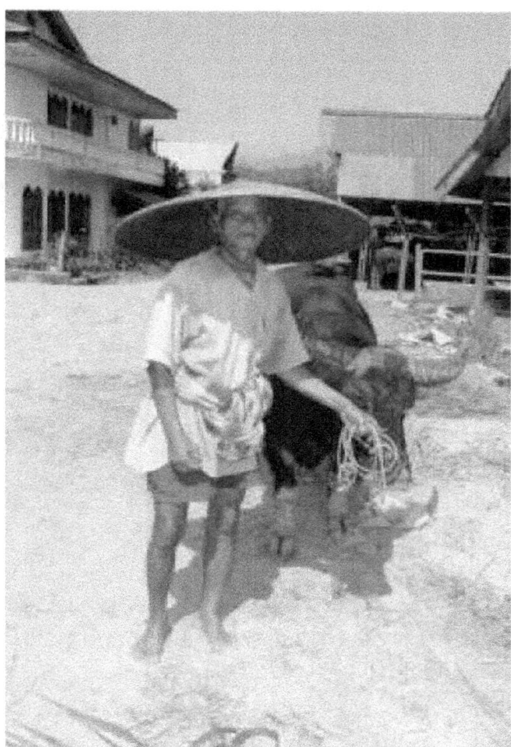

Proud of new purchase

The slopes of the limestone hills show off coconut palms, coffee and pine trees, hiding wet rice terraces and bushes of cloves. The Tana Toraja peoples base their death rituals on their animistic beliefs, which ensure a safe passage after death into the next world. The Torajans believe the deceased will use animals in their next world, so the families of the deceased try to compete for hosting the most guests and the greatest number of pigs and buffaloes sacrificed during the *Rambo Solo,* or funeral ceremony.

Unlike the Western funeral custom of showing respect for the deceased by wearing black and sharing stories in small groups, the Torajans spend years saving enough money for their upbeat ceremonies held after a death. Society includes the dead as well as the living for the Toraja people. The end of the rice harvest season signals the beginning of the funeral festivals. The dramatic ceremony sometimes lasts for many days with a procession carrying the coffin to a cave or wall of a mountain. Since the Torojan believe in life after death, favorite possessions accompany the dead.

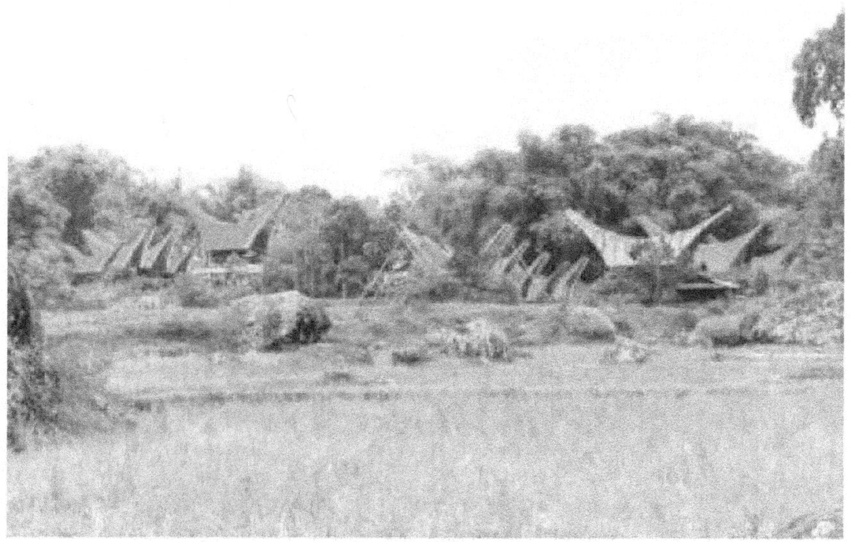

Tana Toroja village

Grave plundering creates a problem, so the people hide the deceased in caves or hire expert stone carvers to create sizeable openings high above the ground in the sides of rock-faced cliffs.

Wooden doors cover these openings, allowing for the addition of others later.

Branches jutting out from the stone facings turn into the poor man's cemetery as coffins hang in solitude high in the air, without worry of thieves, robbing the treasures of the deceased.

Numerous coffins burden the tree branches, clinging to mountainsides. Sometimes they break free and land in piles on top of one another below with bones splattered about the broken pieces of wood slats.

From a distance, the caves speckle the stone facings with the colors of granite.

Inside, skulls line the backs of stone boulders, a reminder of the importance of the permanence of stone.

This helps the living realize the deceased just moved on to their next life, as the stone remains forever.

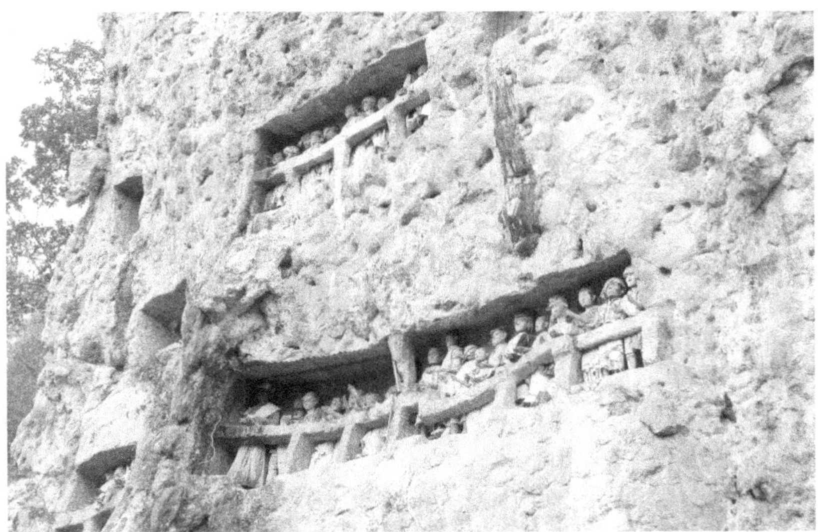

TauTau effigies on the side of a cliff

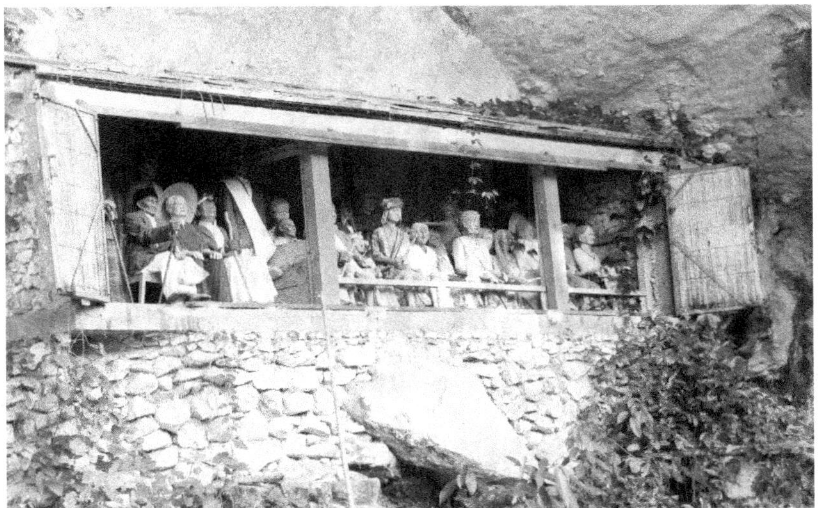

TauTaus, guarding the graves

The smell of fresh cut grass interrupted my thoughts. Movement rustled the thick river growth, seconds before a long bamboo stalk came crashing down in my path! I jumped back, bumping into a mass of cut bamboo, encircled by two bare arms. The invisible man with armfuls of bamboo bent over to pick up the dropped stalks in my path. Playing follow the leader, I realized he had built a ladder to reach a niche, carved in a stone facing for a new grave. Dozens of coffins, some empty and others rotted and weathered shut, zigzagged up the stone base. There, I saw more coffins precariously hanging from horizontal tree limbs.

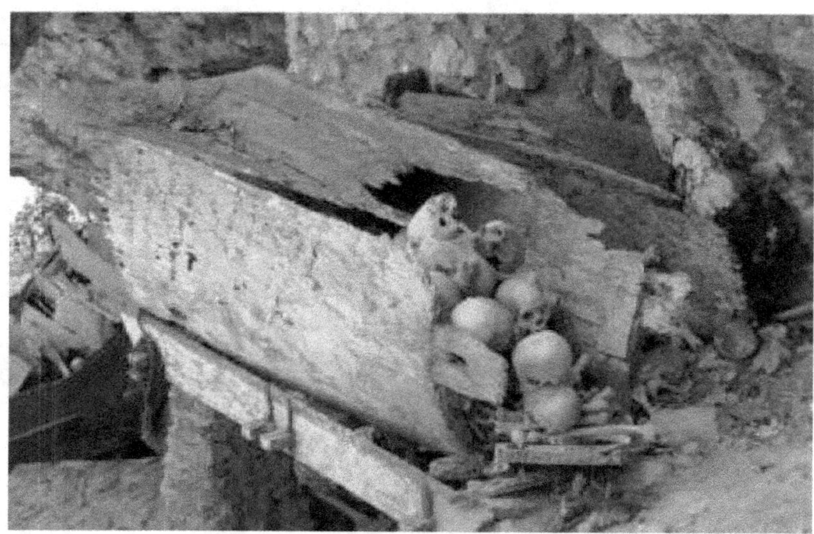

Broken coffin

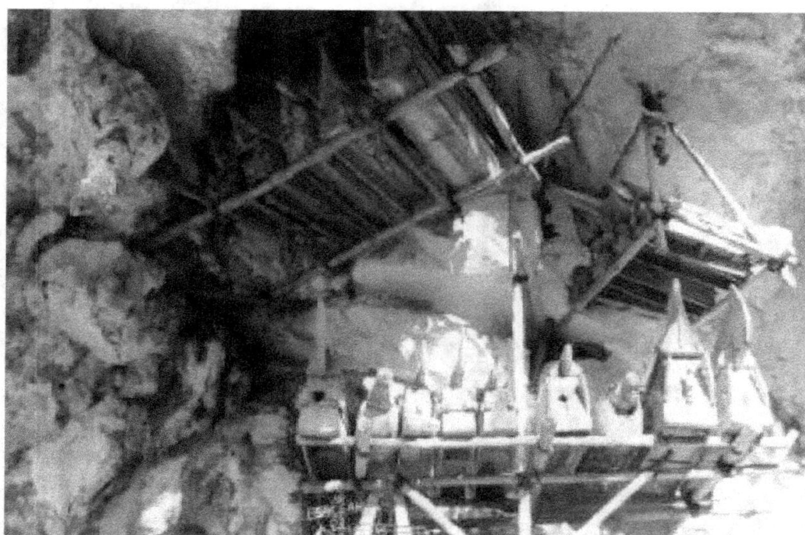

Hanging coffins on cliff

Three or four stories off the ground, to protect these coffins from thieves, stonecutters carve balconies where the *tau taus*, or wood statues, stand watch over the tombs.

A row of male and female figures stood guard in a box carved deep into the stone. From a distance, they looked alive in their sarongs and traditional clothing. With the zoom lens on the camera, I could see the cracks in the elegant wood (Jackfruit), selected for these creations since it represents a status symbol for the wealthy. The Tau Tau effigies, carved to look like the deceased they represent, wore the clothing of the dead and real hair wigs.

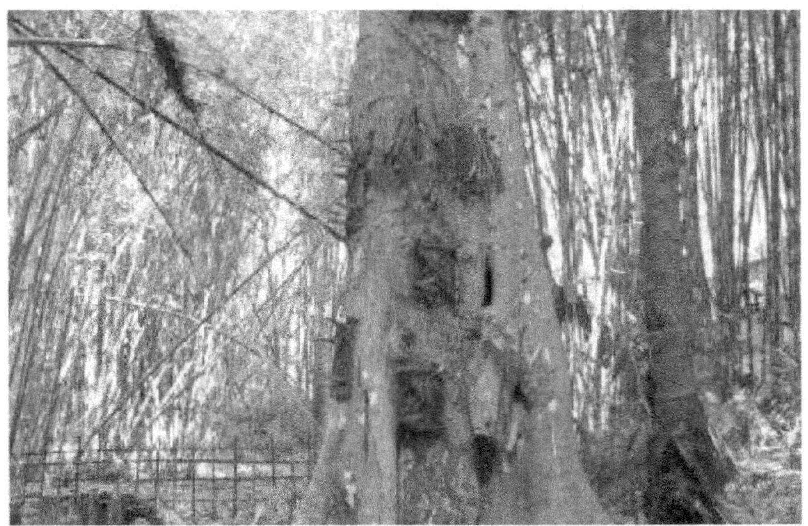

Baby graves in tree in Kambira

The damp fog felt skin deep, nothing compared to the eeriness filling my body while I walked the jungle path to see the baby graves. The animist Tana Toroja people believe in *Aluk to Dolo*, or the way of the ancestor. Their deceased pass into *puya*, or their forever life, on the back of a buffalo, killed at their funeral festival. When a baby dies before teething, it is too young to ride the animal so the villagers bury the baby in the trunk of a tree. Palm fiber or small wooden doors cover the opening, and the tree grows around the baby for sixteen years, followed by a celebration for the baby's spirit, which disappears from the tree for its puya.

An unreadable sign, close to Pana, diverted my jungle walk. The purity of the little ones buried in the trees awakened sadness within me, adding to the effect of the dreary morning. One third of the 300,000 Torajans, living in the Tana Toraja Mountains continue the dramatic funeral ceremonies while living in impressive homes towering over fields of rice and bamboo. The saddle-backed roofs of bamboo remain a trademark of ethnic identity and punctuate the valleys in small clusters, rather than compact villages. The locals call their great homes *tongkonan* (to inhabit with permanence). North-facing doorways allow gods, who rule from the North and East, to enter.

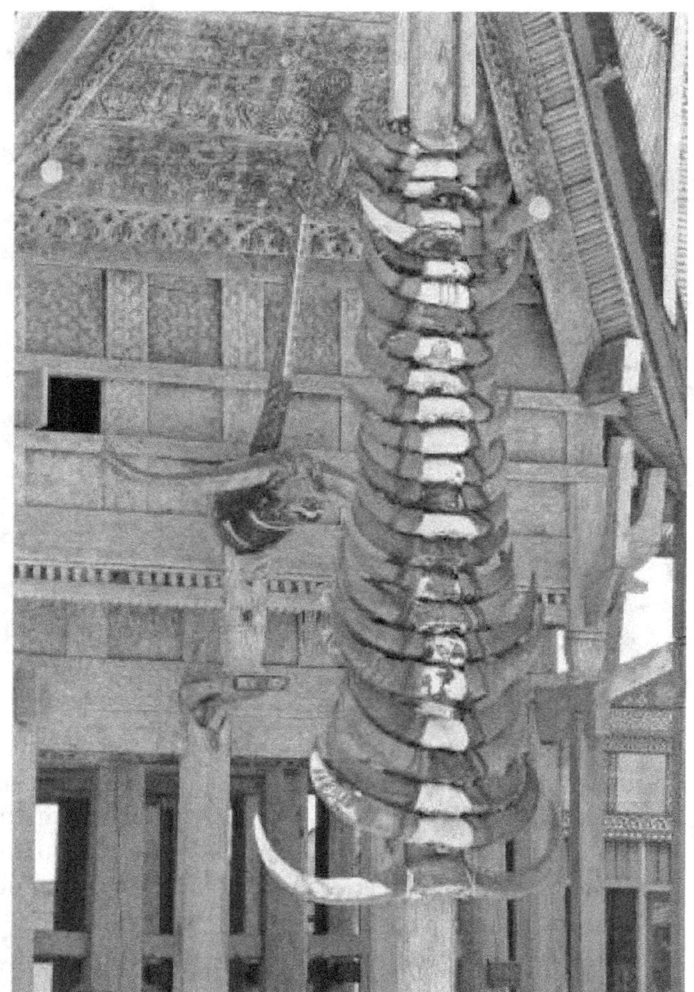

Horns from sacrificed buffalo

Water buffalo horns, the principal symbol of position in the community, sit stacked vertically on the front poles of homes. The wealthier families sacrifice more buffaloes for their deceased members.

Amir, my driver for the week, did not mind that his car had no shock absorbers. Neither did I, considering his hundred-dollar price for a week of chauffeuring me seven hours from Makkassar to Rantepao and back again, plus allowing me to enjoy all the little villages and ceremonies we found along the path. As I slid toward the edge of the seat, my knees slammed against the dashboard, but that felt less painful than the jolts to my bottom from the deep ruts of the roads.

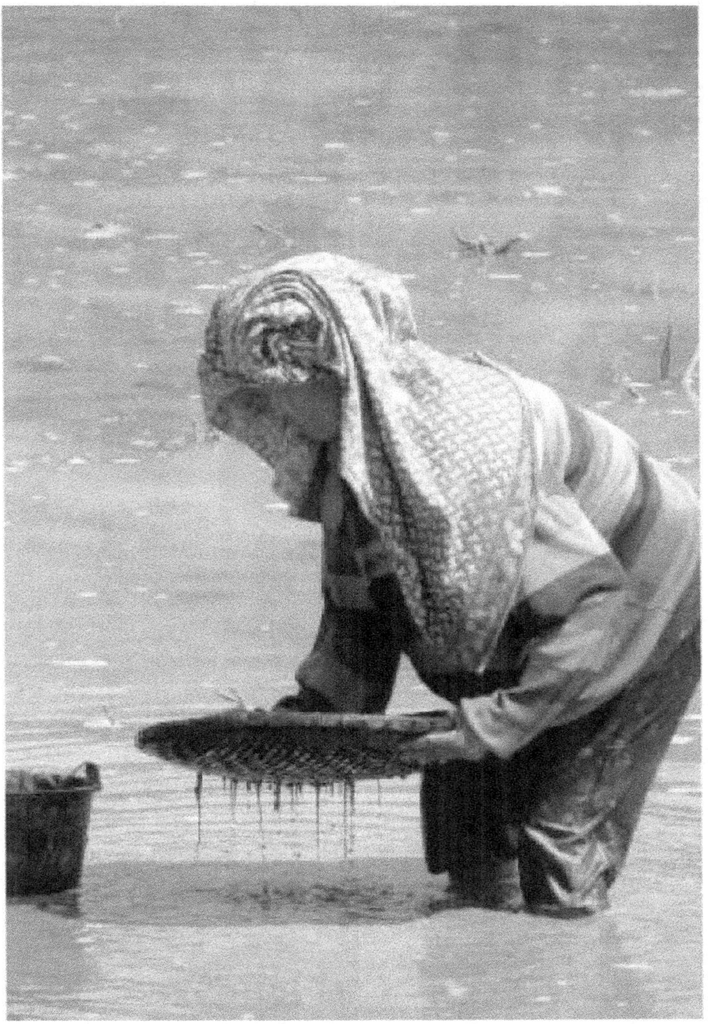

Straining for small fish

After passing the first group of ship-shaped houses, I asked Amir, "Where did the idea of building houses in that shape come from?"

"Many old stories explain," he paused. "Sailors came from faraway lands with their big ships. One year the water dried up, and the ships ended up stuck on the mountainsides. Since the travelers had no other place to live, the ships became their homes."

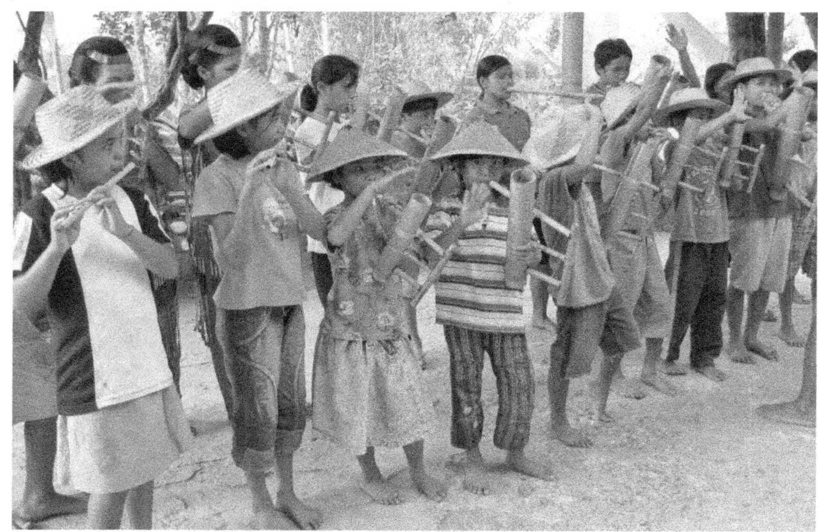

Children at orphanage, playing flutes

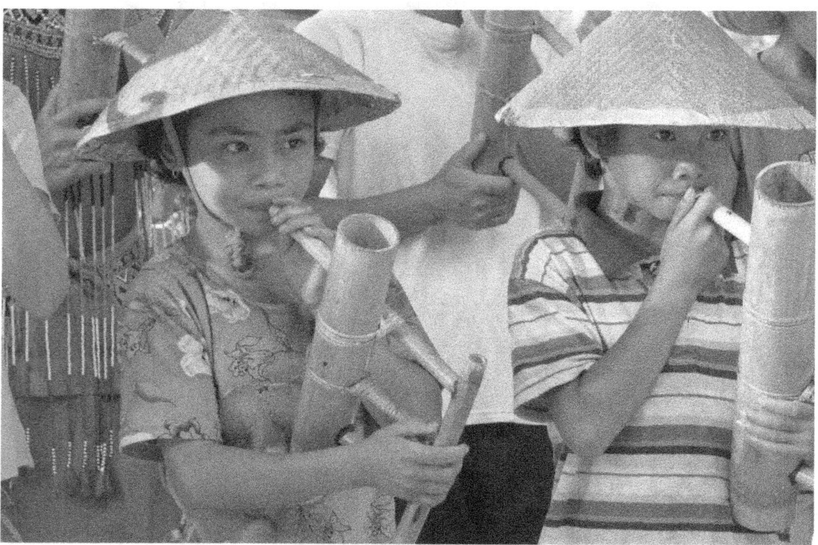

Orphans, playing flutes

Children ranging from around six years old into the teens lined up in front of the house, each holding odd-shaped bamboo flutes. One nod from their foster father, and the front yard filled with music. I sat watching each child play his or her instrument with precision, and each offered joyful smiles between their parts of the song.

Two children about eight years old flirted with me during every song, their body language begging for attention. My eyes kept going back to those kids. Their appearance was unisex. The younger kids dressed in simple tee shirts, long pants, and straw hats covering short black hair. Two of the teenage girls looked lovely, dressed in full, traditional, ethnic clothing, with their long hair braided and clasped with beautiful, flowered barrettes, matching the color of their lipstick and eye shadow.

The orphanage owner did a superb job of raising healthy children with an organized method for teaching responsibility to the community. The foster father of these twenty-seven children explained that his kids performed for community events, and, in return, people provided food and clothing for the children.

The children acted out a couple of simple skits using props and costumes. The two children wanting my attention played the lead roles, knowing the more emotion they exhibited, the more clapping they'd receive. This encouraged them. The music from Mr. Brown's children entertained me for over an hour.

I remembered that, stuffed deep in my pack, I would find the dozen or more blowup punch balls I had brought for special moments with native children, plus the miscellaneous gifts I had picked up at a night market. The two teenage girls traded the fingernail polish and hair barrettes back and forth until each girl had what she liked. The blowup balloon balls scared the children when I bounced them back and forth with the long rubber-band handle.

I waved at the two children in the spotlight to join me, and hesitation caused them to move in my direction, one step at a time. After a few seconds, they figured out the game, and the group laughed and joined in the fun.

Every time I hear the CD I bought from Mr. Brown of these fabulous children, playing their flutes, I will remember those smiles of contentment. A couple of boys playfully tossed some rocks back and forth in some local game under the tipped roofline of the Toroja rice barn.

They wanted to catch my eye, but when I pointed the camera at them, they jumped and hid behind the massive vertical poles, supporting the top storage area. The houses seemed deserted as the ghosts of ancestors played with the wind through the skeleton heads of buffalo, decorating the front of each home and strung from the ground to the top of the roof.

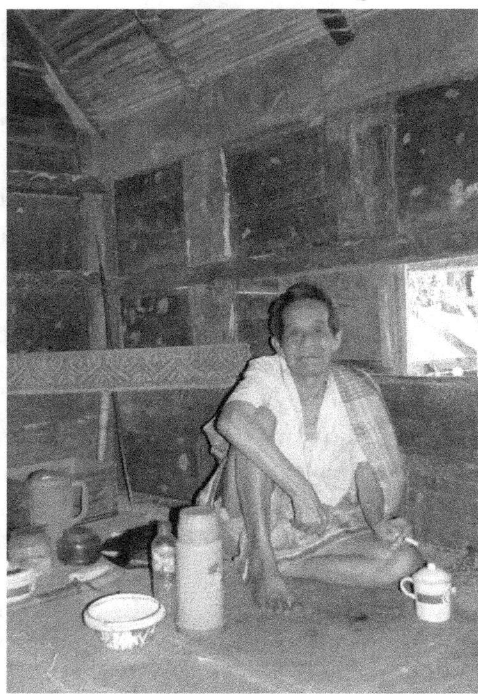

Tana Toroja man by window

A wrinkled face high above in a window came alive as I passed his way along the street and waved at him. I pointed to his home, and then to myself, and he nodded with hesitation. I turned to Amir, who was following me, and explained my invitation to tour the inside of a house.

With each step we took into the pitch-black, lower level of the house, the smell of mold seemed to rise around us. I looked to find the staircase leading to the old man.

As I passed the second floor, I felt as if a time machine had slowed to let me out. He sat cross-legged, close enough to the window for viewing the occasional passerby, but still within reach of a blue thermos, a worn, ragged, filthy pillow and a pile of tobacco leaves rolled into shapes like pencils. My driver pointed to an enclosure like an open cage with vertical poles, half enclosing a linoleum pad covering the wood-planked flooring.

"They use that area for baby making," Amir said as he raised his eyebrows a few times. Amir said something to the old man, and when he smiled, I took his photo.

I showed it to him on the monitor of the digital camera. His smiles increased ear-to-ear as he touched my arm with long skeleton-like fingers. I wanted to give him something special in return for his warm welcome and an inside view of a Torajan's home.

Water bottles and snacks remained in the vehicle. A passport and faded-from-sweat photographs of my four children filled my wallet. He held the photos, one by one, sliding his fingers over and over the faces until one photograph caused him to make questioning sounds. As my youngest daughter had practiced jumping her horse, Chance, I had caught her image suspended over a four-foot tall fence. Maybe he had never seen a horse before.

I told Amir to try to explain the large animal we ride. The old man grasped my hands and held tight. I hoped I had filled a small gap in his quiet day.

After a few days of wandering villages, I felt deluged with bizarre events. I wanted to understand more about this culture but felt the villagers' spiritual beliefs held too many constraints for an outsider. As an adventure traveler, I leave my bed of roses behind while catering to my senses, health, and general safety.

I accept the inconvenience of leaving the creature comforts, like hot water, electricity and fresh salads, all on hold until my return. Caves filled with skulls, animals sacrificed, and coffins hanging about, tend to feed one with emotions.

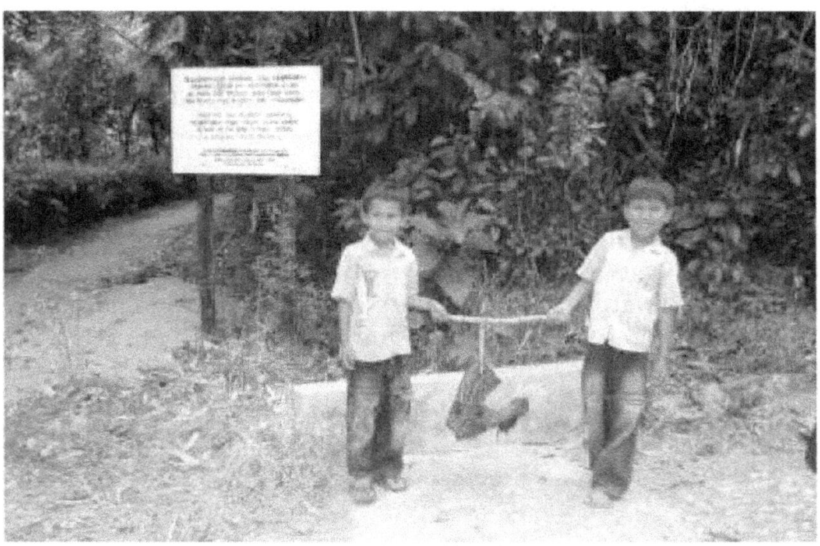

Boys, carrying gift of pork

Two little boys, walking home from a funeral ceremony surprised me with their chattering along a jungle path. They balanced a long bamboo pole on their shoulders with a piece of dripping raw meat, buzzing with flies and swinging between them. I followed them for a bit, but soon I heard music and changed directions to follow it. A group of grey-crowned men, dressed in traditional clothing, played loud, off-tune music. Off to the side, several men sat on their calves, swinging machetes and small axes on hunks of raw meat.

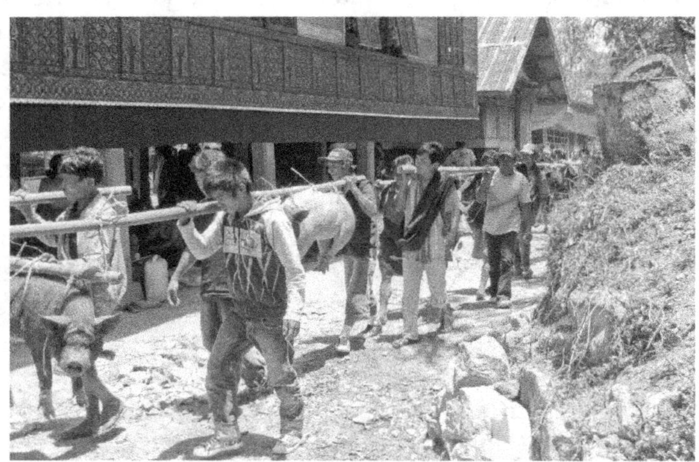

Gifts of fresh meat

A well-dressed man in Western clothing extended his hand to me, saying, "I just finished building my home and want to celebrate with my village. Please stay with us for as long as you like. We have many rooms available."

The energetic Torajans embrace eccentric traditions that have brought them dignity and contentment.

The chilling silences after our walks to the caves or stone graveyards disappeared when laughing children, chasing baby pigs, stumbled in piles on top of one another.

Their welcoming attitude left me with a positive feeling and a yearning for a better understanding of this timeless culture, balancing Christianity with animistic beliefs.

CHAPTER TWELVE

Vietnam: A Series of Unfoldings

"Cook boldly, serve your heart, and what's empty will be filled." Anonymous

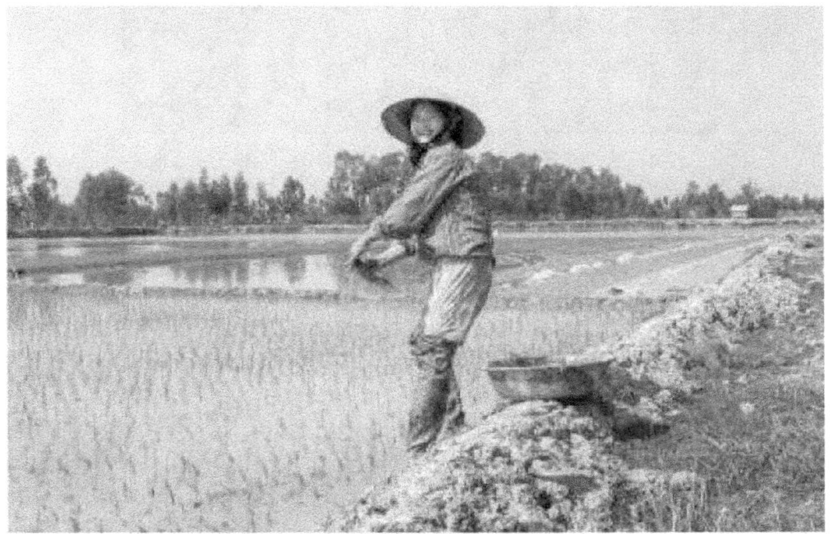

Working rice paddies near Van Lam

The border crossing from Cambodia into Chau Doc, Vietnam via the fast boat happened without cause for concern. My passport stamped "Exit" did not have significance for me at the time. Rickshaw drivers, waiting there for arriving boat passengers, hoped for a few coins to pay for dinner. Stick legs and boney arms moved toward me. His shredded clothing looked like it might fall off the old man before he reached me. His smile had me hiring him for a traditional rickshaw ride to the hotel. The newer *xe loi,* or rickshaws, use pedals like those on a bicycle compared to the older models which required a man to run barefoot between two extended handles in the front of the conveyance, pulling passengers who are seated in the riding compartment behind him. The first two hotels on my list had no available rooms, and so we made our way through the masses of people on the streets. The wheels of the rickshaw scraped the arms of shoppers, staring at goods spread on the ground.

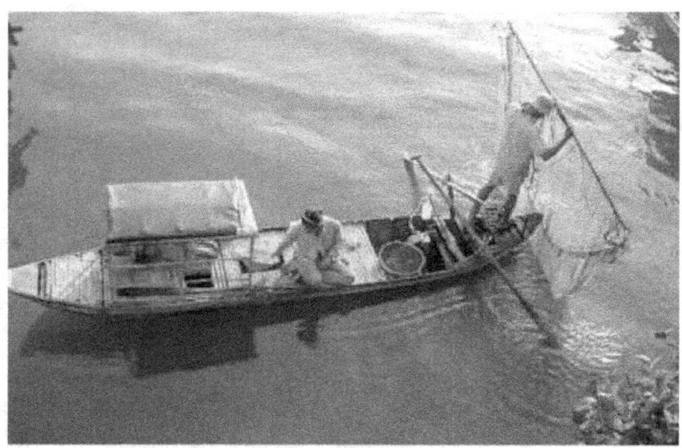

Early morning fishing in Chau Doc

My luggage sat helpless behind me, vulnerable to any thief, having the guts to grab it and run.

Finding a few more full hotels frightened me almost as much as the darkness, framing the tin-roofed shacks on either side of us.

This dear little man continued to run on, dragging me along on his rickshaw, wanting to please me. The man's shoulders hunched over with my weight.

He spoke a few words of English and nodded yes when I asked if he could find a restaurant with some soup. I ordered two, but he refused to come inside.

The wall-less room provided me with a perfect view of my luggage, although the old man had demonstrated his speed in moving his rickshaw and might outrun me if the lure of luggage filled with modern-world toys proved too much for his honesty.

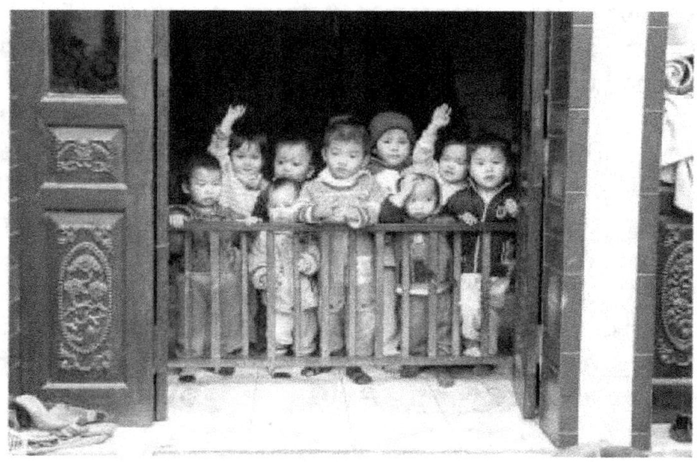

Daycare in Ninh Binh

The restaurant offered no carryout cartons, so the owner dumped the extra soup in a plastic bag, and he knew the old man would consume it quickly, so there was no need to worry about it leaking. The hot broth with a few veggies, half of a chicken foot, and little else recharged us both enough to continue the search for a hotel. A tall place on the river close to where we met ended our search. The rickshaw driver wanted fifty cents for his several-hour sojourn around the town. I pressed coins equivalent to a few dollars into his hands, and he promised to return for my morning departure to Vinn Long.

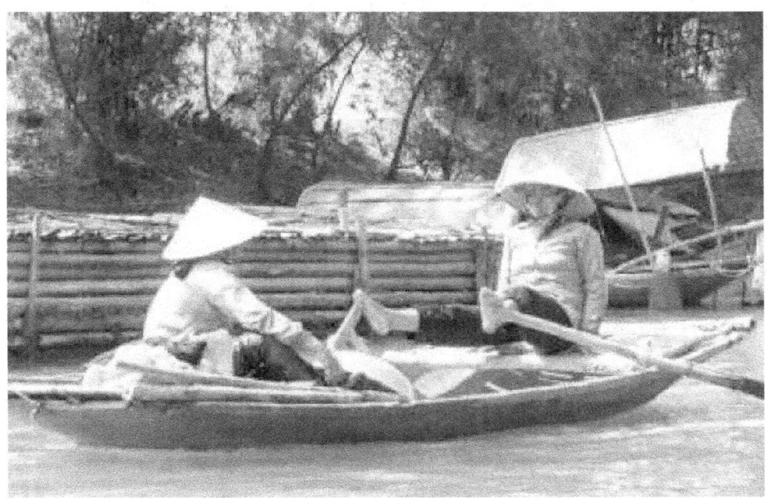

Rowing with feet on the Ngo River

I wanted to sample the many elements of the river town of Chau Doc, 175 miles, or 280 km, from Ho Chi Minh City. A walk down any alleyway immerses the foreign visitor in the atmosphere of this remote Mekong Delta settlement.

The animation of the energetic market full of alert and aggressive locals stops all rickshaw traffic. Frisky fish try to escape their waterless paper boxes.

Carts full of rice sacks bob up and down, pushed by boys too little to move the weight on their own.

People, sitting on the filthy streets, line up in row after row, shouting, eager to catch the attention of a buyer.

Within minutes, the newcomer discovers the truth that Chau Doc, or the kingdom of fermented fish, earns its name every day. Young sweat-covered girls, bloody to their waists, their push baskets full of fish heads and tails dripping with blood trails of gore behind them. The *mam*, or fermented fish products, appear in quantities great enough for a king's ransom.

The smelly fish obscured the path to the *thot not fruits*, or Palmyra palms, made into sugary delights. Expressive Khmer women invite passersby to try the sweet juice of the coconut-like fruit. Thousands of thot not trees envelop the countryside of Chau Doc.

Huge sampans plow the river past evergreen islands that appear like a miniature Venice with crisscrossed, meandering little canals. Sampans with their flat bottoms serve as a permanent habitation on rivers or coastal areas, as they have no means of surviving rough weather. Rent your own for three days for a few hundred dollars, complete with features found in a modern-day hotel. Stop at floating villages to view the *tra* and *basa* catfish cages underwater.

Trap doors in the floors of the sampans allow access to nets under the boathomes where fish wait for the market or that night's meal. Fruit and water hyacinth plantations will fill your viewfinder with trails of smoke, reaching the sky from the faraway brick factories. Life on the floating islands gives one a better understanding of the inventiveness of people who figure out ways to survive.

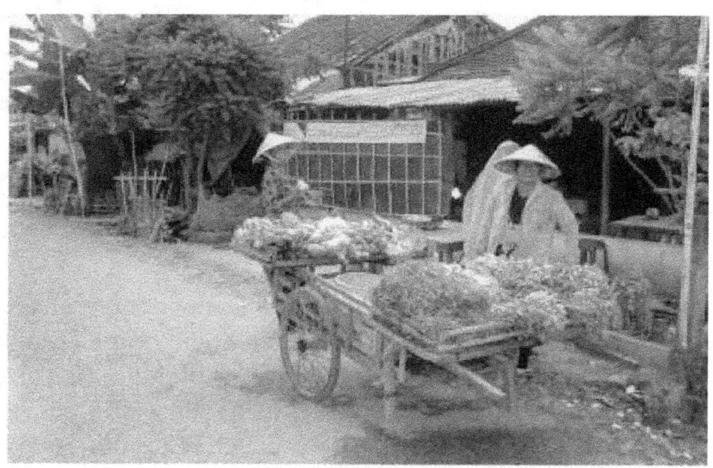

Anxious for that first sale of the day

Her round, brown eyes squinted at me with a smile. She had been my little captain and I her passenger. Our small boat, hard to manage on the mighty Mekong, bumped up against unstable pylons at the shore. The young girl's job was now finished, and she wanted to return home before sunset.

Our departure city, Vinn Long, sat hours away on the shores of Vietnam's Mekong River. I had left after breakfast with the promise of finding a home on the river with villagers who might invite me to stay with them, and the boat driver had found their home, here on the banks of the Mekong.

Layers of fish netting, ropes, clothing rags, and a shoe with the sole missing trapped my feet as I tried to exit the boat. Clumps of tall grass made a great handhold for me as I inched onto shore. Bent over and almost crawling, I found the wooden walkway meeting the house.

The sign language of the girl, hands wildly flailing, signaled her desire for me to keep moving forward.

Words like, "Okay, okay," along with her fake smiles did not assure me that I had the correct address for my invitation. Her departure back to Vinn Long, without any contact with this family, might spell trouble for me.

The frenzy of that crucial moment of my uncertainty vanished like a cloud's shadow in sunlight as a girl in a blue dress suddenly appeared on the shore and held her hands out to greet me.

One of the love/hate relationships with travel that keeps me going, but might detour others from similar travels, comes in the form of language barriers. For instance, if I ask a question of a native, and she nods her head, that does not mean she understood anything I said to her.

You must never assume a total understanding before embarking on a journey with a person who does not speak your language.

If someone speaks in a foreign language, do not ever nod or say yes to them unless every gesture they make and every word they say makes sense to you. And vice versa.

If speaking to people in a foreign country, never assume they comprehend your questions just because they nod or say yes. Agreeing with a taxi driver or potential guide means a commitment, and the end of the story might take you well off the beaten track.

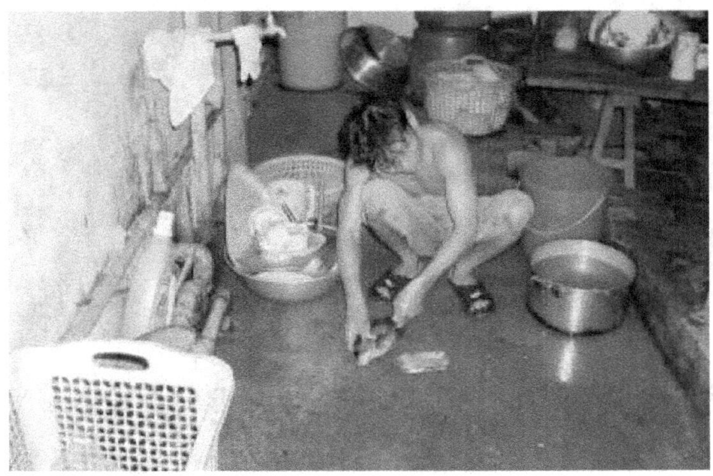

Cleaning fish on the floor in house on the Mekong

Survival techniques for people living on the Mekong River depend on applying lessons learned from their ancestors.

The girl who welcomed me to shore was the daughter of a man and woman who owned a few acres of land, which gave them the ability to channel irrigation and fill pools for fish hatcheries.

In her blue dress, the girl, about twenty, led me on a tour of the acreage. After exploring the compound, she allowed me to help feed her pets: a young duck (on their list for roast duckling, I imagine), and an unhappy little monkey tied inside a cage.

These people spoke not a word of English, so explaining my picky eating habits at dinnertime turned into a chore fraught with embarrassment.

The girl scooped a huge fish from the pond hidden behind the house. I tried to communicate my wish to let the fish live, and for them to throw him back. If fish tails and eyeballs remain attached to their owner, you can take a fish dinner off my menu!

The girl pounded the fish with a mallet until dead, and that did not make my appetite for greasy fish grow! Next, the poor thing landed in a wok designed for a giant, full of bubbling liquid used in the last several weeks of cooking.

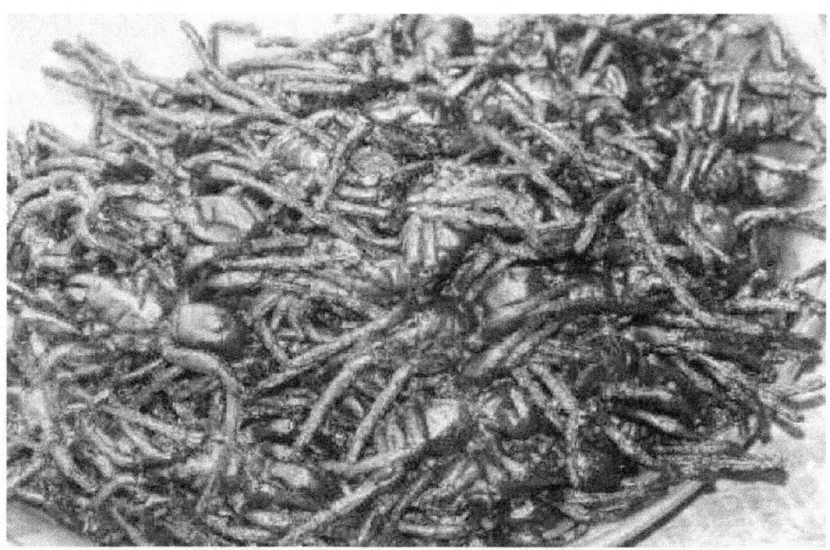

Fried tarantulas, a local delicacy

Ungracefully, a grandmother squatted on the kitchen's dirt floor, chopping onions and other green stringy things.

She smiled a cautious smile without missing a beat with the knife, carving little breaks in the dirt footprints left by barefoot family members.

The blue-dress girl wanted me to rest, out of the way of food preparation, and motioned for me to go back to my little bed area on stilts.

Candle in hand, she approached about an hour later with whispers of what I did not want to hear, something about food to eat.

Several courses graced the table set for a princess. And the fish? He rested upright on a stand, coated in a crunchy-looking batter, empty eye sockets and all.

The geography of Vietnam offers numerous ways to witness the unspoiled mountain trails, explore thousands of hidden islands, and meet the local people with arms wide open to the Western world.

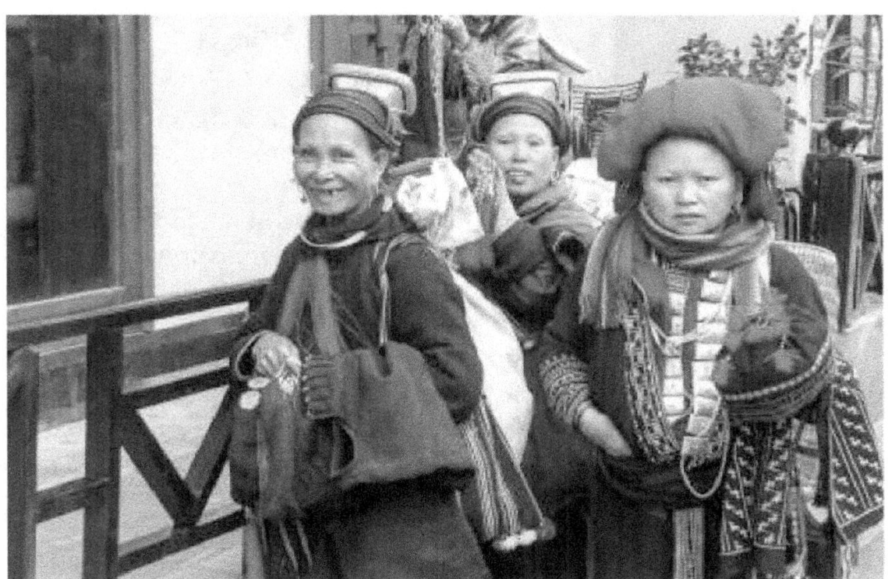

Black and Red Dao women in Sapa

The sign on the window said, "Heated Restaurant."

Sapa had a reputation for cold temperatures, sneaking in at night and deciding to stay.

A light drizzle tickled my eyelashes like snowflakes. Rooms vacant of heat, as well as people, still welcomed warm bodies for overnight stays.

The one restaurant in town advertised warmth and sat across from my hotel.

For Sapa, a $25 dinner shocked me and turned my stomach when served. And the heat?

I had to ask, and, only after I pointed to the sign did a woman carry a black bucket full of cold gray embers and position it close to my feet. Did she think that charcoal, even if lit, would warm my cold bones?

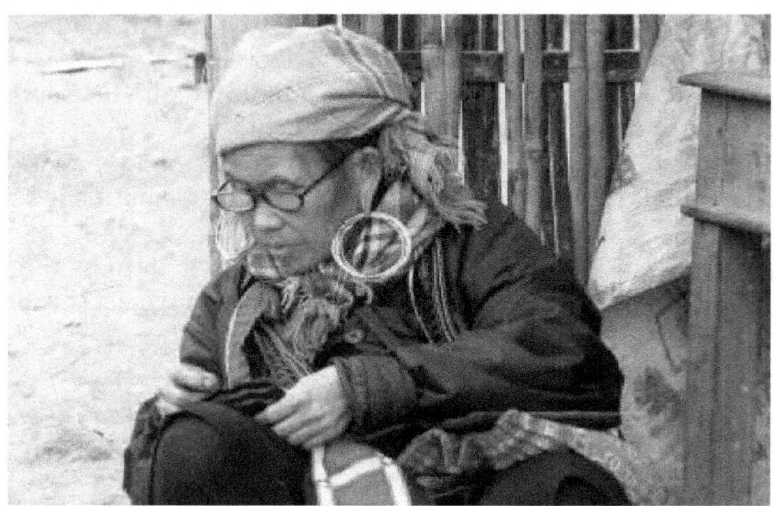

Hmong embroidering in Sapa

Roaming the city's modern streets, tribal women looked like actors in costumes, awaiting their turn in a play. Every female, young or old, held a handful of souvenirs to my face, disrupting the silence I needed to absorb the feeling of the place.

"You remember me," and "You buy from me," echoed from the peaks of Mount Fansipan, Vietnam's highest mountain, shadowing Sapa.

A lone walk into the countryside gives one the feeling of playing the Pied Piper role. Children, even teenagers, follow behind, carrying remarkable amounts of curiosity. Courage takes over as their ice-cold hands grasp mine, wanting to share first a schoolhouse, then a home.

Cat Cat Village sounded like a suitable beginning, and it had a reputation for welcoming people wanting to share their village customs and culture. Names have a way of pulling on my heartstrings. I have to admit that places like Bora Bora, Kathmandu, Shangri La and Timbuktu made it to my wish list because of their names. Time and money get in the way until I begin the research and find that for example, after seeing the movie, *Lost Horizon*, my next trip has to include Shangri La.

Cat Cat Village organized itself like a movie set ready for tourists at the sound of a visitor's footsteps. Except for the burst of work when planting or harvesting rice, the villagers spent their time creating souvenirs. In every few houses, a small group congregates in circles, sitting on child-sized stools and stitching purses, shawls, potholders, and pencils for the tourist crowd. Dogs bark at muddy children in threadbare clothing, both groups stopping to stare at the intrusion of their games. My dream of socks with batteries to provide warmth came to mind after seeing every villager in bare feet.

An H'Mong family's invitation to join the circle around the fire inside their house sounded warm and cozy. A girl speaking perfect English explained her wish for college and a career in the city. After hearing her stories, I wondered how she might make the transition from muddy bare feet to shoes and traffic. She laughed as she covered her face, hiding her quiet voice.

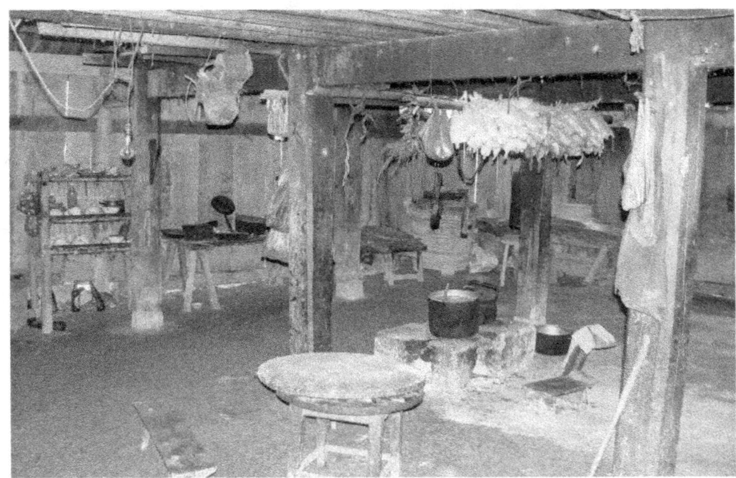

Hmong kitchen area

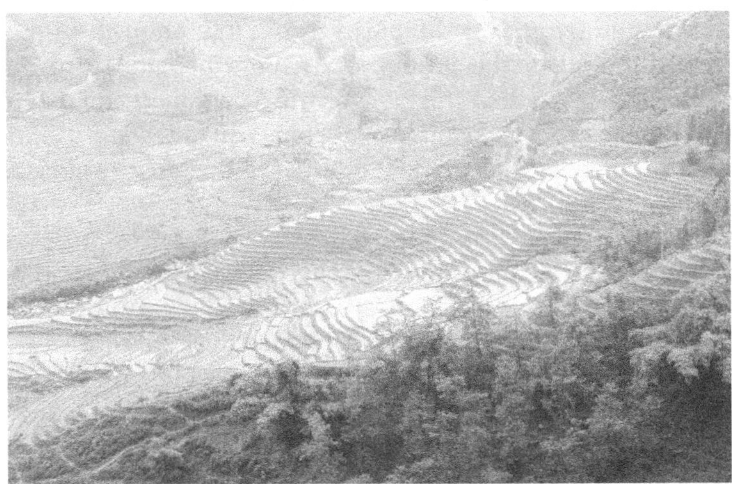

Rice terraces of Sapa

Almost embarrassed, she began her tale of how the Black H'Mong court their wives. "When a boy finds a girl he likes, he kidnaps her and takes her to his parent's home. She must stay there for two weeks, and if she likes it, she stays, and they will marry soon. If she finds herself unhappy, she may return home."

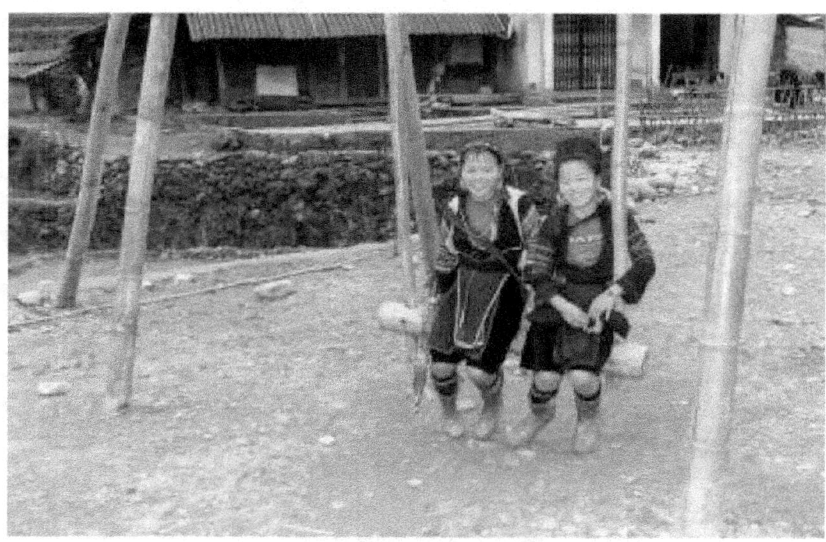

Hmong girls

The H'Mong tribes live in poverty. Therefore, their struggle to survive requires more involvement with tourists, compared to other hill tribes in the area like the Red Dao and Dzay. Narrow paths, running along the edges of rice terraces, provide the way to the Village of Ta Van, a Dzay (also Zay) tribe of around 500 people. If you visit this part of the world, you can ask to help with rice threshing if the harvest season has started. You will separate the grains by beating a handful of cut stalks against a bin, and the loose grains will fall onto a mat used for collection.

Rice fields, stretching to the horizon, were a delight to my eyes while we trekked up and down the steep slopes of the "vertical" valley. Numerous pairs of hands take part in the production of rice in a diverse set of circumstances before the rice ends up on a dinner plate. The merciless sunrays or tropical rainstorms do not slow the hard labor given to the rice fields, an inescapable commonality in Vietnam. From afar the villages looked picturesque, ready for postcard printing.

One day while walking, I heard the sound of roosters squawking, and realized I must be approaching a nearby village. Local women in traditional black dresses with black leggings sat under porch roofs smiling, extending their hands for a shake, not wanting money, just a greeting. A few giggling children rode a water buffalo down the main path, scaring a couple of pigs and ducks into hiding. Satellite television discs, displaying a sign of wealth to all, sat proudly on corrugated metal roofs. Outhouses with squat toilets replaced the need for hiding places on the outskirts of the village.

The sight of bamboo forests indicated water nearby. Children ran past me carrying smaller children. One child stopped to tell his age (ten), but he did not know the age of his brother, riding gleefully on his back. Finally, a rattan suspension bridge underfoot eased my aches and pains after my long day's walk.

The map showed a beautiful silver waterfall ahead, a perfect place for lunch, and a wonderful place for a long rest before my search for Giang Ta Chai Village. The Dao (pronounced Zao) of this area migrated from China in the 13th century.

The women use color and diversity in their traditional clothing and jewelry. Jackets of red or black have embroidered borders to match the black trousers marked with flowers and rich geometric patterns. Turbans of fringed, red fabrics contrast with chunky, silver jewelry. These women regard shaved foreheads and eyebrows as a sign of beauty.

Imagination must have generated the myriad ways to fold and layer yards of fabric edged in fringe for the head. Wealthy families can afford more fringe.

These small villages remain socially connected, and everybody looks after each other.

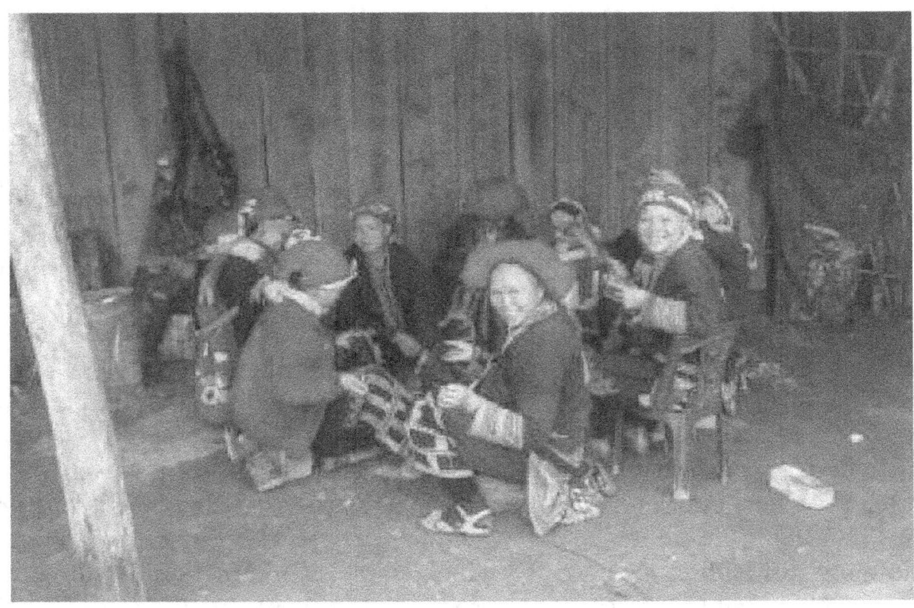

Red Dao

The leggings I bought to wear under my tropical weather nylon travel pants came to my knee. My shoulders drew the line for the height of the local women, which meant their gloves, hats, and socks fit me no better than child sizes. Brr!

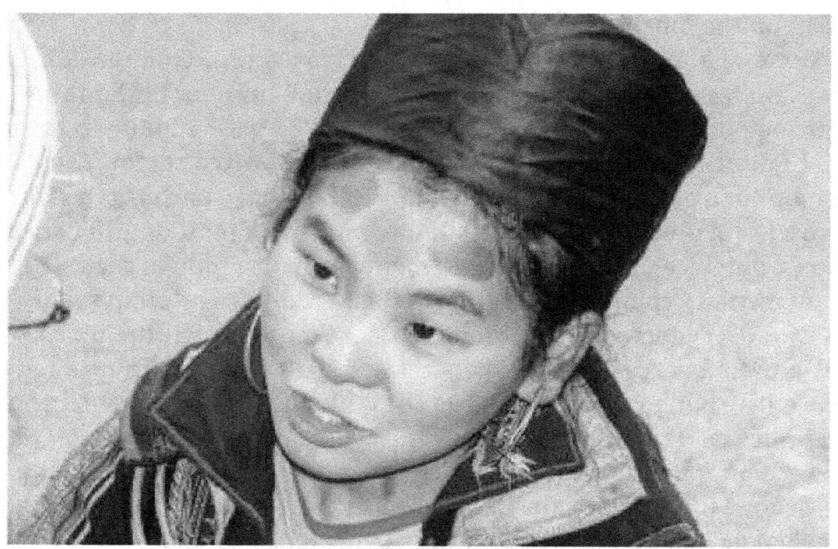

Hmong girl in Sapa

It was time to head back to Chau Doc for the river crossing, prior to going back into Cambodia for a flight to Kuala Lumpur. Two long days of flights and buses found me at the little bus station in Chau Doc, searching for a ride to that hotel on the river. I cannot believe I did not write down the man's name, but from behind a tall van, stick legs and boney arms appeared, and there he was again, dragging his rickshaw! He smiled at once, remembering either his dinner of soup, or my generous tip. However, he also remembered the location of the hotel, and we sped off like lightning.

A young man overheard my stories to the hotel clerk, about the strange attitude I had found directed toward strangers from previous hotel receptionists, and those in the streets not willing to clear a path for the rickshaw. His invitation to me to help him teach in his English class that evening excited me. And what fun we had. The class members ranged from students aged ten to eighty years old, with everyone wanting to ask questions and hear the answers in English. The teacher, determined to leave a positive feeling about his city in my heart, told me to arrive at the dock outside my hotel at sunrise. He wanted to show me small villages of potters and weavers. His interaction with the local people allowed me to witness the sense of contentment the Vietnamese enjoy, which somehow got lost for me in the chaotic traffic of the city and market streets.

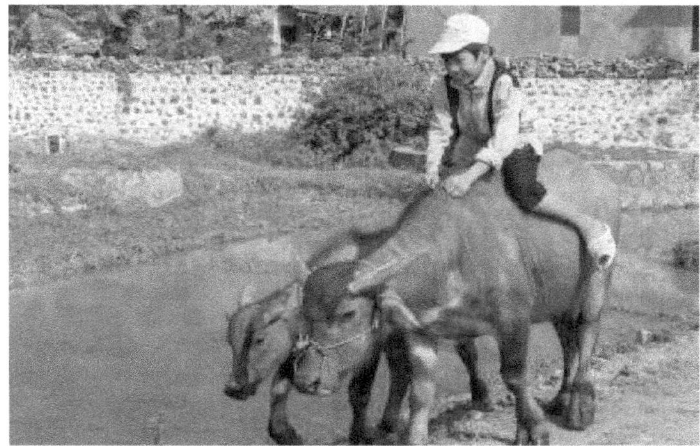

Finding a watering hole in Van Lam

Young girls positioned at weaving looms outside small homes giggled, not wanting to make eye contact as I approached their space. No high-pressure sales clerks here just babies, sleeping in hammocks with life moving at the pace I came to Vietnam to see.

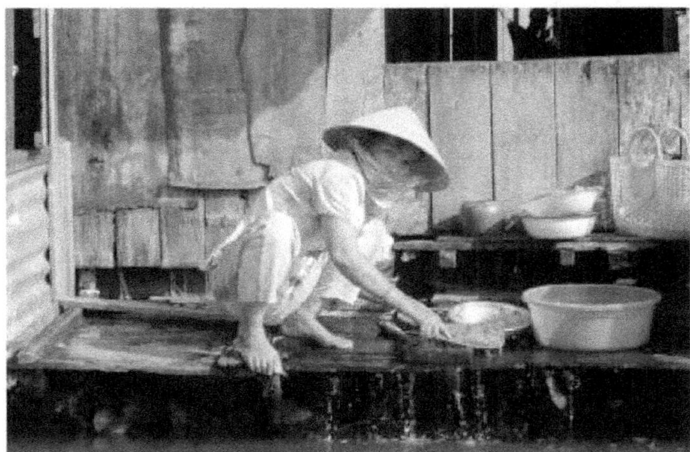

Washing dishes in the river

The young teacher offered his boat for the ride back to the border to cross back into Cambodia. The river journey took about an hour; plenty of time for us to look up details about Vietnam in my guidebook. I decided at the last minute before leaving the boat to give the young man the book to share with his class as a thank you for turning my last day in Vietnam (or so I thought) into a positive experience. The Vietnamese border patrol stamped the exit line on my Vietnam visa. I waved goodbye to my new friend and walked about fifty feet to the Cambodia border station, but without hesitation they refused my entry. When I entered Cambodia, I had paid for a single-entry visa, instead of a multiple entry. I left the country weeks ago, and they stamped the exit on the visa, which cancelled any opportunity to re-enter. I pleaded with the security guards and even offered them two hundred dollars as a bribe. They stood rigid as statues without expression or sympathy. The sandy beach offered no shelter, food, or hope!

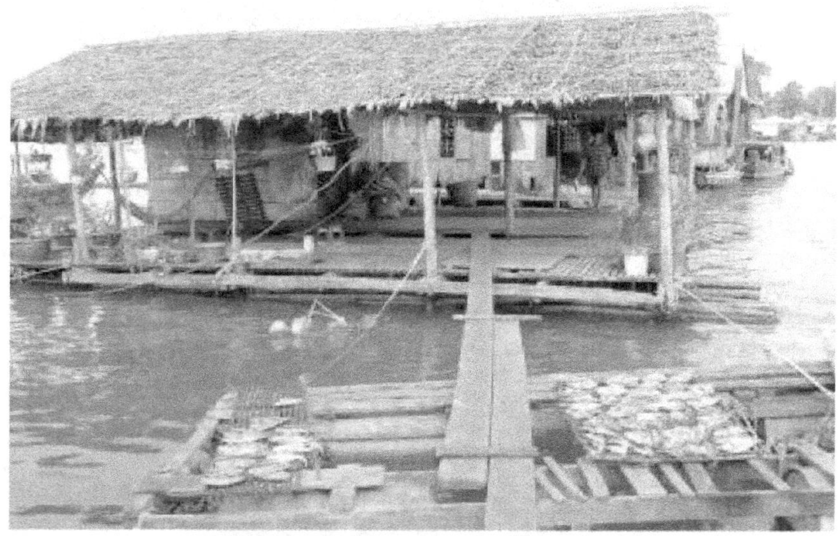

Drying fish on river in Chau Doc

I felt strange and isolated on that sandy beach between two countries. The weight of the disadvantages of solo travel caused my spirits to sink deeper in my discouragement as I pondered the situation at hand.

After dark, perhaps a local man might offer a secret passageway over the border after seeing my bribe refused. Maybe I would share the bribe with him.

Two hundred dollars buys a lot of rice! How would I recognize a prince in white after dark? And, if he robbed me, would he let me keep a sheepskin rug, my sole souvenir, one I had bought the month before in Australia?

A white-as-snow rug might contrast well with a dirt floor, for a few days, anyway!

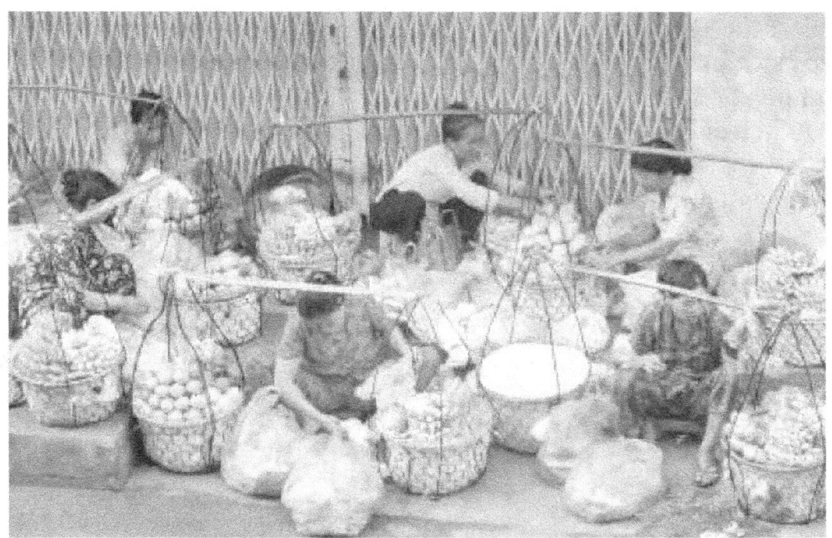

Preparing snacks for sale in HoChiMinh City

My alternative stood fifty feet to my back, the Vietnamese border. Maybe they could help. A slight man, wearing an abundance of badges and ribbons on his uniform, attempted to appear confident as he moved towards me stiffly, like a robot, and asked for my passport.

The passport disappeared with the uniformed man and then suddenly reappeared with that man along with a gust of severity. Ten or more men in uniforms, one holding an official document, circled me as if I looked like an escaped prisoner, caught at last. Their fingers pointed to the paper while one man tapped a pencil at a long black line.

My head recalled television movies about people signing foreign documents, followed by enforced residence in some Thai prison, due to agreeing to some guilt forced on them as a trick.

I shook my head back and forth, explaining, "I will not sign anything that I cannot read."

The pencil tapped harder. The circle tightened as if I might run toward the river and swim to safety.

"English or no sign!" I said firmly. Amazing how shortening a sentence and ignoring all grammar rules could make it possible for foreign officials to understand my words.

Within minutes, the officials walked in single file back behind the fence, leaving me alone with my bags. They refused to let me back into their country without the proper visa and did not care what happened to me.

Behind the Cambodian border line, several people offered hopeful looks. I walked back and forth like a caged lion, wanting freedom from this situation but trapped between two countries.

My watch did not help matters as the minutes raced with the sun in the passing of time. A familiar-looking boat slowed on the beach, and my dear schoolteacher friend jumped to the sand.

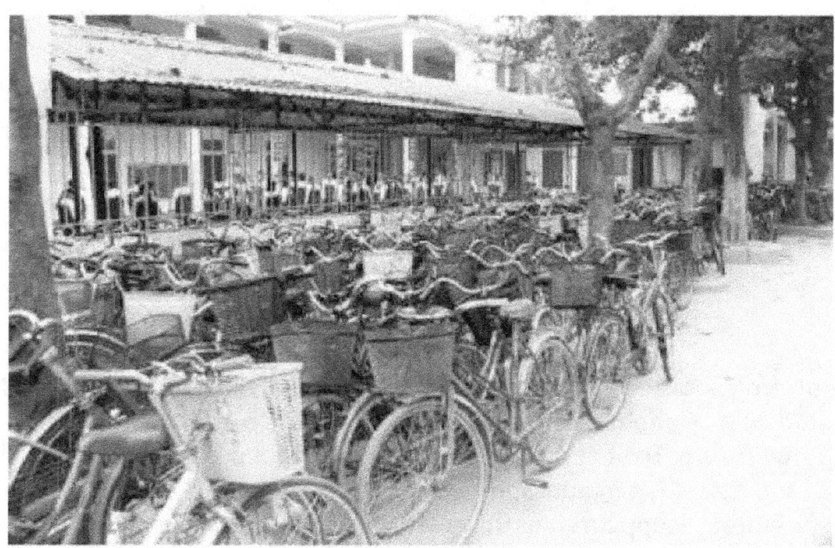

Main mode of transportation in Ninh Binh

"You are in trouble?" His words came to me like magic.

"How did you know?" I asked, tears of joy wetting my eyes. With words of sympathy, he explained, "Someone with a radio called to tell me my friend on the beach had trouble."

After a talk with the Cambodian officers, his expressionless face answered my hopes of getting into Cambodia. In the opposite direction, ten minutes of explanations and a promise gave us the ability to board his boat and turn around toward Vietnam.

I surmised that the schoolteacher promised my appearance in Saigon or Ho Chi Min to sort the matter out. The schoolteacher's gratitude for my gift of the book on Vietnam came back to me tenfold; he not only shared the people of Chau Doc, but also helped me deal with my thoughtless mistake in not getting a multiple entry visa into Cambodia.

The local bus station looked like a used car lot with all sizes of vehicles parked in rows, waiting to fill their empty seats. Six hours of not knowing the driver's destination kept me from sleep, as other passengers' heads fell, limp on neighbors' shoulders. The city on my return ticket spelled Phnom Penh, and I had no departure card with a visa space to stamp exit.

Tiny needles of fear pricked my skin as the van driver managed narrow, rocky paths outside the city limits, dropping passengers one by one. The anxiety overwhelmed me as the last passenger exited the van, leaving only the driver and me. Traffic had long ago gone to sleep. I found my map of the city and the approximate area of my hotel. The driver took his sweet time in finding the right street. Maybe thoughts of kidnapping, or at least robbery, danced in his brain.

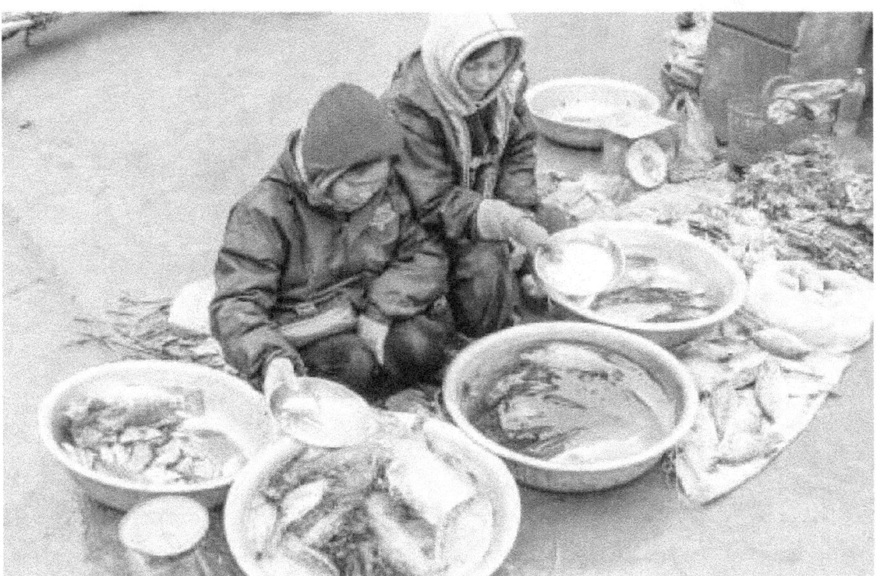

Selling fish in temperatures below freezing in Sapa

"You are going the wrong direction," I told him, in hopes of causing a little distraction from any evil thoughts he might be entertaining. The street sign now matched my hotel's address, and backing up several blocks to find the correct number did not matter at two o'clock in the morning. He asked me to pay for the ride, and it was the third time he had done so.

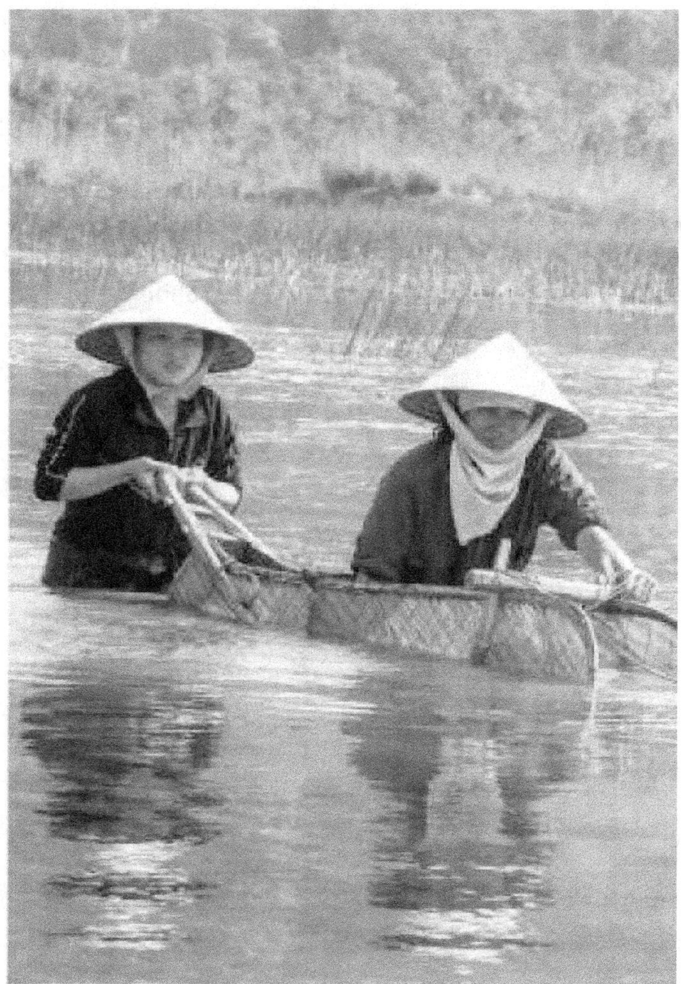

Fishing in Van Lam

"I saw my teacher friend pay you for the entire trip," I told him boldly, wanting him to see I was no easy mark for his tricks. The definition of an entrepreneur applies to one who gets the most out of each situation, I suppose, so I did not blame him for trying. He may not have understood a word I tried to convey.

The streets rested in total silence, except for two men, who happened to sit down on a curb next to the stopped van as if guarding the corrugated tin-roofed hotel bolted down with a huge metal door and four-inch padlock. I ignored their pleas of, "Let me take you to my hotel; this one closed."

That itchy, scared feeling turned into dripping sweat as I pounded on that hotel door, wishing for a change in my luck.

My pounding aroused someone within. I heard mumbling behind the double-locked doors. I was so relieved when a man opened the door to me, and then led me to a room with crisp white sheets. Those lovely sheets coaxed me into a much-needed night's rest.

Next day, the airport cooperated by sending me to a counter to change my ticket and obtain a reissue of an exit visa.

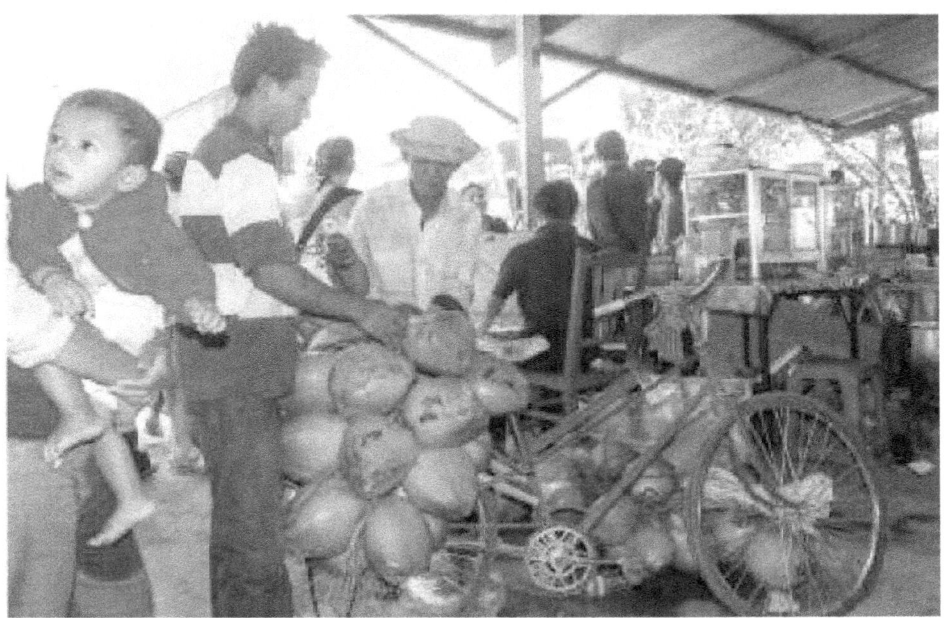

Delivering coconuts to restaurant on bike

The real-life stories of the ancient Oriental still survive in a country favored by nature.

The opportunity for a rare glimpse into mysterious cultural elements stimulates one's curiosity even before the rickshaw ride begins.

The unmistakable conical hats of the Vietnamese gently bow toward the earth, symbolizing the intimate relationship between both the people and their environment.

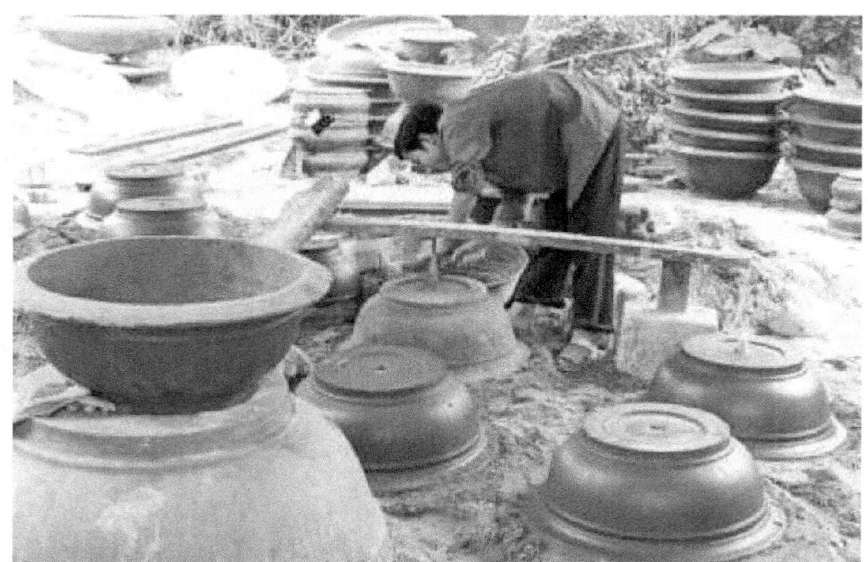

Ninh Binh potter, working on Main Street.

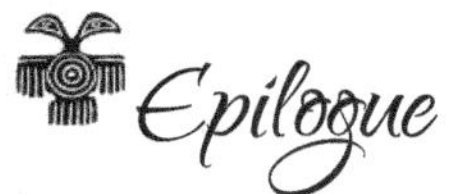

Epilogue

Travel is a reflection of the best of who you really are.

WHY MEET NEW PEOPLE? People of other cultures live in startling ways because of the incredible passages they have taken. Their smiling eyes, honesty, and sincere desire for friendship will mesmerize you into wanting more. Interacting with people of the world builds a base for enriching, life-changing memories. The composition of a travel experience starts with your decision of the place to go and the sights to see, but what you bring back in your treasure chest of memories includes your experiences with people met along the way. As you move through other worlds, you begin to recognize the impact of your unique nature. When connecting with new environments and their people, you soon find no words have ever come together to offer a way to summarize the rewards you receive.

People of foreign cultures remind you of your favorite teacher from school. They bring new ideas to light and offer challenges you have never faced before. You don't realize it at the time, but when you return home, you will witness the positive changes taking place in your own life. As we observe the patient endurance of people of the world, our heartstrings stretch in every direction.

The challenges of meeting new cultures become more diverse than those of the everyday routines we know. What about the language barrier? How does one read a menu, ask for a hotel, or get to the next village or town? Apprehension still swells in my head after I pass through immigration and realize that ten men tug at my sleeve as I await my passage through the airport door in typical Third World countries.

Upon arrival in Bamako, Mali, three men took one bag each to their respective taxis as they waited for my business. I went to the first, and I explained in a language foreign to him that I traveled alone and would he please hand me my bag. His look of deep intent on winning me over soon turned into a shouting match with the other two drivers, all in words I didn't understand. My impatient, feigned smile led to help from a fourth man who spoke English.

Feeling lost on a local bus will turn into the highlight of the day as you get out your maps: Those who speak even a hint of English will seek your friendship. Their stories create your new adventure as you forget where you first wanted to go. If you order a menu item that comes to you as a chicken foot soaked in broth, you order again. You become less uncomfortable as you summon more adaptation from within.

Learning to deal with people of different cultures takes time, but in the twenty-first century, few, distant corners remain. People connect with each other in many ways. Sometimes it feels as if we exist on western technologically advanced islands that float in a sea of cultures, emerging from the past. We have similarities because we share some religious belief, similar parenting and leadership skills, or parallel characteristics like honesty and kindness. Through our differences, we can still learn. Wandering a foreign place, encountering all sorts of peoples, you begin to realize the differences that you noted before transitioning into similarities.

During your travels, you do ordinary things that become extraordinary experiences as you exchange knowledge with new acquaintances. Before you go, you need lots of emotional preparation. You will use it repeatedly during the physical immersion. Haunting as one foreign culture may appear, after that trip you will start packing for your second.

WHY TRAVEL? *"It is not necessarily at home that we best encounter our true selves."* Alain de Botton Is it the lure of an escape that makes one want to travel? Or does adventure lurk in the sounds of places like Kathmandu? Islands like Bora Bora and Bali conjure images of palm trees on deserted beaches and romance. An impulse of spontaneity in your life may cause you to make travel plans and the anticipation compares to getting ready for Christmas. Preparations, or the process of getting there, have rewards as enjoyable as reaching the destination. Have you made a promise to yourself that the mystery around the bend in the road ahead will merit your aspirations for getting there? Travel offers challenges that increase with time. *"A journey of a thousand miles begins with a single step,"* according to a Chinese proverb.

The rewards of travel come from the journey of self-discovery. As you begin to make your own rules and learn to trust yourself, you begin to redefine your individualism. *"I had hoped that the trip would be the best of all journeys: a journey into ourselves."* Shirley MacLaine

While traveling, you will begin to experience the unexplainable change that will take place inside. Removing the masks of everyday life, you participate in someone else's journey by getting involved with their lives and looking at things in a different way. Ask about their customs, religion, food products, how they make a living, their pastimes for relaxing, what they view as important to them, and what they consider as their goals.

That exposure to more traditional customs causes you to change your own lifestyle. By taking these baby steps toward understanding, we remove the barriers we construct in our everyday life. We all wear masks, sometimes many at one time. Do we speak up to an employer when he's wrong, or do we hide behind our job security safety net and keep our feelings private? Do we dress differently when with a different set of friends? What do we say to a group of girlfriends at lunch when they talk about buying red cowboy boots, but you are thinking how odd they will look in them?

While traveling, nobody will judge you, and your body language will not identify you as mother, lawyer, best friend, Little League coach, boss, neighbor, or any other title. *"Are we the same people, I wonder, when all our surroundings, associations, acquaintances are changed?"* Gertrude Bell, a Victorian explorer, once pondered.

Live the definition of serendipity! We often believe that our outer landscape serves as our strongest attribute, and we depend on our dress, manicures, and Botox; by feeding your soul, you realize that the inner landscape has great importance. By expanding your outer world, you'll make invisible inner changes that will last a lifetime.

The value of Tolkien's words, *"Not all those who wander are lost,"* begins to make sense. For a travel virgin, the highs and lows you encounter will complete your experience. You will find your senses, personal habits, patience, attitude and capabilities tested to your limit. You will learn to respect the beauty of a people and their traditions from ancestors past, no matter how difficult it seems. The simplicity of a place may overwhelm you. No running water or electricity? The lack of motivation that concept creates will disappear when you are walking into a small Third-World village and witnessing the men sitting around singing while carving wooden musical instruments. By questioning these realities, you better understand your world. As you walk around with your iPod hanging out of your pocket, don't protest the authenticity of indigenous peoples living centuries-old customs. First, seek to understand before becoming judgmental.

Begin to challenge your abilities. Accomplishments you never dreamed possible will become second nature to you. Greet the unexpected with smiles and patience. All your senses will ignite as you face decisions without computers, newspapers, and televisions with answers for the questions of How? What? Where? Your travels will act like a magnet, gathering experiences that will challenge your curiosity and provoke your questions. When you need to trust yourself for your answers, your fears and insecurities vanish, and the excitement comes as you witness a new you emerging.

We all have the traditional boundaries we make for ourselves as well as the ones others chart on maps and in guidebooks for us. By stepping over those roadblocks, we find we can do things we never dreamed possible. Maybe those rituals serve as a signpost along the road of a much bigger journey.

Riding on the roof of a train from Guayaquil, Ecuador with my fourteen-year-old daughter, I felt helpless when the train stopped without explanation in a town whose name we never knew. The village, off the tourist track, offered no hotels or food or even help to find our way onward. Half a mile up on the main road, I could see what I hoped were bus passengers gathered. Each passing bus held demanding mothers late in preparing dinner or fathers tired from a long day of field work.

After I had shouted "Riobamba" over and again, the group realized my wishes to go north. A few hours passed, and the sun disappeared. A truck filled with green hard-as-rock bananas pulled up, and many from the group yelled to me, "Riobamba, Riobamba." Along with about ten other needy souls, my daughter and I climbed into the back of that truck, and within half an hour, we had taught songs to others journeying with us, shared our nuts and raisins, and wondered where we might land. I could sit on that dirt road all night with a young daughter or take my chances in a truck going somewhere. In my lifetime, I have never hitchhiked and never conceived of getting into a truck filled with strangers who spoke no English. When it started to rain, we pulled a huge tarp over the group and continued our songs and laughter. Within four hours, someone yelled "Riobamba!" We peeked out from under the tarp to see a washed-out sign that we could not read, but the huge parking lot contained many buses. Riobamba!

Whether meeting the black eyes of the Tuareqs of West Africa hiding behind turbans wrapped around their heads and faces, or the welcoming tourist-oriented Indians of San Blas, you will encounter experiences not found in textbooks that will prepare you for the life that awaits you.

What a role our memories play as they lay the foundation for the building blocks of everything yet to come. You do not weigh incredible memories by the ingredients of one experience. Our reactions when meeting new people can turn on the magic.

We take unconscious notes and recognize their import later as we recall the impact people make on our attitudes. As our own expectations of ourselves grow, our confidence and strengths reveal themselves. The real substance lives not around us but within.

Erasing past commitments, your capacity for new circumstances, different ways of viewing the world and making new friendships will grow. By practicing new skills, you will enhance your aptitude for brainstorming new ideas and becoming more self-sufficient. Once you have made a personal connection with a foreign culture, you will change forever.

ADJUST YOUR EYES TO WIDE OPEN WHILE TRAVELING You will open many doors while traveling, and sometimes may come to a door that makes you wonder if you have the strength to push through it. Take care in your responses to the uniqueness of people and their curious customs. Remember, you do not TAKE your photographs and stories. You BORROW them! Let them reflect the soul of your new friends. Find favorable circumstances to help bridge that gap between your country's lifestyle and the ways of foreign ancestors' past. While sharpening the edges of your new adventure, fill your beliefs about those of this new culture with compassion.

Magnify their traditions and stories from the past with compliments. Travel plans seldom play out as expected so remember this: Flexibility and patience will help save the day. Value your health and safety while, at the same time, you comprehend the meaning of the cliché phrase that the journey exceeds the importance of the destination. Open the windows wide and breathe in all that you see. Meeting with new cultures will compel you to value the grand diversity of the places we, as humans, call home. Neither guidebooks nor teachers in classrooms nor even experience on the road can hand you the skills of travel. Travel accomplishments stem from our emotional reactions. What we take from the experience helps to transform us.

"Once you have traveled, the voyage never ends, but is played out over and over again in the quietest chambers that the mind can never break off from the journey." Pat Conroy

What's Inside of Other Books?

Browse the extract below from one of the Jackie Chase other travel books. This example is from: "Walking to Woot" A Photographic Narrative Discovering New Dimensions for Parent-Teen Bonding

The story is about a true adventure shared by Jackie with her 14-year-old daughter in a setting as challenging as the stories about Ethiopia just recounted in "100 People". Over 160 images bring you to the scenes they witnessed; the adventure reads like a novel and is full of fascinating information. Please review Jackie's books on line if you have become a fan and like what she shares.

Excerpt: *"But what do dreams know of boundaries?"* Amelia Earhart

CHAPTER ONE: throwim way leg

Distant voices drowned the stillness in the air. Rustling through the jungle growth, we entered a clearing of burned wild grass, which destroyed any means of concealment or protection. We stopped dead in our tracks within seconds of hearing the swishing sound of flying arrows.

"Did you hear that sound?" Katherine whispered frantically, grabbing my arm.

"Yes, but where did it come from?" I said.

"I'm scared and don't like this," she said with hesitation.

"Katherine, will you ever forgive me if we do survive this?" I said.

She took a few steps backwards but I would hear her say, "It's okay Mom. We'll be okay."

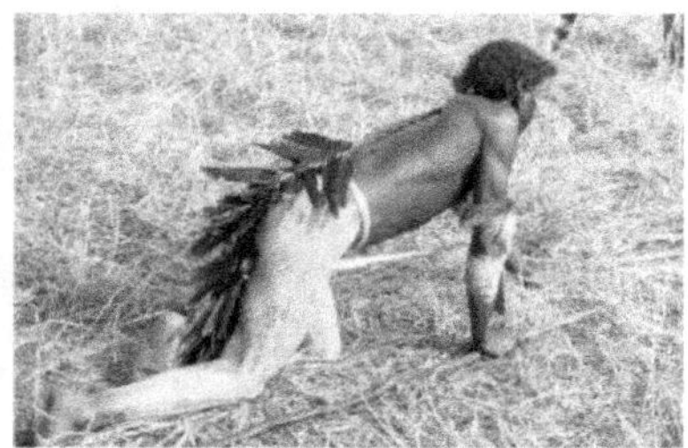

Hiding during war games

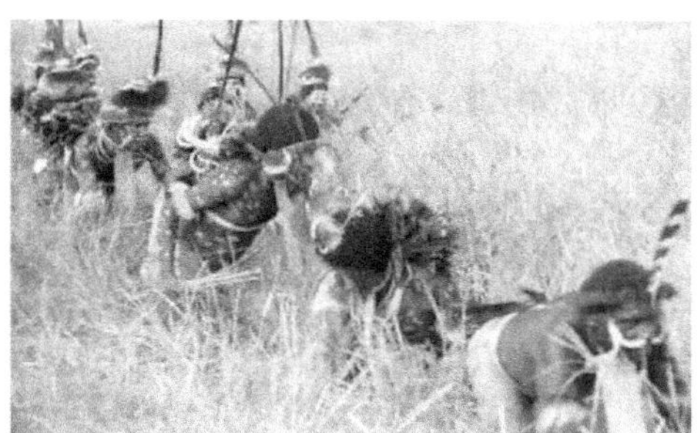

Sneaking up on the enemy

Our eyes caught two groups of local tribal men called Dani crouching in the yellow grass. Crudely carved spears protruded above bodies, glistening with pig grease. Muscled arms waved bows while calloused fingers manipulated arrows.

The opening between the groups equaled the distance of a short arrow shot. The warriors watched with eyes empty of expression and lips drawn in straight lines. The men's silence led us to believe it was imperative we remain still.

Opposite the smallest group, a warrior rose to his full height. He reached for an arrow and shot toward us, high over the heads of the crouched warriors. Lime-powder paint, pig grease mixed with soot, and curly plumes of the bird of paradise decorated the warrior's body.

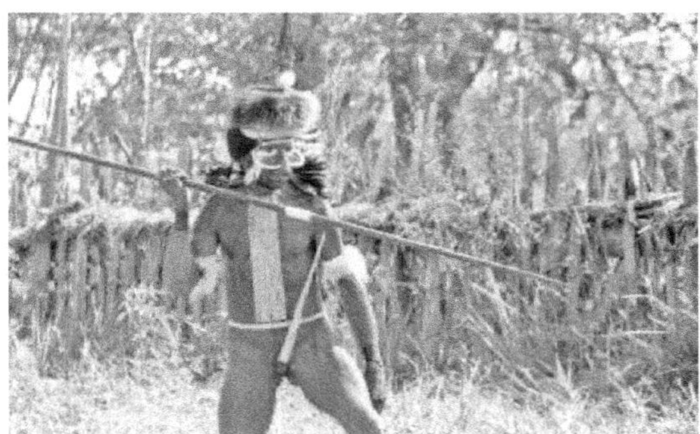

Dani warrior ready for a kill

A form of paralysis swept over my entire body. Sounds of the jungle diminished beneath the drum-like beating of my heart.

My bare knees didn't feel the thorn bushes that I noticed later had left scratches on bare skin.

My brain rushed into a state of crisis. My thoughts came more rapidly when I thought I was going to die.

I had to summon the courage to be stronger than my fears. My mind, fully alert, sensed my body detached. My eyes searched for Katherine's position. Safe and secure?

Our first day in the jungle, and my expectations and foregone conclusions were dissolving.

The sudden yelling, which came from every direction, alarmed me even more. Streams of nervous sweat ran down my cheeks.

Were these cannibals out looking for their dinner or just angry warriors out to rape and kill anything in their sight?

I glanced around but could see only our guide, Julius, above my thorn-bush cover. My body felt heavy like one of those cement statues in a garden.

About six feet behind me, branches from a fallen tree hid slivers of blond hair covering eyes tightly squeezed shut.

I could barely see the tips of Katherine's fingers covering her ears. I remembered, about ten years ago, finding Katherine as a small child standing beside a squished frog in the driveway.

Her eyes closed so tightly they were nothing more than thin lines. Her knuckles were white from pressing her hands hard against her head. I asked her why she covered her ears.

"My eyes can close, but my ears can't," she said.

Without any doubt, I expected our imminent capture. Although against government rules, cannibalism exists in the well-hidden forests of the Asmat tribes.

I knew they fought battles mainly over women, food, and land. Maybe we had trespassed on a sacred burial ground.

My trembling fingers, damp with sweat, untangled the strap of the camera, my witness to the extraordinary scene.

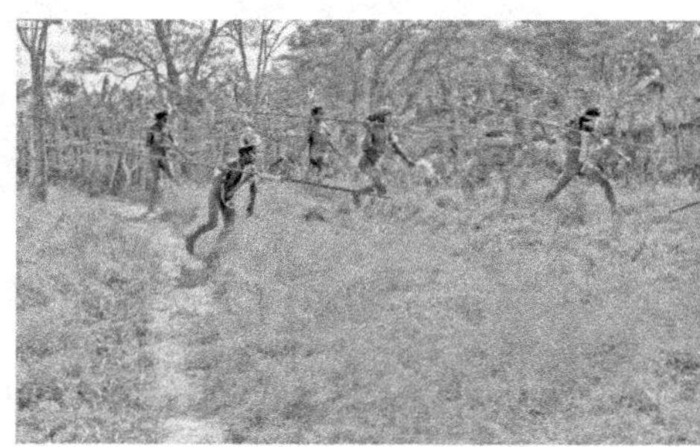

Aiming spears ready for action

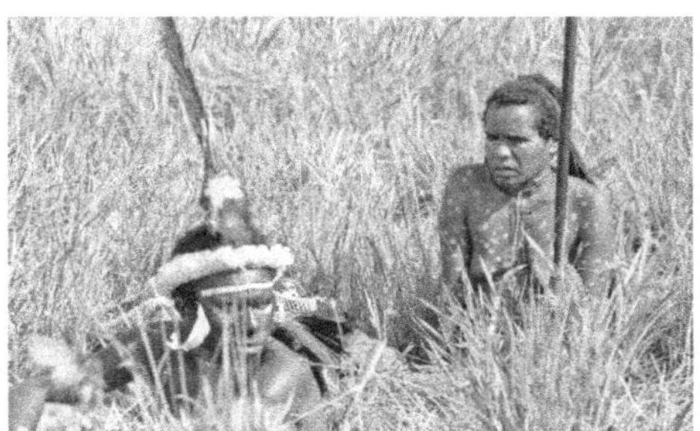

Waga Waga husband and wife hiding from enemy

Would the movement from lifting the camera to my face trigger a barrage of arrows and spears? Ignoring us, several Dani leaped away, whooping and yelling, leaving a curtain of dust in the chaos.

They never looked back and didn't seem to care about the startled intruders interrupting their war games. Laughing and singing, warriors chasing warriors crashed exuberantly down a steep embankment of loose rocks.

A group on the far side of the field ran in the opposite direction, moving their spears and bows up and down to the sounds of their chanting. There were no captives or wounded or even cries for help. Both sides appeared content with the outcome of the battle.

I looked across the field of flattened grass where minutes ago, men had crawled like lions on a hunt. I sighed with relief. Close inspection of an arrow under my boot revealed a long stem of a plant. In lifting my leg, I realized the tightness in my muscles.

Could I take another step? Katherine and I both were breathing hard as if we had just run a mile race. Instead of using the extra adrenaline filling my body for fighting or escaping, I felt satisfied facing that unsettling event.

By not screaming or attacking the warriors with the pepper spray attached to my belt, I may have set a good example for my daughter. Every exhausted muscle in my body felt the adrenaline rush dissipate. I managed enough steps backwards for my shaking hand to reach for Katherine's, cold but clammy.

"It's over. Are you all right?" I said. I hugged her with all the strength I had left to give.

She wrapped her arms around my back and squeezed. And with a half-smile said, "We survived our first real encounter with adventure, didn't we?"

A mock warfare battle between rival villages is an integral part of Dani life. I knew that mock warfare games were common, but when it was actually happening it felt real.

The men play the pretend games to impress their opponents and their women, with much time spent on making weapons and decorations to wear during the battles. Pig grease covers their entire bodies with a coating of soot. Boar's teeth hang from their noses and bird feathers and flowers intertwine to make their head garlands.

Paint and plumage transform their faces into masks. The Dani have a legend about a snake and a bird. The race between the two was to determine the life of humans. If the snake won the race, then man should shed his skin and live forever like snakes. If the bird won the race, man must die. The bird won the race.

Using feathers, the Dani decorated their bodies, their armbands, hair, and the holes in the nose, illustrating their close spiritual relationship with birds.

Katherine later said, "The whole scene looked like a movie set, so the reality of the experience frightened me less because it didn't seem real."

Oh, to be a teen again, I thought. At that moment, I came to realize my assumptions of Katherine's maturity were correct. Acting with discrete confidence, as if nothing threatening had transpired, I absorbed a bit of her teenage courage.

I felt blessed with a new awareness of my own body to summon the strength to move forward. *Throwim way leg* in New Guinea pidgin language translates to "taking the first step in a long journey."

To view more of this story, click on www.AdventureTravelPress.com.

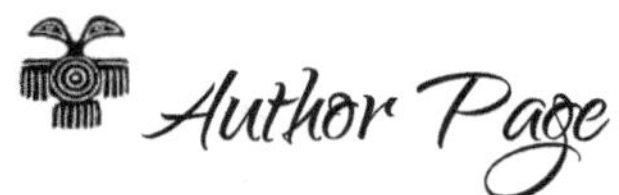

Author Page

Jackie Chase, [www.JackieChase.com, www.WorldTravelDiva.com, and www.CulturesOfTheWorld.com], has traveled to over 100 countries and specializes in staying in remote villages in order to use her keen observations and photo-journalism skills to share her insights with her reader fans. She has traveled alone, with a child, with family, and with friends; she has earned 29 awards from international book contests from 2014 to date of printing; she shares with the public many of the travel secrets she has experienced in her book titled, ***"How to Become an Escape Artist" A Traveler's Handbook.*** The Handbook was tested for several years with students in a college evening class, and they soaked up Jackie's hints and the many ways to avoid disappointment, reduce expenses and frustrations, navigate the issues of visas, language, customs, currencies, accommodations, transportation, attitudes, danger, travel alone, and other problems all covered in over 190 segments in the book.

Her ***"All Hands Working Together" Cruise for a Week: Meet 79 Cultures*** book treats cruising in a unique way to learn about cultures; the reader experiences personal contact with crewmembers from many of the 79 countries they represent, and from many skills they possess.

Jackie Chase has written definitive books on "People to Meet" in contrast to "Places to See". She convinces her readership to look beyond mountains, lakes and buildings to see world inhabitants of all continents as potential friends and shows how much we have in common. She shows how to bridge gaps created by custom and language in ***"100 People to Meet before You Die: Travel to Exotic Places"***. This book, [as well as the others], are available in color, grayscale, and, with stunning images in eBooks that come to life on backlit screens. This anthology contains 321 of those story-telling images ward-winning prose about her adventures in twelve countries. For her fans of a particular country, she has twelve "singles" in print and in eBook format, plus at least one (Panama) translated into Spanish.

For children, from small up through teens, a "winner" of a book is ***"Giraffe-Neck Girl" Make Friends with Different Cultures***. It is about a ten-year-old girl in Thailand who warms the hearts of young and old as she shares her different life and customs.

Jackie Chase's 2016 book, ***"Walking to Woot" A Photographic Narrative Discovering New Dimensions for Parent-Teen Bonding*** has won 15 international awards in the genres of Parenting, Multi-Cultural, and Travel, and it contains both poetic descriptions and visual ones with its 180 images of life with stone-age tribal warriors who haven't changed customs in a thousand years. The New

Guinea unclothed villagers welcomed Jackie and her blond 14-year-old daughter to pig roasts, unusual customs, and dances. Jackie Chase loves to hear from her fans and to see copies of reviews they submit to the web. Contact her:
JakartaMoon@hotmail.com, or Publisher@AdventureTravelPress.com.

These adventures in 12 countries are available on the web as singles, beginning with the name of the country, and this book is available in print with stunning black and white or color images through web book distributors such as:
www.AdventureTravelPress.com, or Kindle, Ingram, Amazon, and Nook.

In electronic download form, these, and other books by the author, can be ordered from all e-book sources. Images from this and other books are available for framing in many sizes upon request. Ask for the catalogue at:
Publisher@AdventureTravelPress.com.

BOOKS BY JACKIE CHASE: 2014/16

All Hands Working Together: Cruise for a Week: Meet 79 Cultures (2014-6)
How to Become an Escape Artist: A Traveler's Handbook (2014-6) Giraffe-Neck Girl: Make Friends with a Different Culture (2014)
100 People to Meet before You Die: Travel to Exotic Cultures (2014-6)

AWARDS (14) FOR THE FOUR BOOKS LISTED ABOVE Royal Palm Literary Award; National Indie Excellence Book Award;
FAPA President's Book Award; Readers' Favorite Book Award; International Book Award; USA Best Book Award; Beverly Hills Book Awards

AWARDS (15) For: "*Walking to Woot*" A Photographic Narrative Discovering New Dimensions for Parent-Teen Bonding
Beach Book Festival; Beverly Hills Book Awards in 3 Categories; Eric Hoffer Grand Prize Awards in 2 Categories; Florida Authors and Publishers Association (FAPA); International Book Award, Montaigne Medals; National Indie Excellence Award; Next Generation Indie Book Awards in 2 Categories; Paris Book Festival; Reader's Favorite Awards in 2 Categories; San Francisco Festival Awards.

All books available at: www.AdventureTravelPress.com

www.ingramcontent.com/pod-product-compliance
Lightning Source LLC
LaVergne TN
LVHW020051110826
845155LV00021B/60

* 9 7 8 1 9 3 7 6 3 0 9 5 9 *